AFRICAN RECRUITS

AND

MISSIONARY CONSCRIPTS

The White Fathers and the Great War
(1914 – 1922)

GW00418152

Aylward Shorter

Aylward Shorter

First Published in Great Britain 2007

Copyright © by Aylward Shorter 2007

Published by

Missionaries of Africa
History Project
Oak Lodge
48 Totteridge Common
London N20 8NB

ISBN

978 095552350 2

Printed and Bound in Great Britain by
Tabbers Ltd.

DEDICATION

In memory of the Missionaries of Africa, the African Soldiers and Carriers who
gave their lives in the Great War,
and the Veterans who lived with the memories and scars of conflict.

Publication of this study was made possible through the generous assistance of the Mrs. L. D. Rope Third Charitable Settlement.

CONTENTS

1. Jean-Marie Le Tohic (seated) with fellow soldiers
2. Deacon Joseph Grison – one of the first to die (Ypres 1915)
3. Joseph Margot-Duclos, novice-priest, died Verdun 1916
4. Novice Henri Guibert one of the last to die (Verdun 1918)
5. Novice Lode de Boninge died in Flanders (1918)
6. Statue of de Boninge (with another seminarian) on the Diksmuide Peace Arch

INTRODUCTION

It is a surprise for many people to learn that over two million Africans served in the First World War as soldiers or labourers and that hundreds of thousands died, or were killed, in action.[1] It is equally surprising for them to learn that large numbers of Catholic missionaries from Africa were conscripted for active service on the Western and Eastern Fronts. Not only did they serve alongside the Africans, as comrades in arms in colonial regiments, but they were involved in the welfare of these often neglected soldiers. Moreover, as chaplains and transport officers, they also played a role in the war which black troops were fighting on behalf of the European powers in Africa itself.

How was this experience integrated into the subsequent life of the Church in Africa, and what difference did it make to relations between white missionaries and African Christians? Moreover, how did it affect relations between both of these and the colonial powers after the war? Remarkably, the war years also saw the ordination, and pastoral initiation of the first African Catholic priests and the beginnings of a Catholic breakthrough in Africa, a continent that is now massively Christian, with the Catholic Church as the majority mainline denomination.

This book begins to answer these questions. It is a story that has not so far been told, and it is narrated here from the point of view of the Society of Missionaries of Africa, popularly known at the time by its nickname "The White Fathers".[2] Published and unpublished sources for the First World War are virtually unlimited. The internet can also testify to the enormous interest generated by the war. Even the questions which this book attempts to address are beginning to receive some attention from historians. However, there is no attempt here to compete with this enormous range of literature. Nor is there any attempt to retell the story of the war in detail as it unfolded in Europe and Africa, beyond what is necessary for contextualizing the war experiences of missionaries and Africans alike. This is not a war history, so much as a contribution to African Church history.

The first three chapters give an account of the missionaries' participation in the war: mobilization, trench warfare and the reckoning of dead, wounded, imprisoned and decorated. Chapter Four examines the spiritual sublimation of these experiences and the leadership role played by Léon Livinhac, the White Father Superior-General. In Chapter Five there is an account of African recruitment, the opposition it aroused and the part played by African troops in Europe and Africa. In all of this the White Fathers had a role to perform. Chapter Six sketches the campaigns that took place in the African continent and their physical and moral effect on the missionaries and their evangelizing work. For an international society with a majority of French members, like the Missionaries of Africa, the presence of Germans in their ranks posed a serious problem after the war. The Church in Africa was also confronted by the wholesale repatriation of German missionaries. Chapter Seven deals with these questions.

The final two chapters look at the aftermath of the war in Africa and the post-war reconstruction of both the Society and the Church under the guidance of Livinhac and Giacomo Della Chiesa, Pope Benedict XV, the long time friend and supporter of the White Fathers. Both were determined to undo the damage inflicted by the war, and to learn its lessons for the missionary future of the Church. The high point for both was the beatification of the Uganda Martyrs in 1920. There is a concluding assessment of Livinhac and an account of his death. Both Livinhac and Benedict XV died in 1922.

This book is one of the fruits of a history project launched by the Missionaries of Africa in 2001. Covering the period 1914 to 1922, it complements an earlier narrative for the years 1892-1914.[3] Taken together, both volumes constitute an account of the thirty year superiorate of Léon Livinhac, though it is to be hoped that a full-scale biography will eventually be written. The General Archives of the Missionaries of Africa are the major source of information for this book. These contain the correspondence of Livinhac and other superiors, the Mission Diaries of the period, records of White Father involvement in the 1914-1918 War, minutes of the General Council's meetings, the report of the General Chapter of 1920, obituary notices of missionaries, their personal dossiers and general statistical reports.

There is also a category of what might be called semi-archival material, the internal publications of the Society, Annual Reports and bulletins. Most important of these is the *Petit Echo*, a monthly bulletin that, throughout the war, printed a selection of the letters written by missionary conscripts from the various war fronts. As a picture of actual trench warfare, it is unsurpassed. A special bulletin, the *Petit Communiqué* was also produced for the confreres on active service. *Echos Binsonnais* was an informal newsletter for soldiers who had been student-aspirants of the Society at Binson Priory. The White Fathers' mission magazine in France, *Missions d'Afrique des Pères Blancs*, is another important bulletin, which reprinted many of the letters from the front. Also of value are Livinhac's circular letters and the Society's juridical documents, Constitutions and Directory. In addition, there are numerous monographs and dissertations, published and unpublished.

Among other archival resources consulted were the British Colonial Office files in the National Archives at Kew, London and the World War I databases of the French Ministry of Defence in Paris.[4] Much of the published literature was consulted in the British Library, the Library of the White Fathers' Generalate Rome, the Library of St. Edward's College London and the Day Mission Library of the Yale Divinity School.[5] I am grateful to the staffs of all these libraries. A select bibliography of this material is given in Appendix VI.

Alas, there were virtually no oral sources available. This project was begun at a time, when no single Missionary of Africa who had taken part in World War I was still alive. However, from 1958-1961 the author was the pupil of Martin Jaureguy (1886-1965), a hero of Verdun, twice wounded and holder of the

Croix de Guerre, who shared many personal experiences of the war with those he taught. The author, when a novice in the Netherlands in 1957-1958, also met Antoon Stootman, "Brother Boniface"(1869-1968), who shared with him personal reminiscences of Livinhac at Algiers. Early in 2004, the author visited Francophone West Africa for archival research, interviews and local visits. He had already spent thirty years teaching, researching and writing in Eastern Africa and was acquainted with local resources there.

Acknowledgements are due to many individuals for help received in the preparation of this book. First place must go to the late Professor Richard Gray, *Emeritus* of London University's School of Oriental and African Studies, who read and commented on drafts of most of the chapters. Tragically, he died on August 7th 2005. The loss of such a mentor and friend is incalculable. Edward Paice of Cambridge University, also kindly placed his recent findings on the Great War in Africa at the author's disposal. The General Archivist of the Society, Ivan Page, was unfailing in the help he provided, as was Herman Konings, Keeper of the Photo Archive. Acknowledgement is also due to the historians of the Society and other Missionaries of Africa, especially Jean-Claude Ceillier who heads the history project, and to Francis Nolan, Hugo Hinfelaar, Wilhelm Grosskortenhaus, Rudi Hufschmid and Diego Sarrio. Also to M. Marinus Rooijackers of Lyons.

The author toured the battlefields of the western front in June 2005. Thanks are due, in connection with this visit, to Roland de Cat and to the author's nephew Damian Hutt. The Great War displays of museums in Britain, France and Belgium were also visited. Finally, a word of thanks goes to the community of Oak Lodge, for their support during the writing of the book.

The spelling of personal and place names conforms to the generally received usage in English publications, rather than to that of purists of the vernacular. This makes for readability, rather than consistency. A Glossary is provided in Appendix IV. Dates of birth and death are usually given after the names of members of the Society. When an asterisk is placed after the second date, this refers to departure from the Society.

It remains for me to say that researching and writing this book has been a moving experience for me personally. The heroism and suffering of those who took part in the Great War in both Europe and Africa are poignant in the extreme, and the goodness of so many of them is unquestionable. The tragedy of which they, their families and missionary confreres were a part has softened with the passing of time, but it is good, to remind ourselves of what happened and to ensure that their memory lives on.

Aylward Shorter
Missionaries of Africa
Oak Lodge,
Totteridge Common,
N20 8NB.

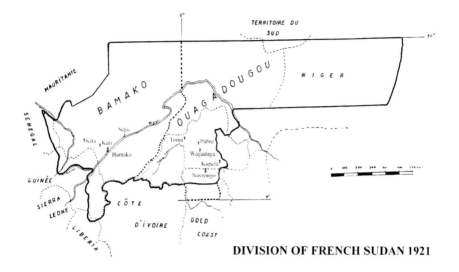

TERRITOIRE DU
SUD

MAURITANIE

SENEGAL

BAMAKO

OUAGADOUGOU

NIGER

Segu

Kita Kati
Bamako

Toma Pabre
Wagadugu
Kupela
Navrongo

GUINÉE

SIERRA
LEONE

CÔTE

LIBERIA

D'IVOIRE

GOLD
COAST

DIVISION OF FRENCH SUDAN 1921

1. Division of French Sudan into Bamako and Wagadugu Vicariates 1921

2. Creation of the Vicariate Apostolic of Bangweolo 1913

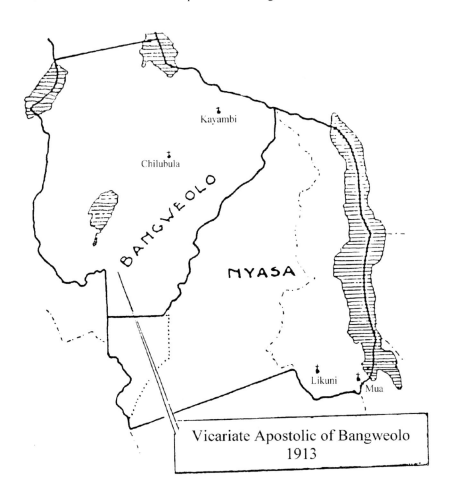

Kayambi

Chilubula

BANGWEOLO

NYASA

Likuni

Mua

Vicariate Apostolic of Bangweolo
1913

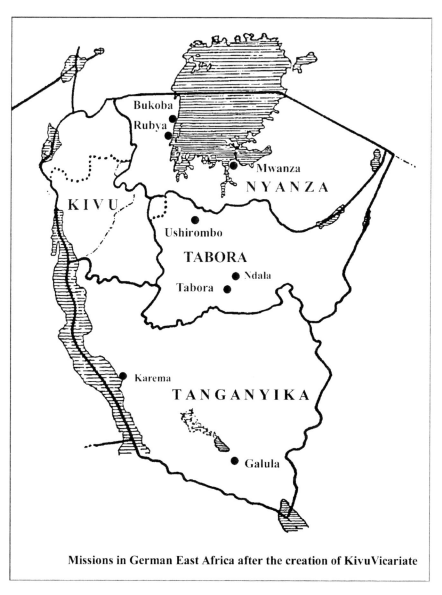

Missions in German East Africa after the creation of KivuVicariate

3. White Father Vicariates in German East Africa after the creation of Kivu (Rwanda-Burundi) 1912

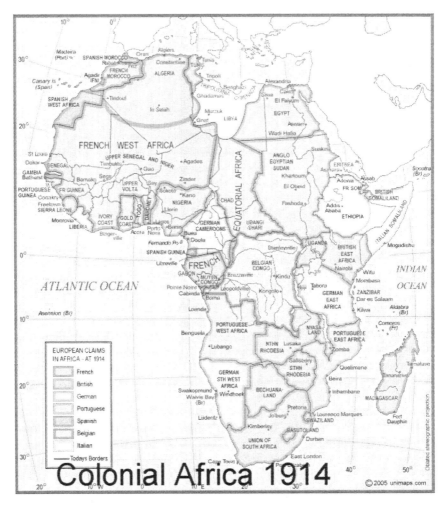

4. Colonial Africa in 1914

5. German East Africa, now Tanzania, Rwanda, Burundi.

CHAPTER ONE

MOBILIZATION

We think we gave in vain. The world was not renewed.
There was hope in the homestead and anger in the streets
but the old world was restored and we returned
to the dreary field and workshop and the immemorial feud
of rich and poor. Our victory was our defeat.
Power was retained where power had been misused
and youth was left to sweep away
the ashes that the fires had strewn beneath our feet.

Sir Herbert Read: *To a Conscript of 1940.*

A World Changed, if not Renewed

There is a sense in which the war poet is correct: *the world was not renewed.*
The First World War did not solve the socio-political and economic problems of
humanity. In fact, it created more problems than it could possibly solve. Social
injustice escalated, particularly with the rise of Fascist and Communist
dictatorships. The unsatisfactory arrangements of the Armistice in 1918 and the
peace treaties that followed could not prevent another world war. Indeed the
legacy of rancour and racism left by the 1914-1918 War made the war of 1939-
1945 inevitable. "The Second World War…was the direct outcome of the
First".[1] Yet there is also a sense in which the world *was* changed. The war
created a new, a modern world. The war dismantled or radically transformed
empires, the Russian, the Habsburg, the Ottoman – even the German colonial
empire - but it was not a war fought for colonial aggrandisement. That was
merely an opportunistic bonus for the Allies at the Versailles peace conference.
The scramble for colonies was basically over before 1914. It was a war that
familiarized the world with military destruction and mass death and that ushered
in unimaginable advances in the technology of war on land, sea and in the air
during the years that followed.

Africa was changed by the war. Under a League of Nations mandate, Britain and Belgium shared the territory of former German East Africa (the modern Tanzania, Rwanda and Burundi), while the former Kamerun (Cameroon) was divided between Britain and France, the latter taking the lion's share. Other adjustments were made relating to Togo and South West Africa (Namibia). Britain now controlled a belt of territory running from the Cape to Cairo. One of the immediate benefits for the Church was that a greater measure of co-operation was now possible between Catholic missionaries in the British territories of Eastern and Central Africa, especially regarding education and the organization of seminaries.

With the disappearance of German Africa and with the record of missionary support for the Allies, the Catholic Church in Africa entered into a changed relationship with the colonial powers. As Bishop Joseph Birraux, Vicar Apostolic of Tanganyika and future Superior General of the Missionaries of Africa, wrote in 1921: "The mission was a light straw which from a human point of view should have disappeared in the great storm. But it survived in spite of everything, respected today as yesterday, moreover the only institution still standing of what existed in the previous order of things."[2] The First World War brought prestige and new recognition to the Catholic Church. It was no longer, said Birraux, an "oasis" in Africa.

The experience of war also accelerated African socio-political maturation and eased the way for a more equal relationship between missionary and neophyte. In the wake of missionary mobilization, the emerging African leadership of the Church acquired greater responsibility, and African conscripts themselves became protagonists of the Gospel.

The terrible human suffering of the First World War is etched into the world's consciousness. We have no precise figures of those who fell so rapidly in its great battles. The total number may reach eight million dead and five million wounded. The "lost generation" accounted for one in three of all British and French men between the ages of nineteen and twenty-two.[3] Out of 140,000 African soldiers from French West Africa who fought in Europe, some 6,000 were killed, a twenty-five percent higher loss than in the French army.[4] The number of carriers who died in the East African campaign is unknown, but it may have reached half a million.[5] The deadly Spanish Influenza and other epidemics, the spread of which was associated with troop movements and trench warfare, killed up to forty million people worldwide in 1918-1920.[6] Remote villages in virtually every African country were affected.

Today, the imposing war monuments and extensive cemeteries of Flanders and Alsace, together with the war memorials in virtually every town and village of Britain and France, are a timeless reminder of what happened. In Dar es Salaam, the *askari* monument and in Nairobi the elegant statues of soldier and carrier, not to mention the urban quarters in both cities named for the Carrier Corps, *Kariakoo* and *Kariokor*, are also a perpetual souvenir. In Dakar, the imposing *Monument aux Morts* commemorates the Senegalese who died in France. There is no single memorial to the sixty Missionaries of Africa who gave their lives in the First World War, but the stories of their heroism are remembered.[7] This book is a tribute to them and to the African troops who served alongside them in World War One. It is also an attempt to assess the impact of that war on the mission of the Catholic Church in Africa, in so far as it was committed to the care of the White Fathers' Society.

French Mobilization

Before August 1914 the great European powers had built up huge armies of conscripts ready to be mobilized when war became likely or inevitable. Mobilization was a dangerous form of brinkmanship, even if it was merely intended as a diplomatic threat. It had a logic and a momentum of its own, not least because the military authorities of the time believed that attack was the only effective means of modern warfare, but also because moving armies depended on railways and the rapidity of this form of transport brought about an inexorable build-up on the various predetermined fronts. For Germany, without any doubt, mobilization meant war, if the race for military advantage was to be won. Pursuing a modified form of the so-called Schlieffen Plan, Germany followed a precise timetable for its invasion of France through Belgium. In the initial stages of the war the Continental powers mobilized some six million professionals and reservists. Germany had a greater reserve of manpower than France, which used every effort to draft its reservists wherever they were to be found, even French missionaries working in faraway African countries.

The French had invented military conscription in the wake of the Revolution of 1789. After their defeat in the Franco-Prussian War of 1871, universal military service was reintroduced even more rigorously than before. At the beginning of the twentieth century anti-clerical legislation abolished the role of military chaplains and any privilege of exemption previously enjoyed by the clergy. Priests, male religious and seminarians were liable to a period of full-time military service as young adults and remained in the reserve until the age of forty. Many White Fathers had done military service in metropolitan France, Germany or Belgium, while still aspirants of the Society. Others had been called up as novices or after the novitiate, during their theological studies. These "scholastics", as they were called, were mostly receiving their formation at the Society's theologate at Carthage in Tunisia. From there, the bulk of the French conscripts were called to serve with the colonial regiments of the Zouaves in North Africa. After becoming clerics or temporarily professed brothers, and especially after receiving minor and major orders, they were usually assigned to non-combatant roles in the medical corps, as orderlies, male nurses and stretcher-bearers. Aspirants were more often potential combatants. In the general mobilization of 1914, this resulted in the anomaly of aspirants and students often achieving a higher military rank than older priests or brothers with lengthy mission experience. A small and inadequate number of military chaplains had been reintroduced into the French army in 1913. Civilian priests were also admitted as volunteer chaplains in the following year. As a matter of course, therefore, priests of the society, called up in 1914, functioned officially or unofficially as chaplains.

Paul Voillard (1860-1946), First Assistant in the General Council, listed the White Fathers by nationality in 1914 for the benefit of the Editor of *l'Echo d'Alger*, to prove that Germans were not numerous in the Society and that the French constituted the majority (some 75%) of its members.[8] Voillard counted 662 priest members and 180 brothers, a total of 842 missionaries.[9] Of these only twenty-three missionary priests were "genuine Germans" and thirty-six were from Alsace-Lorraine.[10] Of the 180 brothers, thirty-eight were German and eighteen were Alsatian. Voillard later explained to the Algerian Commandant of Police, that Alsatians were "French at heart".[11] This assertion is not entirely convincing. In fact, the population of Alsace-Lorraine was mixed, and those born there between 1871 and 1814 were all technically citizens of the German Empire, whatever their attitude might have been towards France.[12]

There were sixteen nationalities among the White Fathers in 1914.[13] Belgians accounted for eight percent of the total, and the Dutch slightly more. Germans were less than five percent. It was clear that a missionary society that was massively French in membership would be hard hit by their country's stringent conscription law. In the event, 367 French Missionaries of Africa were called up, the fourth highest number out of fifteen religious or missionary congregations in France.[14] Only the De la Salle Brothers, the Jesuits and the Spiritans had higher numbers of conscripts. The figure presumably includes an unknown number of aspirants who were not yet part of the Society's official membership. These may have been equal to the numbers of Belgian and German professed missionaries who were also drafted. Thus about forty percent of the Society's official membership was conscripted into the armies of Europe for the duration of the war, together with an indeterminate further number that had not yet entered the novitiate.

In France itself Missionaries of Africa were relatively few and far between. They staffed procures in Paris, Lille and Marseilles, a philosophy seminary at Binson Priory (Châtillon-sur-Marne), an apostolic school at St.Laurent d'Olt (Aveyron) and a sanatorium at Pau in the Pyrenees. Across the channel in England, but still part of the French Province, was the Priory at Bishop's Waltham, which was another apostolic school and seminary for late vocations. The personnel of all these institutions was shuffled as a result of mobilization. At Bishop's Waltham, for example, three teachers reported for call-up. One, Pierre-Marie Travers (1874-1927), was invalided out of the army and returned immediately to take up his function as Superior. Another, Joseph Bouniol (1884-1950) was a prisoner of war for the duration, and the third, Eloi Falguières (1887-1924) saw both active service and captivity, returning as a seriously sick man at the end of the war.[15] Lille was occupied by invading German troops in the first months of the war, while Binson was occupied by the Germans in both the first and second Battles of the Marne, being almost completely demolished by French bombardment in 1918. In France a considerable number of aspirants, former students of Binson and Bishop's Waltham, were called up. At the beginning of 1919, Bishop's Waltham welcomed a variety of students, who had seen active service in both the French and British forces. They included a tank commander, a naval sub-lieutenant, an army sergeant and servicemen who had fought at Heligoland, Jutland and Gaza.[16] French aspirants, like Joseph Watier (1891-1971), who were already undergoing military service when war broke out, found their service prolonged until the Armistice.

Most of the French missionaries liable for call up were to be found in Africa. The chief novitiate of the Society was situated at Maison Carrée, the mother house at Algiers; while the main scholasticate was at Carthage in Tunisia. When mobilization was declared in 1914 sixteen French novices were immediately called up, three of them already priests. A smaller number of French brother novices were also drafted, two of them losing their lives on active service before the year was out. The clerical novitiate ceased to exist and its buildings were requisitioned by the French army. At Carthage nineteen scholastics were called up in 1914, together with eight young priests who were completing their theological studies there. The following year, a further batch of scholastics received major orders in view of mobilization. Altogether, forty-eight scholastics and young priests were called up, most of them serving as non-commissioned officers in the Zouave regiments, or with infantry and supply units. Among the war dead were eleven French scholastics, fifteen novices and at least ten aspirants.[17]

Most of the novices and scholastics reported to military units in North Africa and some subsequently served in Tunisia, Algeria and even Morocco. The majority, however, saw action on the western and Mediterranean fronts. Relatively few of the missionaries at work in Algeria were liable for call-up. In the end, nine were mobilized. These included Henri Bardou (1877-1916*), the Prefect Apostolic of Ghardaia (Sahara), who – together with his successor, Gustave Nouet (1878-1959) – were made to supervise the making of a road from Laghouat to Ghardaia by German prisoners of war. Nouet had originally been called up as a medical orderly. At Thibar in Tunisia six missionaries were called up.

Of all the sub-Saharan missions, the Vicariate Apostolic of Uganda had the largest number of Christians and catechumens. It also had the biggest number of missionaries – one hundred and sixteen, serving no fewer than thirty-one mission stations. In September 1914, call-up papers arrived for more than thirty priests. Others whose medical status was uncertain were also called to the coast. Five were exempted after a medical examination at Mombasa and permission was given for another seven to be examined by a doctor in Uganda. A total of thirty-four were eventually mobilized. Five were to give their lives in the war.

Naturally there was great reluctance in the vicariate to sacrifice a third of the missionary personnel and the mobilization process was accompanied by considerable confusion, recrimination and misunderstanding. This was partly caused by the absence of the vicar apostolic, Henri Streicher (1863-1952), in France for health reasons. In his place the administrator, Simon Moullec (1861-1924) and the regional superior, Antoine Grange (1864-1922), strove to keep pace with events. Confusion was also caused by a failure in communications. Although the postal service was still in operation, there were lengthy delays and some letters failed to reach their destination. Between the end of July and the beginning of October 1914 no letter reached the Uganda region from Algiers. In these circumstances recourse was had to the telegraph, although at that time telegrams in and out of East Africa were notoriously subject to error and misinterpretation.[18]   In early September, the Superior General, Bishop Léon Livinhac (1846-1922), took the initiative by sending a telegram from Algiers to all mission superiors, forbidding the indiscriminate embarkation of missionaries for France. In Uganda this was understood as a comprehensive prohibition applicable to all who were liable for call-up, when in fact it was intended for missionaries suffering from ill health or engaged in making a retreat at the time.[19]   No letter of explanation was forthcoming and Grange telegraphed Livinhac for a clarification. When it came, Livinhac's second telegram was even more garbled than the first, but it convinced Grange and Moullec that a comprehensive prohibition was to be upheld. Moreover, the telegram's obscurity of language conveyed an air of reticence and suggested that an unofficial reprieve had been obtained from the French authorities.

Many of the missionaries who were liable for call-up, however, remained sceptical, and feared that they would be accused of desertion. Grange circularized them, advising them to place their confidence in the decision of their superiors and to avoid publicizing their apparent reprieve.[20] Before the end of September a private interview with British administrators at Entebbe resulted in a telegram from the Uganda Protectorate Government to the French Consul in Zanzibar asking that French missionaries might be allowed to remain in the country. The Consul, however, not only refused to pass on this request but replied by telegram that to exempt the missionaries would be unlawful and could not be approved by the French minister for war.[21] He urged immediate compliance with the call-up, making an exception only for those who had done their initial military service between 1887 and 1892.[22]

The French Consul in Zanzibar and consular agent in Mombasa were adamant and the tone of their letters became increasingly threatening. They had to deal with individual conscripts, who were unable to give a reason for their refusal to obey the mobilization order, and not with religious superiors who, unbeknown to the French authorities, had apparently countermanded it. Grange became increasingly concerned and told Livinhac that he would have to bring his telegrams into the open, however private and confidential they might be, in order to defend the missionaries from the charge of desertion.[23] This brought a third telegram from Livinhac ordering unequivocal compliance with the mobilization order and the conscripts were embarked in November.[24]   The whole saga had lasted two and a half months, perilously close to the three month limit for military call-up in the colonies.

In his correspondence with Streicher during August and September Livinhac made no allusion to the mobilization crisis in Uganda.[25] When Streicher arrived in Mombasa from Europe at the end of November, he was a "little surprised" to find that the "lamentable exodus" had already taken place and he "manifested his displeasure". Twenty-five missionaries had already left for the war in Europe and another ten had just arrived, after being threatened with desertion. Four of these were later exempted. Streicher saw the consular agent in Mombasa who did not insist on a desertion charge.[26]

The French consular agent had no funds with which to pay the fares of the conscripts. For thirty of the thirty-four mobilized missionaries, the British colonial administration at Entebbe met the cost of the journey by lake steamer and rail to Mombasa in second class, as well as all meals *en route* - a not inconsiderable sum. On the ship from Mombasa they were forced to travel fourth class, sleeping on deck. Grange saw that they took blankets for the voyage and that each was give twenty francs for meals on board.[27] A year later, Jean-Marie Le Tohic (1873-1939), a Ugandan missionary who was over age, volunteered for service in the medical corps.[28]

What truth is there in the story of British intervention in the French call-up? There is no reference to such a step in the correspondence of the Uganda Protectorate Government with the Colonial Office in London during 1914.[29] However, Grange sent Livinhac copies of both the British telegram and the French Consul's reply on October 5th. They seem not to have survived either in the Archives of the Missionaries of Africa or in the colonial records of Uganda.[30]

What truth is there in the report that the Uganda Protectorate paid the railway fares of the French conscripts? Again, there is no reference to it in the lists of claims submitted to London. It may, however, have been covered by recurrent travel expenditure, which was at the discretion of the Protectorate.[31] In any case, it is frequently referred to in the correspondence and reports of the Missionaries of Africa, and Julien Gorju (1868-1942), in a note published by the Catholic newspaper *Munno*, thanked the government for securing the conscripts' transport to Mombasa free of charge.[32]

In the four vicariates of German East Africa (modern Tanzania, Rwanda and Burundi) there were eighty-one French Missionaries of Africa when war was declared in 1914, but it was impossible for those liable for call-up to respond. The British Royal Navy maintained a blockade at the coast and the German authorities prevented all forms of communication with the Allied powers. Furthermore, French missionaries were moved away from the borders of the colony and many were also interned at Tabora after Allied forces penetrated the country in 1916. When Tabora fell in September of that year and the colony was nominally in the hands of British and Belgian forces, a half hearted attempt was made to mobilize the French missionaries. The political officer at Tabora passed on an order for the conscription of all French missionaries under the age of thirty-one, but the railway was out of action, and there were no qualified doctors to conduct medicals.[33] French missionaries in Kivu Vicariate (Rwanda-Burundi), the first to be liberated by Allied forces, received a mobilization order, but this was countermanded. In Nyanza Vicariate one father and six brothers were called up and in Tanganyika Vicariate four missionaries. With commendable patriotism, Antonin Nogaret (1883-1945), a missionary in Nyanza, made a heroic effort to report for military service. He reached Mombasa via the Uganda railway and, after waiting for several months, embarked on a Japanese ship bound for Madagascar, intending to take ship there for Marseilles. Providence had other plans, because the Japanese ship caught fire at Zanzibar and, there being no likelihood of further transport, the French

Consul returned him to Bukoba. The British authorities generously gave him a first class ticket for his return rail journey.[34]

In Central Africa, French missionaries in the White Father Vicariates of Bangweolo (modern Zambia) and Nyasa (modern Malawi) were much fewer in numbers. Bishop Mathurin Guillemé of Nyasa reckoned that seventeen were liable for call-up. If all went to war, he would be left with five Canadians and five Dutchmen, not even enough to place two missionaries in each of the six mission stations. Bangweolo (northern Zambia) was in a similar dilemma. With the backing of the British, the French Consul-General in Pretoria was approached, and exemption was granted while the French Government was being contacted. Bishop Guillemé's relief, however, was premature. The exemption was revoked in August 1916 and twelve missionaries were mobilized.[35] The diary of the Jesuit mission at Katondwe reports the arrival of these twelve on their journey west to the railway.[36]

In West Africa the Vicariate of French Sudan – as yet undivided – was more than four times the size of France. This vast circumscription which covered the modern countries of Mali, Burkina Faso and parts of Guinea, Ivory Coast, Ghana and Niger, was served by a mere forty-three White Fathers, most of them French. At different times, a total of twelve missionaries were called up, but two were exempted almost immediately and allowed to return to their missions, while remaining on the reserve. Three or four others were deployed locally for the campaign in Cameroon, or as medical interpreters for the African troops in transit at Dakar. One of those who served in France was Eugène Mangin (1877-1922), brother of the redoubtable General Charles Mangin. After the social upheavals caused by the recruitment of African troops for service in Europe, the colonial government came to the opinion that it was better for the region's stability if missionaries were allowed to remain at their posts.[37]

Some of the White Fathers at St. Anne's, Jerusalem, were also called up, but their plight was forgotten when all the French missionaries were expelled by the Turks and their Melkite seminary closed down. On December 4th 1914 the newly elected Pope Benedict XV inquired of Fr. Louis Burtin (1853-1942), the Society's Procurator in Rome, how many White Fathers had been called up, and how many killed. He was told that there were more than two hundred and fifty members of the Society under arms and that twenty had already lost their lives. "Poor children! Poor children!" exclaimed the Pope.[38]

Belgian Mobilization

Belgium introduced conscription in 1912, but, by the time of the German invasion in 1914, it had hardly taken effect. After the capture of Belgium's eastern forts and the German crossing of the French frontier, King Albert, as Belgian Commander-in-Chief, organized operations from Antwerp in the German army's rear. Antwerp was rapidly besieged and taken, but Albert's broken army recovered and fought alongside the British and French armies in the so-called race for the sea, and the subsequent battles in Flanders, winning the admiration of both friend and foe alike. At the end of 1915, the Belgians mobilized men born between 1890 and 1895. Three Belgian White Father priests, two brothers and three novices responded. Eleven Belgian scholastics were called up from Carthage, including four newly ordained priests. They were joined by two novices from Algiers and two brothers from Thibar. Altogether thirty Belgian members of the Society were mobilized and were camped at Calais and Auvours. This camp contained no fewer than three hundred seminarians and religious who were allowed to continue their theological studies and – in the case of the Missionaries of Africa – the study of Swahili. A Belgian Jesuit was placed in charge, and it was remarked that the establishment was more like a seminary than a military camp.[39]

By the following year, some forty Belgian White Father priests, brothers, novices and scholastics had been called up from Africa (both North and Equatorial) to the Belgian army in Europe. In 1916, another Belgian scholastic was conscripted. This was Joseph de Maeght (1894-1963) who afterwards served as a missionary in Lake Albert Vicariate, Congo.[40] One of the Belgian novices conscripted in 1914 was Charles Raes, who did not persevere in the Society. The Belgian military authorities were good enough to post him to the Congolese army in Africa, where he took part in the invasion of German East Africa in 1916. After the capture of Rwanda and Burundi, he followed the retreating Germans on their withdrawal to Tabora.[41]

German Mobilization

Conscription was introduced throughout Germany after 1870 and an enormous army of serving and potential soldiers was created. The country's standing army was increased by 170,000 men before 1914. Young men were subjected to a compulsory two year period of military training, followed by five years of annual training. Then, until the age of thirty-nine, they were placed in the *Landwehr* or secondary reserve. After that, until the age of forty-five, they belonged to a third-line reserve, the *Landsturm*.[42] The German authorities did not usually conscript priests into the army except as chaplains, but had no compunction about drafting religious brothers during their formation. These remained in the reserve after profession. Clerical aspirants could also be called up, but left the reserve after receiving major orders.

In Germany the missionary vocation seems to have been particularly attractive to working men, eager to learn a trade. Such men became brother auxiliaries. In 1914 German brothers outnumbered German priests in the Society of Missionaries of Africa. There were thirty-eight German brothers to twenty-three German priests. The younger German brothers had been called up for basic military training during formation and were then enrolled in the reserve. Most of them were to be found in Germany and a few were completing their formation and learning trades at Thibar, Tunisia. Two were working as missionaries in Algeria. When war broke out there were also thirty German novices at Algiers. These could not, of course, re-join the German Army. All of them, together with the two professed brothers and those from Thibar, were interned by the French, one of them dying of tuberculosis during the process.

In German East Africa, there were only ten White Fathers who were "genuine" Germans (besides twenty-three Alsatians). The colony was blockaded at the coast and surrounded on its three other sides by hostile allied countries. There was no question of a call-up to the army in Germany. Five of the ten German missionaries, however, did some military service with the German colonial army in East Africa during the war. One of them, Jean-Pierre Blass (Brother John Berchmans 1885-1916*) of Ndala (Unyanyembe) did not wait for call-up papers, but abandoned his mission, volunteering immediately for service in the German colonial army in September 1914. His missionary vocation was already in question and the chauvinism of his French confreres after the outbreak of war was the final straw. He was not allowed to return, but was released from his perpetual oath three years later.[43]

Paul Chylewski (Brother Josaphat, 1875-1948), a German of Polish origin, was called up in 1915, and appeared at Mwazye Mission (Tanganyika Vicariate) at the end of May, dressed in the uniform of a *Landsturmann*. He was carrying 3,000 Rupees for Lieut. Markgraf, a German officer at the border with Northern Rhodesia (modern Zambia).[44] Later in the year, he and Alois Hamberger, a German White Father priest, replaced their non-German confreres at this sensitive border mission, threatened by British invasion. Léon Schneider (Brother Germain, 1883-1959) also appeared at Mwazye in November in the guise of a *Landsturmann*.[45] Jean Borste, (Brother Gaspard, 1873-1948) was another German brother, called to serve in East Africa. He was posted to a supply unit and was captured by the Belgians in 1917.[46] Finally, Conrad Blass (Brother Balthasar, 1877-1959) was also called up from the reserve in 1915 for the East African campaign and was later interned as a prisoner of war in India.[47] In Europe itself, more German brothers and some clerical aspirants were called up. Eight of these died on active service in France.

Chaplains and Transport Officers

White Father priests did not join the French army as chaplains, but some were officially appointed as such while on active service. This happened to Léon Darot (1890-1958) on the Serbian front at the end of 1916, and also to Léon Brossier (1882-1918) at Verdun in May 1917.[48] The latter was killed by an exploding shell at the Vosges in the following year. A former novice of the Society, the priest Charles Umbricht (1873-1941), who left for reasons of ill health in 1912 before taking the missionary oath, was allowed to serve as a volunteer chaplain in 1914, although exempt from call-up. Umbricht became one of the most celebrated and decorated heroes of the First World War – a legendary figure in his own lifetime.[49] For the duration of the war Rome gave all priest-soldiers the same powers and faculties as chaplains, and it was up to them to exercise this ministry as and when their other duties allowed. In fact, the presence of priest-soldiers in the trenches was universally welcomed. Their ministrations were scarcely ever refused and they were regarded by their superior officers as an important boost for morale.

The changed attitude of the French authorities towards the clergy was an important facet of the *union sacrée*, the rallying of all sections of the population to the national cause. Anti-clericalism was forgotten and every trace of the former animosity disappeared. The figure of St. Joan of Arc, long cherished by the Catholic right, now became a patriotic – even a republican – symbol, reaching a climax in the saint's canonization two years after the war. Marshall Pétain, the "victor of Verdun", went so far as to quote Joan's triumphant words at the siege of Orléans in his famous Order of the Day of April 9th 1916: "Courage! We shall have them!"[50]

The Belgians had no reluctance about appointing chaplains, and they welcomed them especially in their colonial army. Missionary priests were reckoned to be a stabilizing factor in the Congolese *Force Publique*, good for discipline and morale. Bishops were asked to offer some of their priests as military chaplains. In August 1915 Bishop Victor Roelens of the Vicariate of Upper Congo began by appointing Augustin Dumortier (1878-1951) chaplain to the troops that were assembling in the north of his vicariate, ready for the onslaught on German Rwanda. In the following year he appointed Joseph Weghsteen (1873-1962) to the southern army on the Northern Rhodesian (Zambian) frontier. By the end of 1916, he had already appointed eight chaplains, and this number was maintained up to the end of the war. Five of these chaplains accompanied General Charles Tombeur and his Congolese troops all the way to the siege of Tabora in September 1916. Others remained with the troops at Kigoma and in Belgian occupied East Africa until they were eventually allowed to return to their mission. Altogether eleven White Fathers served as military chaplains with the Belgians and Congolese in the East African campaign.[51]

Another ten Missionaries of Africa served as chaplains with the British forces in East Africa and several more served at different times as chaplains in native military hospitals in the region. Thousands of the soldiers and carriers that were recruited for the campaign were Catholics and thousands of all categories and denominations succumbed to dysentery, pneumonia, malaria and meningitis. Early in 1916 the British authorities were massing their forces on the Ugandan, British East African (Kenyan), Northern Rhodesian (Zambian) and Nyasa (Malawi) borders, ready for a multi-pronged invasion of German territory. Chaplains were needed to accompany the African *askari* (soldiers) and *tenga-tenga* (carriers). Staff was also required for the native hospitals that were being set up at Dar es Salaam, Kilwa, Morogoro, Dodoma, Fife (Nkawa) and elsewhere as the campaign progressed. The MSOLA (White Sisters) served in many of these hospitals, as did sisters of other congregations. Priests of the Spiritan, Mill Hill and Consolata missionary societies also worked in them as chaplains. Early in 1916 Bishop Henri Streicher of the Uganda Vicariate was also asked to supply missionaries for these functions.

The South African commanders, Jan Christian Smuts and Jacob Louis Van Deventer, pushed southwards from British East Africa (modern Kenya) in two columns. The Canadian White Fathers, Edouard Lafleur (1876-1921) and Joseph Fillion (1881-1930) went with them to the central railway and on to the south-east. Two other Canadians, the future Bishop Edouard Michaud (1884-1945) and Adrien Laberge (1886-1973) were joined by the Frenchman Célestin

Dupupet (1876-1949) as they accompanied the column of Brigadier-General Sir Charles Crewe from Uganda. Crewe occupied Bukoba, Ukerewe Island and Mwanza, before following in the wake of General Tombeur's Congolese in the approach to Tabora. These White Father chaplains were all given the rank of Captain.

At the same time, White Fathers in Nyasaland were urging Bishop Guillemé to respond to the Government's request for chaplains. This was regarded as a necessary proof of loyalty from a missionary society that had members in "enemy territory" across the border with German East Africa.[52] Guillemé offered the services of two Canadians, Ernest Paradis (1881-1945) and Wilfred Sarrazin (1885-1928), and also two Frenchmen, Claude Boucansaud (1881-1958) and Joseph Mazé (1883-1959). These four were given the rank of Lieutenant, and accompanied the forces of Brigadier-General Edward Northey as they moved northwards into German East Africa.

In July 1916 these chaplains acquired another string to their bow, being appointed to the transport service. As transport officers, it was their duty to organize the carriers in the supply caravans. By the last year of the war, as carriers and *askari* were wounded or fell sick in their thousands, the transport officers found themselves increasingly involved in hospital work, and other White Fathers were drafted into the native hospitals with them. Francis Legendre (1886-1920), a Frenchman, was appointed to a hospital at Fife (Nkawa), Northern Rhodesia (Zambia), while the future bishop, Oscar Julien (1886-1961), a Canadian, found himself caring for one thousand two hundred soldiers and carriers, of whom ten died every day.

In 1917 the concept of military chaplaincy provided a solution for the pastoral care of the Bavarian Benedictine missions of German East Africa, after the German monks had been interned and repatriated by the British. Bishop Streicher of Uganda offered another of his missionaries, the Dutchman Joseph Laane (1869-1941) for this apostolate. With the rank of Captain, Laane visited military camps and hospitals and was then asked by the outgoing German Bishop, Franz-Xavier Spreiter, to accept nomination as Administrator Apostolic in the Dar es Salaam Vicariate. As Bishop Streicher colourfully observed, "The Benedictine Vicar Apostolic received him as Jesus at Gethsemani welcomed the consoling angel."[53] Laane begged more personnel from other vicariates and eventually headed a team totalling some fifteen missionaries. He was joined at different times by a total of twelve Missionaries of Africa, working until 1920 at Mahenge, Lindi, Peramiho, and Iringa.[54]

Between twenty and thirty White Fathers, therefore, were appointed military "chaplains" in East Africa during the First World War. It was a sacrifice which nevertheless bore fruit in various ways for their vicariates of origin, as we shall see.

Effects of Mobilization on the African Missions

In 1914 the Missionaries of Africa were responsible for eleven ecclesiastical circumscriptions. In Equatorial Africa there were the Vicariates Apostolic of Uganda, Nyanza, Kivu, Unyanyembe, Tanganyika and Upper Congo, and in

Central Africa, the Vicariates Apostolic of Nyasa and Bangweolo. In West Africa there was the Vicariate Apostolic of French Sudan and in the Algerian Sahara, the Prefecture Apostolic of Ghardaia. To these must be added the Mission of Kabylia also in Algeria. Missionary bishops relied on a regular supply of personnel to staff existing mission stations and to found new ones. The sudden removal of some two hundred missionary priests as military conscripts and chaplains was a bitter blow. It was compounded by the relative absence of any new arrivals, and – in German East Africa – by the repatriation of German missionaries after the war. However, the total number of mission stations declined by only two or three during the war years. Very few had to be closed. On the other hand, the steady expansion of the missionary vicariates that had taken place in the years preceding the war was temporarily halted and virtually no new mission stations were opened during the war.

Growth in numbers depended on maintaining the catechumenates. Fortunately, in some of the vicariates the White Fathers had trained catechists who could carry on the work of preparing adults for baptism, even though – as in Uganda – some catechist training centres were forced to close during the war. The seminaries, however, did not close and the number of seminarians continued to rise.[55] A small but growing number of African priests was also beginning to make a pastoral impact. The overall advantages and disadvantages from a spiritual, social and pastoral point of view that flowed from the war will be considered in a later chapter. All that needs to be done at this juncture is to make a statistical assessment of the missions entrusted to the White Fathers.

Funding was still tied to missionary statistics at this time. Consequently, the returns made to Rome are a notoriously unsafe basis on which to judge the success or failure of missionary work. However, they can offer some indication of how the war affected the White Father vicariates. All of them had relatively large numbers of catechumens, and the momentum of growth could only be sustained by maintaining these numbers. Nearly all the vicariates experienced a drop in the number of catechumens. In spite of the large-scale recruitment of *askari* and carriers and the other social upheavals caused by the war, the smaller vicariates managed to maintain their levels fairly well. The vicariates with massive catechumenates, such as Uganda and Kivu experienced a marked drop in numbers. Uganda, for example, dropped from more than seventy thousand catechumens at the beginning of the war to around fifty thousand at the end. Kivu dropped from eight thousand to four thousand in 1918.[56] Clearly, maintaining these large catechumenates required considerable management, as well as pedagogical skills, which only missionary priests then possessed. In the case of Uganda, the sudden removal of the missionaries coincided with the end of mass conversions in Buganda, though not in other regions of the vicariate.[57] It must be said, nevertheless, that the fall in numbers was a temporary phenomenon in most places. In the decade that followed the First World War the numbers of Catholic missionaries and Christians doubled.[58]

Effects of Mobilization on Missionary Recruitment

Up to 1914, candidates in the Society of Missionaries of Africa completed their formation in North Africa. After novitiate in Algiers, clerics went to the theological scholasticate at Carthage, Tunisia, and brothers to the trade school at Thibar also in Tunisia. The single European province, centred on France, possessed a major seminary at Binson Priory, near Châtillon-sur-Marne, where aspirants studied philosophy and completed a first year of theology before going to the novitiate. There were also embryonic major seminaries with a similar pattern of studies for clerics at Bouchout in Belgium and Boxtel in the Netherlands, combined in these places with a postulancy for brother aspirants. A German vice-province had been erected in 1905 in the hope of attracting German vocations and to provide support for missionary activity in German East Africa. The vice-province included a brothers' postulancy at Marienthal in Luxemburg, a postulancy and major seminary on the model of Binson at Trier, the ancient Roman city on the Mosel, and a purpose-built junior seminary at Haigerloch in Baden-Würtemburg (traditionally Hohenzollern). There were further junior seminaries, or apostolic schools in France, Belgium, the Netherlands and Switzerland, and also – as a result of the anti-clerical legislation – a school in southern England, founded in 1912. This school at Bishop's Waltham embarked on a modest late vocations programme, preparing aspirants for philosophical studies.

Students for the missionary priesthood usually followed a two-year course in philosophy, a year of novitiate and four years of theology, three of them at Carthage. To supply the Society's missions in Africa with about thirty priests annually, Carthage would have had to enrol a total of a hundred and twenty to a hundred and thirty students at any one time.[59] It was difficult to achieve such numbers even in the pre-war period, but with mobilization, the number of theology students fell dramatically. In August 1914, twenty-seven French students were called up and this was followed in 1915 by the call-up of more newly ordained French students and a group of Belgians. Moreover, all the French novice clerics who would normally have moved on to Carthage were also mobilized. The German novices were interned in Algeria, but were eventually moved to Garaison in the High Pyrenees, together with a German father, Leo Pfeffermann (1867-1956). There they continued their internment for the duration of the war. The clerical novitiate in Algiers was closed. Carthage was thus deprived of its normal intake, as well as of a large number of current students. The year ended with a total of only twenty-four. Apart from a small number of exempted Frenchmen, these hailed from neutral or non-belligerent countries. By 1916, the number had sunk to twenty, the smallest total on record.[60]

Even when the war was over, it took some years before the scholasticate could get back to normal. Although relatively few demobilized novices and scholastics who survived the war dropped out of formation, no fewer than twenty-three had given their lives for their country. In 1919 the clerical novitiate re-opened in Algiers with seventy-three, many of them war veterans, and two years later clerical novices numbered fifty-one. In 1919, twenty-nine newcomers reported for theology studies at Carthage, all except four being war veterans. By 1920 the total in theology was eighty-three and by 1921 it had risen to ninety-three.

Ordinations to the priesthood dropped to the all-time low of three in 1915-1916 (two Canadians and one Dutchman), and even in 1919 it was still a "war time ordination" of only five.[61] By July 1921, ordinations had crept up to twenty-one.[62] Recovery was slow and this meant that relatively few new missionaries were available for the African vicariates for several years after the Armistice.

Binson Priory, which had only ten students at the time of its closure in 1914, played a key role during the war, in its liaison with White Father aspirants at the front. Indeed, the seminary was virtually at the front itself, being twice occupied by enemy troops during the first and second Battles of the Marne and suffering final destruction in 1918. Its story will be told in greater detail later in this book. The seminary reopened provisionally at Le Colombier, near Angers, after the war, and then moved to Kerlois in Brittany, where there was a total of forty-three students in November 1920.[63] These were virtually all war veterans.

Bouchout in occupied Belgium was also forced to close. It reopened prematurely with thirty students in 1917, but the students had to be sent home in July for lack of food. By the end of 1922, it had nineteen major seminarians.[64] Meanwhile, at Boxtel in neutral Holland the philosophy seminary continued to operate. To it was added in September 1914 a combined clerical and brothers' novitiate for Dutch and Belgian candidates.[65] In 1918, Boxtel boasted of having almost as many personnel as the motherhouse in Algiers.[66] It had nineteen scholastics in January and as many as twenty-one novice clerics in December. After the novitiate reopened at Algiers, the philosophy seminary continued, and counted fifteen scholastics at the end of 1920. The scholasticate at Trier in Germany also continued throughout the hostilities. It started the war with eight scholastics in 1915 and this number had risen to thirty-two in 1919, eight being theologians.

In 1915 the total membership of the Society actually topped the nine hundred mark, but with a reduction in recruitment thereafter, together with many deaths and departures, it swiftly declined to eight hundred and fifty-six in the year after the war ended. In 1920, it was just beginning the climb back.[67] At the same time, it was being noted that a powerful movement towards the missionary vocation was taking place in the Netherlands. The Mill Hill Missionaries, the Society of African Missions and the Scheut Missionaries were all beginning to attract applicants in large numbers.[68] The same was true in post-war Germany. This was noticed in a memorandum from Georg Steinhage (1876-1962) and was also the subject of discussions at the 1920 General Chapter of the White Fathers.[69] In fact, the Society was shortly to share in this vocation boom that took place in the inter-war years.

"The blood of priests and seminarians shed in the war is the seed of vocations" wrote a White Father correspondent from East Africa in 1916.[70] The reasoning would seem to be similar to that of the original dictum: "The blood of martyrs is the seed of Christians." It is undoubtedly true that the example of heroic sacrifice inspires others, but this truth needs to be placed in the whole context of the First World War. Before 1914, a handful of White Fathers, operating from procures and formation houses, were responsible for mission animation in Europe and North America. The Great War brought up to four hundred Missionaries of Africa to the front line, where they mingled with the youth of Europe, America and Africa. Many of them had already served in Africa, and all were fired by the missionary ideal. The presence of missionary aspirants, novices and scholastics in uniform was perhaps even more persuasive. Friendship in adversity creates the strongest possible bond, and it is not at all surprising that the work of the White Fathers became more widely known and more deeply appreciated and that young soldiers even discussed the possibility of a missionary vocation with them in the trenches. Statistics would seem to support this hypothesis. Total membership of the Society topped one thousand in 1925. By the end of the following decade it was one thousand five hundred and on the eve of the Second World War the total was already two thousand.[71]

This experience of trench warfare on both the western and eastern fronts is the subject of the next chapter. It is largely against the background of this experience that the rest of the story of what happened to the Missionaries of Africa in World War I must be told.

CHAPTER TWO

TRENCH WARFARE

The Western Front

In January 1917 François Viel (Brother Camille 1885-1955) described the trenches in which he lived on the Western Front. They were twelve metres deep, with bunks on top of each other, as on a ship. They were filled with armaments and supplies and some were lit with electric light.[1] The previous June, Father Joseph Delmer (1891-1969) described his trench on the Mediterranean front. "I live in a pretty hole", he wrote "covered with tent canvas...I have deepened it so I can stand upright. A niche takes my altar stone for Mass, the banner of the Sacred Heart and some flowers before the crucifix and (a picture of) *Notre Dame du Retour.*"[2] The war in Europe was trench warfare and these descriptions show the extent to which the trenches had become a permanent feature of every major battlefield.

Missionaries of Africa were present on all the fronts of the First World War.[3] Most saw action on the Western Front. The German invasion of Belgium provoked the so-called Battle of the Frontiers in August 1914, in which offensives by the French Army and the British Expeditionary Force failed to hold back the main thrust into France. The Allies of the *Entente* retreated to the outskirts of Paris, tempting the Germans into untenable positions east of the city. The first Battle of the Marne took place in the first half of September. Faced with the prospect of being outflanked and even of a wedge being driven between the wings of their army, the Germans withdrew to defensive positions on higher ground in the north-west. There followed the "Race to the Sea" and the first Battle of Ypres in Belgian Flanders. On September 15th the first trenches began to appear, as both sides dug themselves into facing defensive positions along a line stretching from the Belgian coast down to the Franco-Swiss border.

These entrenched positions remained virtually unchanged until the final year of the war and were, to all intents and purposes, impregnable. The trenches were protected by barbed wire entanglements and manned by machine-gunners. A maze of saps or communication trenches connected the front line to supply lines, first aid posts and headquarters in the rear.[4] Artillery was also positioned in the rear to give supporting fire. It was incumbent on the Allies to attack the entrenched German invaders. This they did, in large-scale daylight offensives or in night raids. The Allies used the artillery barrage to bombard enemy trench systems and defences before an assault, or to sweep before the troops as they advanced over open ground. Besides giving warning of the impending attack, this heavy gunfire could never effectively destroy the enemy positions. The Germans used their artillery mainly to disperse the attackers, and their machine guns to wipe out those who succeeded in getting through the barrage.

The pointless horror of such assaults was most powerfully illustrated by the Battle of Loos in September 1915, in which a mass of British troops advancing across open grassland was mown down by German machine-gun fire. In the British infantry units and Kitchener's "New Army" of volunteers, sixteen thousand lost their lives and twenty-five thousand were wounded. Those who survived reached the unbroken barbed wire and were forced to retreat, while the Germans, sickened by the slaughter, held their fire.[5]

Communications were largely maintained by runner, since radio telephony had not yet been introduced and fixed field telephone lines were regularly cut by the bombardment. It was also extremely difficult to direct artillery fire on to specified targets. Apart from observers in captive balloons, aerial observation hardly existed. This meant that, while defence was strong, attack was usually unsuccessful. As a result, a situation of stalemate developed in which the opposing armies remained stuck in their trenches for months on end, undergoing regular, mutual bombardment from each other's artillery. Brother Joseph Rollin (Maxime, 1881-1961), for example, spent no less than twenty months in the trenches at Ypres between 1914 and 1916.[6]

The Western Front was a belt of devastated countryside, rutted earth, splintered trees and ruined villages, about four miles wide, stretching some four hundred and forty miles from Nieuport in Belgium to the Swiss border near Freiburg. The country on either side of this belt of destruction was eerily normal. Within, it was a "furnace" of exploding shells and machine-gun fire across a "no-man's land" no more than three thousand to four thousand yards wide, exacting equal numbers of casualties on either side.

In 1915 Allied offensives took place at Ypres and also in Artois and Champagne. 1916, however, was the year of major battles. The German attack on Verdun began in February, defended by the French at immense cost to both sides. By June twenty million shells had been fired into the battle zone, permanently altering the character of the landscape and making it a place of terror and death. Both sides fought for the sake of fighting. There was no prize to be gained only men to be killed. For the French, Verdun was a place of huge symbolic value. It stood on the road to the lost provinces of Alsace and Lorraine, and had to be held at all costs. More than seven hundred thousand soldiers perished before the fighting subsided in December and the Germans abandoned their war of attrition.[7] In many ways, Verdun was a "war within the war".

The other great land battle of 1916 took place in the region of the Somme River. This area had been held by the French until August 1915 and was a so-called "quiet front". The Germans had had time to secure their positions, but when the British arrived to take over the sector, their commander Douglas Haig planned an offensive to break the enemy line. The line proved far stronger than expected. The Germans had dug trenches that were thirty feet deep and were impervious to British shells. In early July the unprotected attackers approached the defenders in their impregnable earthworks and barbed-wire entanglements, only to be mown down in their thousands. Twenty thousand British troops died on the first day of battle and another forty thousand were wounded. This was the greatest loss of life in British military history. Further attempts, aided by troops from Australia and South Africa, and by the French, in their sector across the river, resulted in small territorial gains. The battle rapidly became a "war of attrition". By the end of July, the Germans had lost a hundred and sixty thousand and the British and French over two hundred thousand, while the line had barely moved three miles.[8]

The campaign was prolonged by the appearance in September of a new invention, the tank. After an initial success, virtually all the tanks were disabled. October and November brought no further change. Repeated attacks were repulsed by the Germans. In the holocaust of the Somme, the Allies certainly lost six hundred thousand men, the Germans as many, killed and wounded. The Somme was Europe's "greatest military tragedy of the twentieth century".[9]

White Father soldiers served and died at Verdun and on the Somme. Adrien Sylvestre (Brother Alexis 1887-1918) from Nantes was wounded in the left arm and thigh at the Somme in 1916. He was rescued from the trench in which he lay, unable to move, and attributed his survival to the intercession of (the as yet uncanonized) Sister Thérèse of Lisieux, whose shrine he managed to visit while convalescing from the subsequent painful operation. He went missing near Lassigny in the final year of the war. A confrere writing after his disappearance summed up the war experience of many White Fathers: "What scenes of carnage and death! And what a frightful responsibility has been incurred by those who unleashed such a cataclysm!"[10]

The experience of Verdun called forth the most graphic descriptions of battle in the White Fathers' letters to their superiors. In January 1916 all was still quiet, as Raphaël Ordonneau (1893-1973) started teaching Latin to a young soldier who wanted to be a priest and went for a two hour walk with him one evening in the forest.[11] Then, after some initial "rough engagements", matters became more serious in February. "They will never have Verdun!" exclaimed Joseph Portier (1878-1955), reflecting the general mood of the French infantry. He went on to describe how, as he was celebrating Mass at the forest edge with shells bursting a short distance away, some passing soldiers said: "Let us stop and pray for our comrades".[12] Louis Châles (1891-1961) in March described the repeated German assaults and their determination to take Verdun. He was severely wounded a few days later. On May 18th a scholastic, Ernest Delarse (1881-1916), described "the worst eight days (he) had ever lived". The earth had been turned over and over again by the shells. No trenches were left, only craters and fox-holes. There was "infernal, continuous machine-gun fire", while he snatched a moment to eat at night and to write his last letter. Next day, he disappeared without trace.[13]

Gaston Duiquet (1888-1930*) wrote on June 5th "from the trenches – or rather, a little muddy ditch" - that sleep was impossible in the wind, rain and gunfire. A day later he joined a counter-attack. They reached a shallow communication trench under a "mad deluge of metal", with a raging fire on the horizon. "One can lose one's life here a thousand times!" he wrote. They took cover and nibbled some biscuits and tinned meat. Then he was called to bury two Zouaves.[14] Three weeks later he was himself wounded.[15]

Father Jean-Baptiste Robert (1887-1916), another victim of Verdun, wrote five months before his death: "There are no trenches or saps left, only shell holes with lacerated arms and legs sticking out and a strong stench of putrefaction."[16] The fever-ridden Brother Joseph Loiseau (Pierre 1881-1918) writing also in May, described how he had lived on nothing but water for five days and how his swollen feet were covered with abscesses. He arrived in this state at Verdun to collect the wounded from the "Valley of Death". "The bombardment was so great and the barrages in the rear so concentrated that I am always asking myself how I have managed to come out of this hell safe and sound." Shells were "falling like hail".[17] He died the following year in hospital of a neglected abscess. "We shall appreciate life", wrote Father Charles Joyeux (1885-1936*), "if we ever come out of this war."[18]

Father Jules Pagès (1887-1984) wrote in December of the troops' silent march along muddy communication trenches, carrying their heavy packs. They were in mud up to their knees and every inch of ground had been shelled. They passed the corpses of soldiers in the trenches and more corpses littered the roads on their return. The priest's feet were frozen and his toes had turned black.[19] The scholastic Ernest Potier (1888-1918), who was to die at the start of the Nivelle Offensive, wrote of the "frightful, unimaginable bombardment" and of moments that belong neither to life nor death." Minutes later he was wounded in the shoulder.[20]

During March 1917, the Allies noticed that the Germans were withdrawing along the whole front between Arras and the River Aisne. Considerably stronger positions further back had been prepared by them known as the Hindenburg Line. The Line, however, stopped just short of Vimy Ridge in the Arras sector and the ridge known as the *Chemin des Dames* in the zone of the River Aisne. Canadian troops scored a sensational success at Vimy Ridge in April and penetrated up to three miles of German territory. The Germans, however, quickly rebuilt their positions. With the standoff at Verdun and a threat of unrest in the French Army, General Robert Nivelle planned an abrupt breakthrough at the *Chemin des Dames*. However, the German defences in this area were among the strongest of the entire front and the so-called Nivelle Offensive in April was another failure.

During the remainder of 1917 Allied efforts were concentrated in the region of Ypres, focussing on the village of Passchendaele. Both armies employed similar tactics in the sodden and muddy wastes of this battlefield, without a decisive victory being possible for either. In spite of this, the battle was pointlessly prolonged by Haig until nearly seventy thousand of his soldiers were killed and a hundred and seventy thousand wounded.[21]   Most of the White Father conscripts, especially the Belgians, saw action in and around Ypres, either in 1915 or 1917. Two died at Passchendaele.[22]

The United States declared war on Germany in April 1917 and the first American troops arrived in France in June. American intervention was one of the decisive factors in bringing the war to an end. Germany had no equivalent resources to oppose the millions of soldiers that the United States was able to bring across the Atlantic. Until this became evident, Germany decided to launch a series of Spring offensives in 1918. The first two targeted the British sector in March and April. In May and June the Germans launched attacks on the French sector. The final great push came in July, precipitating the second Battle of the Marne and once more engulfing the White Fathers' seminary at Binson. Allied counter-attacks took place throughout the rest of the year, breaking through the Hindenburg line at several points. In the second week of November the Germans negotiated an armistice with the Allies, and the war officially ended on November 11th. More Missionaries of Africa lost their lives in these closing months of the war than at any other time during the conflict.

The Dardanelles

The Dardanelles is a narrow waterway that joins the Mediterranean to the landlocked Sea of Marmara. This, in turn, is connected to the Black Sea by the even narrower passage of the Bosphorous, guarded at its entrance by the city of Istanbul. The European shore of the Dardanelles was a narrow peninsular belonging to Turkey.   Early in 1915 Kitchener and Churchill planned a diversionary attack on Turkey in this region. An amphibious attack on Gallipoli in February by the Royal Navy and Royal Marines ended in failure. The Turks, under their German commander, were taken by surprise, but proved strong enough to hold off the invaders.   Stronger landing parties were evidently required.

After unnecessary delays and with inadequate preparation and intelligence, an Allied   Expeditionary Force of British, Australian and New Zealand troops attempted to land on the Mediterranean shore of the peninsular in April, while the French *Corps Expéditionnaire d'Orient* created a diversion on the Asian shore of the waterway before joining the action at the tip of the peninsular.[23] The coastline consisted, for the most part, of steep cliffs which proved impossible to scale, and the Allies were pinned down on the beaches or slaughtered in the boats. The worst losses were suffered by the Australians and New Zealanders in so-called "ANZAC Cove". There, it was afterwards said, Australia became a nation. The critically positioned Turkish 19th Division was commanded by the charismatic Mustapha Kemal, later known as Kemal Attaturk, founder of modern Turkey. The Allied survivors clung to the steep slopes and sandy bluffs of the coastline, while the Turks dominated the hillsides from their trenches on the crests. Savage fighting also took place at the tip of the pensinsular as the Allies struggled unsuccessfully to push the line inland. On December 28th, the withdrawal of troops from Gallipoli began. The Allies had lost two hundred and sixty-five thousand men killed, the Turks three hundred thousand killed, wounded and missing.

Sultan Mehmed V of Turkey had declared a *jihad* or holy war against the Allies on November 11th 1914. His call to Muslims in British, French and Russian territories to rise against their rulers fell largely on deaf ears. The Missionaries of Africa were reckoned to be specialists in Islam. Many, if not most, of those called up were serving in North African regiments. Whatever the reason, a relatively large number found themselves fighting the Turks in the Dardanelles. On most fronts, the handful of White Father conscripts knew of each other's whereabouts and tried to meet with them, whenever opportunity arose. In the Dardanelles, there were no fewer than thirty Missionaries of Africa belonging to the French Expeditionary Corps. It was a small force operating in a confined space and they saw and heard a great deal of each other. About twenty White Fathers, mostly scholastics and novices, interacted regularly as medical orderlies and stretcher-bearers. Gaston Duiquet (1888-1930*) envied this missionary companionship. With misguided zeal (he was still only a student) he thought it was entirely appropriate for them to be fighting against Muslims. Writing from "the bitter trenches of the North", he exclaimed: "What a beautiful little army! Thirty White Fathers throwing themselves with the same heart and momentum into the assault on Islam! ...To fly our flag over the palace of the Grand Turk is also part of the glorious work of White Fathers. Forward! It is God's will."[24]

The German General Otto Liman von Sanders was the overall commander of the Turkish armies at the Dardanelles and there were other German officers serving the Turks. One of these was Sebastian Zehetmaier (1894-1969), a White Father aspirant called up from his philosophy studies at Trier. Zehetmaier was a Lieutenant in the Information Services, who saw action with the Turkish army against the Russians in the Caucasus in 1916, receiving decorations from both Germany and Turkey. He does not seem to have put in an appearance in the Dardanelles.[25] Had he done so, it would certainly have given the lie to Duiquet's simplistic religious view of the campaign.

The letters from Gallipoli in April and May convey an atmosphere of excitement, confusion and danger - bombardment, disembarkation, re-embarkation. Some scholastics waiting on board are doing their spiritual reading while others are plunging in among the soldiers struggling ashore. Several White Fathers are wounded. Then, the Turks come at night to throw grenades into the Allies' hastily dug trenches and to bayonet them. The White Fathers make the rounds of the trenches from their first aid post. A Zouave is killed by a British soldier in mistake for a Turk. Bursting shells, grenades, bombs and tracers are all around, "an indescribable spectacle. War is horrible!"[26]

Father Arsène Sabau (1887-1874) describes a "hellish bombardment" in June. The British advance three hundred metres, but have to retreat under artillery fire. There is a new assault and the French take two trenches, but thousands of Turks emerge and push them back. A battalion of eight hundred men is reduced to one hundred and fifteen, and the White Fathers are burying the dead all day. Three Missionaries of Africa are killed: Jean-Baptiste Béraud (1891-1915) receives a bullet through the right eye while leading an assault on recently occupied trenches. Jean Declerck (aspirant) and Adrien Boyer (1895-1915) are wounded. One is evacuated to Bizerta, but dies on board ship. The other dies in hospital at Nice.[27]   Then comes the hasty withdrawal. Having predicted a "victory over Islam" in May, Father Jean-Baptiste Blin (1887-1977) passes over the ignominious retreat of November in the fewest possible words.[28]

Salonika and Serbia

Austria's original war aim was the punishment of Serbia for its involvement in the Sarajevo assassinations, but its first invasion was ineffective and by the end of August 1914 the Serbs had expelled the enemy from their country. The following month the Serbs unwisely crossed into Austrian territory and were forced to withdraw. A short-lived attack on Bosnia invited further Austrian retaliation, but again the Serbs expelled the enemy from their borders. The Austrians and Germans did not resume hostilities against Serbia until the autumn of 1915. In September Bulgaria, impressed by Austro-German victories over Russia and Italy, joined forces with the Central Powers in the hope of recovering its province of Macedonia which had been ceded to Greece in 1913, after the Second Balkan War. The odds were now against Serbia, whose only hope was to attract Allied troops into the Balkans via the Greek port of Salonika.

On October 3rd 1915 an Anglo-French force landed at Salonika, formed in part by withdrawals from Gallipoli and encouraged by the hope that Greece would enter the war on the side of the Allies. Salonika became a vast Allied base and the troops advanced at once into Serbian Macedonia. They were too late to save the Serbs. Austro-German-Bulgarian forces invaded Serbia in October-November, expelling both the Serbian army and the Serbian King from their country, while Bulgarian forces simultaneously engaged the British and French in Macedonia. The remnants of the Serb army crossed into Albania and embarked on Italian ships bound for Corfu. By December 12th the British and French had been pushed back into Greek territory. They were joined in 1916 by what remained of the Serb Army.

Salonika thereafter became an Allied enclave for the remainder of the war. It was a huge encampment of some half a million soldiers, with an enormous stockpile of military material, but it exerted no pressure on the Bulgarians and Germans across the border. On the contrary, it became a medical liability, a vast disease zone, variously described as "an internment camp" or "a great military hospital". Malaria caused ten casualties for every one inflicted by the enemy. Casualties from disease exceeded a hundred percent of the strength of some of the units. Salonika presented yet another form of stalemate.[29]

Nearly all the White Father soldiers from Gallipoli were transported to Salonika and two more joined them from France. Father Arsène Sabau (1887-1974) described the forty-eight hour steamer trip that brought the first eight to Greece on October 2nd 1915. Calling at Lemnos, they found the Bay of Mudros filled with activity. Arriving before Salonika, Mount Olympus was visible in the distance. A field hospital was set up immediately in the former Lazarist seminary. Then they set off for the Serbian front by train on October 17th. On the two-hour journey they passed trains filled with Serbian refugees and retreating Serbian soldiers.[30] Father Léon Darot recalled that this was the land evangelized by Saint Paul. The soldier confreres and aspirants were the modern "Thessalonians".[31] On this front, the Missionaries of Africa were more widely spread out in fox-holes and "endless trenches" than they had been in Gallipoli, but they managed to stay in contact and come together from time to time. On one occasion, in November 1915, Father Sabau joined with six confreres to make a novena in view of the Society's patronal feast of the Immaculate Conception and to pray together at the grave of Gabriel Berthoumieux. At the subsequent Mass, Sabau preached to thirty soldiers on the text: "Come to me all you who labour and are heavy burdened" (Matthew 11:28).[32]

The Serbian front was hilly and the winter weather bitterly cold. The campaign against the Bulgarians had its ups and downs, but the overall experience was one of unrelenting retreat. Even behind the Allied front line in Salonika there was the fear that Austro-Germans and Bulgarians might invade the Allied enclave. "We are always at war, without being at war", wrote one of the missionaries.[33] Gabriel Berthoumieux (1893-1915), a French scholastic from Cahors, was the first to be killed. He received a bullet in the stomach during a reconnaissance patrol on November 16th 1915 and died in the night. Then on May 27th 1916 it was the turn of Régis Delabre (1889-1916), another French scholastic. Sheltering in a fox-hole from a hail of enemy shells on the Serbian front, he received a direct hit. Father Joseph Delmer (1891-1969) identified the almost unrecognizable body at midnight and conducted the burial in the early hours of the following morning. A mournful group of four Fathers and four seminarians stood around the grave. Before departing, they planted a cross with the inscription "Died for France".[34] One of the mourners, the scholastic Clovis Capelle (1888-1917) had scarcely another year to live. A second lieutenant, he was in the act of lobbing grenades at attacking Bulgarians to provide cover for his retreating soldiers, when he was shot in the head. His last word to those near him was a command to leave him where he had fallen and to get out of danger.

Three other White Fathers died in the Salonika campaign, but they were all victims of the endemic diseases rife in the area. Louis Le Dévedec (1882-1916), a priest from the Uganda mission, died in a Salonika hospital from typhoid fever. François-Marie Renaudier (1890-1917), a French Father from Rennes, was evacuated and reached the hospital in his home town before dying of malaria. Father Alfred Courant (1880-1918) died of broncho-pneumonia in a hospital at Veles in Macedonia.

Greece finally joined the Allied *entente* on July 2nd 1917. In the last year of the war, while Bulgarians starved, the German troops withdrew in order to reinforce the Western Front. The Serbs invaded Macedonia once more and Bulgaria agreed terms on September 29th 1918. In competition with the Italians, Greece invaded Anatolia in Turkish Asia Minor during June 1919 only to be defeated at the hands of a Turkey re-energised by Mustapha Kemal, the victor of Gallipoli. At the Treaty of Lausanne in 1923 a beaten Greece and a victorious Turkey agreed to exchange the minorities on each other's soil.[35] Meanwhile, the

White Fathers remained in the muddy, water-logged trenches of Salonika, the breeding ground of mosquitoes, throughout 1917 and 1918, until it was time for demobilization. They had fought alongside Russians in 1916, but Russia withdrew from the war in the following year after the October revolution and the November Treaty of Brest-Litovsk. One White Father veteran of Salonika, Auguste Clavel (1895-1979), was to become embroiled in the Russian Civil War of 1919 – a story that will be told in a later chapter.

Palestine

After their half-hearted assault on the Suez Canal in 1915, the Turks retreated to Gaza in Palestine, and held a line that straddled the Sinai desert. In the following year, the Arab leader Hussein, Sherif of Mecca, launched the Arab Revolt. This revolt was brilliantly led by Hussein's son Feisal ibn Hussein and the famous British liaison officer, T. E. Lawrence, known to posterity as "Lawrence of Arabia". Lawrence and the Arabs captured the port of Aquaba on July 6th 1917. Meanwhile, General Edmund Allenby arrived from the Western Front to direct operations against the Turks in the Near East. While Allied armies under Allenby pushed the Turks northward from Gaza, Lawrence harassed them on the eastern flank, sabotaging the Hejaz Railway.[36] Jerusalem was captured and Allenby made a ceremonial entrance into the city through the Jaffa Gate on December 9th. Marching in Allenby's parade was one Toussaint Cocaud (1881-1928).

Cocaud, who came from Nantes, entered the novitiate of the Missionaries of Africa after his ordination as a diocesan priest in 1906.[37] After novitiate, he was sent on probation to St. Anne's Jerusalem, and this became his eventual appointment. On August 4th 1914 he was called up and served in the medical corps, firstly in a hospital at Nantes and later in Paris helping to transport the wounded by rail. At the end of 1916 he was sent to Palestine and joined the French contingent there after a visit to Cairo. He travelled up the railway to join the troops marching on Jerusalem.

Allenby's entry into Jerusalem was a splendid occasion. Lawrence described it as "the most remarkable event of the war, the one which, for historical reasons, made a stronger appeal than anything on earth."[38] Allied sympathizers, among them the Dutch Superior of St.Anne's, Nicholas Van der Vliet (1876-1966), were at the Jaffa Gate to welcome the conquerors. Allenby and his general staff, with Lawrence and the French High-Commissioner François Georges-Picot, entered the holy city on foot, followed by a mounted escort. Behind them marched the foot soldiers, including Cocaud. To his amazement, Van der Vliet found himself being given the *accolade* by one of the soldiers. It was none other than his confrere and former colleague.[39]

Mesopotamia had been conquered by the British in 1917. During 1918, Allenby reorganized his forces and pushed into northern Palestine where he faced the Turks at Megiddo, the celebrated battle site of Biblical times. His breakthrough of September 19th to 21st brought an end to Turkish resistance and an armistice was signed at Mudros on the Aegean island of Lemnos on October

30th. In May 1919 Cocaud was able to return to Jerusalem and rejoin the seminary of St. Anne's.

Going into the Furnace

For young conscripts, whose sheltered existence in missionary houses of formation had barely been disturbed by the short experience of military service, the plunge into a First World War battle-zone was traumatic and alienating. Many, in their first letters from the front, described the shock they had undergone. It was "something terrible", wrote Father Charles Joyeux (1885-1936*) of his first taste of battle - eight days of terror at Ypres in May 1915. The horror was indescribable. There was nowhere to hide from the hell of fire and steel, the thick smoke and hideous noise. Most of the trench shelters and breastworks collapsed under the impact of machine-gun fire, and more than five thousand shells fell in seven hours.[40] "I left the battlefield", wrote Célestin Paulhe (1888-1919*) in May 1916, "filled with the horror that it inspires."[41] Usually, it was likened to a "furnace" or simply to "hell". "Our division goes straight into the furnace". "We have just emerged from the furnace". I go "to Verdun to take my turn in the terrible furnace".

Bombardment was a "hellish" deluge of iron, a "murderous rain" of shrapnel and shell splinters, an "iron hurricane". Louis Châles (1891-1969) described the effect produced by large calibre shells. "Unless you have seen them, you cannot imagine what large calibre shell wounds are like. To understand their explosive power you must visit the ruins of re-conquered villages. Nothing remains. Everything is destroyed and pulverized. It is difficult to recognize where the houses were, the streets, church and cemetery. It is complete devastation".[42] Under a heavy bombardment there was a feeling of helplessness. One could only cower at the bottom of a trench, curled up in a foetal position and wait for the shells to stop falling. Bombardment induced a numbness, a kind of insensibility. Emerging after a bombardment, soldiers lurched like sailors on a heaving deck. Strange to say, the numbness helped them cope with the frightful sights they saw around them. "The front line has been levelled", wrote Paulhe in July 1916. "At night we bury the bodies in shell-holes. There are only forty left alive in this company...Hardly an area as big as a man's hand has not been turned over several times by shells. Everywhere there are bloodstained uniforms and shattered limbs".[43] Father Pierre Gallerand (1887-1976) described an assault after an artillery barrage at Verdun. The troops advanced in full view of the enemy and under the withering impact of their machine-gun fire. Word spread from mouth to mouth as they went forward: "So-and-so is killed. So-and-so is wounded." More and more gaps appeared in the line of advancing troops. A Zouave fell beside him. Hastily, the Father dressed his stomach wound and prepared him for death. The soldiers continued forward, trampling the victims of the machine-gun. They found a dead German at the bottom of a trench, then a dead French soldier. Gallerand jumped into a shell-hole beside a dying Frenchman to give him the last sacraments.[44] There were "frightful sights everywhere", wrote Châles, "skulls, legs, arms, a piece of torso, half a human body."[45]

Jean-Louis D'Hervé (1890-1966), wrote in March 1916 that he had been eight days under bombardment. His only shelter was "abandonment to Providence".[46] Joseph Portier (1878-1955) wrote in the same month from Verdun. They were under a very fierce bombardment, but he experienced great happiness and interior calm in abandoning himself into the hands of the Father. "Into your hands, O Lord, I commend my spirit."[47] This was the only approach possible for a man of faith to this experience - a more positive form of resignation than mere passivity.

After several weeks in the "furnace" a quiet retreat at Binson Priory was like being in paradise. "I am out of the horrible furnace", wrote Châles on April 15th 1916. "I am at Binson Priory. (I have gone) from hell to paradise.[48] "Several days at Binson", echoed D'Hervé, "were like being in paradise. I came out of a long nightmare into another life, but this life was also a dream."[49] Many soldiers who experienced the terrible bombardments of World War I suffered from what we nowadays call post-traumatic stress disorder, and which, in those days was called "shell-shock" or "neurasthenia". Joseph Watier (1891-1971) suffered from a lesion in the brain, probably as a result of a lengthy bout of unconsciousness following a shell explosion. He continued to have fits into the 1930s.[50] Camille Cormerais (1894-1979) had headaches and migraines all his life.[51] And Léon Pignide, a French aspirant, suffered a stroke while swimming in the river La Truyère in 1917. This may have been due to a brain disorder attributable to post-traumatic stress.[52] Many White Father veterans had eccentricities of character, but not many seem to have been typical shell-shock victims. On the other hand, confreres in the medical corps frequently had to help evacuate "poor soldiers with nervous troubles."[53]

One of the hazards of sheltering in a trench during a bombardment was the risk of being buried alive. This was especially the case in the Dardanelles, where the trenches had to be dug hastily in poor positions. Joseph Watier was covered in earth from a shell that exploded a few feet away underground. He was lucky to escape death.[54] Early in the campaign, Sabau had to bury a Zouave who had been stifled under a collapsed trench.[55] And Father Paul Verdouck (1889-1932) described how four of his men were buried alive after seventy-three shells fell on their position. While he was rescuing them, others were buried. Verdouck moved to dig them out, but his lieutenant forbade it. They had to retreat. As they moved back, Verdouck could hear the stifled voices crying pathetically for help.[56] The worst experience of a White Father in this regard was that of Joseph Lautour (1875-1943) who was buried in a communication trench at Verdun. He managed to get out of his "tomb", but his eyesight was so seriously affected afterwards that he could not see what he was doing in the medical section and had to be sent back from the front. He was given an early discharge in 1917, but his eyesight remained poor and he was also deaf. A specialist was able to improve his eyesight many years later, but during the Second World War Lautour failed to see or hear a German military vehicle coming towards him near Toulouse in 1943 and was killed in the ensuing accident.[57]

Kill or Be Killed

Most of the White Father conscripts were non-combatants, but many - whether they were combatants or not – had to shoot to kill and even to take part in bayonet charges. It goes without saying that the experience of killing other human beings was as distasteful as it was new to priests and seminarians. On the other hand, it was a question of kill or be killed. Pierre Valléau (1892-1915), a French novice cleric, took part in a bayonet charge at Ypres in 1915. He was wounded and earned a mention in dispatches. Shortly afterwards he went missing and his body was accidentally found a year later.[58] From the start of the war there was an almost mystical fascination with the machine-gun. "The Germans advanced in columns of four", wrote a missionary from Ypres. "Our two machine-guns scythed them. In two minutes the enemy was in headlong flight. Several minutes later they advanced again, shooting…A hidden machine-gun sowed death in their ranks." There were three more attempts by the Germans and then, "after five minutes of murderous (artillery) fire, a few survivors were seen crawling through the grass to what was left of their trenches." The correspondent's conclusion was unexpected. "The friendships forged under machine-gun fire", he wrote "are strong and pure."[59]

It was the same story at the Dardanelles. Sabau described how the Turks carried out a bayonet attack at night. "Our machine guns mowed them down."[60] In another vivid report from the same front, Léon Lebouc, Brother Euthyme, described how the French went "over the top" on July 12th 1915. They advanced two hundred metres under a rain of bullets. The Turks fled "like rabbits", but then counter-attacked realizing that the French were few in number. They came waving white handkerchiefs and the French did not know whether they were British or Turks. However, soon some of the Zouaves began to fall and two officers were killed. "I fire at a group of three Turks: *touché*! Then I am hit in the neck hand and eye. I am taken to a first aid post."[61] The Brother nearly lost an eye, but recovered sufficiently to be posted to Serbia. Joseph Loiseau, holding a Turkish trench, had an unexpected clash with the enemy in a sap. "I shot one down", he wrote, before discovering some fifty or sixty more a few metres away. Loiseau offered the sacrifice of his life, but the bullets took another direction. He was able to take cover and eat a supper of sardines and bread.[62]

The novice cleric, Benjamin Durand, a sergeant, found himself in a wood at Verdun in March 1916. It was bitterly cold and there was snow on the ground. He and his men took up position at 3 a.m. in a ravine behind Douaumont Fort, recently captured by the Germans. Enfiladed by German machine-gun fire, they retreated to another position. Through his binoculars Durand could see a group of Germans in a clearing four hundred metres away. He gave the order to fire. The whole group fell, but horses and men were observed to be still moving. "A second burst brought immobility". Shortly afterwards, Durand himself was wounded. His Zouaves carried him to safety. "You will all get killed for my sake", he protested. "So what, Sergeant?" was the reply. The party struggled back along roads strewn with overturned vehicles, dead horses and human corpses.[63]

Trench Life: Mud, Rats and Gas

Mud was a typical feature of trench warfare. Rain turned trenches into troughs of liquid mud which seeped through a soldier's boots and rotted his feet, a condition known as "trench foot". Roads were coated with "gluey mud", while a combination of heavy rain and persistent bombardment created a great sea of mud through which troops had to pass in order to get to the front line. If a soldier slipped off a duckboard into it, he could drown.[64] Mud was a chronic problem in the water-logged fields of the Flemish lowlands, especially after the sluice-gates were opened on the river Ijser in October 1914. It was on this front that Missionaries of Africa had their worst experiences of mud. A White Father aspirant reported in December 1915 that several soldiers nearly drowned in the mud, as they were returning from the trenches. Two soldiers spent a whole night in it up to their chests and it needed eight men to pull them out.[65] The stench of the mud was atrocious, because the pools contained the decomposing bodies of men and horses. Mud was less of a problem on the Somme or at Verdun, but White Fathers complained of it in both places. At Verdun, a missionary complained of being immersed in mud up to his knees, with no food for three days while enduring a precision bombardment. "Mud was everywhere, in our shirts, jerseys, tunics and greatcoats."[66]

The combination of mud and cold weather was especially painful when soldiers were obliged to march on frozen mud.[67] Although it was warmer in Salonika, missionaries experienced the ever present mud there as well. Camille Cormerais (1894-1979), an aspirant from Binson, described the celebration of Mass, with mud-covered soldiers kneeling to receive Communion.[68] "On Pentecost Sunday 1916," wrote Célestin Paulhe, "we appeared like lumps of mud".[69]

The opposing armies of the First World War shared their trenches with another army – an army of rats. These were not small, domestic rodents, but giant "super-rats" that grew fat on dead bodies. A British soldier claimed that they could even be as big as cats.[70] At night they ate the soldiers' rations. Under bombardment, they became hysterical, cowering with the troops in their quarters. Needless to say, rats had no gas-masks! Gas attacks had a stupefying effect on them, and soldiers stumbled over their sluggish bodies.

Rats spread disease. In the First World War, rat fleas caused typhus and other fevers, as well as the highly contagious pneumonic plague. Rats also caused bacterial contamination of food. Killing rats in the trenches could be counter-productive. It only added to the general stench, and a dead rat was often more dangerous from a medical point of view than a living one. When trenches became waterlogged, both men and rats were often forced out.[71] And, in any case, rats were equally at home in the encampments and first-aid posts behind the front-line.

Louis Châles (1891-1969), on the Western Front in October 1916, found himself commanding a squad of rat-catchers. With eight men, he methodically destroyed the vermin in one encampment after another. Using dogs, poison and even explosives, they counted hundreds of victims every day. "We inflict heavy losses on this enemy!" he wrote exultingly. One has a feeling that the rats had the last laugh.

Another hazard for troops who had no opportunity for a regular bath or change of clothes was the appearance of body lice. These lived in the seams and linings of the uniform and were a constant irritation, driving men into a sort of frenzy.[72] They also spread diseases such as trench fever and typhus.

All the armies of the First World War used poison gas and suffered deaths from gas in their thousands, especially the Russians. The French used tear-gas grenades against the Germans in August 1914, and the Germans used them against the Russians with little or no effect in January 1915. The Germans, however, gave serious study to the development and large-scale use of chemical weapons. In April 1915 they fired Chlorine gas from pressurized cylinders against the French infantry and Zouave regiments at Ypres. It was like a yellow-green cloud with the smell of a mixture of pineapple and pepper. Chlorine gas had the effect of stimulating over-production of fluid in the lungs, leading to death by internal drowning. Asphyxiation by Chlorine gas was a slow and extremely painful death. At first Allied soldiers had no defence against such gas other than to hold a handkerchief or sock soaked in urine against their mouth and nose. By July, however, gas-masks and respirators had been developed. Gas fired from cylinders was unpredictable. The wind could blow it back in the faces of the attackers, and it could hang about in the trenches of the defenders rendering them impossible to capture. The problem was solved by the development of gas shells fired by the artillery.

By this time, the more deadly Phosgene gas had been developed. This was a highly toxic and corrosive gas that had a delayed, but often fatal effect on the respiratory system. It caused much less coughing and so led the victims to inhale it in greater quantities. However, respirators also became more sophisticated, and the Germans introduced Mustard Gas in September 1917, firing it in high explosive shells. Mustard Gas blistered the skin of its victims, causing internal and external bleeding, and attacking the bronchial tubes. A person seriously affected by Mustard Gas usually took three or four weeks to die. Protection against Mustard Gas proved more difficult than against Chlorine and Phosgene. Tear-gas was sometimes used as an irritant to make the enemy remove their gas-masks and so make them more vulnerable to a deadlier gas. Mustard Gas had the drawback for the attacker in that it remained active in the soil for many weeks after delivery. Although the opposing armies quickly copied each other's chemical innovations, gas became less and less effective, once the crucial element of surprise had been lost and the number of gas casualties diminished as the war went on.[73]

The White Father soldiers and their Algerian Zouaves were among those who felt the effects of poison gas at Ypres in 1915.[74] Eighty-seven gassed reservists were hospitalized at Binson Priory in late 1915.[75] One scholastic wrote in December that his "skin was worth little at the moment" after a counter-attack by Germans, using gas and flame-throwers.[76] In December 1915, Camille Cormerais reported a "new gas that kills those without masks in eight days after terrible suffering".[77] This may have been Phosgene. An aspirant from Binson wrote in the same month: "I don't know why I am still alive. I was gassed in one and a half minutes. I coughed sneezed, expectorated, suffocated. They gave me cold milk and next day I spat blood. But it did not last."[78] And another student from Binson told of the precautions they were all taking against gas. The Germans were apparently well supplied and were sending over "steel buckets" of the murderous powder.[79]

The wearing of a flowing beard was a strict rule in the Society of Missionaries of Africa. However, a beard interfered with a gas-mask and had to be sacrificed if one wished to avoid being asphyxiated.[80] Louis Châles on the Western Front claimed to have been gassed at least twenty times in October 1916. This was mostly tear-gas.[81] Even as late in the war as March 1918, a White Father student reported "I have been much hampered by gas. I have not been able to speak for three days. However, it is not serious and after a rest behind the lines, this discomfort will go away."[82] Another student called Chauvet was not so lucky, finding himself in a Cognac hospital for six days, blind and with lesions in the throat and right lung. [83] Several White Fathers suffered the after effects of poison gas long after the war was finished. Auguste Clavel (1895-1979) was "chesty" throughout his life, due to Mustard Gas, and Eloi Falguières (1887-1924) died from the effects of Phosgene Gas six years after the Armistice.[84] Coughing blood and unable to swallow even liquids, he lost strength and voice. He finally choked to death in the Society's sanatorium at Pau on September 28th 1924.

Aerial Warfare

Aerial warfare hardly existed before the First World War, and although airships, aircraft and balloons underwent rapid development during the conflict, their role was never decisive. At the beginning of the war their task was mainly one of observation and reconnaissance, but they rapidly acquired the function of bombers and fighters. Germany set the pace, but air superiority swung backwards and forwards between the opposing armies as technology progressed.[85]

Rigid airships first appeared at the beginning of the twentieth century with the invention of the Zeppelin. At the outbreak of war, these mammoth ships, more than five hundred feet in length, came into their own, outstripping the speed of contemporary aeroplanes, bristling with machine-guns and carrying a deadly load of bombs. The first Zeppelin bombing raid on London took place on May 31st 1915. The White Fathers' school at Bishop's Waltham near Southampton lay directly in the Zeppelin's path and the Fathers were obliged to black out their windows. They did this none too soon, for a couple passed overhead that very evening. Later in the year they observed a Zeppelin, "looking like a great vulture", caught in the converging beams of the searchlights. The Fathers' interest in these sinister craft seems to have been interpreted by the local police as making signals to them. The accusation, however, could not be upheld.[86]

As bombers, the Zeppelins were far from accurate. In any case, aeroplanes soon acquired stronger engines with which to catch them and artillery started to fire incendiary shells at them. These quickly ignited the hydrogen they contained and brought them down. The Missionaries of Africa first experienced Zeppelins in battle at Salonika in early 1916, when an airship dropped fifteen bombs without doing any reported damage. A month later a Zeppelin attempted unsuccessfully to bomb their headquarters at night, but the bombs fell wide of the target.[87]   Almost at the same time, Camille Cormerais at Verdun saw a Zeppelin hit by an incendiary shell.[88] However, it is Henri Le Veux (1879-1965), the Luganda language expert and future novice-master, who has left us the most graphic description of the downing of a Zeppelin on the Oise in March 1917.[89]

"On Saturday I had the enviable opportunity of watching a Zeppelin crash. Our batteries announced its appearance at around 5.30 p.m. The airship was some three thousand five hundred metres up and looked like a black caterpillar, gliding through the clouds which occasionally hid it from view. The rockets sent up by our guns seemed to lack (the) strength (to reach it). The engine of murder and devastation just kept coming on, braving our powerless efforts. Little by little, the rockets gained strength and reached its level. Realizing the danger, it slowed down and started to tack in order to find its way back to its own lines, trying all the time to gain altitude...Suddenly, a bright light shone at its tail point. 'Got him!' exclaimed the onlookers, scarcely daring to hope for such luck. The flame grew longer, licking the sides of the long cigar, and then all at once enveloped it completely. After a few seconds, the Zeppelin toppled over and broke up. The first fiery debris fell at once. The larger section held together and sank more slowly, leaving a trail of smoking foam in the greyish sky. All the soldiers broke into applause. The twisted, half-melted carcass of the broken monster now lies in a Compiègne garden. The crew were all killed."[90]

Although the Zeppelin was superseded as an engine of war, it developed into a passenger airship during the inter-war years, stimulating competition in Britain and America. The last of the gigantic passenger dirigibles was the Graf Zeppelin II completed shortly before World War II.[91]

Bomber and fighter planes were already fast developing by the end of 1914. The Germans mounted machine-guns on their Fokker monoplane, and their Fokker tri-plane, when it appeared, had the edge over its British and French counterparts. The huge Gotha heavy bomber, which was improved throughout the war, took the Zeppelin's place in bombing raids on London and Paris, and provoked the formation of the Royal Flying Corps, the world's first independent air force, in 1918. In the last year of the war aerial warfare was no longer the preserve of heroic aces engaging in individual combat but became a matter of co-ordinated strategy and liaison with ground forces.

Already at the start of the war, Germany possessed an all-purpose fighter-bomber and surveillance plane, the Rumpler Taube ("Dove"). It was a weird, birdlike monoplane, resembling a Leonardo da Vinci sketch, rather than an actual aircraft. Originally of Austrian manufacture, it was very light, but, although it could not mount a heavy machine-gun, it was able to carry half a dozen bombs. The Taube was the plane most frequently encountered by White Father soldiers on the Western and Mediterranean Fronts. Arsène Sabau witnessed bombing and aerial dog–fights in Salonika in January 1916 and another White Father observed German planes carrying out an unsuccessful bombing raid at the beginning of the Battle of Verdun. Allied planes seemed more numerous.[92] Marius Gremeret (1873-1959), missionary in Uganda, was also at Verdun when a *Taube* bombed his first aid post, wounding a medical orderly. The victim was on the operating table when the plane returned and dropped four more bombs a hundred metres away.[93] Hervé Quéinnec (1896-1946) had a miraculous escape at Fleury, but luckily bombing was not accurate in the First World War.[94] The ubiquitous *Taube* appeared at Salonika and Julien Chabot (1892-1926) watched it drop two bombs in June 1916. It was driven off by Allied artillery, but returned to let fall its remaining four bombs wide of the target.[95] A similar "bird of ill fortune" made three sorties on an Allied hospital at Verdun, even though the Red Cross was clearly marked on its roof. Célestin Dupupet (1876-1949) reported that it set fire to the hospital building, killed four medical orderlies, two of whom were priests, and bombed others as they fled the compound. One of its bombs fell between the legs of a patient and went through his hospital bed into the ground without exploding. Another patient got up and ran to the door, only to see his bed shattered behind him.[96] According to Jules Pagès (1887-1984) soldiers moving along the communication trenches at Verdun were also bombed.[97] German planes operated far a-field. The White Fathers' procurator in Rome, Louis Burtin (1853-1942) reported on the panic when German planes flew over the Eternal City in December 1917 and January 1918. They had recently bombed Naples, killing sixteen people. The Mayor of Rome immediately started to organize air-raid shelters.[98]

Balloons were used by both sides in the First World War for observation and as a barrage against enemy aircraft. An early German variety was called the *Drachen* (Dragon). It had a single fin and was completely cylindrical. It was nicknamed "Sausage" by the Allies. The Fathers at Binson rejoiced when French fighter planes brought down a *Drachen* at nearby Oeuilly.[99]

White Father conscripts seem to have had little to do with the Allied air force. Only Pierre Bringuier (1875-1957) was actually posted to a French air base.[100] In the limited area occupied by the Allies at Gallipoli, Léon Darot (1890-1958) found himself next door to the British airmen's camp. One of the pilots ditched his plane in the sea, because his badly fixed bombs made it dangerous to land on the ground. He swam out to his machine to try and salvage it, but blew himself up in the attempt. The pilot was a Catholic and Darot conducted the funeral at the camp in front of a group of curious Britons.[101] After the Germans captured Lille in 1914, White Fathers reported that a British pilot flew over the town to bomb telegraph installations. His plane was forced down, but citizens helped him escape to the frontier, whence he returned to scatter leaflets.[102] Soldiers at Verdun, among them a White Father aspirant, admired the "remarkable liaison" between planes, artillery and infantry.[103]

Combatants and Non-Combatants

French conscripts from the Missionaries of Africa served in a variety of infantry regiments but the majority saw action with the Zouaves. The name is said to derive from an ethnic group in Kabylia that joined up with the French colonial army in 1830. By 1914 it had become a regiment of Algerian settlers and assimilated natives, with elements from Morocco and Tunisia, enjoying a reputation that outshone that of the Foreign Legion. Over the preceding decades Zouaves had distinguished themselves in desert conflicts, in the Crimea and in the Franco-Prussian War. Known for their swashbuckling bravado, their reckless courage and unconquerable fighting spirit, the Zouaves wore a colourful uniform of baggy red trousers, a collarless blue jacket and a red *chechia* or fez. Such finery was out of place on the twentieth century battlefield which demanded camouflage, not colour. By mid-1915 the exotic uniform had been exchanged for a mustard-coloured battle-dress and the *chechia* for the steel helmet.

The Zouave battalions collected many battle honours in the First World War. They took part in the recapture of Douaumont Fort at Verdun and the assault on the *Chemin des Dames*. The Fourth Zouaves captured Malmaison Fort in October 1917 and were credited with having "saved France" by blocking the German advance on Paris in the Spring of 1918.[104]

White Father students who did military service during their formation in Algiers or Carthage usually did so with the Zouaves in North Africa. They were therefore called up to Zouave battalions in 1914. Those who did military service in France, or who were mobilized, earlier on in their missionary formation, were more likely to join other infantry regiments. Those from North Africa had the distinct advantage of knowing the Zouaves and their homeland already and they had numerous personal contacts in the regiment. Jules Pagès had acted as a warrant-officer instructor for many young Zouaves at Tunis.[105] He went with them to France and fought alongside them at Verdun. Zouave Officers knew the White Fathers and several were personal friends of White Father superiors.

The vast majority of White Father conscripts served in the medical section of their unit as non-combatants. This was especially the case with ordained priests and with those who were more advanced in their priestly training, but there seems to have been no hard and fast rule. Pagès was called up shortly after his ordination in 1915, serving as a combatant and achieving the rank of Lieutenant.[106] The citation he received in 1917 for action at Verdun stated: "Harassing the enemy ceaselessly with his machine-gun fire and raising the morale of his men at every moment, he contributed very largely to the success of our recent operations."[107] In 1918, he was wounded by a machine-gun bullet in the thigh in the final glorious episode of the Fourth Zouaves before Paris.

The distinction between combatant and non-combatant, however, was somewhat academic. It was often dangerous for troops to leave the relative safety of their trenches, but stretcher-bearers had regularly to move from one dug-out to another and to make their way back under fire along the shallow communication trenches to first-aid posts and dressing stations in the rear. These were frequently targets in themselves. When accompanying assault troops, non-combatants also had to defend themselves. Belonging to a medical unit demanded equal, if not more, courage than being a frontline combatant. This was recognized by the troops themselves. The courage of Father Jean-Baptiste Robert (1887-1916) was a byword among the Zouaves whom he served as a medical orderly. Appointed "nurse in the trenches" in 1915, he was continuously at the front from the end of 1914 until his death at Douaumont, Verdun in 1916.[108]

Those who served with medical units received some training, but they were essentially what we would call today "paramedics", supplementing the work of the medical staff. They were emergency professionals, giving the first healthcare to the sick and wounded in battle and ensuring their rapid and safe removal to wherever qualified medical care was available. They had to assess the state of a patient and stabilize his condition. Besides having a genuine desire to help people, they needed to be calm and quick-thinking. They also needed a fair amount of physical strength for lifting and carrying people back from the frontline. Mostly, they spent their time dressing wounds and evacuating the wounded, struggling with the stretchers down the narrow communication trenches under machine-gun or shell fire. At times, they were put in charge of further evacuation and transport to hospitals away from the front. Usually, they were also responsible for giving the dead a first burial, either in shallow graves near the front or in cemeteries and churchyards further back. Carrying bodies through the trenches was another duty requiring stamina and physical strength. They were responsible for preserving letters and personal possessions of the dead for identification by their military units and for their families at home. At Gallipoli one of the terms of the armistice was a commitment to bury the dead. Three thousand Turkish corpses lay unburied and Arsène Sabau found himself trying to find room for four hundred in an area measuring thirty feet by twenty-five.[109]

Jean-Marie Le Tohic was exceptionally heroic, miraculously escaping death on the Champagne front at the end of the war by pushing and pulling a wounded soldier in a wheel chair a distance of twenty kilometres under heavy bombardment.[110] "I treat the wounded Germans who fall into my hands", wrote a White Father paramedic in 1915, and Joseph Portier (1878-1955) told a moving story from his experience of transporting the wounded from a first-aid post to a field hospital. In February 1915 he had three wounded Germans in his lorry. A wounded Frenchman offered his shoulder to one of them as he was getting down from the vehicle. "Think nothing of it, old buddy", he said. "This morning I tried to bump you off, but this evening you are my brother." He even gave the German his own gas-mask. "War can be waged without hatred for the enemy" added Portier.[111]

Many paramedics spent time in the field hospital itself. Auguste Bazin (1881-1946) has left us a vivid description of one such "hospital" not far from the trenches.[112] The wounded were brought in, covered in blood and mud. The first task was to clean them up and then to extract shrapnel and shell splinters. In addition they had to be ready to take cover in a nearby cellar at a moment's notice if there was a bombardment. Pierre Saclier (1876-1917) reported in June 1915 that the military hospital at Dijon, where he worked, had treated four thousand three hundred and fifty wounded soldiers in the first six months of the war. Two hundred and thirty of them died, only ten without the last sacraments.

He had administered forty.[113] Saclier himself collapsed and died of exhaustion at the same hospital in 1917.

Soldiers in the First World War respected the stretcher-bearers and other paramedics who looked after them. They represented practically their only hope of survival when wounded or gassed. The Missionaries of Africa who gave them this service were ideally placed to provide the consolations of religion. For their part, the soldiers were extremely receptive to such ministrations, especially the "colonials" from Algeria, Senegal and French Sudan who had no hesitation in asking for the sacraments. "You know from where to draw strength", a Chief Medical Officer, who had nearly twenty White Fathers in his division, told them.[114] "The spiritual life is better here than in the (army) reserve" wrote a missionary from the Western Front in 1915, "because of the danger and nature of the work I do. You cannot treat the suffering members of Christ without thinking of him." The missionary in question was a medical sergeant in the mountain infantry (*Chasseurs Alpins*). Thirty of his stretcher bearers had been mentioned in dispatches, six had been killed and five seriously wounded. On top of this, he himself had stopped a bullet that lodged between his jersey and shirt above his heart. The bullet had already passed through a tree and had lost velocity before reaching him.[115]

At a purely human level, the young victims of World War I found it comforting to have a priest or seminarian to help them face the loneliness of death or disfigurement. A Belgian White Father student Victor Vuylsteke (1892-1962) was a stretcher-bearer in Flanders. He wrote in 1917 that a nineteen year old soldier, fatally wounded by a shell, had died in his arms. The official chaplain had been to anoint him and he had also been visited by the major in charge of his unit. Shortly afterwards, the major was killed outright and the chaplain mortally wounded.[116] Father Jean-Marie Le Tohic found that conversion took place at critical moments. In January 1916 he heard the confession of a young man about to have his leg amputated and gave him communion. Le Tohic was at his side during the operation and even held the leg as it was being severed. Back in bed after the operation, the young amputee shed tears of emotion and asked if he could embrace the priest. Another young soldier lost both an arm and a leg. Taking the Father's hand he begged: "Father, don't leave me. Stay here!" A twenty year-old Zouave, whose amputation came too late to save him, died in Le Tohic's arms. He bade a personal farewell to all the wounded in the ward and entrusted the priest with a message for his sister. At the moment of death he too asked to be hugged. Yet another amputee wanted an embrace before an operation that was successful. Le Tohic who experienced a strong bond of affection with these soliders concluded: "When the heart speaks, these brave men do wonderful things."[117]

Chaplains

By now it should be abundantly clear that a dividing line between paramedic and chaplain hardly existed, especially when the paramedic was himself a priest. "I wish I were a priest" wrote Gaston Duiquet from Ypres in May 1915. "I could help these men more. They are almost going to confession to me. 'If you were a priest' (they say) 'I would make my confession to you.'"[118] This was one reason why several White Father conscripts and prisoners of war, who were on the threshold of the priesthood, received early ordination. Duiquet was one of them and received the news joyfully in October.[119] On the Western and Mediterranean Fronts official chaplains were few and far between among the Missionaries of Africa. Léon Darot became a chaplain in time for Christmas Midnight Mass 1916 in Salonika. "Without a priest", remarked the soldiers who had had no priest for three months, "we were like animals".[120] René Burtin also acted as chaplain on the same front in 1916. With the General's permission, he enjoyed the use of an abandoned Bulgarian Orthodox church which had survived bombardment and desecration as a stable. Burtin cleaned it up and celebrated Mass, Vespers and Benediction in it every Sunday, attracting congregations of five hundred and eight hundred soldiers. "The saints on the icons smiled on us in the light of our one hundred and fifty candles".[121] Eighteen months before his death in the Vosges, Léon Brossier (1882-1918) began duties as a chaplain at Verdun.[122] About the same time, the Belgian Government which was not so averse to appointing full-time chaplains as the French, was asking the Missionaries of Africa for one or two.[123]

All of this was in stark contrast to the wide-ranging activities of officially appointed White Father chaplains in Equatorial and Central Africa. They baptized and confirmed literally thousands of African troops and carriers, and their ministry was seen as an extension of missionary work in the area. As Bishop Auguste Huys (1871-1838) reported at the end of the war, the work of these chaplains had borne fruit for the entire mission.[124] Their story will be told in a later section of this book.

In what did the ministry of chaplains – official and unofficial – consist on the European fronts? Reconciling the wounded and the dying and taking communion to soldiers in the trenches were the important activities. Gaston Duiquet was called to help two dying comrades on the Western Front in May 1915. He hesitated before moving out of his safe position to brave the enemy machine-guns. Then he dived in among the bullets and reached the two fatally wounded soldiers.[125] Joseph Delmer (1891-1969) also ran the gauntlet of enemy fire in Salonika in 1915 to reach a wounded soldier. "I am grateful for the priesthood which enables me to help souls", he wrote simply, on hearing that he was to be mentioned in dispatches.[126] Charles Joyeux took the sacrament to the soldiers at Verdun who practised frequent communion. As he passed with the Blessed Sacrament, the sentries presented arms.[127] General absolution was frequently given on the eve of an assault, and sometimes, if the troops could be gathered for it, there was a group Viaticum, as happened at Rojani in Serbia in 1917.[128]

Organizing the public celebration of Mass and finding suitable places for it were also important. Masses were celebrated for the stretcher-bearers. Or there was an official "military Mass" on Sundays for an entire unit. Louis Deléry (1879-1959) organized a Christmas Midnight Mass for his battalion in 1915 on the Western Front. A seminarian prepared song sheets and there were choir rehearsals. Before Mass thirty people went to Confession. During the Mass itself traditional Christmas Carols were sung and a Passionist preached a patriotic sermon.[129] In the following year, Deléry organized Sunday Masses in a forest on the edge of the Verdun battlefield. Soldiers were summoned by a bell, and though the singing was poor, there was plenty of goodwill. The climax of the celebration was the consecration to the Sacred Heart. Each soldier present read and signed his declaration.[130] Small chapels or oratories were sometimes constructed for Mass in the trenches themselves, or a cabin set up behind the lines and decorated with statues salvaged from bombed out churches in the neighbourhood.

There was little opportunity for baptizing a non-Christian or reconciling a Protestant to the Catholic Church. However, a scholastic on his way to the Dardanelles found two African soldiers on the boat. The rosaries around their necks proclaimed their Catholic allegiance. One, from Dahomey (modern Benin) was already baptized. The other a Bambara from French Sudan was a catechumen. Both were in need of instruction, and they were thrilled to find themselves in the company of a White Father. The scholastic took time on the voyage to give them both a complete catechesis "beginning with Adam and original sin".[131] Reading the accounts of pastoral ministry by White Fathers on the European fronts, one feels that it was driven by a zeal that was missionary and that – in these situations of extraordinary hardship - it was characterized by a spirit of missionary asceticism.

The Ministry of Charles Umbricht

Charles Umbricht was born in 1873 of Alsatian parentage and studied for the diocesan priesthood in the major seminaries of Nancy. After military service in 1894-1895, he received major orders and was ordained priest in 1897. Following three years of pastoral ministry in the diocese and seven years as a French teacher of college students from Alsace, he applied to join the Missionaries of Africa at the age of thirty-six. He entered the novitiate in Algiers in September 1909 and was posted to St. Anne's Jerusalem for his probation. His health however was poor and he was obliged to give up the idea of a missionary vocation. He left the Society in May 1912, without applying to take the missionary oath.

Although the doctors had given him only three months to live, Umbricht was determined to serve his country when war was declared in 1914. Being medically unfit for military service, he volunteered as an unofficial chaplain. In view of the inadequacy of official chaplains in the French Army, the Ministry of War, at the urging of the Comte de Mun, admitted the principle of priests who had no military duties volunteering as chaplains. Umbricht was accepted in this capacity, serving with the 20th Division that comprised soldiers from Normandy and Brittany, and took part in the battles of the Argonne and the Somme.

Umbricht became a byword for bravery and devotion, encouraging survivors, caring for and transporting the wounded, and giving burial to the dead. It was said that he was, "the moral leader of the Division". He was mentioned in dispatches ten times, receiving the Cross of the Legion of Honour as early as November 1914 and Officer of the Legion in May 1917. Oblivious to danger, he spent his time continuously in the trenches. In 1915 he retrieved the body of a captain from within thirty metres of the German trenches. The dead officer had important documents in his pockets.[132] In August 1916 a large calibre shell exploded near him as he was moving a wounded soldier and rendered him completely deaf. Umbricht even took part in assaults, accompanying the regimental colours right up to the captured enemy trenches.

The heroic chaplain was at Verdun in 1917 and in the Second Battle of the Marne in the following year. On November 22nd 1918, he entered Strasbourg with the French Army, taking his place at the head of the parade, directly behind the flags and regimental colours. Thereafter he was entrusted with organizing the chaplaincy to the French army of occupation in Alsace-Lorraine and the Rhineland and was made a Commander of the Legion of Honour in 1920. When the remains of Blessed Charles de Foucauld were re-interred at El Golea in 1929, Umbricht went to Algeria to be present.

At the outbreak of the Second World War in 1939, Umbricht was a prison chaplain in France. He again volunteered his services as military chaplain, and after the fall of France in 1940 offered to serve with the troops from West Africa. Before he could achieve this final ambition, Umbricht died on October 23rd 1941 aged sixty-eight. Charles Umbricht was a hero and an inspiration to the White Father conscripts of the First World War, who followed his exploits throughout the conflict and who regarded him – as indeed he did himself - as morally a member of the Society.[133]

In the following chapter we shall attempt to render an overall account of the Society's participation in the 1914-1918 War and to submit what might be called "The Golden Book" of the Society.

CHAPTER THREE

THE GOLDEN BOOK

Those who gave their lives

It was the custom of religious and missionary institutes in France to list members who gave their lives for their country in a "Golden Book" of remembrance. To this was added the number of those who saw active service, those decorated, and those mentioned in dispatches. Many of these were posthumous awards or honours given to soldiers who later died in the war. At Livinhac's request the Missionaries of Africa, like other societies, drew up their own Golden Book and also contributed statistics to a general Golden Book of all the congregations. In spite of this, no manuscript or published version of the White Fathers' Golden Book of the Great War survives, but the names and statistics were certainly compiled.[1] Forty-three White Fathers are recorded as "killed". However a complete list of members of the Society who died as a direct result of the hostilities must now number sixty, and even this number is not definitive.[2]

One of the reasons for the original under-estimate is that the Golden Book was a French enterprise and only counted the French confreres who died. It ignored the five Belgian confreres who also gave their lives on the Allied side, as well as the nine German confreres who lost their lives during the conflict. Another reason is that it concentrated on confreres who had taken the missionary oath or who had at least started their novitiate. Novices who had been clothed in the habit of the Society were entitled to its suffrages on the same footing as those who had taken the missionary oath. Consequently, for the students who died it is these names that appear in the Society's necrological calendar. The original list apparently includes four aspirants who had not yet begun their novitiate, but there are at least six more who gave their lives. In fact, the total of number of aspirants may be greater than ten, since the exact status of some students aspiring to be White Fathers is unknown. No doubt, among those who died were some who should be described as "former aspirants". The names of aspirants can only be gleaned from the pages of the Formation Registers, from *Petit Echo*, and *Echo Binsonnais*.

Another reason for the restricted number in the first list is that it only counted those killed by shells or bullets, or who went missing, on the field of battle. It did not count those who died from other causes associated with the fighting – those who died from diseases contracted in the trenches or during internment and enemy occupation, from post-traumatic stress disorders, from the after-effects of gas, or even as a result of what is now called "friendly fire". Yet, all these can be said to have given their lives in the war. Two brothers who were missionary aspirants, Joseph and Léon Pignide lost their lives during the war. Joseph served in the Dardanelles campaign and afterwards in Champagne-Ardennes, where he was killed on September 30th 1918 in the attack on Courlandon near Fismes. He was a corporal in the Ninth Zouaves.[3] His brother, Léon, died on July 20th in the previous year. As already mentioned, he suffered a stroke while swimming in the river La Truyère, possibly triggered by post-traumatic stress.

Jean-Marie-Joseph-Eloi Falguières (1887-1924) has already been mentioned in Chapter Two. He was a White Father priest who had taught for two years at the Priory, Bishop's Waltham, before being called up as a stretcher-bearer in the Medical Division in 1914.[4] He served at Malmaison in 1917, on the Somme in March 1918 and later in the same year at the Chemin des Dames. Refusing to leave his First Aid Post, he was taken prisoner and suffered a short, but harsh experience of captivity. He was mentioned in dispatches in 1919. Freed in November 1918, he was demobilized the following year and went back to Bishop's Waltham and afterwards to St.Laurent d'Olt. However, he had not recovered from his experience at the front or as a prisoner of war. Phosgene asphyxiating gas had damaged his respiratory tract and caused him to cough blood continually. In spite of receiving treatment, he found it more and more difficult to swallow even liquids and finally to speak. He died of suffocation at Pau on September 28th 1924, six years after the cessation of hostilities. There is no doubt that he deserves to be listed with those who gave their lives in the First World War.

Some of the following who died in, or on the way to, hospital have already received a mention in Chapter Two. Jakob Nilges (1887-1916) was a German novice cleric from Trier, "one of our best seminarians".[5] When war broke out he was in the novitiate in Algiers and was promptly interned as an enemy alien. Held in deplorable conditions in Fort L'Empereur, he contracted tube-rculosis and was moved to the hospital at Mustapha, where he died on April 29th 1916. Gustav Apitz, Brother Ludger, from Cologne (1895-1915) saw active service in the first year of the war. He died in hospital at Châtel (Rhône) on August 28th 1915, probably from wounds received in battle. Adrien Boyer (1895-1915), a French novice cleric from Rodez, died in the military hospital at Nice on June 16th 1915 from wounds sustained on the Dardanelles Front. Joseph Buatois (1884-1915), a French priest, served as a medical orderly in Tunisia, but died of cerebral malaria at Teboursouk on June 5th 1915. Henri Chiron (1889-1915), a French novice cleric from Luçon, died in the military hospital at Poitiers on February 10th 1915, of typhoid, contracted in the trenches. Alfred Courant (180-1918), a French priest from Quimper, died in the hospital at Veles (Macedonia) on November 2nd 1918, of broncho-pneumonia contracted on the Serbian front.

Jean Declerck, a French aspirant, served with the Zouaves in the Dardanelles, where he was wounded. He died on the boat to Bizerta in July 1915. Lucien Gomé, Brother Barnabé (1889-1918), a French novice brother, served firstly with the Zouaves and then with the Eighteenth Regiment of Artillery, after which he was given work in a munitions factory. He died of the dreaded Spanish influenza in Castelsarrasin Hospital, Carcassone, on October 7th 1918.

Other victims of illness were Louis Le Dévédec (1882-1916) who died of typhoid fever in Salonika on October 7th 1916; Joseph Loiseau, Brother Pierre (1881-1918), who died in the military hospital at Tunis on November 26th 1918; George Maeyaert (1884-1917), who died in enemy occupied Antwerp on February 13th 1917; François-Marie Renaudier (1890-1917) – already mentioned – who died of chronic malaria on October 18th 1917; and Pierre Saclier (1876-1917) who died of exhaustion on May 31st 1917.

One Missionary of Africa seems to have died from so-called "friendly fire". This was Arthur Mechau (1874-1916), Brother Fulgence, a German.[6] In Rwanda - at that time a part of German East Africa - German troops made a short stop at Mibirizi Mission on April 21st 1916. They were surprised by invading Belgian troops and an exchange of rifle fire took place around the mission. Although the mission walls were thick enough to absorb the bullets, Brother Fulgence was wounded, presumably by Belgian fire. Perhaps, he had emerged unwisely from the mission buildings during the fire-fight. He became unconscious and died the same evening. The mission diary and other sources are so tight-lipped about his death as to suggest acute embarrassment that the brother was killed by Allied invaders. The fact that he was German may have added to this embarrassment. He remains, nevertheless, a victim – the only White Father victim – of the East African campaign.

We can be sure that forty-seven confreres on active service were actually killed on the field of battle or died immediately afterwards from wounds sustained in battle.[7] Of these, thirty-six were French, eight were German and three Belgian. Most of them were shot by machine-gun fire. Typical was the case of Jean-Baptiste Béraud (1891-1915), the French scholastic from Le Puy, described as a "valiant and devoted corporal", who was shot in the right eye on June 21st 1915, while courageously leading an assault on recently occupied enemy trenches in the Dardanelles.[8] Clovis Capelle (1888-1917) was another scholastic, who came from Arras. As a second lieutenant in the Dardanelles, he was wounded in one arm, but continued to care for his men. As we have seen in Chapter Two, he was eventually shot in the head on April 17th 1917 in Macedonia. He was awarded the Legion of Honour, the *Croix de Guerre* and the Silver Medal for Bravery.

Pierre Lhomme (1886-1917), a young priest from Rennes, showed outstanding courage as a stretcher-bearer in the medical corps. He was killed by machine-gun fire on July 31st 1917 in the Anglo-French offensive at Ypres. Joseph Margot-Duclos (1881-1916) came from Gap. Ordained a diocesan priest in 1904, he went for further studies and then did pastoral work in his cathedral parish. In 1914 he entered the novitiate of the Missionaries of Africa and was called up after three months. He served first as nurse and stretcher-bearer, and then – after the disbanding of his regiment – as chaplain to the Verdun Redoubt of Froide-Terre. This was a fortification on a slope to the east of the city, facing the German front line.[9] On June 22nd 1916, the Feast of Corpus Christi, he celebrated Mass and decided to keep the Blessed Sacrament on his person.[10] The following day, June 23rd he went to the help of a wounded officer, but was machine gunned through the heart and kidneys. The bullet that pierced his heart passed through the pyx containing the Blessed Sacrament he was carrying and particles of the consecrated host were mingled with his blood. The striking symbolism of this detail was not lost on his confreres. He was buried in the courtyard of the redoubt and his grave was visited by General Charles Mangin. A memorial tablet on the wall of the Froide-Terre Redoubt now commemorates all those who died in its defence.

Louis-Félix Meyronin, a French aspirant, served with a machine-gun company in Champagne where he was mentioned in dispatches. He was shot in the stomach on either September 26th or 27th 1915 and was buried in the cemetery at Suipes.[11] Ernest Potier (1888-1918), from Nevers, "one of our best scholastics", who served as a sergeant in the Fourth Zouaves , was shot in the forehead on Maundy Thursday March 28th 1918 on the Champagne front, and Frans Van Der Wegen, a Belgian aspirant was also shot in the head on September 29th 1918. His last words were: "My God, I love you with all my heart".[12]

Seven Missionaries of Africa are known to have been killed by exploding shells or shrapnel from shells. Léon Brossier (1882-1918), a French priest from Angers, had been a missionary in Uganda. He served as a stretcher-bearer in the 116th Alpine Regiment and fought at Verdun, taking part in the recapture of Douaumont Fort. On November 13th 1916 he wrote: "I return safe and sound from Verdun for the second time, thanks be to God. How many times did my heart not cast an appeal to the Blessed Mother of heaven and our dear saints of Buganda ?" He received the *Croix de Guerre* and was four times mentioned in dispatches. He was killed by a shell splinter at the Vosges towards the end of the war on September 18th 1918.[13]

Léon Cadet (1878-1916), a French priest from Cambrai, had also been a missionary in Uganda. He, too, fought at Verdun. In his last letter, dated April 24th 1916, he had written: "Our ordeals accepted by us are the path that leads to future glory and eternal reward…If God wishes to keep me for Uganda, he will. Those he keeps are well kept. If he wishes to call me more quickly to his side, I will not be any less happy." On April 27th, he was killed by an exploding shell that took off one foot and broke the other leg in two places, besides wounding him in the chest. Both his legs were amputated and he remained lucid till the end. His agony lasted three hours, and he was buried in the churchyard at Jubecourt (Meuse).[14] His name is inscribed on the high altar of the Douaumont Ossuary Chapel at Verdun.

Lode or Louis De Boninge (1896-1918) was a Belgian (Flemish) novice cleric from Malines-Brussels. He had been called up from the evacuated novitiate at Boxtel in neutral Holland and rediscovered his Flemish roots in the army. Having learned of the many injustices perpetrated on Flemish soldiers, he joined their patriotic movement in spite of the opposition of his chaplain. Arrested by the military authorities, he was visited in remand by his White Father superior, Edouard Leys (1889-1945), who urged him to apply for a pardon. De Boninge, who felt no guilt about the matter, refused. He was sentenced to seven months detention and a fine in February 1918. On appeal, the sentence was reduced and suspended, and he rejoined his comrades in the trenches. At St. Joris, near Nieuport, he was killed by a shell from a Howitzer while on his way to care for the wounded on May 7th 1918.[15] His dismembered body was first buried in the military cemetery of Duinhoek, De Panne, and later reburied in the family grave at Wekelgem. His statue in the *gandourah* and *burnous* of a White Father, carved by Karel Aubroeck, appears on the Peace Arch at the Ijser Cross Memorial in Diksmuide. In 1932 his father refused permission to remove his remains to the crypt of this memorial, but his mother consented in 1936. It is not certain whether his grave is, in fact, there. Although he had technically disobeyed his missionary superior, there is no evidence that he was excluded from the Society.[16]

Auguste De Langhe, Brother Liévin (1890-1917), was another Belgian, a temporarily professed brother from Ghent. He had only been a few hours in the trenches when a piece of exploding shell pierced his heart on August 24th 1917. He died instantly.[17] Régis Delabre (1889-1916) was already mentioned in Chapter Two. He was a French scholastic from Le Puy, who was due to be ordained priest at Carthage when he was called up in August 1914. He served with the Zouaves as a sergeant in Macedonia. On the evening of Saturday May 27th 1916 he took shelter with a warrant officer on the Serbian front under a hail of enemy shells. The fox-hole in which he was sheltering received a direct hit. The shell took off his right arm and virtually beheaded him.[18] The mournful funeral conducted by his confreres, which took place next day, has already been described. Henri Guibert (1888-1918) was a French novice cleric from Nantes. As a sergeant and stretcher-bearer in the Ninth Zouaves, he took part in several early engagements at Verdun, being awarded the *Croix de Guerre*. He was killed by a shell splinter through the heart at Landifay in the Aisne Offensive on October 30th 1918. He had been in the act of reconnoitring a forward site for a First Aid post. He was buried at Landifay.[19] Finally, the French aspirant Louis Souton, who had just completed his philosophy studies was wounded by an exploding shell at Mount Kemmel in Flanders and died after a long agony on April 29th 1918.[20] Five thousand two hundred and ninety-four soldiers of the Thirtieth Regiment of Infantry died in the defence of Mount Kemmel on April 25th 1918, but only fifty-seven of the dead were identified. Souton, because of his lengthy agony, was among them. They are commemorated on the monument at the French ossuary on Mount Kemmel.[21]

A small number of White Fathers were killed by a bomb or grenade. Adrien Guillou (1889-1917), a novice cleric from Nantes was a second lieutenant in the 1st Regiment of Zouaves/Rifles. He was killed on May 11th 1917 on the Chemin des Dames in Champagne-Ardennes. The most reliable account of his death, given by Albert Claverie, the chaplain stretcher-bearer who carried him from the front, was that he was killed by a grenade. He was buried at Vendresse.[22] Albert

Malavieille (1892-1916), another novice cleric came from Mende. He served with the Zouaves in Flanders where he was wounded by shrapnel in the buttocks in July 1915. On recovering, he was posted to Verdun where he was killed by a grenade in the fighting around Douaumont Fort on March 5th 1916. "He had the soul of a saint" was the verdict of a fellow missionary.[23] His name is inscribed on the high altar in the chapel of the Douaumont Ossuary at Verdun. Joseph Moussié (1889-1915) was a scholastic from Toulouse. He was "literally blown to pieces" by a bomb on the front at Arras on January 25th 1915. There were virtually no recognizable remains.[24]

Some of those who lost their lives were fatally wounded on the battlefield and lived for a greater or lesser time before dying. Alphonse Pascal Boissay, Brother Martial (1891-1914), a novice brother from Orléans was killed at a very early stage in the war. Serving with a mounted troop of Zouaves, he was wounded at Arras on October 23rd 1914 and declined to be taken to a First Aid post. "I am fatally wounded", he said to the stretcher-bearers. "I feel I am going to die and I want to be left alone to prepare to appear before God."[25] Earlier, he had declined the award of the Military Medal. The case of Adrien Boyer (1895-1915), a novice-cleric from Rodez, has already been mentioned above.[26] Pierre Gaillard, a French aspirant, studying at the White Fathers' seminary of St. Maurice, Switzerland, fought with the colonial infantry at Verdun where his leg was shattered by a shell on October 8th 1917. He died twelve days later at Roanne (Rhône-Alps) on October 17th.[27]

Joseph Grison (1889-1915) from Lille had already been ordained deacon when he was called up. His thigh was shattered by a shell at the River Ijser, Ypres, on April 30th 1915. His leg was scheduled for amputation and he received absolution from his confrere, Charles Joyeux (1885-1936*), but died of his wounds at Dunkirk on the same day, before the operation could be carried out.[28] Pierre Huguet (1889-1916) was a scholastic from Nantes. He was wounded in the region of the liver at the Dardanelles, but recovered and was sent to Macedonia. There he was wounded again in an engagement with the Bulgarians at a railway station on September 21st 1916. He was anointed by Etienne Farrussenq (1889-1953) and died later the same day. In his last letter he wrote: "I submit myself entirely to God's will. Whatever happens, I have already said my *fiat*." His last words were: "I am happy, I did my duty". He was the subject of a moving testimony from his fellow scholastic, Paul Verdouck (1889-1932): "He died a saint. He is now with God and the Blessed Virgin Mary. He died for France, the Church, the Society and the dear scholastics. He was my companion at Binson, in the novitiate, at Carthage and my brother in arms."[29]

Georges Pecheberty (1894-1915) was a French aspirant, serving with the Second Zouaves. Wounded in the thigh on June 7th 1915, the eve of an assault in the Tracy-le-Mont region, he was taken by ambulance to Choisy-le-Bas and died later the same day.[30] Emile Vanlaere (1892-1918), a Belgian scholastic from Bruges, served as stretcher-bearer in the Belgian army. He was fatally wounded while returning from a patrol near Nieuport on the Ijser front and died after several hours on April 9th 1918 in the presence of several of his confreres, who administered the last rites. He offered his life for the conversion of the Africans.[31]

Seven Missionaries of Africa who fought in the First World War are listed as "missing". This is a category of enormous dimensions. For example, at the Thiépval Monument in northern France, the number of missing listed in the Battle of the Somme reaches a total of seventy-three thousand three hundred and sixty-seven soldiers without a known grave.[32] On the Menin Gate at Ypres are recorded the names of fifty-four thousand soldiers who "simply disappeared".[33] This could come about because they were victims of a direct hit by a shell or a bomb, which meant there were no – or insufficient - remains to identify. Alternatively, their remains might never have been found, because of changes in the landscape as a result of bombardment. On the other hand, their bodies may have been found, but were unidentifiable for other reasons, e.g. lack of identity discs or personal documents. Paulin Bros, a French aspirant studying philosophy at Binson, was a corporal of infantry who went missing at the Somme (Moreuil) on April 4th 1918.[34] We noted in Chapter Two that Ernest Delarse (1881-1916), a French scholastic from Moulins, disappeared without trace at Verdun on May 19th 1916. He was a warrant officer, who had already been wounded at Arras in June 1915. Three weeks before he died he wrote to Paul Voillard: "As for me I am entirely submitted to God's will. I know that the least little shell burst or single bullet will not touch me without God's permission...This very evening we are going back to the same place, at the moment one of the most dangerous on the front. If I remain there, Father, rest assured that my last thought will be for our dear Society, which I have wanted to join, and for its venerable superiors. Please present my respectful good wishes to Monsignor the Superior General and ask him to bless me."[35]

Félix Jory, a French aspirant serving in the infantry, went missing in August 1918. Some two months earlier he had written that he was on his way to the front line.[36] Pierre Le Cléac'h (1889-1914) was a French scholastic from Quimper. He was due for ordination when he was called up in August 1914. He served as a warrant officer in the Zouaves and went missing in Champagne on October 5th 1914.[37] Adrien Sylvestre, Brother Alexis (1887-1918), was a French brother from Nantes who had been on the staff of St. Anne's Jerusalem. In 1916 he was wounded in the left arm and left thigh at the Somme, but was luckily rescued. After a painful operation he visited the grave of the as yet uncanonized Thérèse of Lisieux, to whose intercession he attributed his survival. He went missing in the German lines at Boulogne-la-Grasse, west of Lassigny, on Maundy Thursday April 15th 1918.[38] Léon Valette (1888-1915) was a French novice cleric from Rodez. He went missing on the River Ijser on April 30th 1915. Finally, Pierre Valléau (1892-1915) – already mentioned in Chapter Two – went missing on the banks of the River Ijser on the same day as Léon Valette.[39] However, when soldiers were digging a trench there a year later, his body was discovered and identified from his identity disc and personal letters. He was buried under a small cross amidst the shell holes that covered the landscape. Some time later, Victor Vuylsteke (1892-1962), then a soldier in the

Belgian army, saw the cross and added the words *Père Blanc* to the inscription.[40]

The sixty Missionaries of Africa who gave their lives in the First World War comprise fourteen priests of the Society, eleven brothers, eleven scholastics (including one deacon), fourteen novices (including one priest) and the ten aspirants who are known.

Wounded Veterans

It is impossible to give a precise figure for all those who were wounded in the First World War.[41] In Chapter One the figure of five million was hazarded. However, if one takes into account all the various ways in which those who survived were affected by the war, physically, psychologically, socially, spiritually, the figure must exceed the eight million estimated to have lost their lives. War veterans were traumatized, dehumanized, emotionally distressed, often angry and embittered, even if they were not physically wounded or mentally impaired. Missionary of Africa conscripts were perhaps well prepared by their Christian faith and vocation to face the horrors of the war, but there is no doubt that everyone who enlisted was changed in one way or another. Many had to live with physical or mental disabilities for the rest of their lives and carried these back with them to their missions in Africa. Often they evinced a greater sensitivity towards other sick and handicapped people, as a result of their own experience. For some, active missionary work was no longer possible. The stories of some White Fathers who survived the experience of being wounded have already been told. In this section, some more examples are given.

Julien Chabot (1892-1926) had finished his novitiate and was doing military service when the war broke out. He served in a dressing station at the Dardanelles and was later moved to Salonika, where he was attached to a mobile column in Macedonia. He returned to the scholasticate after the war and was eventually appointed to Wagadugu in 1921 after his ordination. However, he suffered from an acute infection and congestion of the lungs that eventually killed him in 1926, a mere five years after his arrival in West Africa.[42]

Louis Châles (1891-1969), called up in 1914, was severely wounded in the hip by a piece of shrapnel, the last fragment being removed years later, after he had suffered abscesses and inflammation. Throughout his life he had a stiff leg that made walking and even sitting difficult. He served as curate at Carthage Cathedral for forty-three years, but his sufferings continued. He was unable to put on or take off his right boot by himself and developed ankylosis of the right hip. He could only perch on chairs, and preferred to work standing up. The distinctive mark of his missionary life was the way in which he accepted this disability.[43]

Camille Cormerais (1894-1979) was called up as a novice in 1914 and spent several years in the trenches. In 1917 he was wounded in the right arm. Part of the humerus was missing and no natural joint was possible. He wore an appliance for the rest of his life, but had difficulty moving his arm. An outstanding missionary in the French Sudan and the Sahara, he nevertheless suffered from migraine and nervous crises. He died at the age of eighty-four at Tassy, France.[44] Jean-Baptiste Cormerais (1890-1941) saw action on the Eastern Front and was wounded in the thigh. After ordination, he was posted to the Sahara and later became a seminary teacher in Bamako. He suffered thirty years of discomfort on account of his wound.[45]

Léon Darot (1890-1958) was studying Canon Law as a young priest in Rome when he was called up. He served as a stretcher-bearer with the Fourth Zouaves in the Dardanelles and was then posted to Salonika where a bullet took off the top of his right ear in 1916.[46] Then, later in the same year, he remained behind with the wounded while the rest of his unit retreated. In this exposed situation he was briefly taken prisoner by the Bulgarians, before becoming the victim of a cavalry charge. A Bulgarian cavalry man dealt him a heavy sabre-blow on the head. The blow dented his steel helmet and wounded him on the scalp. The Bulgarians then abandoned the area and Darot made his escape. It later turned out that the sabre-blow had affected his spine and crushed nerves in his back. He served as a missionary in parishes and seminaries in Malawi, but experienced a creeping paralysis which caused him great suffering in the last years of his life.[47]

Achille-Pierre Decloedt (1876-1921) was a teacher at St. Anne's Jerusalem, from where he was called up in 1914. He spent most of the war in the medical corps, stationed at Angoulême. After demobilization, he fell ill with recurrent fevers and headaches. He went to Beirut for convalescence in 1921, and died there in the same year.[48]

Pierre Gallerand (1887-1976) had just been ordained priest in 1914 when he was called up. He joined the Fourth Zouaves and served with great courage in Flanders and at Verdun as Warrant Officer and ultimately as Lieutenant, being idolized by his soldiers. He was wounded in the arm at Verdun and refused to be evacuated from the front line. In the final German offensive of March 1918 he fought alongside the British and was seriously wounded in the attack on Boulogne-la-Grasse, west of Lassigny (Oise) on March 29th. He was taken to an advanced dressing post with shell splinters in the chest, right elbow and hip. He then underwent a series of painful operations in various hospitals until he was demobbed in 1919. He was awarded numerous decorations, including the Legion of Honour. After the war he worked as a missionary in Kabylia and was noted for his military approach to religious obedience.[49]

Martin Jaureguy (1886-1965) was studying for a doctorate in Canon Law in Rome when he was called up in 1914. He fought at Verdun as a Corporal stretcher-bearer in the 249th Infantry Regiment and received the *Croix de Guerre* for an act of charity to a wounded comrade. After Verdun he was promoted sergeant. In May 1917 he was wounded in the right side by a shell splinter during an attack on the Chemin des Dames. After a spell in hospital, he rejoined his regiment on the Italian Front, and had an audience with Pope Benedict XV who enquired about his wound. Returning to France during the final German offensive of 1918, he was seriously wounded at Rouvrel on the Somme (near Beauvais) in April. A bullet passed through his mouth, lightly fracturing his upper jaw, but damaging the lower jaw more seriously. "It pleased God to keep me alive. May his holy will be blessed and glorified forever", he wrote at the time. In a painful operation without anaesthetic, part of the jaw-bone was removed. "A light sacrifice!" was his comment. He spent lengthy periods in several hospitals and was demobbed in 1919. Martin Jaureguy became a seminary professor at Kipalapala (Tanzania) and Eastview (Canada), where the author was taught moral theology by him. Throughout his life he suffered a speech impediment as a result of his wound.[50]

Emile Laroche (1890-1979) was called up in 1914 at the end of his novitiate. He was seriously wounded in 1915 by a machine-gun bullet that fractured his right femur and severed some nerves. He was treated at Rouen and had his leg shortened by six centimetres. There was also a general atrophy of the leg. He received an early discharge in 1916 and worked in French Sudan, North Africa, Argentina (for promotion) and France. His apostolate was deeply marked by his mutilation and other illnesses.[51]

Xavier Le Doaré (1887-1941) served as a warrant officer on the Eastern Front where he was wounded in the arm. Although he served for many years in French Sudan, the wound gave him trouble for the rest of his life and his arm was partially paralysed.[52] René Marcant (1882-1961) joined the Zouaves after his ordination in 1914. He was seriously wounded in France in 1915. His shoulder was shattered by a shell and he was invalided out of the army the following year. During his treatment in Paris, he walked in the city with an apparatus for supporting the elbow. Marcant joked that passers-by thought it was a gas projector. He remained all his life in European formation houses and procures.[53]

Jules Pagès (1887-1984) was ordained priest at Carthage in 1915, after which he was called up and became a sergeant instructor with Zouaves in Tunisia. He accompanied them to France where he fought at Verdun in 1916-1917 and in the German offensive of 1918 with the rank of lieutenant, at which time he was wounded in the thigh by a machine-gun bullet. He was demobilized after the Armistice and served as a missionary in Malawi, Kabylia and Jerusalem. Although his health was not good, he lived to be ninety-six.[54]

Arsène Sabau [formerly Sabeau] (1887-1974) was called up after priestly ordination and went as a stretcher-bearer with the Zouaves to the Dardanelles and Macedonia. In September 1916 he was seriously wounded as he went – under machine-gun fire - to assist a wounded soldier. A shell burst a yard from him and he received splinters in the right arm, leg and back. He was taken to a hospital in Toulon, France, for treatment. All his wounds took a long time to heal, but his arm was infected. Gangrene set in and it was amputated early in 1917. Since there was virtually no stump, it was impossible to fit an artificial arm. He remained in France until 1922, when he was allowed to go to Bamako. He took to riding a tricycle and is remembered as an eccentric character of military appearance. He lived to be eighty-seven.

Pierre Valex (1888-1972) was called up in 1914 after novitiate and served in the Dardanelles. There he was wounded and evacuated to Bizerta in 1915. On his recovery he was sent to Salonika and Serbia, where he suffered from persistent malaria and also jaundice and bronchitis. Demobbed in 1919, he finished his studies, was ordained priest in 1922 and posted to Bamako. He suffered from palpitations, breathlessness and cramps and had to return to

France for treatment before serving thirty more years as a missionary in Kabylia (Algeria).[55]

Paul Verdouck (1889-1932) was one of the celebrated White Father characters of the war and a prolific correspondent from the front. One of his letters even had a hole from a bullet that had passed through his haversack. Verdouck was a scholastic at Carthage when he was called up to the Dardanelles Front. He was promoted from sergeant to warrant officer and eventually to warrant officer first class. At Gallipoli a shell wounded him in the thigh and he was evacuated by hospital ship. The splinter was removed and he was posted to Macedonia, where he was wounded a second time in an engagement with the Bulgarians on the Serbian Front, this time in the arm. It was some time before there was a boat to evacuate him to France. Ordained in 1921, he was posted to Bamako. Shortly after returning there from his long retreat in 1932, he appears to have missed his footing in the dark and to have fallen from the Medina Bridge at Kayes. He was found dead the following day.[56]

A final example is provided by the aspirant from Bishop's Waltham, Hervé Quéinnic (1896-1946) who took part in the Battle of Verdun. At the end of June 1916 he was in an observation post at Fleury thirty metres from the German front line, under artillery and aerial bombardment. An exploding shell wounded him in the head and arm. He was given a trepanning operation and survived to work as a missionary in Wagadugu (Burkina Faso), "It was a miracle that I escaped alive" was his only comment.[57]

Prisoners and Internees

Imprisonment was another form of trauma, in which servicemen frequently felt themselves estranged from human society. It was an experience of boredom and alienation that could lead to feelings of abandonment and resentment. Two Missionaries of Africa were taken prisoner early in the war and more than a dozen others were captured and imprisoned later on - most for a short time in the war's final year.

Joseph Bouniol (1884-1950) is well known as the historian who wrote *The White Fathers and their Missions* in 1929 and also as the founder of the Society's missionary magazine in Britain.[58] He was teaching at the Priory, Bishop's Waltham when he was called up in 1914. He took part in several engagements in the North, the Vosges and Lorraine, and was nearly killed before being captured south of Ypres on November 2nd 1914. He remained a prisoner of war for four years. He was held firstly at Mecklenberg, then at Güterloh in Westphalia and finally at Wesel in the same region. The Germans treated priest prisoners like officers and they lived out their captivity in relative comfort. Bouniol was incarcerated in a Franciscan retreat house, in what he called "a second novitiate". His fellow prisoners were French, Polish, Belgian and British officers, a hundred of whom were Catholics. There were also four other French priests. Each prisoner had a small room, containing bed, desk, chair, washstand and a crucifix on the wall. Bouniol's cell also had a picture of the Prodigal Son. In the dining-room there were portraits of Pope Pius X and the Kaiser. There was central heating and a library of 200 books. The food conformed exactly to the requirements of the White Fathers' Constitutions, which meant that it was plain, adequate and wholesome. The only blights on this monastic idyll were the walls and barbed wire that surrounded the house and the relatively small exercise area, a hundred yards in length.

Bouniol was allowed to send four cards and two letters a month, to receive letters from Bishop's Waltham and to read German newspapers. He celebrated Mass daily in the Church, with an English officer as server. He studied German, perfected his English and taught Latin and French. He was visited several times by a German confrere, Georg Steinhage (1876-1962), who brought him a breviary and other books. Later, in 1916, he was moved to a converted isolation hospital nearby, where he had his own room and ministered to two hundred and forty wounded French and British prisoners. Then, in 1917, he was transferred to Eutin, near Lübeck. He was liberated at the end of 1918 and returned to Bishop's Waltham the following year. He remained there until 1938, receiving other appointments in France and North Africa during the last twelve years of his life. During the Second World War Cardinal Archbishop (later Cardinal) Francis Joseph Spellman made him Vicar Delegate for American troops in North Africa.[59]

Auguste Thézé (1890-1920*) was already a deacon when he was called up from Carthage in 1914. He was taken prisoner in France the following year and was held with other clerical prisoners at a Catholic seminary in Münster. There were two priests among them and the chapel in which he heard daily Mass was next door to his room. He was able to receive letters, parcels and books. Among the latter was the biography of Auguste Achte (1861-1905). He also revised Noldin's moral theology manual. In 1917 he was joined by Jules Casthelain (1894-1959), who reported on the piety, discipline and excellent spirit of the seminary. It was well run and theological studies were taken seriously. The organizer of this prison seminary was the celebrated mission theologian of Münster, Josef Schmidlin. Through his good offices Thézé obtained permission to be ordained priest in March 1917. The ordination took place in the cathedral and a reception was held for him attended by the other seventy seminarians. His first Solemn Mass took place on the Sunday following and a subscription was got up for a Mass box. After ordination, he moved into the presbytery with the other priests. In 1918 Thézé was transferred to Magdeburg. In 1919 he was finally released and returned to Carthage to follow a theology course for young priests.

The story, however, did not end happily. Thézé's lengthy isolation from the Society made him suspicious and resentful. He attributed the cold reception he received from the superiors in North Africa to a delation by Schmidlin, accusing him of chauvinism and lack of apostolic charity. As a result, he was allowed to leave the Society and join the archdiocese of Carthage. In 1922 he applied to the diocese of Périgueux.[60] It seems that his was one of the few departures from the Society caused by the deterioration in Franco-German relations during and after the war.

In 1917 François Bellaue (1860-1923) was imprisoned in German occupied Belgium and condemned to three years of forced labour. At the time of his imprisonment, he was provincial treasurer of the White Fathers in Belgium. Aged fifty-seven, he was arrested at Louvain, taken to Antwerp and held at Reinbach and later Limburg along with eight hundred other prisoners of war. Although he was given a clean cell, the diet was inadequate. There was weak coffee in the morning with stale bread, a litre of soup at midday and half a litre of soup in the evening. He was released after the armistice in November 1918 before the expiry of his sentence.[61] Throughout the war the White Fathers at St. Maurice-en-Valais, Switzerland, sent food parcels to prisoners of war and forwarded up to eighty letters a day. This was the salvation of François Bellaue.[62]

Alfred Ernest Howell (1892-1962) joined the British Army as a layman before the war broke out, serving as a regular soldier in the Royal Welch Fusiliers and rising to the rank of sergeant. Posted to Malta with the first battalion, he was sent to Flanders in October 1914. Outnumbered and outgunned, his battalion suffered a devastating German attack at Zonnebeke on October 20th during which Howell was taken prisoner. He spent almost the entire war in prison camps at Göttingen and Limburg. As a prisoner, he was encouraged by a German priest and Latin tutor to follow a missionary vocation. Released in the Netherlands on March 11th 1918, he declined to claim the bar to his 1914 Star, to which he was entitled for being under fire in France. He joined the Missionaries of Africa, becoming eventually provincial of Great Britain.[63]

With the German offensive in the final year of the war there was a spate of captures. At least thirteen Missionaries of Africa were taken prisoner on the western front, among them Eloi Falguières (1887-1924), already mentioned, Jean-Marie Andiole (1886-1950*), Jules Lemoine (1898-1963) and Germain Aymard (1896-1964). At this juncture in the war the conditions in which they were taken and held were harsh, but the experience was mercifully short. All were released after the Armistice and returned to their communities in 1919.[64]

There was no lengthy captivity for prisoners taken on other fronts. In the confused situation of the Serbian Front, Léon Darot (1890-1958), already mentioned, and François Robin (1883-1948) were able to escape shortly after capture.[65] Joseph Mazé (1883-1959), serving as a transport officer with British troops in East Africa in 1917, was held as a prisoner of war by a German column for ten days. Before giving his captors the slip, he had heard the confessions of six German soldiers.[66] The most famous escape was that of Auguste Clavel (1895-1979) from the Bolsheviks in the Ukraine after the war – a story told in the next section of this chapter.

The need to intern missionaries in Africa is a commentary on the "anomaly" of an international missionary society caught up in a world of warring nationalisms. Indeed, the Missionaries of Africa witnessed to a deeper human unity, transcending national hostilities and cultural differences – a unity that finds its roots in Catholic Christianity. This is true, even though the French element in the Society was dominant at the time and in spite of the tensions caused by the war in what was, as yet, a fledgling multi-national institute.

Experiences of internment in Africa varied considerably and the full story of the harassment of missionaries that accompanied the East African campaign will be told in a later chapter. Since German East Africa's coast was blockaded and all its land borders faced hostile Allied powers, it was only a matter of time before the colony was invaded. In these circumstances, missionaries whose nationality was that of an Allied power were regarded by the Germans as a liability and steps were taken to remove them from mission stations in the vicinity of the frontiers.

At first it was not agreed that they should be interned, it being enough to remove them to their other missions further inland, and make them swear an oath of neutrality. Those sent to Tabora from Rwanda-Burundi in early 1915, through the personal animus of the German commander Max Wintgens, were sent back by the Governor, Heinrich Schnee. In August 1915 nineteen missionaries from Nyanza (South) were sent to Ushirombo Mission (Unyanyembe), and others from Burundi were ordered to Bujumbura and then Kigoma. They were allowed to take camp-beds and cooking utensils. As the Germans retreated before the invading Allies, they were loath to leave non-German missionaries in their wake. Many were forced to accompany the retreating troops who fell back on Tabora.[67]

In Tabora the French, Belgian and Italian missionaries were interned in one large hall. However, they were placed at the disposal of the Vicar Apostolic of Unyanyembe, Henri Léonard (1869-1953), for pastoral purposes, and the Italians Giovanni Cottino (1883-1959) and Alessandro Isola (1887-1958) were allowed to stay at the nearby mission of Itaga. When the Allies liberated Tabora eighteen Missionaries of Africa were released, including Eugène Welfelé (1877-1956) and Louis Guillerme (1874-1960) who had been travelling back to Central Africa when war was declared. Altogether, they spent two years and four months as internees at Tabora.[68]

It was now the turn of the British to intern the Germans and to make them swear an oath of loyalty to King George V. The British policy was to send German nationals to an internment camp in Cairo or to Ahmednagar camp in India. Three German brothers in Uganda had been spared exile in India and were allowed to stay under surveillance at Kisubi Mission. Lucien Schmitt (1884-1919) an Alsatian priest, working among the Iraqw in eastern Unyanyembe was also allowed to go to Uganda.[69] Alois Hamberger (1874-1921*) who had co-operated with German forces on the southern border of the colony, was taken to Blantyre (Nyasaland) and from there to Uganda also. Another casualty of post-war Franco-German relations, he found it impossible to live with French confreres and requested repatriation. Arrived in Europe, he found it repugnant to speak French and to represent in Germany a Society that was mainly French in membership and government. He was released from his missionary oath by *Propaganda Fide*, and joined the archdiocese of Munich.[70]

The fate of the German brothers in the conquered colony, many of whom had been military reservists, was more harsh than that of the priests. Apart from Nicholas Jäger (1867-1935), who was an older man and who was allowed to stay at Ushirombo, the other six were taken first of all to a holding camp at Mombasa. Here they were well treated and could take a daily walk and bathe in the sea. This holiday did not last long. Three were sent to Tanga and then on to

Cairo. These were Laurent Molitor (1876-1926), "Brother Castule", Paul Chylewski (1875-1948), "Brother Josaphat" and Jean Borste (1873-1948), "Brother Gaspard". The last named had unhappy memories of his capture and internment. He had worked in a German military supply unit and was taken prisoner in 1917 by Congolese troops who took him with them. In the absence of the Belgian officers from the camp, there was a massacre of prisoners. Chylewski was providentially far from his tent, making his morning meditation and escaped death. After an unpleasant internment in Cairo, he reached Germany in 1919. In 1923 he was posted to Northern Rhodesia (Zambia) and worked there until his death.[71]

Three other German brothers were sent to the camp in India. These were Johannes Hadeler (1874-1944), "Brother Irenée", Conrad Blass (1877-1959), "Brother Balthasar" and Martin Grzeskowiak (1877-1924), "Brother Rogat". Blass had served with the German colonial army in the East African campaign, but Grzeskowiak was a civilian and Polish by birth. He was nevertheless taken prisoner by the British in 1916 and had unhappy memories of his internment in India. Released in 1919, he finally disembarked at Trieste the following year and went home to Poland. Later in 1920 he was appointed to Congo (Lake Albert) and died there of cancer four years later.[72]

The French also interned German residents in their colonies, and, as we have seen, German White Fathers in Algeria and Tunisia were affected. The conditions at Fort L'Empereur where the German novices were interned in Algiers were far from ideal and they were transferred firstly to Berroughia and then, with their novice master, Leo Pfeffermann (1867-1956), to Garaison in the High Pyrenees.[73]

Altogether between sixty and seventy Missionaries of Africa were imprisoned or interned as a result of the war. Prison probably places a greater strain than battle on the relationship of the nationalities involved. However, it is remarkable that relatively few of these prisoners of war and internees abandoned their vocation within an international missionary society.

Auguste Clavel

The story of Auguste Clavel is one of the most extraordinary tales of the war. Auguste Clavel (1895-1979) was due to begin his novitiate in Algiers when he was called up.[74] He served first of all as a stretcher-bearer in the Dardanelles, where he was mentioned in dispatches. Then he had a brief experience of the western front where he was gassed. After this, he joined the expeditionary force to Salonika, stopping on the way in Rome. After the Armistice in 1918, his regiment was detached to assist Baron Piotr Nikolayevich Wrangel (1878-1928), the General commanding the White Russian army in the civil war with the Bolsheviks. The fighting took place along a railway line in Ukraine. Clavel's field hospital was installed in the waiting-room and restaurant of Berezowska railway station, a hundred miles north of Odessa. Under attack from the Bolsheviks, the French and Greek joint force withdrew, leaving three doctors, eight nurses and five wounded soldiers at the station. The Medical Officer in charge ordered his staff to evacuate the station, while he and a single volunteer – Clavel himself – remained to look after their patients. The evacuation, however, failed and the medical staff soon returned. On the night of the 18th/19th March 1919 the Bolsheviks counter-attacked. A Greek machine-gun post held them at bay until an armoured wagon came up the line and wiped out the machine-gunners.

The Bolsheviks surrounded the station, firing through the doors and windows of the waiting-room while Clavel prepared for death. The Medical Officer took his own life, but in the process shot dead a stretcher-bearer standing beside him. Clavel persuaded the restaurateur, a Mr.Camper, not to commit suicide and ordered everyone to go out and surrender. Nobody moved, so Clavel led the way. The Bolsheviks seized them, killing one who tried to flee. Clavel and his companions were then stripped and lined up to be shot. At this juncture a Russian sailor, serving as an officer in the land forces, appeared and forbade the killing of the French. However, he ordered the massacre of all the Greeks and they were immediately shot in spite of their entreaties. The wounded patients were then also killed with blows from rifle butts and revolvers. The massacre took about an hour. One of the French medical orderlies was in fact a Russian called Smolensky who had joined the Foreign Legion. He managed to calm the aggressors telling them that the French were Bolshevik sympathisers. Clavel and his compatriots were then ordered to be taken to Kiev by train.

The train journey took five days, under bombardment from French war planes overhead. At Kolosovka station Clavel was made to treat wounded soldiers of the Red Army, and at every other station where they stopped he and his companions had to bargain for their lives with Bolshevik soldiers who wanted to kill them. At length they arrived in Kiev and were thrown into prison. Forced to attend a propaganda meeting, Clavel was made to praise the Revolution and the local press reported that the French supported Bolshevism. Clavel was a prisoner of war for nearly seven months under a brutal regime and was the witness of many horrors. At one point Leon Trotsky arrived in Kiev. Hearing that there was a French student among the prisoners, he summoned Clavel and engaged him to teach his son French.

Towards the end of September 1919 gunfire could be heard on the outskirts of Kiev. This announced the arrival of the White Russian generals, Symon Petliura (1879-1926) and Anton Denikin (1872-1947) with their volunteer army. Chaos ensued in the city and the Bolsheviks prepared to quit Kiev, taking their prisoners with them to Moscow. In the confusion, Clavel made his escape and took refuge with a Polish family, who gave him civilian clothes. The Bolsheviks were routed in the streets and Clavel was rescued by the Cossacks. A month passed before he could begin his journey to the Black Sea coast. The railway line had been cut and there were bands of Bolsheviks roaming the roads. Eventually, Clavel took an easterly direction through the Kharkov, Don River and Caucasus regions, travelling on goods trains, all the time in danger of death or recapture. He finally reached Odessa and found a French patrol boat that took him to Istanbul. After a further journey of two weeks he reached Marseilles.

In March 1920 Clavel arrived at Algiers, ready to begin his novitiate with the Missionaries of Africa. The novice master made light of his horrific experiences. Clavel, he said, "(was) completely restored after his arduous journeys". Unfeelingly, his fellow novices gave him the nickname of "Bolshevik", and having missed a month of his novitiate, he was made to stay on to complete it in 1921, after the others had left. However, he had already done some theological studies here and there, and he was fast-tracked through the Carthage scholasticate to be ordained priest in July 1923.

In spite of the novice master's unthinking optimism, the war years had indeed left their mark on Clavel and his captivity in Russia had weakened him. He suffered from headaches and the slightest effort exhausted him. He also suffered the after-effects of mustard gas. At first the Superiors were reluctant to appoint him to equatorial Africa and for several years he taught at the junior seminary of St.Laurent d'Olt. At length, with the doctors' approval, Clavel was posted in 1928 to Bangweolo Diocese in Northern Rhodesia (Zambia). Although his health was not good, he lived to be eighty-four and is remembered in Zambia as an active and dedicated superior of several missions. He died at Tassy, France. Clavel remains a legend in the Society of Missionaries of Africa, a man of lively imagination, robust faith and enormous courage.

Citations and Decorations

French anti-clerical legislation was largely based on the premise that priests and religious were disloyal and that they were subject to an authority outside of France, namely the Vatican. In other words, that they evaded French government control. For this reason they were excluded from social and public service, such as teaching or tending the sick. Illogically, however, priests, male religious and seminarians were liable for military service, and in this service, they usually acted as medical staff. The fact that priests and religious in the army distinguished themselves during the war was the best possible argument against anticlericalism. It epitomized the *rapprochement* between the Church and French society which the war helped to bring about. Missionaries of Africa served their country and earned the respect of their compatriots.

Prejudice, however, died hard and there were those who did not want to believe that priests and religious had been anywhere near the battlefield. After the war, an absurd calumny was circulated that conscript priests had never been to the front at all, but had been held in safety behind the lines. To counteract this false rumour, Livinhac ordered that White Fathers should wear their medals and decorations when travelling or visiting officials and European centres. They were to wear them pinned to their *gandourah* (cassock) at all religious and civil ceremonies.[75]   Missionaries of Africa, of course, tended to be somewhat ambivalent about receiving honours. Ignatian spirituality taught that one should not wish for honour rather than dishonour.[76] Pierre Lhomme (1886-1917), for example, remarked on receiving the news that he had won the *Croix de Guerre*, "The will of God is more important than such honours", and Léon Darot (1890-1958) on receiving similar news, piously quoted Psalm 115: "Not to us O Lord, but to your name give the glory".[77]   Others, like Céléstin Paulhe (1888-1919*), receiving the Legion of Honour, *Croix de Guerre* and palm in 1916, prayed:

"May this honour fall on our dear Society".[78]   And   Charles Joyeux (1885-1936*) saw his citation in the same year as a recognition of his ministry.[79]

All of which is not to say that White Fathers were not pleased to receive these honours. In fact they joyfully reported them to their superiors, who were equally pleased to publish them in the Society's bulletins and to list them in the proposed Golden Book. René Marcant (1882-1961), who had been so severely wounded at Arras, was in Paris when his *Croix de Guerre* arrived in 1916. Alfred Louail (1851-1921), the Provincial of Europe, proudly pinned the decoration on the young priest's *gandourah*.[80]

Not every act of courage could be known, let alone rewarded, but the Missionaries of Africa certainly had their fair share of military honours. In fact, as stretcher-bearers, medical orderlies and chaplains, they repeatedly risked their lives as they moved back and forth in the trenches and saps, quite apart from taking part in assaults and bayonet charges. When Jean-Baptiste Robert (1887-1916) was promised the *Croix de Guerre* in 1915, he told the colonel that he was a White Father. "Ah good, that does not surprise me", was the reply. "There is no need to say more".[81]

The French system of military honours was older and more developed than those of Belgium or Britain. It was certainly more profuse. The most common form of recognition was to be mentioned in dispatches (*citations*). This could happen at virtually any level in the military structure, the higher the level, the more signal the honour. With it went the right to wear a palm or star affixed to a medal ribbon: a bronze palm for mention in an army dispatch, a silver gilt star for an army corps dispatch, a silver star for a divisional dispatch and a bronze star for a brigade or regimental dispatch. The Golden Book of the Society reckoned that there were one hundred and fifty such mentions. Several people, such as Charles Umbricht (1873-1912*), Charles Joyeux and Ernest Clément (1877-1953) received more than one. Umbricht, in fact, received no fewer than ten, and Joyeux five. The mention recorded a particular act of bravery and assessed its contribution to the military operations in progress. Similar citations accompanied the award of most decorations. The Golden Book reckoned that there were ninety-nine of these.

Joseph Loiseau (1881-1918), "Brother Pierre", was mentioned for holding a conquered enemy trench; Eugène Burdet (1876-1969) was cited for managing to save explosives after being half buried in a munitions explosion in Alsace.[82] One of the most fulsome mentions was that of Jules Pagés (1887-1984), serving with the 4th Zouaves at Verdun in 1917, and already quoted in Chapter Two.[83]

The *Croix de Guerre* ("War Cross"), a large Maltese Cross in bronze with a crossed swords design, was created in 1915 to reward feats of bravery by individuals or groups. The highest French military medal, it could be conferred on any member of the armed forces, on French citizens and even foreigners, who had been mentioned in army dispatches. Martin Jaureguy (1886-1965) received his at Verdun in 1915, for bravery on the Plateau de Vauclerc and there were similar awards to White Fathers on virtually every war front.[84]   The Golden Book lists eighty-four awards of the *Croix de Guerre*.[85]

The Legion of Honour was created by Napoleon Bonaparte, then First Consul, in 1802 as a general military and civil order of merit. There are five classes: grand cross (limited to eighty members), grand officer (two hundred members), commander (one thousand), officer (four thousand) and *chevalier* or "knight" (unlimited). When it was awarded for extraordinary military bravery, it automatically carried with it the award of the *Croix de Guerre*. The Golden Book lists eight awards of the Legion of Honour.[86] Charles Umbricht was eventually admitted as Commander of the Legion. Marie François Clément (1887-1941) of the 9th Zouaves became *chevalier* for evacuating wounded comrades under machine-gun fire and then taking part in a bayonet charge, in the course of which he was himself severely wounded. Céléstin Paulhe received the cross of a *chevalier*, together with the *Croix de Guerre* and palm for having raised the morale of his soldiers, in spite of being wounded himself.[87] Nicholas Van der Vliet (1876-1966), although he was Dutch and a civilian, was made *chevalier* of the Legion in 1921, for having preserved the Basilica of St. Anne's Jerusalem (it was French property) during the war.[88]

There were other French decorations. Sixteen Missionaries of Africa received the Military Medal, eight of them posthumously.[89] Eight received the Medal of Honour for Epidemics, one of them for treating Serbian soldiers suffering from cholera and typhus. One also received the Medal "*Reconnaissance Française*".[90] The Golden Book estimates that there were fourteen foreign and "diverse" decorations.[91] Although White Fathers serving in the Belgian and British armies were not so generously rewarded as those in the French Army, several received Belgian military decorations and one received the Order of Leopold.[92] Achille Joseph de Paepe (1890-1941*), a Belgian stretcher-bearer, received the Belgian Croix de Guerre in 1919 for showing bravery under bombardment in the previous year. He refused to leave his post, being subsequently buried by a shell and severely wounded.[93] Lucien Avignon (1890-1957) was decorated by the King of Serbia.[94] Another student received the Cross of St. Stanislas Third Class from the Czar if Russia in 1916.[95]

Laurent Denis (1880-1936) a Frenchman, Oscar Julien (1886-1961, later Bishop) Canadian and Albert Scholte (1875-1952) "Brother Sébastien", a Dutchman, were mentioned in British dispatches for their contribution to the East African campaign. Seven other missionaries of the Nyasa Vicariate (Malawi), along with two MSOLA (White Sisters), also received the bronze oak leaf clasp that accompanied this honour. Joseph Fillion (1881-1930) another Canadian, was awarded the Order of the British Empire in King George V's 1919 Birthday Honours, for his work as a military chaplain in the same campaign.[96] The Most Excellent Order of the British Empire was instituted by George V towards the end of the war in 1917 to reward both civilian and military wartime service. However, in 1918 a separate military division of the order was created. There were five classes: Grand Cross, Knight and Dame Commander, Commander, Officer and Member. Fillion was made Officer of the Order.

More important than the citations and decorations was the personal letter of thanks sent to Bishop Mathurin Guillemé (1859-1942), a fervent anglophile, by

Brigadier General G.M.P. Hawthorne on January 23rd 1919 in recognition of the White Fathers' services to the British forces in Central Africa, as transport officers and chaplains. "I can declare in all sincerity", wrote the General, "that nobody among our troops gained the respect and esteem of their comrades so much as the members of these missions."[97] For good measure, Guillemé was also decorated by the British. Two years later, at a public ceremony in Algiers, the French Naval Minister praised the Missionaries of Africa for their role in the war. *Union Sacrée* and *Entente Cordiale* were by now visible realities.[98]

The Role of Binson Priory

For the Missionaries of Africa in the First World War Binson Priory played an important, and ultimately a "sacrificial", role. There had been an ancient chapel on the site since the sixth century and this had been rebuilt by Miles de Châtillon, the father of Pope Urban II two centuries later. In 1885 the Archbishop of Rheims, in whose diocese it lay, restored the chapel and built a large "priory" on to it to house a religious community. In 1895 the White Fathers became tenants of the priory which was opened as a seminary of philosophy and theology.

Binson Priory was situated near the River Marne, north east of Paris. In 1914 it was an imposing collection of buildings, with cloisters and a fine Romanesque chapel. The latter boasted a high church tower and steeple. At the back was a spacious courtyard and park. There was also a home farm to supply the material needs of the seminary. François Heulin (1880-1961) became rector in 1908 and stayed throughout the war. In 1914, he remained with a handful of students, but these had all dispersed by the beginning of September.[99] Standing in the path of the German army as it thrust towards Paris, Binson Priory became engulfed in the first battle of the Marne and Heulin feared it would be shelled. This did not happen just yet.

As the gunfire drew nearer in the first week of September 1914, the community huddled in the cellar.[100] One night they heard footsteps in the corridors above, but dared not investigate. Next morning they found a detachment of German soldiers in the courtyard who rapidly searched the house and climbed the tower, while the Sisters made coffee for them.[101] Soon afterwards, their commandant arrived, a polite captain in his fifties who came from Osnabruck. He allowed the White Fathers to stay, and even to celebrate Mass in the neighbouring parishes. In the chapel a congregation of soldiers from Westphalia and Poland assisted at Sunday Mass. The only sour note was struck when the Captain was upset at being given the "unlucky" Room No.13. The Germans boasted that the war would be over in a month, while all around the battle continued to rage. By September 9th there were already signs that the Germans were preparing to retreat. "Our army is carrying out a change of front", announced the Captain. By September 10th all the German soldiers, including twenty wounded, had departed in the direction of Rheims, leaving the Priory intact. Shortly after this, a small group of French cavalry appeared, to be followed by a succession of detachments and ambulances, while gunfire continued in the distance. The German advance had been halted.

In October 1914 the Priory was requisitioned as a military isolation hospital for typhoid and paratyphoid patients. Forty-five of these arrived in early November, to be followed by more and more convoys of sick, wounded and dying. Wooden huts were put up in the courtyard to take the overflow, and five nuns came to join the hospital staff. By the end of January sixteen patients were already dead.

Throughout 1915 and 1916 this state of affairs continued. Meanwhile Binson Priory took on a distinctive role with regard to its alumni and other White Father students serving on the Western Front. Heulin had been able to retain the use of a dozen or so rooms for the community, and throughout 1916 and 1917 the Priory was host to a succession of soldier confreres who came to spend their leave there, to rest or to make a retreat. The nostalgia of its former students for the "paradise" of Binson, its "charm and solitude" was boundless.[102] In this way, Binson became the centre of a network of communication and contact among young White Father conscripts. In 1916 Heulin decided to launch a newsletter which he called *Echos Binsonnais*. Written by hand, it was reproduced by jellygraph, an old device for copying, that used a plate of jelly. This continued to appear until 1919.[103] *Echos Binsonnais* became henceforth a reliable source of news about the movements and fortunes of confreres in the war.

Heulin was on excellent terms with the Cardinal Archbishop of Rheims, Louis-Henri-Joseph Luçon (1842-1930). In 1916 Luçon visited Binson for a Confirmation and took the opportunity of giving a conference to soldier priests gathered there.[104] The archdiocese of Rheims had been much battered by the war and its magnificent cathedral, the ancient coronation church of the French monarchy, had been extensively damaged by fire and bombardment. The Carmelites of Rheims, who had been holding the church's most precious reliquaries, were forced to move to Dijon and the Cardinal deposited these treasures with the White Fathers at Binson.[105] They included the relics of Saint Remy (Remigius), Apostle of the Franks, which were kept "incognito" on the top of the sacristy cupboard and an entire altar-shrine containing the body of Saint Celestina or Céline, martyred at Metz in A.D.300.

Meanwhile, the hospital continued to function at Binson, receiving eighty-seven gassed reservists in 1916.[106] In January 1917, a big shake-up took place and the Priory became a Red Cross field hospital with thirty-eight nurses, the majority of them English and Scottish, looking after a hundred and twenty patients. The whole place was renovated, garages were built and the Bishop's Room was turned into a state of the art operating theatre. By the end of the year the number of patients had risen to three hundred. Many died and Heulin officiated at their burials.[107]

On May 28th 1918 the German offensive got under way that led to the second battle of the Marne and the evacuation of Binson began. Some valuable objects were hidden. Others – including the reliquiaries and metalwork of the chapel - were rescued blindly in the dark, loaded on to a baggage cart and taken to a safe house at Romilly. Five vehicles took the farm animals. Heulin moved into a farm twenty miles to the south, and made a few more trips back to Binson, to rescue furniture, for which Cardinal Luçon lent a lorry. The French colonel in charge helped to rescue the vessels, vestments, books and personal belongings of the missionaries. The beds and library were left to the medical service and the soldiers were invited to take all the food that was left. By June 12th, with the advancing Germans three miles away, the medical personnel and the Missionaries of Africa had gone.

By this time, the bombardment had begun in earnest and shells were raining down on Binson and its surroundings. Already, the chapel roof and some walls had been shattered. Soon after this, a German battery in the park did further damage and the Priory fell into enemy hands. Towards the end of July, the counter offensive began and Binson Priory became the target of the French artillery. The damaged building was now totally destroyed and its ruins "liberated" by the French who re-crossed the Marne on July 27th. The White Fathers crept back to view the wreckage. Abel Couturier (1858-1931) accompanied Heulin back to Binson on August 5th to see what was left of the buildings.[108] As extant photographs reveal, there were nothing but ruins. The spire and bell tower had fallen, the vaults, roof and organ had gone and the upper floors had collapsed on to each other. The courtyard was a mass of debris. Saddest of all were the corpses of the wounded - both German and French -, crushed in their beds and enveloped by the fallen upper floors. Couturier did not have the courage to go down into the cellars to see if there were more bodies. The farm had been completely devastated. Three quarters of all the trees in the park had been burnt or cut down and every single station of the Cross had been damaged. All that was intact was the kitchen and the big granite statue of Pope Urban II on the hill behind the Priory. Heulin went in person to report on the disaster to Cardinal Luçon.

The Missionaries of Africa re-opened their philosophy seminary in 1919 at Le Colombier (Maine and Loire) and then moved into the *château* of Kerlois in Brittany, a former novitiate of the Eudists. François Heulin went on to spend forty years as a missionary in Zambia. Cardinal Luçon died in 1930, but he had obtained war damages and lived long enough to see the rebuilding of his cathedral as well as Binson Priory. In the year of his death the Salesians of Don Bosco opened a college in the restored buildings.

Victims of the Torpedo

In the First World War the submarine offered Germany the only real chance of challenging the naval strength of Britain. It did this not only by attacking warships and troopships, but also by threatening supply lines and targeting merchantmen. Although technology improved, the early U-Boats did not have the range or capacity of their Second World War successors. They therefore chiefly patrolled European waters, the North Sea, the Channel and the Mediterranean. Unrestricted U-Boat warfare came near to defeating Britain, but it helped bring the United States into the war after the controversial sinking of the giant Cunard Liner, the *Lusitania* in 1915. The submarine war became particularly deadly in the Mediterranean, and by the time of the Armistice in

1918, the Germans had sunk some five thousand Allied ships for the loss of only a hundred and seventy-eight U-Boats.

A missionary society that needed to move its members and students from one place to another by sea was especially vulnerable to submarines. In 1916, for example, French parents were unwilling to send their sons across the channel to study at Bishop's Waltham for fear of torpedoes.[109] And in the last stages of the war the British Colonial Secretary refused to sanction the journey of two White Fathers to Equatorial Africa, because of the torpedoing of a steamer to Cape Town, the *Galway Castle*.[110] Given their vulnerability, it is therefore surprising that only four Missionaries of Africa were aboard a ship that was torpedoed and all four survived. Although they were not considered worthy of the Society's official Golden Book, their stories are sufficiently dramatic to be recorded at the end of this chapter.

Remi Coutu (1887-1919) was returning to Canada on the liner *Hesperian* when it was torpedoed on the 4th September 1915. The ship, which was on its way from Liverpool to Montreal, was off the Irish coast when it was hit, as the *Lusitania* had been four months earlier. Coutu's life was saved but his luggage went down with the ship.[111]   More dramatic was the experience of Louis Fontugue (1892-1978) returning to Salonika from home leave on December 16th of the same year.[112] This scholastic had embarked three days earlier at the Italian port of Taranto, on the cruiser *Châteaurenaud*, which was escorted by two torpedo boats. The warship was a large one, being over four hundred feet in length, with four funnels. It was carrying nine hundred and fifty passengers and a crew of four hundred.

Approaching the Gulf of Patros, in Greece, scene of the historic naval battle of Lepanto, it was struck by a torpedo, which penetrated the hold. This was full of charcoal and the explosion was muted, but thick black smoke emerged from three of the funnels. In the general panic Fontugue failed to find room in a lifeboat, but slid down a rope to the water and was taken on board one of the torpedo boats. No sooner had he reached safety than a second torpedo struck the abandoned ship and blew up the ammunition store. The explosion was enormous. The ship began to list, the stern up-ended and the huge vessel began to sink. It disappeared in less than two minutes. Meanwhile the torpedo boats gave chase to the submarine. Depth charges were directed at it and the enemy vessel soon surfaced, up-ended and sank. The twenty man crew were rescued along with their German commander who claimed that everyone on board the cruiser would have died if he had managed to fire his second torpedo sooner. Those in the lifeboats were also taken on board by the torpedo boats and soon everyone arrived safely at the Greek port of Itea seven or eight miles away.[113]

René Burtin (1875-1951) was also shipwrecked in the Mediterranean.[114] He was on his way from Marseilles to Salonika when his troopship, the *Caledonian*, was struck by a torpedo (or possibly a mine) near Port Said. The ship had tacked in many directions during the nineteen day voyage in order to avoid U-Boats, but in the end it was unlucky. Burtin was celebrating Mass in the saloon and had just reached the Communion antiphon when there was a terrific explosion amidships. He rushed to his cabin to get his life-belt and pith helmet and, passing the saloon on his return, he grabbed the chalice and put it in his pocket. Hot steam was issuing from the engine-room and prevented him getting to his designated lifeboat. He jumped over the side and swam towards some floating wreckage. The ship had been blown in two and the bow section sank first. The stern section remained afloat for twenty minutes which allowed for the rescue of those still on board, but there were only fifty-one survivors. Eventually, the stern up-ended with screws and rudder in the air and disappeared.

Burtin remained in the water for twenty minutes, still in his Mass vestments, and was picked up by a torpedo boat. He disembarked at Port Said still in the same garb and several religious communities offered to make good the clothes he had lost on the ship. A fellow survivor was Captain Rosario Pisani, the French explosives expert, who was on his way to join T.E. Lawrence and the forces of the Arab Revolt.[115] The first Turkish train that he blew up on the Hejaz Railway was, he said, in revenge for the Caledonian.[116]

Yet another Missionary of Africa to be torpedoed in the Mediterranean was Jean-Baptiste Blin (1887-1977).[117] He was travelling from Bizerta to Salonika and had embarked on the Sant' Anna on May 10th 1918. On May 11th the ship was torpedoed near the small, rocky island of Pantellaria, in the channel between Tunisia and Sicily. In the darkness there was total confusion. Some people jumped into the water and many of the lifeboats and rafts sank because of the haste and disorder. Blin remained on the sinking ship with several others, trying to get a raft ready, and giving general absolution to those struggling in the water. However, an overloaded lifeboat crashed down from the boat-deck into the water drowning everyone in it. Blin and his companions got into the now tragically emptied boat, and took command when an officer panicked. They rowed to a gunboat a few hundred yards away and were taken on board. In the meantime, the waves swept over the Sant' Anna's bows and the ship's propellers appeared above water at the stern. Many still on board jumped into the sea, but there were still a hundred Arabs, clinging to the ship in fear of the water. The vessel rose vertically and took them to the bottom. It was a frightful spectacle and the cries of the victims were heart-rending. Estimates of the number drowned varied between seven hundred and a thousand. After this tragedy the only other torpedo incident that affected the Missionaries of Africa was the loss of a hundred and fifty-five packages destined for the African missions on another ship torpedoed in the Mediterranean in August 1918. Luckily, the packages were insured.[118]

Before dealing with Africa's contribution to the war in Europe and the Near East, and with the war in Africa itself, the next chapter examines the spiritual integration of the White Fathers' war experiences and the way they made sense of them in terms of their African missionary vocation. It tries also to assess the leadership role of Léon Livinhac, their Superior General, during the war.

CHAPTER FOUR

A WAR OF THE HUMBLE

Spiritual Life on the Front

"Modern warfare is no brave show (*panache*). It is a war of the humble who hold fast in spite of the privations, fatigue and moral depression that result from seemingly endless painful conditions."[1] Martin Jaureguy (1886-1965) made this observation in 1916 from the trenches at Verdun. There were seldom any dashing feats of gallantry in this war. There were few if any romantic cavalry charges or spectacular sieges, let alone colourful squares drawn up on the open plain. Trench warfare was a drab affair. Soldiers were virtual "cave men" clinging to their semi-subterranean defences and earthworks under almost constant bombardment. "Far from civilization", wrote another Missionary of Africa, "I am a bit of a savage".[2] Humility and tenacity were the order of the day.

A fair idea of the spiritual life of missionary conscripts can be gained from the letters they wrote from the frontline. The Directory of the Constitutions laid down that each missionary was to engage in regular correspondence with the major superiors.[3] This "correspondence required by the rule", as it was called, was to be characterized by great simplicity and openness. It was not to be a vehicle of antipathy, discontent or resentment. Moreover, it was expected to deal with mainly spiritual matters. Given this stipulation, one might expect such letters to be fairly one-sided, perhaps even somewhat sanguine – not perhaps a witness to the real feelings and fears of young men caught up in a war situation. In peacetime, the writers might have been tempted to paint too rosy a picture of their spiritual state and to present themselves to the superiors in the best possible light. This was not the case with the priests and seminarians conscripted in the First World War. The conditions of trench warfare and the imminent possibility of violent death or serious wounding give these letters an unmistakable ring of truth and sincerity.

When war broke out in August 1914 it was feared that regular communication between the houses of the Society would be interrupted. For this reason publication of the *Petit Echo,* the Society's main internal bulletin, was suspended until further notice. By June 1915, it was recognized that communication with most houses was fairly regular and publication of the bulletin was resumed.[4] It was then decided to publish in every issue extracts from the correspondence of the missionary soldiers. These give an authentic picture of the conditions they were experiencing and of their state of mind.[5]

Léon Livinhac, the Superior General, confessed that he was consoled and edified by the letters from the front.[6] However, by 1916 he was in his seventieth year and had only six more years to live. In Holy Week that year, he suddenly became very tired and was understandably unable to carry the principal burden of this correspondence. Thereafter, he shared the task of answering the letters with Paul Voillard (1860-1946), his eventual successor, and Joseph Malet (1872-1950), to both of whom the letters were increasingly addressed.[7]

Conformity to the rule, strict adherence to the prescribed spiritual exercises and scrupulous fidelity to one's duties of state were always emphasized by Livinhac as the infallible path to sanctity and perfection. It was inevitable that the missionaries at the front should examine their consciences with regard to these matters. It was also inevitable that they would lament the impossibility of such fidelity in the circumstances of war. Organizing the spiritual exercises was difficult, if not impossible, especially without the support provided by community life. This particular "exile" was the worst suffering.[8] One confrere wrote that he made his meditation before his comrades woke up. The rest of his spiritual exercises were done in the evening, if he could get hold of a candle.[9] Another confessed that it was very difficult to find a moment for prayer. "Every now and then I do a little reading. I manage the spiritual exercises by rising early. If only there was a church nearby!"[10] "On guard duty I make my meditation and say my rosary", wrote a missionary from Serbia in 1915. For spiritual reading, he had the *New Testament*, the *Imitation of Christ* and the *Letters of St. Francis of Sales.*[11]

Pierre Lhomme, who was to be killed the following year, wrote in 1916: "I have passed several Sundays and many weekdays without celebrating or hearing Mass. When I can, I do. Mass is one of the great consolations of the priest-soldier, the only time when we feel once more that we are priests. For twenty-two months I have not recited the office. (But) I subscribe to the breviary of *The Priest in the Army*. With courage and goodwill one can recite it often."[12] Adrien Sylvestre, destined to die in 1918, also wrote that he tried to keep the timetable he followed at St. Anne's Jerusalem with regard to work, vigils and meditation, but the big void in his life was caused by the absence of Mass.[13] For some, merely holding the rosary continually in their hand was a form of material prayer. "The language of a *poilu* (French soldier) is not picturesque in the mouth of an ecclesiastic", wrote another conscript. "Prayer is difficult after such conversations.[14]

Before long, the White Father soldiers came to accept that this state of affairs was God's will and that if he deprived them of the spiritual exercises and sacraments, God would help them in others ways.[15] They went even further than this, in recognizing that such privations had positive consequences. Although there would be many departures from the Society in the aftermath of the war, at the height of the conflict itself missionaries often felt that their vocation was strengthened. "This long war, with its horrors and bad examples", wrote a novice cleric, "has never once given me the idea of abandoning my vocation".[16] "I never stop thinking of the Society, its major superiors, members and works", wrote Pierre Gallerand (1887-1976) from Nieuport in 1915. "I pray in long vigils at the parapet (of the trench) for God's blessing on the Society."[17] "One result among many others of this long war", wrote another Missionary of Africa, "is to draw more tightly the bonds that bind us to our dear Society".[18] "Let us hope", wrote Gaston Duiquet (1888-1930*), "that the war will strengthen the bonds of charity between members of our society."[19] And Joseph Bouniol (1884-1950) from his Westphalian prison assured Livinhac, "I never cease to think of the Society".[20]

Livinhac had written that he did not fear a decrease in the supernatural outlook of those on active service. "You were right", replied a White Father conscript in 1915. "I am spending the sweetest moments of my life."[21] "My spiritual life is strengthened" was another comment.[22] A year before his death, Joseph Loiseau was told by his colonel, "You know where to draw strength from".[23] The source of his spiritual strength and that of his White Father companions was faith in God's providence and complete trust in his will. "Your children do their duty, that is to say, the will of God", wrote a Missionary of Africa to Livinhac in 1915.[24] "God's will be done and may Mary help us to fulfil it with holiness up to the last moment." "Why do I survive?" asked another, "Because God wants it". "I commend my whole being into the hands of God. If he wants my life, it will be my happiness to give it for the Church, for our dear Society and for France."[25] "I am entirely submitted to (God's) holy will", wrote Ernest Delarse three weeks before he died at Verdun.[26] To be "a good soldier of Christ" was the missionary conscript's duty of state.

Submission to God's will and trust in his providence was the logical attitude in a situation of great danger. It was this danger that enhanced the spiritual life. The gun was "the most eloquent preacher", and its harsh lessons changed people's attitudes to religion. The constant threat of death could produce great religious fervour. One White Father went so far as to place "German machine guns" on a par with the sacraments as a cause of supernatural growth.[27] The painful conditions of trench warfare were relatively easy to sanctify and ardent acts of love and contrition arose spontaneously in moments of danger. "Pray for me, dear Monsignor", wrote Loiseau to Livinhac in 1916, "that I may never cease to sanctify myself through contact with death and with the God who preserves my life and health, so that I can return to my dear Uganda…I like to think that my army service will benefit souls and give glory to God."[28]

The presence of African soldiers on the Western Front was a reminder of the missionary ideal and another help for the spiritual life. Again and again White Father conscripts made an explicit offering of their sufferings and even of their lives for the missions, for the non-Christians of Africa and for the Society. "The blood of those who have given their lives is not lost for Africa", wrote Arsène Sabau (1887-1974) to Livinhac in 1917. "The salvation of the (Africans) is the goal of our daily sufferings."[29] One missionary identified himself with the so-called "uncivilized world" of Africa which he contrasted with the "civilization" that had unleashed this terrible war. "Our Society", he concluded, "has chosen the better part".[30]

Notre Dame du Retour

"O Mary, formidable as an army in battle array, help us!" Ernest Potier made this prayer at Verdun in 1917, quoting the military metaphor with which the lover addresses his beloved in the Song of Songs.[31] Potier was killed on the Champagne front the following year, but on that afternoon at Verdun he felt the powerful presence of Our Lady at his side, as he carried a wounded soldier under fire. Although he received wounds in the shoulder and feet, an "invisible hand" deflected the bullets from his head and that of his wounded companion. It was "an unforgettable pilgrimage" across the battlefields of past days. Devotion to the Mother of God was a characteristic of the Society of Missionaries of Africa and conscripts on active service felt her miraculous protection. It was Mary who brought rescuers to the trench of a wounded confrere, Mary who saved a limb from being amputated, Mary who prevented a nearby shell from exploding. It was even Mary who caused the Germans to retreat, and who protected soldiers from "friendly fire". "I am firmly convinced", wrote a White Father from the Western Front in 1915, "that the Blessed Virgin Mary in person reduced these lumps of steel to dust as if by magic", and Joseph Delmer (1891-1969) in Serbia exclaimed: "We have blue steel helmets, but our real helmet of salvation is the Blessed Virgin".[32]

It was a simple faith that placed Mary firmly in the sphere of divine Providence. Although missionaries felt that she gave them tangible protection from danger in the present, she was also the one who prayed for them "in the hour of our death". Her presence was a comfort when they were wounded and she presided at the supreme sacrifice of those who gave their lives. Celestin Paulhe (188-1919*) was severely wounded in the jaw and in the eye cavity. "At the moment of being hit," he wrote afterwards, "I felt I was in the presence of the special and efficacious protection of the heavenly Mother. This thought helped me bear my misfortune with true apostolic patience."[33] And Joseph Delmer described the death of Régis Delabre on the Serbian front in May 1916, as the Blessed Virgin completing the month dedicated to her by taking to herself one of Livinhac's children.[34]

Mary was very often invoked by White Fathers, as by other soldiers, under the title of Notre Dame du Retour ("Our Lady of the Return"). This devotion which was popular in both world wars had a curious origin. A statue of Our Lady occupied a prominent position on the roof of Clermont Cathedral near a bell tower from which the canons were called to return to choir. This statue was known as Notre Dame du Retour. It became a symbol of the soldiers' desire for a safe return from the dangers of the front, as well as from imprisonment or internment. White Fathers had pictures of the statue and invoked Mary under this title on every occasion. One vowed to give his medal of honour as an ex voto to her and another who escaped serious injury to his spinal column promised her a "fine candle". In Uganda, a mission church was even dedicated to Notre Dame du Retour. Kitabi mission had been finished in 1914 and its opening delayed until the "return" of the missionary soldiers. In expectation of their demobilization the church acquired its dedication.[35]

Another name that was frequently on the lips of Missionaries of Africa in battle was that of the Carmelite, Thérèse of Lisieux. Thérèse died in 1897 and although she was not canonized until 1925, she was regularly invoked as a saint by White Fathers and even given the title of "saint" by them. However, she was more frequently and more correctly called "Sister Thérèse" or even "the venerable little Sister Thérèse of the Child Jesus". Her patronage of the missions was known to the Missionaries of Africa, as was her friendship with their late confrere, Maurice Bellière (1874-1907). In fact, her doctrine of God's merciful love was widespread by this time and helped to counteract the pessimistic theology of salvation that often prevailed among missionaries. In their prayer for deliverance and in their acts of thanksgiving the name of Thérèse was joined to that of Mary.

The Leadership Role of Léon Livinhac

In 1914 Léon Livinhac, at sixty-eight, had another eight years of life, continuing as Superior General of the Missionaries of Africa until his death in November 1922. Charles Lavigerie, the Cardinal Archbishop of Algiers who founded the Society, had been dead for more than twenty years, and although Livinhac lived very much in the founder's shadow, his own prestige in Africa and in the Society was enormous. He was already older than Lavigerie had been when he died. In a Society of some eight hundred members there were only three older than himself, but he was the patriarch.[36] As the first Catholic Bishop of Equatorial Africa and a hero of the first missionary penetration of the African interior, he had an intimate understanding of the conditions under which his missionaries laboured, a fact of great practical significance for his governance of the Society.[37] He was a deeply spiritual man – many would say a saint – who had the spiritual welfare of his missionaries passionately at heart. His realistic experience of the hardships of missionary life, his asceticism and humility brought into relief his natural tendency towards pessimism. True to form, he gave vent to the direst apprehensions when the First World War broke out. Prophetically, he foresaw a "terrible trial" for the European nations and predicted disastrous consequences for the Missionaries of Africa, their missions and resources.[38] As he reported in a circular letter of February 1915, his fears had been largely borne out in the first six months of war. He concluded: "Pray above all for the poor old man who writes to you".[39]

Old and fearful he may have been, but the war was to be his "finest hour". Livinhac rose to the occasion, guiding his missionaries through the ordeal and holding the Society together. The First World War provided him with the opportunity to demonstrate remarkable powers of leadership, the consequences of which were entirely positive. During his superiorate Livinhac wrote one hundred and thirty-four circular letters to the whole Society, twenty-six of them in these eight final years of his life, the last one being sent out some six months before he died. His thirteen war circulars were among the most poignant that he wrote. Three of them were lengthy newsletters, describing what was happening on the various war fronts and in the mission territories. Their value consisted in giving his readers a global picture of the Society at particular moments in the war. Two were written in 1915 and one at the beginning of 1918.[40]   They showed to what extent the Missionaries of Africa formed a united family and in them he begged for prayers on behalf of those on the battlefields and in the hospitals. They also testify to his compassion and to his longing for an end to the carnage and suffering.

"The letters from the front", he wrote in 1915, "excite in us lively feelings of compassion for their sufferings, admiration for their courage and spirit of faith...We have, therefore, at this moment a greater number of our (confreres) exposed to all the engines of destruction invented by...modern science, and it is a duty for those of us who enjoy calm and security in our communities to pray with greater fervour than ever for them...Nothing can happen without God's permission. We abandon ourselves body and soul to God's will, and have confidence in Mary to whom our Society is consecrated."[41]

Four other war circulars, written in 1916 and 1917, dealt with spiritual topics: providence, patience, consecration to the Sacred Heart and chastity. "War has tightened the links that bind our society together", he wrote in the first of these. "Never have you so loved the Society or felt happier to be members. This is a great consolation for me."[42]   He then went on to develop the theme of providence and to demonstrate that evil as well as good helps to realize God's plan. He exhorted White Fathers not to criticize providence, but to love it and be grateful to it.

The letter on patience was prompted by those who complained that the war was taking too long. God is the model of patience and Missionaries of Africa must develop the qualities of a patience that is supernatural, universal and continual. Practising patience was an important means of sanctification.[43]   The letter on consecration to the Sacred Heart mentioned the courage of the missionary soldiers who were living their vocation in a special way, and who were in need of grace to realize their missionary ideal in such circumstances.[44] The circular on chastity began by asking God to watch over "those whom duty exposes night and day to murderous engines that cover with blood and ruins the most immense battlefield that the world has ever seen."[45] Nevertheless, Livinhac felt that White Fathers in physical danger at the front and the overworked missionaries they had left behind in Africa could always be exposed to dangers of another kind. Hence an essay in practical spirituality.

In his final news circular, Livinhac dwelt on events in the East African campaign.[46] He bore in mind the African Christians who had been forced to become soldiers or carriers and who had been deprived of religious instruction and the sacraments. He also lamented the sudden death of Bishop Adolphe Lechaptois (1852-1917) his former co-novice of 1873.[47] But he exulted in the ordination of ten African priests in three of the White Father vicariates.

Besides the general circulars addressed to the whole Society, Livinhac also composed special circulars for the soldier missionaries at the front, the *Petit Communiqué*. These spoke of the war in Africa and listed the names of those killed or missing in Europe and the Near East. They contained expressions of affection and compassion for the soldiers and a very real appreciation of the affectionate letters that he received from them.[48] Livinhac also made a practice of adding messages in his own handwriting to the printed circulars sent to the front. This delicate attention was especially prized by confreres in the trenches. It demonstrated both Livinhac's thoughtfulness and kindness as well as the informality of his relationship with the younger members of the Society.

Few of these personal messages survive. However, there are three in the Society's archives. They are in his own handwriting and are worth quoting at length.[49] François Viel, Brother Camille (1884-1955) received the following after he was wounded at Verdun in 1917: "My Dear Brother Camille, I was very sorry to hear that you have been wounded in both legs and that you are suffering a great deal. Father (Pierre) Viel who gave us the news does not know if your wounds are serious or not and you can imagine my anxiety.[50] I beg the divine Master to relieve your sufferings and to guide the surgeons' hands in getting your limbs back in good order. I pray that he will give you the patience that will turn your pain into a source of merit. You have been wounded in carrying out your duty at the risk of your life. God knows this and will reward you one day. I don't have to tell you that we are praying for you. I bless you with all my heart, my dear child and sign myself, affectionately and wholly devoted in Our Lord, +Léon."

To another missionary (possibly Charles Joyeux 1886-1965), who had been wounded and decorated, he wrote in November 1915: "You have been told of my joy when I heard that your bravery had been recognized and rewarded, but I wanted myself to send you my most sincere congratulations. We missionaries await an eternal glory and do not set much store by the glory we achieve in this world. Nevertheless, whatever redounds to the honour of our holy religion and of our dear Society makes us happy, and that is the case with the distinction you have been given. It is with my whole heart, therefore, that I congratulate you. May Our Lord soon heal your glorious wounds and, in the meantime, give you the patience that will make your sufferings meritorious."

To Father Gabriel Binel (1879-1942), a missionary from Uganda, detained at Bizerta, he wrote on October 14th 1918: "Offer to Our good Saviour, through the hands of Mary, our good Mother, all your work and all your troubles. They will then be very meritorious and will confer on you and your friends the grace of conversion and sanctification. It is a pity that you lack a place in which to make your spiritual exercises in common with the other confreres now at Bizerta. Try to do your best on your own, and if there is no time make up for them by being united with Our Lord in the depths of your heart, and by making frequent ejaculatory prayers. It seems that this terrible war which has torn you from your mission cannot last much longer and will finish by defeating our enemies and allowing the return of some of our conscripts before very long. The certainty of a brilliant victory and the thought of your approaching return to your dear Buganda must make up for your present upsets…Carry out to the best of your ability the duties imposed on you and if, in spite of all your care, you are unable to escape reproaches and punishments, accept them with a spirit of faith and offer them for the conversion of sinners."

Another vehicle for Livinhac's thinking and teaching about the war was provided by his speeches of thanks for the good wishes presented to him at the New Year and on his patronal feast day. He spoke repeatedly on these occasions about both the consolation and the anguish he felt, and he invariably gave the soldier confreres his special blessing.[51] At the New Year of 1917 he said: "The conscripted are true missionaries accomplishing their priestly and patriotic duties. They show everyone how we love one another in the Society".[52]

Livinhac's communications evoked an enthusiastic response from those at the front. In 1915 Louis Glass (1886-1919*) and Léon Darot (1890-1958) in Gallipoli told him how much his circular to the soldier confreres and aspirants was appreciated.[53] Eloi Falguières (1887-1924) read and re-read the circular on patience. "Thank you", he wrote, "for the resignation you give us and thank you for your prayers."[54]   One soldier correspondent thanked Livinhac for the personal message added to the circular which was so appropriate to his present situation. "I hear the sound of your voice and see your gestures, and I imagine myself still at your feet with all the confreres of my class, those on mission, those at war and the one already in heaven. Since I started keeping (the circulars) they form a book, which I could wish was a bit smaller (to carry), but to which I am much attached."[55]

Frans Van Volsem (1893-1967) wrote in 1916: "Before leaving (for active service), dear Father, I must thank you for all you have done for me during the sweet years of the scholasticate and all during the past nine months of my mobilization. You cannot imagine the good you do for your children through the *Petit Communiqué* and the little word that you add to it."[56] "Your last letter, Monsignor", wrote another soldier in 1917 "caused me the greatest joy" and Camille de Chatouville (1871-1927) wrote after the war from Kigonsera, East Africa, about his happiness in receiving Livinhac's circular on chastity.[57]

The soldier missionaries wrote frequently asking Livinhac's blessing or calling down blessings on him in their turn. The novice cleric Adrien Guillou, soon to give his life, asked his blessing in 1916 before departing for the front and Céléstin Paulhe (1888-1919*) wrote in 1916: "I will never forget, Monsignor and Venerable Father, the sentiments of tender solicitude that you have graciously shown me on the occasion of my being wounded."[58] "May the good Mother of heaven", wrote Arsène Sabau (1887-1974), "keep you still a long time in our affection. May she obtain for you from her divine Son the numerous graces you need to guide our dear Society with wisdom and firmness in these troubled times."[59]   It was a deeply felt wish and one that was repeatedly expressed.

Nostalgia for Africa

The thought of Africa was never very far away from the minds of the missionaries at the war fronts of Europe and the Near East. They offered Mass, when this was possible, for the missions and accepted their sufferings, as well as the prospect of death for the redemption of the Africans. "The mere thought of our missions", wrote Eloi Falguières in 1916, "puts sweetness into the bitterness", and Adrien Guillou added that he had no other ambition than to devote himself entirely to the African missions. He prepared for this by simply doing his duty as a soldier.[60] For a student to die during the war, without ever working directly for the evangelization of Africa, was something that did not bear thinking about, but there were those who made that sacrifice and said their *fiat*.[61]

As we shall see in the following chapter, there were occasions when White Father conscripts served with African troops on the European fronts or came into contact with them. This was a welcome reminder of a past or future posting in Africa. Some even managed to remain in contact with their former mission station. Postal links with Uganda remained intact throughout the war, and Joseph-Marie Verpoorter (1884-1972) received regular news from his mission of Gayaza. He longed to return to his dear catechumens and neophytes, and he had a copy of the grammar written by Henri Le Veux (1879-1965) with him in the trenches, reading some *Luganda* every day.[62] Another missionary from Uganda regretted that he did not have a book of *Luganda* hymns with him, so that he could make the people of Buganda known.[63]

The Uganda Martyrs' cause for beatification was being pursued during the war years, and Uganda missionaries at the front took the opportunity of preaching about them on numerous occasions. Marius Gremeret (1873-1959) gave an eloquent sermon about the martyrs at Limoges in March 1916. The homily made Louis Hamon (1880-1930) forget the snow and cold of France. [64] "I miss the warm sun of Uganda", he wrote, "and – let's face it – a strong African porter to carry my kit-bag and haversack!"

Henri Le Veux's *Luganda* grammar may have been studied by others in the trenches, but Le Veux himself was also present at the front. Called up in 1914 as a medical orderly and stretcher-bearer, he remained in the front-line throughout the war. Incredible as it may seem, he worked on his great *Luganda*-French Dictionary in the trenches, for most of the time under bombardment. His dictionary is regarded as irreplaceable for the study of *Luganda*.[65] The example of Le Veux epitomises the linguistic talents of the White Fathers.

Theology in the Trenches
We have already come across the Belgian "seminary-camp" of Auvours and the German "seminary-prison" of Münster, in which organized theological studies were pursued by mobilized seminarians. It seems, however, that scholastics whose studies had been interrupted by the war seized on every opportunity to continue their theological formation by themselves. In a period of boredom one missionary conscript reported that he re-read his scholastic manuals and Meschler's commentary on the Spiritual Exercises of St. Ignatius. He even managed to carry out all the exercises of a thirty day retreat in succession.[66] An aspirant in Salonika revised his philosophy, refreshing his memory about such things as "essence" and "existence", and another soldier tried somehow to "live the life of a scholastic" albeit in the trenches.[67] It was not easy. As Gaston Duiquet (1888-1930*) at Verdun remarked, "One thinks less of theology and syllogistic combat after guns and grenades."[68]

An aspirant "living in the woods and in the rain" found time to read an issue of *Études*, and another spent time teaching Latin under a hail of shells to "a young man of twenty-three to whom war has given a vocation".[69] As we have seen already, there was also language study. After *Luganda*, *Swahili* was the favoured subject. *Swahili* studies took place at Auvours, and Joseph Fillion (1881-1930), a missionary in Uganda, prepared for chaplaincy work in German East Africa by brushing up his English and beginning *Swahili*.[70]

For scholastics who were on the verge of completing their priestly studies when they were called up, the question of ordination was uppermost in their minds. As the time for ordinations at Carthage came round each year, they yearned all the more for priesthood. "In four days time", wrote a scholastic from the Serbian Front in 1916, "my confreres will be priests forever. I meditate on the dignity of the priest-hood…every day. My thoughts, prayers and sacrifices are for the future priests."[71] "When will I be ordained ?", asked Auguste Thézé (1890-1920*), the prisoner of war, "When Africa ? When the missions?"[72]

In March 1915, Gaston Duiquet heard that soldier deacons at the front were likely to be ordained. "Will I be one?" he asked. Then he received a joyful affirmative and hurriedly borrowed a theology book from another scholastic to make a last minute revision. The thought of his future ordination obliterated all fear of death.[73] In July of the same year Etienne Farrussenq (1889-1953) and Joseph Delmer (1891-1969) were also called to priest's orders. As priests, it was decided, they could do more for their fellow soldiers. They were to complete their studies after the war. A similar reason was given by the General Council for Auguste Thézé. As a priest, he could help his fellow prisoners of war. After consulting the seminary staff at Carthage, Joseph Malet (1872-1950) sent him the good news.[74] Emile Laroche (1890-1979), who had been invalided from the front because of his mutilation was among the five first priests to be ordained at Carthage when the war was over.[75]

It is now time to turn to Africa and to examine the involvement of its countries and their peoples in the First World War, as well as the White Fathers' ministry to African troops both in the African continent and in Europe. It must be said however that, quite apart from such direct contacts and involvements, it is not possible to separate the experience of the missionary conscripts in Europe and the Near East from the whole impact of the War on the African Church. The traumatic experience of the trenches affected their missionary outlook and commitment. In most cases it helped to deepen their spiritual life and this was reinforced by the spiritual exercises they made at Maison Carrée when the war was over. Moreover, the experience humbled them and made them less prone to temptations of chauvinism and colonial arrogance. In some cases, they were even disgusted by the so-called "civilization" that perpetrated so much suffering and destruction. Besides spiritual maturity, they evinced a greater respect for Africans, especially for the African soldiers who fought alongside them, and a greater fondness for the mission field from which the war had temporarily banished them. The mobilized of 1914 were markedly different from those who returned in 1918, and the Church which they came back to serve would also be different.

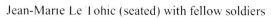

Jean-Marie Le Tohic (seated) with fellow soldiers

Deacon Joseph Grison

Joseph Margot-Duclos

Novice Henri Guibert

Novice Lode de Boninge

Statue of de Boninge

Martin Jaureguy

Charles Umbricht

Charles Joyeux

Binson Priory before the 1918 bombardment

Binson Chapel after
the bombardment

Auguste Clavel

Binson after the bombardment

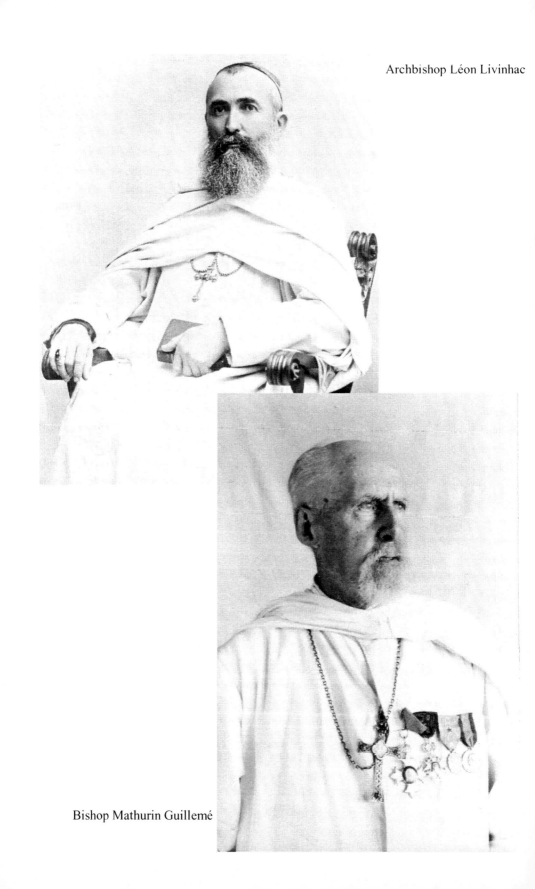

Archbishop Léon Livinhac

Bishop Mathurin Guillemé

Théophile Avon

Louis Burtin

Pope Benedict XV (Giacomo della Chiesa)

Archbishop Alexis Lemaître in a flute duet

The Congolese Force Publique salutes the White Fathers

Group with Paul Voillard (front row centre), Joseph Laane (front row right),
Joseph Mazé (back row extreme left)

Oger Ulrix with Belgian priests and seminarians in uniform at Antwerp

The 1920 Chapter. Livinhac is in the centre front row, flanked by Bishop Victor Roelens of Upper Congo (left) and Bishop Henri Streicher of Uganda (right)

Rubaga Cathedral, Uganda, symbol of a Catholic breakthrough.

CHAPTER FIVE

AFRICAN RIFLEMEN, ASKARI AND CARRIERS

Recruitment in French West Africa

The fact is not well known, but more than a million African troops were recruited to serve as combatants in the First World War.[1] In addition, more than a million Africans were recruited to participate in the war effort as labourers and carriers. African *askari* (soldiers) of the German colonial army, the *Schütztruppe*, were enlisted - as the name implies - for the defence of the German colonies. Ranged against them in West Africa were African Riflemen (*Tirailleurs*) from Senegal and French Sudan, as well as African regiments from the British colonies of Nigeria and the Gold Coast (Ghana).[2] The last two units also served in the East African campaign, together with *askari* of the King's African Rifles from Kenya, Uganda and Nyasaland (Malawi). In the Congo, the Belgians recruited *askari* into the *Force Publique*, but as this was basically a force for policing the colony, it experienced an initial difficulty in taking offensive action in German East Africa. The opposing armies in East and Central Africa also recruited well over a million African carriers, of whom more than twenty percent are known to have died from malnutrition and disease.

Between 1914 and 1918 over one hundred and eighty thousand Africans fought in Europe, mostly in the armies of France. The British also brought twenty-five thousand Africans to Europe from South Africa to serve in the Native Labour Contingent, which was barred from a combatant role. Six hundred and fifteen were drowned when the S.S. Mendi sank off the Isle of Wight in February 1917. Those who arrived safely lived in segregated compounds, serving as manual labourers in the French docks and behind the trenches. They received no rewards, medals or ribbons when they were disbanded at the end of the war. When the United States of America entered the war, two African American divisions sailed to France in 1918 and one hundred and sixty thousand army labourers preceded them to handle supplies and build the necessary facilities.

However, it was chiefly France that recruited troops in Africa and brought them to Europe. The French Army included three hundred and forty thousand North Africans (French settlers and native North Africans), two hundred and fifty thousand West Africans and thirty thousand blacks from the French West Indies. A thousand Senegalese were shipped to Gallipoli where three quarters of the force were killed or wounded within the first ten days. A hundred and forty thousand black Africans fought in Europe for France, mostly on the Western Front and twenty-four thousand of these were reported killed.[3] Thousands were listed as missing and thousands more were wounded.

One of the great advocates for using black troops in Europe was General Charles Mangin, whose brother Eugène was a White Father and a member of the recruiting commission in French Sudan.[4] General Mangin had served in French West Africa and had written a book about the value of African troops four years before the war started.[5] Mangin and others argued that sources of manpower had to be found outside France and they extolled the fighting qualities of these "warriors". Although the French army was more open than others to the drafting and even the promotion of non-white troops, the reality of their recruitment and conditions of service was altogether a different story.[6]

The number of African combatants recruited into the French Army in the First World War has never since been surpassed. In Senegal, it accounted for half the able-bodied men of military age in the colony. One historian has argued that this enforced recruitment was a more intense expropriation of manpower than the slave-trade and that it used comparable methods.[7] In 1914-1915 three "drives" took place in rural Senegal employing various means. Mobile commissions were sent out with interpreters to examine potential recruits. Chiefs and other local agents received bounties and other benefits for assembling them. For example, they could receive up to twenty-five francs per head of those recruited. On the other hand, they risked being fined or imprisoned if they failed to produce the quota required. Medical examination of the recruits was cursory, and many who had infirmities and disabilities were passed.

When recruitment was left entirely in the hands of Senegalese chiefs and *marabouts*, recruits were simply kidnapped or captured in armed raids, as slaves had been in the past. Agents were paid per head captured. If local headmen or family heads were slow to co-operate, their parents and relatives were taken hostage, and "volunteers" entered the army so that their family members could be released. Domestic slaves were often the first to be put forward. People fled to avoid recruitment or bought exemption through bribery. At best, those enlisted were reluctantly complying with the wishes of their family. At worst, they were the victims of an armed *razzia*. Forced enlistment for service overseas caused as much terror as a slave raid, and people made the obvious comparison, fearing that those recruited would never return. In fact, up to twenty-five percent never did. It is even claimed that the mortality rate of African soldiers on the western and other fronts was proportionately higher than that caused by slavery.[8]

By 1917, there was growing social unrest in French West Africa and revolts took place in Senegal and other colonies, as a result of military recruitment. In spite of this, there was still an urgent need for more African soldiers. The equivocal saviour of this situation was Blaise Diagne (1872-1934).

Blaise Diagne

Blaise Diagne was a Senegalese politician, whose family enjoyed French citizenship and who, in alliance with the majority Socialist party, was elected a deputy to the French National Assembly in May 1914. He spoke perfect French and had married a French woman.[9]   During 1915-1916 he obtained a clarification of native civil rights in the four original communes of Senegal, to the extent that African *communards* became subject to the same conscription laws as white Frenchmen. The enthusiasm for military service in the communes which followed the passing of this law contrasted with the adverse effect of the recruiting drives in the protected regions of Senegal and the other French colonies. Georges Clemenceau, who came to power in France towards the end of 1917, turned to Diagne for a solution to the problems caused by recruitment in the French African colonies. He came to an understanding with the Senegalese deputy and signed a decree on January 14th 1918, naming him commissioner for recruitment in French West Africa.

Diagne was vilified by French colonials at the time as a Bolshevik, and subsequently by African nationalists, as an agent of French imperialism. In fact he demanded – and was given – sweeping powers by Clemenceau and, as a price for his co-operation, an amelioration of pre-war colonial servitude in Senegal. Recruits were to be exempt from forced labour after the war and given preferment for jobs in the public sector. Those who had received decorations were to be eligible for full French citizenship. Diagne's return to Senegal in 1918 coincided with the home-leave of four hundred Senegalese Riflemen, some of whom had been highly decorated. These became agents of propaganda for Diagne. To all intents and purposes, Diagne's recruitment drive was extremely effective. He was empowered to dismiss unco-operative French officials and even to commission blacks as officers. Diagne's campaign throughout French West Africa exceeded the goal of forty thousand recruits. He actually enlisted sixty-three thousand. Very few of these, however, served as combatants before the Armistice was signed in November 1918.

Diagne's post-war prestige was enormous and he was re-elected as deputy by a landslide majority. Although the French did not keep all their promises to him, and although Africans did not have any say in the peace-making process, Diagne's intervention ensured an end to many abuses and injustices and created a more egalitarian vision of human relationships in colonial Africa and in the world at large. Beyond any doubt, his intervention altered the whole psychological environment of military recruiting in French West Africa.

Recruitment in Eastern Africa

The *Schütztruppe* was the Defence Force of the German colonies. In Cameroon and East Africa it was a mixed force of white and black soldiers. In South West Africa (Namibia) it was a wholly white force, under the command of Ernst Göring, the father of Hermann Göring, Nazi leader in World War II. The East African *Schütztruppe* was established under a law of 1891 and was directly controlled by the colonial office in Berlin.[10] It was highly organized. In 1914 it counted two hundred and sixty white officers and specialist personnel and 2,472 *askari* or black soldiers, including two black commissioned officers and one hundred and eighty-four black non-commissioned officers. The East African *Schütztruppe* was divided into fourteen companies. These were deployed throughout the colony for the purposes of defence and security and for suppressing local revolts. The *askari* were recruited from well-known fighting tribes, the Hehe, Ngoni and Nyamwezi. Although they were relatively poorly armed and endured a draconian discipline, they were well trained and well paid. In fact, they received twice as much pay as their British counterparts. The British were happy to enrol surrendered *Schütztruppen* into the King's African Rifles as the campaign progressed. They created two battalions of former German *askari* but could not give them the pay to which they had been accustomed. On occasion, the *Schütztruppe* was assisted by African irregulars, known by the traditional name for such levies, *ruga-ruga*.[11]

The *askari* of the *Schütztruppe* were experts in bush fighting. In fact, under their imaginative commander Lieutenant Colonel Paul Von Lettow Vorbeck (1870-1964), they virtually invented it. They were mobile, resilient and highly resourceful. The force was eventually expanded to sixty companies and by the end of 1915 it was composed of 2,998 Europeans and eleven thousand three hundred *askari*. Von Lettow wanted a limited and controlled expansion which would not dilute its effectiveness or undermine its structure of command. By the end of the campaign, however, when the undefeated column of Von Lettow surrendered near Kasama (in modern Zambia) after the Armistice in Europe in 1918, it counted one hundred and fifty four white officers or specialists and 1, 156 *askari*.[12]

"The King's African Rifles" (KAR) was the name given to informal territorial forces that had been raised in the pre-war period for internal colonial policing in Uganda, British East Africa (Kenya) and Nyasaland (Malawi).[13] At the outbreak of the First World War they were dangerously under strength and totally unprepared for a campaign against the *Schütztruppe*. Indeed some victims of KAR cut-backs even joined the *Schütztruppe* for want of any other unit to join. The KAR units were controlled and financed by the local colonial administration of each territory, not by the War Office in London. All this was changed by the First World War. By 1916 there was a central command structure under the direct control of Whitehall. From seventeen scattered companies, making up three battalions and comprising sixty-two officers and 2,319 *askari* in 1914, the KAR expanded to thirteen battalions in 1916, and finally to twenty-two battalions, totalling 31,000 *askari*, in 1918.[14]

At the height of the war, the KAR accounted for half the British fighting force in East Africa. The other half was made up of contingents from Britain, India, South Africa, Nigeria and Ghana, with smaller detachments of white and native troops from Gambia, the West Indies and from Northern and Southern Rhodesia (Zambia and Zimbabwe). There were several reasons for this rapid expansion of the KAR. At the beginning of 1916 the South African General, Jan Christiaan Smuts (1870-1950), took over as Commander-in-Chief, and by September of the same year had overrun much of the German colony. His claim to a victory, and to a specifically South African victory, proved premature. Thanks to the tactics of the legendary Von Lettow, the dwindling *Schütztruppe* was able to tie down a force fifteen times its number. In fact, when the Armistice was declared, the German commander was ready to continue fighting for at least another year.[15] Smuts had reluctantly to admit that the Germans could only be defeated by overwhelming numbers and also that African troops were better adapted to the war conditions of East Africa than whites or Indians. These were reasons enough for the rapid expansion of the KAR. There was also the reason that the East African campaign could not be fought at the expense of the war in Europe. Unlike the French, the British did not send African combatants to the Western Front, but by increasing recruitment in Africa itself, they precluded the need for sending more troops from Europe to Africa.

British recruiting policy was explained in terms of martial and non-martial ethnic stereotypes.[16] The reality was that recruiting drives took place among illiterates from marginal areas where men were attracted by the relatively high rate of pay and were likely to accept a harsh military discipline that, until as late as 1946, included flogging. Ethnic groups, such as the Kikuyu, who had a higher level of education and were more politically aware, were shunned as potential cowards and "bush lawyers". The Masai, who were probably the most "martial" tribe in East Africa were not interested. Their cousins, the economically precarious Samburu, however, responded positively, as did the Kalenjin peoples and the disadvantaged Kamba.

In Nyasaland (Malawi) recruitment was also fuelled by economic motives and by the prospect of post-war employment.[17] Recruiting began in the wake of the Chilembwe Revolt, (discussed below) and many came forward in the hope of paying off old scores against other tribes, only to find they were fighting the Germans. As in British East Africa (Kenya), military bands were used as a recruiting device and many people thought they were joining the army as bandsmen. By the end of 1917, nine thousand had enlisted in the Nyasa battalions. They were given four months of basic training, but it was only when they experienced the actual horrors of battle that they knew they had been tricked. As the KAR advanced into the "enemy" territory of German East Africa, "the gloves were taken off" and the liberated populace was impressed as *askari* or carriers. The KAR developed its own military culture, with a simple form of Swahili as its *lingua franca*, conformity to the army's sense of time, hygienic regulations that included two baths a week, a style of dancing that influenced the *beni* (discussed in Chapter Eight) and an anarchic form of Rugby known as "Karamoja Football". The recruits were also exposed to Christian teaching and practice. As the Missionaries of Africa discovered, the *askari* carried their religious beliefs, prayers and hymns with them, helping to spread Christianity throughout the region.

If the KAR was uncoordinated and unprepared for war in 1914, this was much truer of the Congolese *Force Publique*. From its inception in 1886, it was merely a number of small armed units at the disposal of Belgian officials in the Congo, each district having a company of varying size. Its purpose was the effective occupation and policing of the district. The first members of the force were East African Zanzibari, Hausa from the West African interior and traders from the Gold Coast. Little by little, local inhabitants were recruited in annual drives. According to one historian, they were "in effect slaves".[18] Ill paid, ill fed and flogged with the *chicotte* (hippo hide whip) for the smallest offence, many tried to desert, and in the early days white officers spent much of their time trying to recapture deserters. To guard against desertion, conscripts were posted to faraway districts. However, the soldiers' frustrations boiled over into a massive mutiny that lasted from 1897 until virtually 1908. Memories of the mutiny and of the force's role in the atrocities of the so-called "Red Rubber Terror", gave it an evil reputation which it found difficult to live down.[19]

By 1914 the *Force Publique* numbered some seventeen thousand men. There were no specialized units of artillery, engineering, medical support or commissariat. Above all, there was no command structure higher than the company. Only in Katanga was the force better organized, armed and equipped. There were some twenty-five companies, varying in size from two hundred to nine hundred men. Conscripts were enlisted for seven years active service and a further five years in the reserve. A British liaison officer was appointed in 1915, in the person of the celebrated Kenya pioneer, Ewart Grogan, who had traversed Africa from the Cape to Cairo in 1899-1900. Grogan helped the Belgians set up lines of communication and supply.[20] In 1916 Lieutenant-General Charles-Henri-Marie-Ernest Tombeur (1867-1947) was appointed commander-in-chief and given the unenviable task of expanding numbers and unifying the command. By the time he was ready to engage the German *Schütztruppe*, Tombeur had under his command in Eastern Congo, two brigades, each composed of two regiments comprising three battalions. Each battalion had an artillery battery, a company of engineers and a telegraph company. There were also independent battalions guarding Lakes Tanganyika and Kivu. The *Force Publique* suffered heavy losses in the East African campaign: nine thousand and seventy-seven killed, among them fifty-eight Europeans. This was more than the eight thousand, two hundred and twenty-two KAR *askari* who lost their lives in the war.

The greatest scandal of the East African campaign, however, was the fate of the carriers or porters who transported all the necessary supplies for the armies involved.[21] They outnumbered the fighting troops, sometimes by four to one, were often the unwilling victims of brutal recruiting methods and died in enormous numbers from disease, exposure and exhaustion. In East Africa alone the Allies employed something like a million carriers, including thousands brought from West Africa. In Nyasaland the carrier corps was known as *tenga-tenga* and was nothing more than forced labour. Chiefs and headmen were required to produce a quota and used force to achieve it. Runaways were rounded up and wives and cattle were taken hostage. There was a great deal of physical violence. Villagers fought the recruiting agents and there was organized group resistance on the part of the *Nyau* secret society and its branches. In spite of this, recruitment efforts continued. By the end of 1917 two hundred thousand men from Nyasaland had been enrolled as *tenga-tenga*.

Everywhere the mass levy continued. In British East Africa (Kenya) and Uganda one hundred and fifty thousand were recruited in two years. By the end of the war, as we have seen, the total figure of carriers recruited by the British and Belgians in East, Central and West Africa amounted to over a million. They were given a cursory medical examination and expected to carry a load of twenty-five kilos, in addition to their blanket, tools and cooking-pot. Usually the weight of the load was exceeded. In 1916 Joseph Mazé (1883-1959) and his fellow White Father transport officers in Nyasaland (Malawi) found themselves accompanying a convoy of one thousand, one hundred and twenty carriers from Karonga to Fife in Northern Rhodesia (Zambia), a distance of one hundred and eighty-seven miles.[22] It was a continuous journey of twenty-seven days and the consignment consisted of all the materials and equipment required for setting up a wireless station. The loads varied from one hundred and twenty kilos to four hundred kilos and each was carried by from four to sixteen porters. A hundred carriers dropped out from sickness *en route*.

At the beginning of the war the British paid volunteer carriers from East Africa the generous sum of twenty shillings per month, but this was not something that could be taken for granted, and after conscription was introduced it fell to two shillings. Many of the *tenga-tenga* from Nyasaland were tax defaulters and were presumably working off their debt to the government. Many carriers, particularly those recruited by the Germans, received no remuneration at all.

The Missionaries of Africa reported that the Belgians were recruiting carriers in their thousands in the Congo, and that retreating German armies in Rwanda in 1916 left in their wake a "deluge" of *askari* and porters.[23] Although the Germans did not go in for a mass recruitment, their carriers outnumbered the fighting troops. When Von Lettow surrendered in 1918, he still had more carriers than soldiers.[24] By the end of the war, the Allied carrier corps was a mixture of nationalities, languages and tribes. In Bangweolo Vicariate (Zambia) the White Fathers who heard the confessions of the porters, found themselves speaking Swahili, Bemba and Chewa in turn.[25] The recruitment of carriers depopulated the countryside and contributed to food shortages and famine. In the former German colony a third of the male taxable population had been taken by both sides in the campaign.[26] The missionaries complained that the movement and recruitment of carriers made mission work impossible. Large numbers of Christians and catechumens were recruited and it was difficult to assemble congregations for catechism or worship.[27]

In the very exceptional cases where road transport could be used, one Ford car could carry the loads of three hundred porters.[28] General Northey was one of the few commanders who attempted road-making, hiring hundreds of labourers for the purpose. As a rule, however, there were no roads and all supplies had to be carried by human beings. Mobile operations demanded at least two or three carriers for every *askari*. White officers required up to nine. The longer the line of march, the more carriers were needed and the more food they consumed. There was therefore a trade-off between the rations of the carriers and those of the *askari*. The consequence was that the carriers were underfed and their resistance to disease undermined.[29] Hunger, long marches and exposure to the elements combined with a lack of sanitation made them vulnerable to dysentery, meningitis, typhoid and contagious diseases of all kinds.[30] Carriers were not usually as fit as *askari*. They had to make do with unfamiliar food and they lacked the culinary skills of their womenfolk. In any case, conditions for cooking food on the march were normally lacking. Starving carriers were seen foraging for roots and berries in the bush. Many who did so died of alkaloid poisoning.[31] Carriers were exposed to differences of climate and nearly naked men from the warm plains were seen shivering in the cold air of the highlands.[32] In the last year of the war many were also victims of the Spanish Influenza pandemic.[33] Although some were killed through exposure to hostile fire, the vast majority who died perished from disease or exhaustion.

After the capture of Tabora at the end of 1916, the Ugandan carriers were sent home in batches of roughly a thousand. Many never reached their destination.[34] Starving carriers on their way home were seen stripping the maize and cassava from the fields. In Rwanda missionaries saw returning carriers dying by the roadside.[35] A White Father in Tanganyika Vicariate commented: "Many widows are weeping for their husbands who died in the carrier corps".[36] Officially, forty-five thousand carriers from British East Africa (Kenya) alone died – one in eight of the country's adult population. It is probable, however, that of the carriers recruited by all parties in the East African campaign, up to half a million died. No one knows the exact number.[37] The carrier corps, as one historian has written, was "an epic of dogged courage and endurance".[38]

The Revolts

In both French West Africa and British Central Africa rebellions took place after the First World War broke out. In both cases they were partly triggered by forced recruitment, and in both the White Fathers were affected.[39] In the French Sudan, the revolt which started in the region of the Black Volta and Bani rivers in 1915, in what is today south western Burkina Faso and south eastern Mali, escalated so rapidly in extent and scale, that it has been dubbed by some historians the "Volta-Bani Anti-colonial War". [40] The entry of the Ottoman Empire into World War I on the side of the Germans and the Sultan's declaration of a *jihad*, led to a clash between the French colonial administration and local Muslim leaders. The conflict seems also to have been fomented by Germans in their neighbouring colony of Togoland.[41] Henri Maubert, the French administrator, contributed still further to the alienation of the Muslims by his repressive campaigns which were designed to pre-empt any conspiracy. Administrative and military forces had been scaled down in the area because of manpower needs in 1914. In the light of this weakened state of the colonial forces, campaigns of recruitment and tax collection towards the end of 1915 proved to be the last straw. While the Mossi remained loyal to the French, armed resistance began among the Gurunsi of Dedugu in the last week of November. A colonial force of two hundred African riflemen was obliged to retreat after inflicting much bloodshed on the tribesmen. Another bloody encounter took place on December 5th when Maubert was forced to withdraw from the village of Bondokuy. Late in December the largest colonial army ever assembled by the French in West Africa, consisting of eight hundred Riflemen together with a unit of artillery, had yet another costly standoff with the rebels.

In mid-February 1916 a vicious, month-long campaign of reprisal was carried out by a French force of one thousand, five hundred riflemen and some two thousand auxiliaries. Rebel losses were high and the French victory was followed by a scorched earth policy. The rebels then undertook punitive raids on loyalist villages. Among them was Toma in the country of the Samo on the edge of the disaffected region. Joseph Dubernet (1875-1966) was largely instrumental in persuading the Christians of Toma Mission not to join the rebellion and other White Fathers helped prevent the revolt from spreading.[42] The French authorities ordered the missionaries to evacuate the mission station and the rebels attacked the abandoned post on May 6th, destroying the mission house itself. Not much had been left for them to steal or destroy, and the African caretaker escaped with his wife and children.[43] In a second attack on May 27th the rebels violated church vestments and sacred vessels.[44] The local population vented its anger on the perpetrators and a man seen wearing the cassock (*gandourah*) of a White Father and mimicking them was brutally punished.[45]

Alfred Diban, catechist and first Christian of Burkina Faso, was placed in charge of the mission and organized its defence until the missionaries returned.[46] When they did, they found a pill-box outside the main gate, and a sentry armed with a rifle and fixed bayonet. A detachment of forty-five riflemen was also installed in the compound. These finally left at the beginning of October. The ring-leaders in the attack were rounded up and taken to Kudugu where the White Fathers helped in the interrogation that led to their conviction and imprisonment.[47] Rebuilding began at Toma and also at Reo, where the mission had likewise suffered in the revolt. Although it was a new mission, Toma soon attracted candidates for baptism. In 1920 six hundred entered the catechumenate.[48] In view of all these events it is easy to understand why the French colonial authorities were not keen on the call-up of Missionaries of Africa in the Sudan to active service in Europe.

The violent movement associated with the name of John Chilembwe, sometimes grandly called "the intertribal Nyasaland rising", seriously threatened British rule in Nyasaland (Malawi) for a brief period of three days in early 1915.[49] Like the Volta-Bani rebellion in West Africa, it was partly triggered by military recruitment and also targeted Catholic Missions. John Chilembwe (c.1860-1915) is now hailed as a charismatic nationalist martyr because, although he had no clear, long-term goal, his movement was the first notable resistence to colonial oppression in Malawi. Chilembwe was converted by the radical missionary, Joseph Booth, who took him to the United States where he studied at a black Baptist seminary.

He returned to Nyasaland in 1900 as an ordained Baptist pastor and founded Providence Industrial Mission. He taught racial equality and a morality that emphasized temperance and the work ethic. Although at first he did not himself espouse millenarian doctrines, he was surrounded and supported by followers who did. These belonged to the smaller Protestant sects which were virulently anti-Catholic, and were influenced by Watchtower groups that had abandoned that movement's official pacifism. They believed that many Africans would be killed in the coming Armageddon, but that Chilembwe's followers would enjoy supernatural protection. By the beginning of 1915, Chilembwe was beginning to move towards a messianic consciousness and the desire to inaugurate a "New Jerusalem".

Although the political ideas of Chilembwe and his followers grew out of the Bible, they developed against a background of very real social grievance. Forced labour recruitment, massive migration of workers, the pressure of tax collection and, after 1914, the recruitment of *askari* and carriers for the KAR in Nyasaland brought about a growing alienation from British rule. In particular, the cruelty of local European settlers towards their African workers sparked protest and resistance. Chilembwe planned an attack on the worst of the plantations which developed into an armed rebellion of some nine hundred Africans.

The loyalty of Catholics to an institutional Church tended to make them respectful of the colonial government, but the Missionaries of Africa and the Montfort Missionaries were not sufficiently versed in English for communication with the colonial administration or for debates with Protestants. In spite of their isolation, the loyalty of Catholics made them targets, yet the Catholic missionaries' early warnings of impending trouble were discounted by the government as a product of inter-mission rivalry. Besides killing three plantation managers, Chilembwe's followers attacked Nguludi Catholic Mission on January 26th. Nguludi was an abortive foundation of the White Fathers which had been taken over by the Montfort Missionaries in the 1910 ecclesiastical division of the country. The mission was destroyed and a child perished in the blaze, but the Dutch Catholic priest who had been left for dead in the cemetery survived the ordeal. The colonial response was immediate and ruthless. Many rebels were killed and Chilembwe himself was captured and shot without mercy.

The rebellion of John Chilembwe marked a watershed in the relations of the Missionaries of Africa with the British administration in Central Africa. At the outbreak of the war, the government viewed the Society with suspicion since it had numerous members in "enemy" territory - German East Africa.   After Chilembwe, however, Catholics were increasingly placed on a "pedestal of civic virtue".[50] The turn-around was due in large measure to the realism and tact of Mathurin Guillemé (1859-1942), Vicar Apostolic of Nyasa. Guillemé, a Frenchman who was an ardent admirer of the British, set out to improve relations with them, and an opportunity to do this occurred at the Commission of Enquiry set up in Blantyre as a result of the rising. In view of the rebellion's religious character, the leaders of all the Christian denominations were called by the commission and subjected to a lengthy interrogation. Although Guillemé had not been noticeably vocal about the underlying socio-economic causes of the revolt, he and other Catholic missionaries believed that its religious motivation was clearly the fruit of private judgement in matters of faith.[51] The commission was particularly concerned about the influence of the Bible and Bible teaching in African instituted Churches.

On taking the stand, Guillemé tabled a Dutch Reformed Church tract entitled *The Fruits of Romanism*. This prejudiced and ill-informed document accused Catholics, among other things, of forbidding Bible reading and even of murdering translators of the Bible, an accusation that was presumably a reference to the execution of William Tyndale in Flanders in 1535! No doubt, the tract was a piece of mischievous slander, but in the circumstances it helped, rather than harmed, the Catholic cause. Guillemé testified for two hours, explaining that Catholics did not forbid the reading or translation of the Bible, and thought every Christian should possess a New Testament. The Old Testament, however, required more careful explanation. Guillemé did not think it wise to put the whole Bible into the hands of catechists. For the time being, a catechesis based on Bible stories was sufficient. Although he had as yet no African priests, he stressed that, in the future, they would be under the hierarchical authority of the Church, and would not be allowed to act independently. Biblical interpretation was the prerogative of the Church's *magisterium*.

A second topic which interested the commission was the sacrament of Penance. Guillemé declared that the Catholic clergy exercised a far-reaching influence through Confession, obliging penitents who knew about plots against the government to reveal them to the authorities. They could not, however, compel penitents to denounce themselves. Guillemé's testimony made a good impression on the commission, one of whose members wrote to him afterwards: "In not putting the Bible in the hands of everyone without distinction, (you) demonstrate great wisdom".[52] Basking in the light of this new found esteem, Guillemé offered the services of the White Fathers as military chaplains, medical and transport staff in the approaching conflict with German East Africa.

White Fathers' Ministry to the Riflemen

In order to terrify the enemy on the western front, French authorities spread alarming tales of African Riflemen butchering German soldiers and these stories were eagerly repeated by the Germans as evidence of the exploitation of African brutality by the French.[53] In fact, the Riflemen were more sinned against than sinning. They were, if anything, the victims of a situation that was not of their making. The charge has also been laid that African troops were deployed as "cannon fodder" to spare the lives of French soldiers, and there is more than a hint of truth in this accusation, although it was strongly denied by the authorities at the time. When the war started the French were sceptical of the Africans' military qualities, and up to 1915 the Riflemen were used mainly as garrison troops. In 1916, however, they appeared as combatants on the Somme and at Verdun. A tactical group of Riflemen and colonial infantry was responsible for the most celebrated military action of the war, the re-taking of Fort Douaumont. When French morale began to collapse in 1917, the Senegalese, in spite of their losses, were dispersed along the front as tactical spearheads for larger French units.

Generally, colonial infantry, such as the Zouave regiments, were integrated with the French Army, but – except in combat - the black Riflemen were segregated. In 1917 Mangin created "mixed regiments" of Riflemen and colonial infantry and employed them as shock troops in advance of the metropolitan formations. In such situations there is "compelling evidence" that French commanders readily sacrificed African Riflemen to spare French lives, especially at the moment of assault.[54] The policy led to proportionately higher black casualties (some twenty-five percent higher) than French.

Modern war conditions were completely alien to the African troops in Europe. If the white European soldiers suffered from the cold and wet, living throughout the winter in the open, these soldiers from the tropics felt the harsh climate, the cold and the snow, even more.[55] Alcohol and martial music did not compensate for the torment they endured. Some even lost their reason, especially as amputees in hospital. Needless to say, the Riflemen had only the vaguest understanding of the reasons for the war. Nobody informed their families when they were killed and their sudden reappearance at home when the war ended was unexpected. It was assumed they had been lost forever. Many found that the wives they abandoned had remarried.

In spite of all this, a romantic image of the African Rifleman persisted in France. They were praised for their bravery and their loyalty to France. Many received the *Croix de Guerre*. Although contacts with French women were resented, the Riflemen frequently had a (usually platonic) relationship with a girl from a good family, known as a "wartime godmother". The picture of a smiling African Rifleman was even used as a trade-mark for various household goods and patent foods during and after the war.[56] On the whole, French prejudice against black Africans was eroded, albeit to a limited extent, by the military performance of the Riflemen.

The French White Father conscripts served for the most part in the Algerian Zouave regiments or in metropolitan infantry units. Although the first Zouaves were native auxiliaries from Kabylia, by the mid nineteenth century the Zouaves were composed exclusively of Frenchmen. Native Algerians, Moroccans and Tunisians were thereafter recruited into units of colonial infantry. The Missionaries of Africa rarely met the Riflemen during combat, unless – like Adrien Guillou (killed in 1917) – they served in a so-called "mixed regiment". Otherwise, they mainly encountered the Africans in hospital during the course of their medical duties, when acting as interpreters or by chance when travelling. As already mentioned, one of the Missionaries of Africa who witnessed the slaughter of the Riflemen during the disembarkation at the Dardanelles met several African soldiers on board a troopship in 1915. Jules Lhomme (1891-1955) was a scholastic at the time and saw two blacks with rosaries. He showed them a photograph of himself in the White Father habit. One of the two, from Dahomey (Benin), was already baptized, the other was a Bambara catechumen. With a zeal that was no doubt misplaced, he gave them "a complete catechesis, beginning with Adam and original sin". Later, he found a young Senegalese from the White Fathers' mission of Kita and baptized him.[57]

In June 1916, Eugène Ratisseau (1883-1933), who had served with Bambara Riflemen in Cameroon, accompanied them to France where he recognized several of his Christians and catechumens among those who disembarked at Bordeaux. In the following year he witnessed their sufferings in the snow.[58] Louis Hamon (1880-1930) encountered a fine, black soldier from Senegal in one of the mountain regiments. He spoke fluent French and attended Sunday Mass regularly.[59] Joseph Lautour (1875-1943) instructed a Mossi and a Malinke whom he found with five black Christians on the Aisne Front.[60] Another letter from this front reported that the Africans had been tested by machine-gun fire, as well as by mud and snow.[61] During 1916, the French colonial government in West Africa asked for missionaries to go to France as interpreters for the Riflemen. Five White Fathers were designated. On arrival at Marseilles, they were appointed Corporals and sent to the Africans' camp at Fréjus on the Riviera.[62] Marius Ferrage's (1880-1962) Bambara manual was issued for the use of black troops and their officers.[63]

Ratisseau met a black chaplain from Guinea in 1917, but there were few priests attached to the Riflemen's battalions. It was in the hospitals, that the Missionaries of Africa came into their own as unofficial chaplains to the African troops. Louis Glass (1886-1919*) wrote letters for the Riflemen he found in hospital. Léon Darot (1890-1958) encountered a Rifleman, suffering from tuberculosis and "looking like a skeleton", in a hospital in Salonika. He instructed him for a month and a half before baptizing him by the name of Peter. He even started learning Bambara in order to instruct another dying African soldier. Joseph Loiseau, "Brother Pierre" (1881-1918), prepared another Bambara soldier for death and astonished a Jesuit colleague in the hospital, who had not thought white men could speak an African language.[64]

The White Fathers found that many Africans were being baptized in the hospitals without instruction and did their best to remedy this defect. Auguste Bazin (1881-1946) was edified by the openness of the Africans and other "colonials" who were not afraid to ask for the sacraments. A black Moroccan, a former Bambara slave, impressed Marcel Vanneste (1884-1963) at Calais-Virval by his devout confession.[65] A notable apostolate was carried out by Louis Burtin (1853-1942), the long-serving procurator of the Missionaries of Africa in Rome. Large numbers of troops passed through Rome, among them many African Riflemen, and Burtin made a practice of visiting the principal railway station where they boarded trains for various destinations. Burtin went among them distributing pictures and medals of Pope Benedict XV and seeking out those who wished to go to confession. One who did so was a soldier from Madagascar, who made his confession out loud, receiving absolution bareheaded and kneeling in the mud.[66] For his services to troops in transit, Burtin received the bronze medal *Reconaissance Française* in 1918.[67] However, the most important contribution by a White Father to the welfare, spiritual and material, of the Riflemen was that of Alexis Lemaître.

Brigadier-General Lemaître

In 1911 Alexis Lemaître (1864-1939) had been a missionary at Ghardaia in the Sahara and had spent five years as Superior of the Thibar domain in Tunisia, when he was appointed Vicar Apostolic of the vast and, as yet ecclesiastically undivided, territory of French Sudan.[68]   He was a man of many accomplishments – among other things, a musician who enjoyed playing the flute. Possessed of a strong will, Lemaître set out to restore a largely demoralized vicariate, improve relations with the colonial authorities and find staff for his depleted mission stations. His plans, alas, were overtaken by the war, and in 1914 he faced the call-up of twelve missionaries, one of them being Eugène Mangin, brother of the general. In June 1916 Lemaître himself followed them to France, having become seriously ill as a result of amoebic dysentery. After a stomach operation in Paris, he convalesced for several months at a military hospital in Rochefort-sur-Yveline.[69]   At the end of 1917 General Mangin's influence secured a meeting for his brother with Henri Simon, the Minister for Colonies, who in turn expressed a wish to meet Lemaître.

Lemaître saw Simon in January 1918 and learned that a new recruitment of African Riflemen was planned in French West Africa. The minister asked for the Bishop's support and went so far as to offer the return of mobilized White Fathers to help gain acceptance for the measure. Lemaître thought it best to accept the offer, although the condition could have been compromising for the Church.   The situation was even further complicated by political events in French West Africa itself.

Joost Van Vollenhoven, a naturalized Frenchman of Dutch descent, had been appointed Governor-General in 1917, but had a violent disagreement with the French government over the further recruitment of African soldiers. As a result of this difference, he resigned and returned to France. After an audience in January 1918 with the President of the Council, Georges Clemenceau, he rejoined his regiment and was killed near Soissons in July. At his final audience with Clemenceau, the President of the Council told him that it was his intention to consult Lemaître over the issue and the Bishop was duly summoned on Saturday January 26th. During a wide-ranging discussion lasting fifty minutes Clemenceau picked Lemaître's brains on French achievements in West Africa, on the Africans' state of mind and on the situation of African soldiers in Europe. To Lemaître's way of thinking, the campaign of recruitment could not be separated from the question of the African soldiers' welfare in Europe. Clemenceau, who was also Minister for War, asked the Bishop to return on Monday for a joint meeting with Simon.

At the joint meeting, the President of the Council famously declared to his Minister for Colonies that Lemaître had taught him ten times more about the colonial question in five minutes than he had learned throughout his whole parliamentary career.[70] Thereupon Clemenceau as Minister of War and Simon, holding the portfolio for the colonies, commissioned Lemaître to put his ideas into operation. The Bishop complied. On February 19th Clemenceau signed the order entrusting Lemaître with the special mission of studying all the questions relating to the moral and material interests of the West African troops serving in

Europe and North Africa. The aim was to improve their conditions of living and to make their service overseas profitable for themselves, while furthering French influence in their home countries. Lemaître was enjoined to forward his reports, observations and proposals to the high command. Furthermore, while visiting the African troops, he was to enjoy the status, emoluments and travel facilities of a Brigadier-General.

Lemaître began by making Paris his base, after which he started a tour of the African camps on the *Côte d'Azur*. During these visits he ate with the high-ranking officers, some of whom accompanied him to the billets of the African Riflemen. Here they could see for themselves how happy the soldiers were to hear their own language spoken. Everywhere Lemaître sowed the seeds of his own ideas on colonial policy. His journeys took him almost up to the enemy trenches in some places, and he did not neglect to visit Verdun. Nor did he fail to visit the wounded and sick Riflemen in the hospitals. During the year he also continued his visitation in North Africa. Before the Armistice in November he had submitted his report, proposing, among other things, a corps of colonial interpreters consisting of Europeans who could speak African languages and Africans who could speak French.

Lemaître's mission to the Riflemen ceased with the end of the war and he was present in Notre Dame for the *Te Deum*, as well as at Meaux Cathedral for the celebration of the victory on the Marne.[71] In May 1919 the Bishop commenced an appeal in France on behalf of the demobilized African Riflemen, especially those who were mutilated or sick, and for the widows and orphans of African soldiers. In October, with the support of the Cardinal Archbishop of Paris, he circularized all the Bishops of France concerning the appeal. Lemaître was to decide how the money collected would be spent, although Livinhac in Algiers was sceptical and feared a bad press if the funds collected did not go directly to the Africans themselves.[72]

By this time, Lemaître was preparing to return to French Sudan and had sent a telegram: "Prepare my return for July - +Alexis".[73] Once again, his plans were overturned. Not only did he have a recurrence of his amoeba problems, but he was shortlisted as coadjutor to the ailing and elderly Archbishop Combes of Carthage. Lemaître was by now well known to people of influence in France and had even received a prize worth ten thousand francs from the *Académie Française*.[74] Not surprisingly, it was the French Government that made the explicit request for Lemaître.[75] In Rome for the canonization of St. Joan of Arc in May 1920, he was informed of his new appointment by Pope Benedict XV. Lemaître who had been hoping to remain in the French Sudan, was persuaded to accept his new posting without too much difficulty.[76] He was made coadjutor at Carthage, with the personal title of Archbishop of Cabasa on July 28th 1920.[77] Mgr.Combes died on February 20th 1922 and Lemaître succeeded him automatically as Primate of Africa. In the same year he had the privilege of receiving the President of France, Alexandre Millerand, at Carthage.[78]

The General Council of the Society had had misgivings already about Lemaître as bishop in the French Sudan. He was thought by them to be a seductive speaker, whose projects were utopian, and who tended to be harsh, authoritarian and indiscreet. "It is a misfortune", wrote Livinhac, "that Benedict XV named him coadjutor with right of succession at Carthage, a succession which is now a *fait accompli*."[79] However, the appointment did not lie in their hands, and for good or ill Lemaître became Lavigerie's successor at Carthage.[80]

White Fathers' Ministry to Askari and Carriers

In spite of its horrors and the sufferings it caused, the East African campaign helped - paradoxically - to spread the Christian faith. Catholics were most numerous among the Congolese of the *Force Publique* and among Ugandans in the KAR, but they were also substantially present in the colonial forces of Kenya and Central Africa and among the carriers. White Fathers did not serve as chaplains in the German *Schütztruppe*, but they accompanied the Congolese and the British columns, as they invaded German East Africa from north, west and south. The *askari* themselves helped to spread the faith, recruiting candidates for baptism and promoting piety and a deepening of spiritual consciousness among those already baptized. Most of the soldiers and carriers had only known the Church, as it was found in their own home regions. Now, they discovered men from other regions who were Catholics like themselves and worshipped with them in the common liturgical language, Latin. As a result of the war, they had an enhanced understanding of the Church's universality.

Prejudice, however, still dogged the attitudes of Europeans – even missionaries – towards the African soldiers. The Congolese *Force Publique*, in particular, had an evil reputation to live down. Not only was Brother Fulgence (Arthur) Mechau accidentally shot dead at Mibirizi Mission, but Nyundo Mission also became the focus for several unsavoury rumours, as the Congolese invaded Rwanda from the west. Jan van der Burgt (1863-1923) was the celebrated Dutch ethnographer of Rwanda who had been decorated by the German government. A staunch Germanophile, he believed the worst of the invading Congolese. As a retired missionary in neutral Holland, he gave out in 1915 that the Belgian forces had ravaged Nyundo and that only three hundred, out of four thousand Christians could now be found at the mission.[81] After the war he followed up this exaggeration with an article in a German periodical, extolling the German handling of the natives and criticizing British and Belgian treatment of Africans. German newspapers cited van der Burgt's views as evidence of cruelty perpetrated by the Congolese troops. Needless to say, this created a bad impression in Belgian colonial circles. There was also consternation in the General Council of the Missionaries of Africa, which asked the Belgian Oger Ulrix (1874-1954) to set the record straight, and rejected the appointment of van der Burgt to the sanatorium at Autreppe, in case the Belgian authorities refused him entry to their country. For a year, van der Burgt, who remained a thorn in the side of the White Father superiors, was allowed to chaplain to a community of Bavarian Benedictine Sisters in the Netherlands. He died at Utrecht eighteen months later.[82]

Another curious accusation concerning Nyundo was made in 1915, by Bishop Victor Roelens (1858-1947), Vicar Apostolic of Upper Congo. Roelens was very far from being a Germanophile and was prepared to believe a story brought to him by Belgian officers that the superior of Nyundo, a German called François Knoll (1880-1951), had a drawn a revolver and fired three shots at Congolese *askari* who came to the mission. Roelens believed the story and promptly denounced Knoll to the General Council of the Society, which ordered his immediate exclusion from the Missionaries of Africa. A year later, Roelens had, somewhat sheepishly, to admit that the story was a pure concoction by the *askari* concerned in order to excuse their disobedience. They had been sent to the mission, but had not gone there, inventing this story as an excuse.[83]

Missionaries of Africa who served as chaplains to the Congolese troops found them for the most part "regular and honest".[84] Even before the invasion began, Congolese soldiers were being baptized in large numbers at Baudouinville and Mpala missions. Bishop Auguste Huys (1871-1938) thought that at least six hundred had been baptized in the northern part of the vicariate.[85] Joseph Weghsteen (1873-1962), who was one of the chaplains, reported that Congolese *askari* at the frontier with Northern Rhodesia (Zambia) were nearly all Christians, that they attended catechism regularly and that there had been many converts among them since the war began.[86]

Raphaël Roy (1879-1943) went from one Congolese camp to another in 1916, over a distance of two hundred and fifty kilometres. He found the troops proselytizing one another. No one wanted to die before being baptized. "What are my sergeant's stripes worth?" a soldier asked him. "What I want are the stripes of baptism." So zealous was one *askari* that he baptized a dying comrade, using his own saliva. An amputee told Roy: "This bullet which has deprived me of a leg is a punishment for my innumerable sins."[87] Soldiers begged their chaplains for baptism. *Nataka Mungu* ("I want God") said one.[88] Although the missionaries found their soldiers full of goodwill, it was clear that they lacked instruction. This was especially the case with those from the other vicariates that had not introduced the White Fathers' four year catechumenate. A high point in the Congolese army's Catholic practice was reached when General Tombeur and his staff attended a Requiem in Tabora on November 2nd 1916. The town had just been captured, and Mass was offered at the White Fathers' mission for all the *askari* who had fallen during the siege. The Congolese troops presented arms at the consecration. A fortnight later, a *Te Deum* was sung on the feast of King Albert of the Belgians.[89]

It is a commonplace of war that soldiers occasionally seize the opportunity to take revenge on a superior officer. This happens in every army. That it occurred in the *Force Publique* is not surprising. Roy was obliged to assist at three executions of Congolese *askari*. All made the exemplary death of a "good thief". In one case, at Kigoma, André Makambo from middle Congo had shot his platoon commander in a fit of anger. After making his final confession, he thanked the chaplain and said "Now I am ready to die". He then distributed his clothes among his comrades and asked Roy to write to his wife. On the way to execution he recited the rosary and on arrival placed the beads around his neck. The troops were drawn up in an open square, with more than two hundred whites and their servants in attendance and a large crowd of curious onlookers.

The sentence was read and André died at the hands of the firing squad shortly after beginning another Hail Mary.[90]

On some occasions the chaplains were able to intervene in disputes between officers and men. This happened when a Congolese *askari* killed an officer who had punished him. The officer was unpopular and the culprit was supported by his entire Company. A Missionary of Africa intervened to prevent further bloodshed and to end the mutiny.[91]

The White Father chaplains in the KAR also found Christians as fervent as those in the *Force Publique*. Ernest Paradis (1881-1945) was lodged in a former Protestant mission after the battle of Lupembe at the end of 1917. He found many Christians among the *askari* and carriers. Large numbers came to him for confession at week-ends, and Sunday Mass in their camp was well attended. In the final year of the war Oscar Julien (1886-1961) celebrated Easter at Mbamba Bay on the German shore of Lake Nyasa (Malawi), with an international congregation of soldiers and carriers. All sang the *Kyrie, Gloria* and *Credo* with great enthusiasm. "They thought", added Julien, "that they were in their own church at home."[92]

Much of the chaplains' ministry consisted in hospital visiting. One White Father reported that, since coming to Tabora, he had baptized more than a hundred and fifty dying soldiers, carriers and houseboys, most of them suffering from meningitis or tick fever.[93] The chaplains from Nyasaland (Malawi) in particular found they had to be stretcher-bearers, medical orderlies, interpreters, organizers of transport and even intermediaries with the enemy. They received the pay of a simple soldier and ate the same rations.[94]

The kindness of the missionaries to the carriers was never forgotten, although it has been claimed that some of these unfortunates were whipped by missionaries. According to Melvin E. Page, the men were "surprised at seeing the kind missionaries they knew at home beating tired, hungry and sick men".[95] In the context of this remark, Page quotes Hector Duff's opinion that a White Father who had been assigned to carrier duty was "rather too martially minded for his job". Page adds: "That priest and several of his fellows may have been trying to end doubts about their loyalty, which had been occasionally questioned, since others of their order worked for the Germans. One means of accomplishing that goal in the carrier service was to exact greater performances from their men."[96]

This seems to be a gratuitous slur. Sir Hector Duff, was the Scottish Chief Secretary of Nyasaland. In the book of reminiscences that he published nearly two decades later and which is the source of the quotation, he told a story about Ernest Paradis, one of the White Father transport officers. The story is a light hearted account of an excitable missionary in his mid-thirties. Although Duff admits his preference for married Presbyterians and Moravians over the less domesticated Roman Catholic celibates, there is no serious criticism implied in his tale. It is merely a diverting anecdote told by a staid Scotsman, amused at the antics of a French foreigner. Also, it has nothing to do with anyone beating the unfortunate carriers. This is the yarn in full.

Père Paradis of the French Roman Catholic Mission "was employed as a civilian transport officer, a genial, amusing fellow, popular with everyone, but rather too martially minded for his job, the result being that, instead of keeping to his proper place in the rear, he was constantly getting himself mixed up in battles, much to the embarrassment of his superiors. In the excitement of one such occasion he so far forgot himself as to get hold of a rifle and begin firing madly in the direction of the enemy, whereupon a scandalized officer approached him and the following dialogue took place: 'Look here, I say, Father Paradise (*sic*), stop it ! This won't do, you know; you're a civilian, you mustn't go shooting at people.' 'That's alright, Sir, (replied the missionary). Don't worry, I am such a bad shot, I never hit anyone.'[97]

From his base at Tukuyu, Duff administered the region of German East Africa occupied by General Northey and his troops. The anecdote rings true, and Duff may have heard it at first or second hand. Needless to say, he does not speculate about Father Paradis attempting to prove his loyalty by exacting greater performances from the carriers.

Page refers to another cleric also, as evidence for his criticism.[98] This gentleman, however, can hardly be included among the "fellow missionaries" of Ernest Paradis, since he was a member of the Church of Scotland with no Presbyterian colleagues in German East Africa. This was Robert Hellier Napier, who served as a transport officer two years earlier at the Battle of Karonga in September 1914. Napier, on his own admission, "brandished and used a stick freely".[99] However, he did this in the heat of the moment under enemy gunfire, in order to save the lives of his carriers and urge them out of a deep water-filled gully where they and their precious loads were in danger. The only Missionary of Africa known to have carried a bamboo cane when supervising carriers was Joseph Mazé (1883-1959). However, there is no evidence that he whipped them with it. The cane, which he carried in lieu of a more lethal weapon was an object of admiration, rather than reprehension.[100]

The work of chaplain took the Missionaries of Africa far beyond the borders of their own mission stations and vicariates. In so doing, it made them better known and extended their influence over the entire region. The First World War not only helped to give Africans their first national experience, it also helped to unify and extend the Catholic Church. Henceforward, "African society opened up to missionary influence more widely and more easily".[101] In the next chapter the immediate impact of the East African campaign on the White Fathers' missions in the German colony is examined.

CHAPTER SIX

EUROPE'S WAR IN AFRICA

Last Glimmer of the Scramble

An unintended side-effect of the First World War was that it became the final act of the Scramble for Africa. Transporting Africans to fight a war in Europe was bad enough. To fight a European war on African soil has been called "the climax of Africa's exploitation".[1] From the outset of the war, however, the Allied Powers cast envious eyes on the relatively undefended German colonies, and the war ended with the disguised annexation of these territories as "mandates" or trusteeships under the newly founded League of Nations. In 1914 Germany possessed four African colonies: Togo, Cameroon, German South-West Africa and German East Africa. It was only in the last-named colony that the Missionaries of Africa were at work and had, in fact, four of their oldest missionary vicariates. These were directly affected by the lengthy, four-year East African campaign. Of the other German colonies, it was merely in the eighteen month Cameroon campaign that White Fathers from French Sudan served as non-combatant conscripts.

Germany's hold on its four African colonies was precarious. All of them were isolated territories, surrounded by hostile powers. Although each possessed a coastline and boasted some excellent harbours, they were too far away for adequate protection by the German Navy. In spite of this, the harbours offered necessary land support for the steamships employed in Germany's "Cruiser War". The German colonies were also part of a worldwide system of communications, with strategically placed wireless stations and transmitters. These, as well as the harbours, inevitably became favoured targets for the Allies.

The very first bullet shot by a soldier in British service during the Great War was fired on August 12th 1914 in Togo.[2] This tiny colony, sandwiched between the Gold Coast (now Ghana) and Dahomey (now Benin), was easily captured by Senegalese Riflemen and a British contingent of West African Rifles, the Gold Coast Regiment, in August 1914.[3] The population numbering half a million Africans and two thousand Europeans was defended by a *Schütztruppe* of two hundred white officers and one thousand, five hundred *askari*. The British alone could field an army from the Gold Coast which was three times that number and the campaign lasted barely three weeks. The port of Lomé was captured on August 12th and the Germans destroyed the all-important wireless station at Kamina on August 25th, rather than allow it to fall into enemy hands. The surrender took place on the following day. After the war, the League of Nations divided the region into two mandates, one British and one French. The British administered their section as part of the Gold Coast colony and protectorate, to which it was formally joined in 1957 to constitute the independent state of Ghana. Except for a short period of three years, the French section was administered as a separate unit and became the independent Republic of Togo in 1960.

Cameroon was a different proposition. It was more than five times the area of Togo and equalled in size both France and Germany combined. Except for the tiny Spanish enclave of Rio Muni (Equatorial Guinea), it was bounded by vast territories administered by the French and British.[4] In mid-August an Anglo-French conference in London authorized the invasion of Cameroon. The colony was defended by a *Schütztruppe* of one thousand, six hundred *askari* under two hundred and five white officers and NCOs. The local police force was incorporated in order to double its strength. The British, under Sir Charles Dobell (1869-1954), brought troops from Gold Coast, Nigeria and Sierra Leone, and these were joined by French colonial infantry and Riflemen from Senegal, as well as Belgian troops of the Congolese *Force Publique*. Together with thousands of carriers, the Allied army reached a total strength of twenty-five thousand. In spite of this preponderance of numbers, the Allies encountered stiff German opposition. The Cameroon forces were controlled by civil authorities who believed in the merits of German colonization and relied on local support that was readily forthcoming. The Germans intended to conduct a protracted campaign in order to be in a strong position at the end of the war. Both British and French failed to understand this intention.

Early Allied efforts were costly and for the most part unsuccessful, but on September 27th 1914, with the support of British and French cruisers and gunboats, the port of Duala, which was also the colonial capital, was captured, together with its wireless masts and those of neighbouring Victoria. During the remainder of the eighteen month campaign, the Allies were dogged by a lack of direction and co-ordination. They also encountered sustained and skilful German resistance, as well as a torrential rainy season. After a disastrous engagement in which Nigerian troops broke and fled under an artillery counter-attack, the capture of the strategic town of Garua on June 10th 1915 deprived the Germans of their lifeline to the northern plateau.[5] The town of Yaounde then became the new centre of gravity and source of supply, but this fell on January 1st 1916 and the last German post at Mora surrendered in February. Allied forces sustained twenty percent casualties, chiefly through disease, and most of the defeated Germans and their *askari* took refuge in neutral Rio Muni. The capture of Cameroon released the Gold Coast Regiment and West African Frontier Force for service in East Africa. German missionaries were interned and evicted, precipitating an educational crisis in the colony.

The two Missionaries of Africa who served with the French forces in Cameroon were Eugène Ratisseau (1883-1933) and Claude Chevrat (1886-1921*). The first was attached to a unit of Bambara Riflemen, whom he afterwards followed to France (as we saw in Chapter Five). After being posted to Edea, a centre south-east of Duala, in 1915, he returned to Duala the following year *en route* for Dakar and Europe. He reported that there had been twenty-five consecutive days of rain and that the retreating Germans had destroyed hospitals, bridges, railways and locomotives. Both he and Chevrat, who followed Ratisseau to Edea, were favourably impressed by the state of the Catholic Church in Cameroon. Ratisseau estimated that there were twenty-five thousand baptized Catholics in the country and went so far as to compare the Cameroon mission to that of Uganda.[6] Although the comparison was far-fetched, the German Pallotines had been remarkably successful. After the Allied victory however, German missionaries - Pallotines and Spiritans - were deported, and Cameroon Catholics went without a priest for two and a half years. Following the division of the country, the celebrated Irish Spiritan Joseph Shanahan, Prefect Apostolic of Lower Nigeria, was put in charge of the British section, and the senior French military chaplain, Douvry, was made superior of the rest of the country, before it was confided to French Spiritans.[7]

Chevrat was so struck by the desperate need for pastors and evangelizers in Cameroon that, when he was finally demobbed in May 1920, he was reluctant to return to French Sudan, with its penury of baptized Catholics.[8] Instead, he sought permission to remain as a missionary in Edea. The General Council of the White Fathers gave him permission to approach *Propaganda Fide* to be released from his missionary oath, and he left the Society in the following year.[9]

General Smuts and the Germans

In 1916 Jan Christiaan Smuts (1870-1950) became commander-in-chief of the British army in East Africa and this included a substantial expeditionary force from South Africa of some twenty thousand white soldiers. When he and the South African troops left the field in the following year, Jacob Louis van Deventer (1874-1922), another South African, eventually succeeded him as commander-in-chief. Boer settlers in East Africa had no particular animus against the Germans, rather the contrary. However, the campaign in German East Africa was seen in some quarters as a South African campaign – even as a South African victory. There was even a faint hope that South Africa might profit territorially from the success, through a possible bargain with the Portuguese in Mozambique.[10] All of this may seem strange in view of the fact that some fifteen years earlier Smuts and van Deventer had been fighting the British in South Africa, both leading invading columns into the Cape Colony. The war left a legacy of bitterness among the Boers, but Smuts believed that the future greatness of South Africa depended on collaboration with Britain. He identified himself with Cecil Rhodes and the task of promoting European civilization in Africa.[11] He shared this view with another South African soldier-statesman and Anglophile, Louis Botha (1862-1919), who became premier in 1907. Smuts joined his cabinet and together they helped to create the South African Union in 1910, for which Smuts wrote the constitution.

At the outbreak of war in 1914, Botha mobilized South African troops for war against the Germans and Smuts rejoined the army. South Africa's campaign against German South West Africa was not merely a contribution to the First World War, it must also be set in the context of Smuts' and Botha's ambitions for South Africa. London supported the conquest of South West Africa for the long-term security of the Union and for binding it more firmly to the British Empire.[12] It was in fact a form of "sub-imperialism". South African troops were stationed along the German colony's border, but several units led by Lieutenant-General Manie Maritz and other Boer Nationalists, amounting to some twelve thousand men in all, allied with the Germans. The rebellion was destroyed by Smuts and Botha, with van Deventer commanding the force that defeated Maritz on October 24th. There were up to a thousand casualties on both sides. Smuts and Botha represented the only political power which could counter South African divisions and create a "Greater South Africa" alongside the British Empire.

German South West Africa was a huge and largely arid country, six times the size of England and populated by only eighty thousand Africans, with some seven thousand settlers. The German colony's all-white *Schütztruppe* numbered three thousand and was opposed by a South African army comprising fifty-thousand whites and thirty-three thousand black Africans. South African troops were landed at Walvis Bay, while van Deventer travelled overland with five thousand horsemen. The strategic objectives were the ports and wireless stations which were speedily attained. Windhoek, the colonial capital, was captured in May 1915. The commando-style operation resembled the Boer War and was all over in six months, the Germans being outnumbered and outgunned. The German surrender in July deprived them of valuable harbours and wireless communications, and the country was thereafter administered by South Africa under a mandate until 1988. It became independent in 1990 and is now known as Namibia. By the end of the First World War South African immigrants already outnumbered German residents.

With the victory over German South West Africa under his belt, Smuts appeared the obvious choice to replace Sir Horace Smith-Dorrien as Allied commander-in-chief in German East Africa in February 1916. Although the German *Schütztruppe* there was far from being comprehensively defeated, a major part of the colony was occupied by January 1917, when Smuts handed over his command. Henceforward, Smuts was to play a role on the world stage, as a member of the Imperial War Cabinet and as a key negotiator at the Paris Peace Conference together with Botha. In a famous memorandum on the League of Nations, he spelt out the terms under which the Allied Powers were to exercise their mandates.[13]

Missionaries of Africa in Equatorial Africa

In 1914 the Missionaries of Africa served four ecclesiastical circumscriptions or vicariates apostolic in German East Africa. In the north-east, the Kingdoms of Rwanda and Burundi, together with Buha, formed the vicariate of Kivu, with a general population of some two million inhabitants, at that time half the population of the entire German colony. There were some sixty missionaries, staffing seventeen mission stations, under the veteran Alsatian Vicar Apostolic, Jean-Joseph Hirth (1854-1931), aged sixty. The people were well disposed to the Church and the vicariate claimed more than eighteen thousand baptized

Christians and eight thousand catechumens. It had about eight thousand children attending its schools.[14]

The southern half of Lake Victoria lay in German East Africa, with its lake ports of Bukoba, Mwanza and Musoma, and its islands, the largest of which was Ukerewe. The vicariate of Nyanza served the multi-chiefdom societies that inhabited these shores and islands. On the eve of the war, there were fourteen mission stations staffed by some fifty missionaries under their Dutch vicar apostolic, Joseph Sweens (1858-1950). There were more than ten thousand baptized Christians in the vicariate and between seven and eight thousand catechumens. There were around three thousand children in school.[15]

Further south lay the immense and sparsely populated vicariate of Unyanyembe, occupying the whole centre of the colony and stretching, in a narrow corridor, as far as Lake Natron and the border with British East Africa (now Kenya). In the north of the vicariate was Ushirombo, the oldest of its ten mission stations. In the south, Ndala was its most successful recent foundation. Ndala lay a short distance from Tabora town, founded by Arabs in the previous century at an intersection of trade-routes and now receiving a new lease of life from the central railway line that joined Lake Tanganyika to the coast. The Vicar-Apostolic of Unyanyembe, who resided at Tabora, was the energetic Henri Léonard (1869-1953) from Metz. He had thirty-eight missionaries and four and a half thousand baptized Christians, with half that number of catechumens plus fifteen hundred children in school.[16]

Finally, the vicariate of Tanganyika lay along the eastern shore of Lake Tanganyika, stretching westwards to the River Ruaha, and comprising the Kingdom of Ufipa and other smaller chiefdoms. It included several lake ports, the most important being that of Kigoma. Its Vicar Apostolic was the gentle and saintly Adolphe Lechaptois (1852-1917) from Laval. Between Lakes Tanganyika and Rukwa, and in the Rukwa plain to the south, the vicariate's thirteen mission stations were strategically sited to cover the whole region. Beyond Rukwa, and in the Southern Highlands, there were no Catholic mission stations, since the Germans had imposed a ban in favour of the Moravians in this area, a situation that lasted until 1922. Tanganyika vicariate had forty-eight missionaries in 1914, around twelve hundred baptized Christians and half that number of catechumens. It had some twelve thousand children in school.[17]

Surrounding the German colony on its three land borders were hostile colonies of the Allied Powers, in all but two of which the White Fathers had extensive missions.[18] Surrounding the north western shores of Lake Victoria and serving the highly populated lake kingdoms, as well as the peoples of north-eastern Congo, was the Vicariate Apostolic of Uganda under its vigorous and authoritarian bishop, Henri Streicher (1863-1952), another missionary from Alsace. Uganda claimed around one hundred and sixty thousand baptized Christians and half as many catechumens.[19] This was easily half the total of Christians in all the missionary circumscriptions of the White Fathers at that time. Its thirty-one mission stations were served by one hundred and sixteen missionaries, a number soon to be depleted by the departure of conscripts and military chaplains.[20] And there were over 21,000 children in the vicariate's schools.[21]

Across Lake Tanganyika, on its western shore, lay the vicariate of Upper Congo, stretching westwards to the Congo River (or Lualaba) and northwards to Kivu Province, bordering the kingdoms of Rwanda and Burundi. This province was the most densely inhabited region of the vicariate. The whole population of Upper Congo was reckoned to be around eight hundred thousand and in the three oldest of its twelve mission stations, a third was already baptized. Catechumens outnumbered the baptized by three to one. The vicariate was clearly set for enormous numerical expansion. There were around fifty White Fathers, led by the formidable Victor Roelens, their Flemish Vicar Apostolic. More than ten thousand children attended the vicariate's sixty or so schools.[22]

In the south, the sparsely populated Vicariate Apostolic of Bangweolo covered two thirds of Northern Rhodesia (now Zambia). It included the southern tip of Lake Tanganyika, the whole of Lake Bangweolo, and shared Lake Mweru with the Congo in the north-west. The vicariate was centred on the Bemba and related peoples of the north. In 1914 it had eight mission stations and counted eleven thousand baptized Christians, together with eighteen thousand catechumens. There were thirty Missionaries of Africa, led by their French Vicar Apostolic, Etienne Larue (1865-1935). Thirteen thousand children attended the vicariate's seven hundred schools[23]

Finally, further east lay the vicariate of Nyasa, covering roughly two-thirds of Nyasaland (now Malawi). The vicariate ran the whole length of the western shore of Lake Nyasa (Malawi) and was relatively densely populated. This is shown, for example, by its schools, which were only half the number of Bangweolo's, but which were attended by twice the number of school children. The vicariate, which focussed on the peoples of Angoniland, was more recent than Bangweolo. It had only six mission stations in 1914, with six and a half thousand baptized Christians and slightly more catechumens. However, it was clearly an area of promise, as the school numbers demonstrated. It was served by twenty-seven White Fathers and its Vicar Apostolic was the perspicacious Mathurin Guillemé (1859-1942) from Rennes.

This then was the situation of the Missionaries of Africa on the ground, as the campaign in German East Africa began. It was clear that the Society was strongly committed to the area. These territories for which it was responsible to *Propaganda Fide* were vast, and more than half of the Society's total membership (nearly four hundred and thirty missionaries out of eight hundred and forty) was actually at work in the region when war broke out. The East African campaign and its outcome would clearly affect the situation and future of the White Fathers in Africa.

Fighting on the Frontiers

Although the British showed no immediate inclination to attack German East Africa, and although the German Governor Heinrich Schnee invoked the provisions of the 1885 Congo Act to the effect that African colonies should remain neutral in the event of a European war, both sides soon became committed to an East African campaign. In this section and the next, a summary of the campaign is given, before describing in greater detail the various episodes which affected the Missionaries of Africa.[24] The first encounters took place at the German colony's frontiers on land, sea coast, lakes and rivers. The war in East Africa began on August 8th 1914, when the British cruiser *Astraea* bombarded Dar es Salaam, aiming for the German wireless station and landing a small party of Marines, who negotiated a truce with some townspeople enjoying the support of Governor Schnee. The truce was immediately repudiated by London. The Germans had earlier blocked the harbour entrance with scuttled ships, thus depriving both navies of its use as a base.

The Royal Navy's three cruisers, *Astraea*, *Hyacinth* and *Pegasus* patrolled the East African coast attempting to blockade the more formidable German cruiser *Königsberg*. The German ship slipped through the cordon and shortly afterwards *Astraea* and *Hyacinth* were recalled to the defense of the Cape. This left only *Pegasus* to confront the heavily gunned *Königsberg*. On September 19th *Königsberg* caught up with *Pegasus* in Zanzibar harbour whither she had retreated with engine trouble. In less than half an hour the British cruiser was destroyed. In the meantime two things had happened. Although the British had the greater strength on Lake Victoria, a German force supported by their gunship *Muansa*, landed at Karungu on the eastern British shore of the lake and briefly occupied Kisii on September 9th. This was a bid to attack the railhead at Kisumu. Gusii warriors joined in the battle against the British colonial forces and the Mill Hill Fathers were obliged to evacuate their mission stations at Nyabururu and Asumbi.[25] The invaders were driven off by the King's African Rifles and North Lancashire Regiment. Guns from the *Pegasus* were mounted on British lake steamers, and eventually in March 1915 the *Muansa* was scuttled by the Germans and later became an Allied supply ship. After this, British control of Lake Victoria went unchallenged.

The other event was the occupation of Taveta across the border with British East Africa (Kenya) by von Lettow-Vorbeck and the German *Schütztruppe*. From this vantage point the Germans attacked the Uganda Railway and fought an engagement at Tsavo. Their main target was Mombasa and they were within twenty-five miles of this vital port when they were halted by the British. In October a minor battle took place between the Germans and a mixed force of KAR and colonial police at Karonga, a port in Nyasaland on the northern tip of Lake Nyasa (Malawi). The Germans were driven back.

The Indian Ocean port of Tanga was crucial to the German colony's export trade, being linked by rail to the settlements and plantations of the north-east. On November 1st 1914 eight thousand troops of the North Lancashire Regiment, the KAR and the Indian Expeditionary Force, which had arrived in Mombasa in August, attempted an amphibious landing at Tanga from transports and escorts of the Royal Navy. The action was an unmitigated disaster. Major-General Arthur Edward Aitken held the overall command, and both he and the other senior officers seriously underestimated the military capacity of the *Schütztruppe*. The assault was dogged by unnecessary delays, administrative confusion, lack of intelligence and the woeful inexperience of some Indian regiments. The British were confronted by a German force of one thousand under von Lettow-Vorbeck, who had rushed to the scene and who rapidly reconnoitred the British position. With him were two companies commanded by the legendary Tom von Prince, nicknamed *Sakalani* by the Africans.[26] The invaders were routed, losing three hundred and fifty-nine dead and an almost equal number of prisoners. Total German casualties were one hundred and forty-eight, one of the dead being *Sakalani* himself.[27] In the hurried British re-embarkation that followed the battle a huge arsenal of weapons and munitions was left behind for the Germans.

It had been intended that the British, if successful at Tanga, should meet up with another force under Brigadier-General James Marshall Stewart, who was simultaneously invading the German colony across the border west of Mount Kilimanjaro. A brief, but decisive action took place at Longido and Stewart's force of one and a half thousand was easily dispersed by three German field companies and a mounted column. After the ignominy of Tanga and Longido, Aitken was relieved of his command, ordered home, and reduced to the rank of Colonel. Major-General Richard Wapshare became commander-in-chief.

Apart from immeasurably raising the morale of the German *Schütztruppe*, the Battle of Tanga had another important outcome. Lieutenant-Colonel Paul Emil von Lettow-Vorbeck (1870-1964), a newcomer to the colony, emerged as the unrivalled leader of the German forces in East Africa. Aged forty-four, he had served in the German army for a quarter of a century. Not only had he made a study of German military policy in the colonies, but he had served in South West Africa and had been wounded in the Herero uprising. A brilliant and highly imaginative commander, he inspired the utmost devotion among his *askari*, whose fighting qualities he fully appreciated. He was to be the major adversary of the Allies throughout the entire campaign, undefeated to the very end.

After the reverses of the first six months, the War Office ordered the British forces to undertake only defensive action in East Africa. This breathing space gave von Lettow the opportunity to perfect his army. However, the calm was prematurely broken in January 1915 in a skirmish at Yasini, a small coastal settlement on the German side of the border, where a British force had captured a stone fort. On January 19th the British surrendered to the besieging Germans and Wapshare received a reprimand from London. Three months later he, too was relieved of his command and was posted to Mesopotamia, his place being taken by the competent, but alcoholic, Major-General Michael Tighe. Before the change-over had taken place the Germans had started to infiltrate British East Africa again and to attack the Uganda Railway.

Lake Tanganyika was controlled by the Germans who had mounted guns on their steamers and were effectively blockading the Congo lake shore. The only Belgian ship on the lake, the unarmed *Alexandre Delcommune* was attacked by the *Hedwig von Wissmann* in August 1914. In October it was beached and then disabled by a German landing party.[28] The British-owned ships *Cecil Rhodes* and *Good News* were also sunk. From their position of strength, the German ships shelled the Congolese lakeside towns throughout the first half of 1915 and attempted to mount raids across the lake. The Congolese *Force Publique* prevented any significant disembarkation, but a bloody battle took place at Tembwe Point, between Kalemié and Moba, on March 27th. On Lake Kivu, the Germans requisitioned a motorboat from Protestant missionaries, on which they mounted a gun. With this they captured Ijwi Island and attacked the Congo border, where they were once again repulsed by a small Congolese force. Meanwhile in June, British forces from Nyasaland (Malawi) captured the important German port of Sphinxhaven (Mbamba Bay) on the western shore of Lake Nyasa, where they sank the steamer *Hermann von Wissmann*.

While the shelling of Congolese lakeside towns continued on Tanganyika in June, Lake Victoria was under overall British control and an Allied commando raid was now feasible. The War Office reluctantly authorized a foray on Bukoba town to destroy the German wireless station there. The force, composed of KAR, British troops and Indian *sepoys*, was led by Stewart. Four lake steamers ferried them across the lake and the attack took place on June 22nd. German resistance crumbled on the second day and both the German wireless station and arsenal were blown up. At the request of the commander of the Royal Fusiliers (or "Frontiersmen") Stewart imprudently gave permission to loot the town, and there followed a disgraceful orgy of violence, drunkenness and rape. Not a single household or building escaped. With all semblance of discipline gone, there was nothing more to do than re-embark.

In July, on the Northern Rhodesia (Zambia) frontier, the Germans besieged the fort of Saisi to the east of Abercorn (Mbala) at the southern tip of Lake Tanganyika. After a Belgian relief attempt the Germans raised the siege, but later in the year turned their attention northwards to the Congolese Fort of Luvungi on the River Rusizi, between Lakes Kivu and Tanganyika. Captain Schimmer and a force of irregulars made a determined attempt to capture the fort, but were beaten back by the *Force Publique*. Meanwhile, the British battleship *Goliath*, and a flotilla of smaller warships was hunting the *Königsberg* at the sea coast. The German cruiser had taken refuge in the maze of channels that formed the Rufiji River delta. It was eventually located and put out of action on July 11th. Scuttled by its captain, the *Königsberg's* guns were salvaged and thenceforward played a major role in von Lettow-Vorbeck's land battles. The crew also joined the land forces. One of the *Königsberg's* guns was placed on the *Graf von Götzen*, a large steamer assembled at Kigoma and launched in 1915, which had helped to ferry troops to Luvungi.

In the spring of 1915 the British admiralty put into operation an audacious plan to regain control of Lake Tanganyika. They did this by transporting to Africa two motor launches armed with three pounder guns. The expedition was under the command of the highly eccentric Geoffrey Spicer-Simpson. The two launches, *Mimi* and *Toutou*, were carried by rail from Cape Town to the railhead in Katanga.[29] They were then drawn by traction engines through some five hundred miles of virtually unexplored bush and over a six-thousand feet high mountain range to the Lualaba (Congo) River at Bukama. Floated down the river to Kabalo, they were then transported by narrow gauge railway to the lake at Albertville (Kalémié). In November they were launched on Lake Tanganyika.

Their surprise appearance and speed soon put paid to German superiority on the lake. By February 1916 all the German ships had been sunk, commandeered or run aground. Fatally crippled, the *Hedwig von Wissmann* was scuttled by its German captain to prevent its capture, and sank. Four Allied sea-planes bombed the *Graf von Götzen* in Kigoma harbour. This was the largest of the German steamers. It too was scuttled by the departing Germans - in the relatively shallow waters of the Malagarasi delta with a view to being raised again. It was recovered by the British in 1924 and began service as a passenger-cargo ship, the S.S. *Liemba*.[30]

At the beginning of 1916, General Tighe was ordered to India. His replacement, Sir Horace Smith-Dorrien resigned because of illness, before taking up his command, and the stage was set for Lieutenant-General Jan C. Smuts to become commander-in-chief. Following his victory in German South West Africa, he arrived at Mombasa on February 19th. Van Deventer and the South African Expeditionary Force landed in March. A new and decisive chapter was about to open in the East African Campaign.

Invasion and Evasion

The appointment of Smuts broke the stalemate in East Africa, allowing the Allied invasion of the German colony to begin in earnest. However, Smuts' commando experience in the Boer War was largely irrelevant in East Africa, and according to Richard Meinertzhagen, he was an indifferent general.[31]

Moreover, his appointment of South African commanders seemed to be turning the campaign into a "family affair". He and the South Africans had no idea of the climatic, health and supply problems that faced them. "Steely and humourless", Smuts provided the co-ordination that was hitherto lacking, but ultimately aimed to manoeuvre rather than fight.

Smuts targeted the north eastern region where German settlement and commercial interests were concentrated, carrying out a two-pronged attack from British East Africa on either side of Mount Kilimanjaro. The Germans withdrew as the Allies invaded. Smuts knew that the Germans would seek to avoid an open battle. On the other hand, he could not himself risk engagements that would cost large numbers of casualties and make him unpopular at home. His tactics were to attempt to encircle the enemy and inflict a swift defeat. To his continual frustration, the *Schütztruppe* slipped through the net each time. It was not difficult to occupy territory vacated by a retreating army, but to take complete control of the country, the enemy had to be defeated. As long as they refused to make a stand, defeat was impossible. Rapid advance was also hampered by problems of supply. On the other hand, the Allied commanders came to admire von Lettow and there is an oral tradition in Central Africa that they did not really want to defeat him, let alone be sent to the Western Front after doing so.[32]

Von Lettow exercised his very considerable skills to avoid a confrontation. He knew that the German colonial forces were outnumbered and that he would not be able to save the colony through military action. However, he intended to keep the German imperial flag flying somewhere as a basis for negotiation when the war was over. His aim was also to pin down the Allies in East Africa and prevent them from reinforcing the European fronts – possibly even forcing them to divert troops from Europe to Africa. He was not fighting a guerilla war in the strict sense. His strategy was not one of lightning raids on Allied troops and installations, so much as one of unrelenting withdrawal, drawing the enemy on to ground of his own choosing, where he could inflict maximum damage from prepared positions. Here, as in Europe, the machine-gun came into its own as a weapon of defence.

Although Smuts was soon able to link the Uganda railway with the (German) northern railway, the latter was repeatedly sabotaged by the Germans after they had made use of it. Smuts' army was moving further and further away from its supply base in British East Africa, whereas von Lettow was continually moving into German settlements and plantations that could supply his army. The German colony was unfamiliar terrain for the British, who had virtually no maps, whereas von Lettow and his *askari* knew the topography well. The vastness of the country and the interminable bush made the campaign "a huge night operation".[33] There were no motorable roads and in the south no railway system. Indigenous Africans in the north did not necessarily welcome the Allied incursion, but waited cautiously for the outcome of the conflict. In the south, however, the tribes were less well disposed towards the Germans, especially the Hehe whose resistance in the 1890s had been overcome with difficulty and who had old scores to settle.[34]

Initially Smuts was hampered by the incompetence and exaggerated caution of his commanders. In early March an indecisive action took place at Latema Nek, but on the 14th, van Deventer entered Moshi town. Three days later, Smuts' forces advanced on Kahe Station, fifteen miles south of Moshi. Here the Germans occupied a strong defensive position, from which they launched a series of assaults, supported by a heavy gun from the Königsberg. Serious casualties were suffered on both sides, before the *Schütztruppe* escaped encirclement at the last moment.

In early April a German company surrendered to van Deventer's troops in an action at Lolkisale Hill, the *Schütztruppe*'s first clear defeat. Van Deventer then pushed down to Kondoa Irangi in the direction of the central railway line. Von Lettow chose to defend the rail link with the colony's war time capital, Tabora, and sent fifteen field companies to Kondoa Irangi. On May 9th a fierce engagement took place in which German artillery bombarded the Allies and German bayonet charges developed into a hand-to-hand battle. South African sharp-shooting eventually won the day and the Germans suffered a tactical setback. Meanwhile, Smuts' eastern division continued to push down the northern railway line, taking Handeni on June 19th.

The division was brought up short at Kangata twenty miles to the south, where it walked straight into a German trap. After inflicting terrifying slaughter on a South African brigade, the Germans once again dispersed rapidly. At the end of June, a flying column forced a German retreat from a bridgehead on the Lukigira River, and both Dodoma and Tanga were taken in the first days of July. Kilosa fell at the end of August and von Lettow abandoned Morogoro on

August 26th in order to keep his force intact. By September, the coastal towns of Bagamoyo, Dar es Salaam and Kilwa were all in Allied hands. Von Lettow made another stand at Kisaki on the Mgeta River, south of Morogoro, and withdrew yet again after a hard fought engagement. From this point the Allies' southwards push petered out.

Rwanda's frontier with the Belgian Congo consisted of Lake Kivu, with its Island of Ijwi and the towns of Gisenyi and Shangugu to the north and south of the lake. Burundi's western border followed the Rusizi River which connected Lake Kivu to Lake Tanganyika in the south. The town of Bujumbura lay near the northern tip of Tanganyika near the Rusizi Delta. As control of Lake Tanganyika was gradually wrested from the Germans towards the end of 1915, General Tombeur's *Force Publique* began to press harder on these borders, attacking the towns of Gisenyi, Shangugu and Bujumbura. Eventually in May 1916 a full-blown Belgian invasion began. The "fiercely competent" Captain Max Wintgens, the German Resident in Rwanda, commanded a small force of a thousand *askari* and a hundred white officers. He was opposed by a force of eleven thousand and fully realized that his only course would be a strategic withdrawal to Tabora. However, he took advantage of Tombeur's slow build-up of reinforcements and supplies to offer what resistance he could. Further south, in Kigoma and Ujiji, Kurt Wahle, the retired general who had been pressed into service when the war interrupted his holiday visit to the colony, disposed of some two thousand troops.

The Belgians captured Shangugu and the Rusizi Delta, fanning out into three columns. Ijwi Island was taken and the Germans fell back on Kigali, the Rwandan capital, occupied by the Belgians on May 8th. In June the column led by Lieutenant Philippe Molitor (1869-1952) took Bujumbura and in the following month, Gisenyi. Fearing he would be cut off from Wahle, Wintgens was forced to evacuate Kigali. Tombeur had captured Rwanda and Burundi almost without a fight.

The centre column moved westwards into Kagera District on the south western shore of Lake Victoria, while the Molitor column moved on to Biharamulo and Ushirombo and the Olsen brigade went south to Kigoma on Lake Tanganyika's eastern shore. Also in July, the South African Brigadier-General, Sir Charles Crewe, began operations on the German shores of Lake Victoria. From Uganda his "Lakeforce" occupied Bukoba, Ukerewe Island and Mwanza, the last being evacuated by the Germans before he arrived. Bukoba and Mwanza were the two most important German ports on the lake. All the German forces from the north-east, representing slightly less than half the *Schütztruppe*, now converged on Tabora.

According to an agreed plan, Tombeur and Crewe were supposed to combine for the assault on Tabora. However, the Belgians had the ill-concealed ambition of adding the whole of their conquests between Tabora and the lakes to their Congo colony, and they won the race to Tabora.[35] The siege lasted ten days, with some of the fiercest fighting at Itaga to the north-east of the town. The battle of Itaga took place on September 13th and 14th 1916. Taken by the Belgians, it was re-taken by the Germans, before being captured again under heavy bombardment. An eyewitness described the hill as being strewn with corpses. The troops then closed in to find Tabora town abandoned. General Kurt Wahle, and Captain Max Wintgens had struck out in a south-easterly direction to join forces with von Lettow in Mahenge. Tombeur entered Tabora on September 18th and Crewe arrived shortly afterwards to offer his congratulations, before disbanding his Lakeforce in Uganda. German prisoners, taken in the town, were given humiliating tasks, such as street sweeping, cleaning latrines and shoveling manure.[36]

The Belgians continued to administer their conquests until 1919, when the Paris Peace Conference decided they could retain Rwanda and Burundi, but surrender the eastern shore of Lake Tanganyika to Britain. Sir Horace Byatt, who headed the British colonial administration from 1917 to 1924, conducted a take-over ceremony at Kigoma in 1921.[37] All the White Father vicariates in former German East Africa lay in the Belgian sphere for the remainder of the war. At Karema the Belgians set up a military hospital in which the renowned doctor-catechist Adrian Atiman also practised. Such was the impression he made on the Belgian medical authorities that he was decorated by them after the war.[38]

Nyasaland and Northern Rhodesia were unprepared for war in 1914. Moreover, British control was tenuous along the border regions of these colonies. Only a scorched-earth policy deterred serious German incursions. The British commander, Brigadier-General Edward Northey had not only to build up an establishment but also to overcome horrendous communications and supply problems over a vast, but thinly inhabited region. By May 1916, however, he was leading four columns, totalling two thousand five hundred men, from Nyasaland and Northern Rhodesia into German East Africa. These swiftly occupied the major German posts on the southern border and by forced marches penetrated two hundred miles into enemy territory in the direction of Iringa and the Kilombero Valley west of Mahenge. On the road to Iringa Northey encountered and overcame German resistance near the village of Malangali. On August 29th he entered Iringa town, abandoned by its garrison. He then had to face Wahle and his three columns as they swept south-east from Tabora. Iringa was besieged by Wahle and then relieved by elements of van Deventer's division from the central railway. The column led by Wintgens proceeded to attack Northey's supply depot at Lupembe, a village at the head of the Kilombero Valley. A five-day battle took place that included bayonet charges and sustained machine-gunfire, while Wahle's main force passed by at a distance. Wintgens was repulsed with heavy casualties. At the end of November a British column was able to cut off Wahle's rearguard and force its surrender. The Germans lost a heavy gun and more than two hundred prisoners, including a senior commander and six other officers. The remnant managed to slip away to Mahenge.

Von Lettow now veered towards the sea coast, followed by the British who captured the German Fort of Kibata north of Kilwa. In December 1916 von Lettow attacked Kibata and the surrounding British trenches with heavy artillery and machine gun-fire. The battle resembled the Western Front in more ways than one, and was distinguished by a counter-offensive led by the Gold Coast Regiment and by the first use of Mills grenades in East Africa. There were heavy casualties on both sides. Although the Germans continued their withdrawal south of the Rufiji River, the British were in no position to follow up their advantage immediately.[39]

Von Lettow's Endgame

In January 1917 the campaign entered a new phase with the departure of Smuts. His invitation to join the imperial war conference in London was a heaven-sent opportunity for him to withdraw from an impossible situation. His outflanking manoeuvres had failed to bring about von Lettow's defeat and the large numbers of South Africans invalided home were contributing to his growing unpopularity there. On the other hand, the fact that most of the German colony was now in Allied hands allowed him to claim that victory had already been achieved.

Major-General Reginald Hoskins replaced him in the East African command. He had the unenviable task of winding up Smuts' hopeless offensive, while Smuts himself in London proclaimed that the war was over. Partly as a result of Smuts' propaganda Hoskins was unfairly recalled in March and his place taken, on Smuts' recommendation, by van Deventer at the end of May. Smuts had already built up the KAR to a strength of eight thousand and Hoskins speeded up the regiment's expansion into twenty battalions. This was partly necessitated by the exodus of white troops and Indian units many of which were invalided home. It was also slowly dawning on the leadership that African *askari* were much more suitable for this kind of warfare than Europeans, South Africans and Indians, who were unused to the terrain and who more easily succumbed to tropical disease. To the surprise of many, especially the South Africans, the African soldiers were also proving themselves to be competent fighters. In addition to the KAR and the Gold Coast Regiment, five thousand Nigerian volunteers joined the Allies in East Africa at the end of 1916.

The Germans had now abandoned more than two thirds of the country. The undefeated von Lettow-Vorbeck concentrated on the coastal region of the south-east, with a small contingent of a thousand whites and some seven thousand *askari*. With him were Wahle and the unfortunate colonial governor, Heinrich Schnee. In the final end-game, von Lettow's genius came into its own and he grew to be a respected and even a legendary adversary for the Allies. He has been compared to Rommel in the Second World War.[40] His talent for improvisation and self-sufficiency knew no bounds. Not only did he live off the farms and plantations he traversed, but he harvested all that was edible in forest and bush. As a mycologist, he possessed expert knowledge of edible fungi. He also developed his own herbal medicines. He baked home-made bread on the march and manufactured soap, candles, cigarettes and even petrol. He hunted for bush meat and drove his own herd of domestic cattle. He also manufactured army boots and sewed uniforms. When malaria medicine was no longer available, he manufactured his own quinine, by boiling the Peruvian *chinchona* bark, and producing a foul-tasting liquid known as "Lettow Schnapps".

The health of his *askari* was comparatively better than that of the Allied troops and their diet of local food was healthier. A form of "natural selection" was practised in which only the fittest soldiers were retained. Thirteen doctors travelled in his column and the seriously sick and wounded were left behind in a series of *ad hoc* hospitals, each with a doctor, to be picked up by the British. There was also a camp following of African women who cared for the menfolk and more than eight hundred were with him when the war ended. Several had given birth on the march, rejoining the column within hours.

Earlier, von Lettow had even managed to obtain military supplies from two blockade-running cargo ships. The *Rubens* was sunk north of Tanga in 1915, but a large proportion of the armaments and supplies she carried was salvaged by the Germans. The *Marie* arrived in Sudi Bay in March 1916 and 50,000 porter loads of supplies were taken from her and carried up to the central railway in three weeks. Through all these contrivances von Lettow maintained an effective fighting force, enjoying unfailing mobility.

Nevertheless, there was a darker side to von Lettow's improvisation. He left behind him a path of destruction: ransacked fields and stores, empty, plundered villages and starving people. More than three hundred thousand people died of famine in the former German colony before the end of 1917, a twentieth of the total population. African interests were subordinated to those of Germany. It was exploitation on a massive scale. Although von Lettow's genius was to recognize and make use of his askari's experience of bush war, and although he inspired loyalty in them, he practised a harsh discipline. The hippo hide whip was in continual use for every kind of misdemeanour. Fifteen lashes were administered for disobedience and twenty-five for lying.[41]

In March 1917 Max Wintgens, who headed one of Wahle's columns struck north on his own, taking with him five hundred men, thirteen machine guns and three field guns. He did this on his own initiative and without authorization. Von Lettow's view of this manoeuvre was ambiguous. It was a dazzling exploit, but one which was unlikely to achieve much in isolation from von Lettow's own force. Nevertheless, Wintgens' dash northwards across the Rungwa River towards Tabora inspired fear and uncertainty in the minds of the Allies who believed their northern conquests to be secure. As British troops gave chase in the rear or tried to head him off from the front, Wintgens' adventure caused a major disorganization. On May 21st, however, Wintgens surrendered to the British, having become seriously ill with typhus at Kitunda in northern Ukimbu and being in need of proper medical treatment. Before his surrender, he handed over the column to Captain Heinrich Naumann.

Naumann, a ruthless "psychopath", crossed the central railway line and captured Singida town without firing a shot. He then laid siege to the British occupied fort of Mkalama some fifty miles to the north. An Allied relief party forced him to lift the siege and he turned west towards the northern railway and the town of Moshi after easily capturing the small fort at Ikoma. One of his raiding parties managed to strike at Kahe station, burn military stores and capture three British officers. By this time, however, momentum had been lost. Naumann had been obliged to disperse his column into a number of independent units. Most of these were captured and Naumann himself surrendered on October 2nd. He was tried in Britain for the murder of Lieutenant Sutherland at Ikoma and for cruelty to native women. His death sentence was commuted to a seven year prison term, but he was deported to Germany in the year after the war.

In July 1917 another pitched battle with von Lettow took place at Narungombe, forty miles southwest of Kilwa. It was a hard fought engagement in which the British enjoyed the advantage of mortars, a weapon the Germans did not possess. From October 15th to 18th von Lettow fought his last set-piece battle at Mahiwa-Nyangao, west of Mtwara. It was the most savagely fought engagement of the entire campaign, "an equatorial Gettysburg".[42] Although he claimed victory, and although his casualties were a fraction of those sustained by the Allies, he had no reserves to fill the gaps. After blowing up his last Königsberg gun, von Lettow retreated across the Ruvuma River into Portuguese East Africa (Mozambique).

In November 1917 the attempt was made to bring supplies to the beleaguered German column by air. The Zeppelin, a naval L.59 airship, left Jamboli in Bulgaria with fifteen tons of arms, ammunition and stores. After a difficult crossing of the Mediterranean, the airship set course for the two thousand mile flight across Africa to the Makonde plateau. Over Khartoum a wireless message was received ordering the mission to be abandoned. It was afterwards rumoured that this was a piece of British disinformation. In any case, the Zeppelin flew back into furious gales that necessitated the jettisoning of half her cargo. She returned to her airport of origin, after a record-breaking flight lasting more than four days and covering more than four thousand miles.

Von Lettow had hoped to be joined by a thousand-man detachment under Captain Theodor Tafel. However, with his troops near to starvation, Tafel was forced to cross back into the former German colony and surrender to Northey. Portuguese resistance proved ineffective and their contribution to the campaign a liability to the Allies. Von Lettow continued south in 1918, after capturing a Portuguese camp. He now became a genuine guerilla, giving more importance to mobility than striking power. He fought to feed his troops, attacking Portuguese camps and other sources of supply.[43] Dividing his force into smaller foraging groups, he raided Portuguese supply depots. At Namacurra he captured quantities of weapons, ammunition, fresh uniforms and hundreds of tons of food. In June Northey left to become Governor of British East Africa. Meanwhile, van Deventer, who had reluctantly entered Mozambique to stiffen the Portuguese resistance, suspected that the Schütztruppe was about to threaten the port of Quelimane. But after routing a British detachment at the Namirrue River, von Lettow turned sharply west towards Lake Nyasa and once more slipped away from the Allied forces.

During August the Germans pushed northwards along the eastern shore of Lake Nyasa, engaging in inconclusive skirmishes with the KAR along the way. Before re-crossing the Ruvuma on September 28th, von Lettow discarded his sick and wounded, including General Kurt Wahle, who was now aged sixty-four and was suffering from a double hernia and malaria. Back in his former colony, the German commander rounded the northern tip of Lake Nyasa and unexpectedly crossed south into Northern Rhodesia (Zambia), striking at the Allies' weakest point. It would have been difficult to find supplies, had he remained in the former German colony, as the British expected him to do. Also he would have suffered more desertions by *askari* and carriers in their homeland. After pillaging several missions for supplies and especially hospital stores, he occupied the town of Kasama on November 12th. The following day, a British motorcyclist was intercepted near the town with dispatches that announced that an Armistice had taken place in Europe on November 11th. Before obeying the order to give himself up at Abercorn, von Lettow sent a telegram to Berlin on November 14th. No reply was forthcoming. There was nothing for it but to surrender to Brigadier-General W. Edwards. The formal ceremony took place at Abercorn on November 25th. [44] The War Office decreed that the German officers' swords should be restored to them in a ceremonial parade "in recognition of their gallant efforts".[45] Von Lettow travelled by Lake Steamer to Kigoma and by train to Dar es Salaam, where he took ship for Rotterdam. He was given a triumphal reception in Berlin.

Von Lettow's achievement was to have successfully contained for four years an army of at least one hundred and thirty thousand. The campaign had cost Britain seventy-two million pounds, quite apart from the costs incurred by Belgium and Portugal. Whereas the German *Schütztruppe* had lost two thousand five hundred men through death and disease, the Allies had lost around fourteen thousand, more than five times the number of the German dead. The proportion of deaths to wounded and prisoners was much higher in East Africa than in the other fronts of the First World War.[46]

War in the White Father Vicariates

The war in East Africa was felt both indirectly and directly by the White Father vicariates. The first side-effect of the campaign was the blockade of goods and information experienced by the missionaries in German East Africa and Upper Congo. A few messages from Bishops got through to Algiers, but on the whole there was a "black-out" during 1915 and most of 1916. When fighting started in the Kivu Vicariate, the Germans forbade the White Fathers to correspond with their confreres in Bukoba under pain of death.[47] Missionaries in East Africa had little idea of the progress of the war in Europe, or even of who was fighting whom. Confused French missionaries, relying on local German newspapers, were at first unsure whether Britain was an ally or an enemy.[48] In many ways the mission stations were self-sufficient, but some essentials had to be imported and the war made this impossible. Altarbreads, Mass wine and candles, needed for liturgical celebration, had to be rationed, but it was remarkable that supplies never failed completely, and that mission stations could supply each other. In some Burundi missions Mass was only celebrated on Sundays and no more than a teaspoonful of wine was allowed. Bishop Streicher sent a crate of Mass wine from Uganda after the departure of the Germans.[49]

Hardest hit at the beginning of the war was Upper Congo. Until the blockade of Lake Tanganyika, the normal way of travelling the length of the diocese was by boat. When the newly appointed military chaplain, Augustin Dumortier (1878-1951), reported to his unit in Kivu Province, he had to travel overland by bicycle and had a narrow escape from German shells on the lakeside in Uvira.[50] During the blockade there was no transport or sale of goods in the vicariate. After the Belgian invasion of Rwanda-Burundi, it was possible to obtain supplies from Uganda and Pierre Colle (1872-1961) was sent to Kampala in 1916 for the purpose. Especially necessary were cloth and beads for paying the mission workers. He found that some goods destined for the vicariate had been detained at Bukoba, and engaged two hundred and twenty-five porters in western Uganda to carry loads back to Upper Congo.[51]

The lakeside missions of Upper Congo were the first to suffer when the shelling started on Lake Tanganyika. The old fort on to which the Missionaries of Africa had built their church and station at Mpala was due for demolition, but this had been prevented by the war. Instead, it was requisitioned by Belgian artillery and machine gunners of the *Force Publique*. Early on January 7th 1915 a German steamer appeared on the horizon. The missionaries knew it would take an hour to get within range and so there was time to evacuate everyone. The Blessed Sacrament was transferred to the basement and everyone took refuge in the hills behind the mission. Two priests took care of the children and the sick. The steamer's two guns fired on the fort without inflicting any damage and not a single roof tile of the mission was broken. The Belgian artillery responded vigorously and the German ship retired before any disembarkation could take place. A solemn promise was made by the White Fathers that a Lourdes Grotto would be erected in the square after the war, if the mission was preserved by the Blessed Virgin. The promise was fulfilled.[52]

Katana Mission lay on the south-western shore of Lake Kivu, opposite the German occupied Island of Ijwi. On the morning of October 27th 1914 Belgian troops, installed at the mission, fired on an approaching German flotilla and drove it away in disorder. The Germans returned on January 9th 1915, with their newly acquired (Protestant) gunboat, and sprayed the mission with machine gun-fire. The Belgian troops returned fire and the gunboat withdrew. Ten days later the gunboat returned and opened fire once more. This time the defending garrison had been increased to fifty soldiers and strengthened by a field-gun battery. One Belgian shell was enough to ensure the gunboat's withdrawal.[53] Meanwhile, the *Force Publique* built up its reserves on the border. A hundred *askari* and four white officers were billeted on Katana mission for a year.[54] The mission of Nya Gesi had to give hospitality to six thousand *askari* and a hundred officers.[55]

The White Fathers' mission suffered when the British raid on Bukoba took place on June 22nd 1915. During the bombardment that preceded the landing, a shell pierced the church roof and exploded on the Bishop's *prie-dieu*. Bishop Joseph Sweens had been reciting his breviary on the spot moments before, and was coming out of the church when the shell struck. The British apologized afterwards to the Bishop for the damage to the church, giving the excuse that they were aiming at a German gun that had been installed in the mission compound. Local Africans continued the pillage of the town after the British re-embarked.[56]

Smuts' and van Deventer's big "push" southwards from Kilimanjaro in 1916 only affected the extreme north-east of a White Father vicariate, Unyanyembe. At Iraku Mission, near Mbulu, the Missionaries of Africa were caught in the ebb and flow of war. On May 11th van Deventer's column occupied Mbulu Fort on its way to Kondoa Irangi, and the missionaries dutifully went to swear allegiance to King George V. In spite of attempts by the officers to control them, the British troops pillaged the mission. Bands of Germans re-appeared and engaged with the invaders, leading to the accusation that the White Fathers were helping and welcoming the Germans. On June 8th the missionaries were ordered out of Iraku and sent to the Spiritan mission of Ufiomi, east of Mbulu. They were allowed to move around within a two-mile radius and send people to keep an eye on their abandoned station. During this time they ministered to *askari* from Uganda and British East Africa (Kenya), as well as to Christian South African, Mauritian and Indian soldiers. At length, on September 19th 1916 they were allowed back to Iraku and found their stores and barns empty and their fields cleaned out. Many of their schools had been broken into and local people feared to associate with them. A small core of Christians, however, remained faithful and the Catholic commander of Mbulu Fort gave some help. All the Spiritan missionaries from the neighbouring missions of the Kilimanjaro Vicariate had been removed and the White Fathers found themselves extending their ministry eastwards to Ufiomi and Mbugwe.[57]

Turu Mission Station near Singida town fared worse. The British took Singida on August 21st and a week later the missionaries were ordered to go to Kondoa Irangi. Four German and Dutch White Fathers from Turu were then taken by car to Nairobi for internment, but two French missionaries, liberated by the British from their German imprisonment in Tabora, were eventually allowed back to Turu in December. In the meantime Captain Hutchins at Singida had kept an eye on the mission and even reimbursed the fathers for anything that had been stolen. Pillage had been avoided.[58]

The Vicariate Apostolic of Kivu (Rwanda and Burundi) was more heavily populated and its mission stations were closer to one another than was the case in other vicariates. The Belgian invasions of April-May 1916 had a devastating impact that was both complex and far-reaching. To give a coherent account of what happened is far from easy.[59] The mission stations were, of course, not only a focus for the worship and instruction of a Christian community. They were also important centres of human and socio-economic development in their own right. Many of them were requisitioned in turn by the opposing armies.[60] In Burundi, the missions of Buhonga and Kanyinya were occupied twice by both armies. Requisitioned mission stations lost practically everything: cattle, donkeys, saddles, tools, wood, furnishings, medical appliances. Occasionally, the Germans paid for the losses in bank-notes that were soon to become worthless. In some cases, missionaries of "belligerent" nationalities were ordered to leave their stations, but some were allowed to stay or were able to return later. Those of Buhonga in particular were sent to Bujumbura and from thence to Kigoma and Tabora. Some mission stations became battle grounds and several were abandoned to pillage and plunder. In general, the north of the vicariate fared better than the south, since the Germans had to avoid being bottled up there. Consequently, the fighting tended to move south. Before the invasion, the Vicar Apostolic, John-Joseph Hirth, who was in poor health and had failing eyesight, was moved out of Nyundo to Kabgayi and then to Save.[61]

The *Force Publique* began its invasion of Burundi in April 1916, crossing the Rusizi River south of Lake Kivu. With them went the White Father novice, Charles Raes who had been conscripted into the Belgian Army and was posted to the Congo.[62] He witnessed the capture of Shangugu in May and the burning of Bujumbura by the departing Germans in the following month. Mibirisi Mission lay to the south of Shangugu and Belgian troops from the direction of Bujumbura reached it on April 21st. They arrived before it had been vacated by the Germans and before the missionaries had had time to get away. A battle developed, in which, as we have already seen, Brother Fulgence Mechau was killed. After the Germans withdrew, the Belgians occupied the mission buildings and the missionaries were put into nearby grass huts.

In Rwanda, although the *Schütztruppe* was not numerous enough to resist the Belgian invasion, Max Wintgens, the German resident, was determined that the Kingdom should be strongly defended. He was also determined to maintain a security black-out and forbade the Missionaries of Africa to communicate with the enemy (their confreres of Upper Congo) under pain of death. At the beginning, he allowed missionaries of "belligerent nations" to remain in their stations, giving his opinion that the war would be over in three months. Later, three missionaries of the vicariate fell under suspicion and had a short internment at Tabora. When Italy declared war on Austria, Italian missionaries were reclassified as "belligerent". Threatened at first with internment at Tabora, they were allowed to stay in up-country missions away from the frontier.[63]

The White Fathers saw Wintgens as "ardent, energetic, courageous, upright but severe".[64] In spite of these qualities, he could only retreat to a fortified hill overlooking Lake Kivu, as the Congolese army swung round the northern end of the lake at the beginning of May, capturing and burning the town of Gisenyi. The first mission station in the path of the advancing *Force Publique* was Nyundo. The Germans occupied the mission, while the White Fathers retired to the forest of Kandamira. The Congolese reopened the offensive in the night of May 10th and the opposing forces occupied positions in the hills around the mission. At length, Wintgens evacuated the whole district of Bugoyi in order to avoid encirclement and ordered the German superior, François Knoll (1880-1951) to go south with him to Murunda. The other two missionaries left the forest and crept back to Nyundo under a hail of bullets and shells. Two days later the Belgians arrived at Nyundo. The Germans had used the church as a barrack-room, magazine and kitchen, while the mission house was turned into a blockhouse. The White Fathers were lucky that the mission was not destroyed and that the Belgians did not bombard it. Only two shells struck the church and slightly damaged the *façade*. The Belgians, however, occupied half the parish territory and the missionaries were prevented from setting foot there for a year. The Catholic population was thus effectively halved.

At Murunda Mission Wintgens once again requisitioned the church as a billet for his soldiers, sending the missionaries away from the station one day ahead of himself. Two days after the Germans' departure the Belgians arrived, flushed with their victory at Shangugu. In the interim, the mission was pillaged by local people and many cows were taken. Hundreds of planks had been burnt for fuel by the Germans. The Belgians ordered the return of the stolen cattle, but the effects of the war in Nyundo and Murunda were dire for both missionaries and their people. Famine spread, as people were uprooted from their farms, while soldiers and carriers pillaged the fields. People took refuge in the forests, eating grasses and roots. Brigandage of all kinds increased, chiefly cattle rustling and food theft. Many were ready to commit murder to obtain food. Some priests went so far as to sell their personal chalices in order to buy food for the starving. At Nyundo, the White Fathers estimated that half the Christian population – two thousand in all – had died in the fighting and its aftermath.

The invading Belgians were surprised to find missionaries of belligerent and neutral nationalities still at their posts, and suspected that this was because they had collaborated with the Germans. The anti-clerical Belgian governor of Bujumbura even deported three White Fathers to the Congo, where they were held at Mpala Mission until May 1918.[65]

Nyanza suffered more than the other vicariates from the forced closure of missions and the expulsion of French missionaries by the Germans. More than thirty priests, brothers and sisters were sent to be interned, with others from Kivu, at Ushirombo in neighbouring Unyanyembe. Several mission stations and even a leprosarium had to be abandoned.[66] Everywhere, there was a lack of medicines, clothes and shoes. At Ushirombo there was no new intake to the seminary and it was possible to give each internee a room. The unwilling visitors whiled away the time, going for walks and making retreats. The occupation of Mwanza and Bukoba by the British Lake Force in July 1916 was virtually painless, since the Germans had already departed. There was, however, a touching story connected with this action. At Bukumbi, Equatorial Africa's oldest mission station near Mwanza, an African servant was acting as caretaker at a nearby German house, vacated by its owner. Masai irregulars of the Lake Force broke in and were about to shoot the servant when a KAR *askari* from Uganda intervened, shouting: "He is wearing a rosary! He is a Christian! Don't shoot him!" The caretaker's life was saved.[67]

In Unyanyembe, although troops from both sides ravaged the countryside, the actual fighting was focused on Tabora, the interim colonial capital, and it was there that most of the missionaries were concentrated either as refugees or internees. The latter spent their time in prayer, study, growing cabbages, practising bicycle-riding and giving retreats to sisters.[68] The Tabora Mission Diary provides a picture of events and conditions inside the besieged city.[69] In early July the missionaries had already been told that the town would not be defended, if it was attacked. Towards the end of the month it was learned that the missionaries at Ushirombo had been ordered to go to Tabora and on July

24th twenty priests arrived. Eleven were given bed space in the school class-rooms. Four days later the White Fathers of Ndala Mission were ordered to Tabora and General Wahle and his column were expected the following day. In the event, it was the worn out Captain Wintgens who arrived with his troops and who immediately took a train to the east, where he joined Wahle.

On September 9th a "Surrender Council" took place at the Catholic Mission, which had for some time been requisitioned as the interim Government House. Monsignor Henri Léonard, the Vicar Apostolic acted as interpreter. Gunfire became more and more distinct during the following three days and the remaining German troops prepared their withdrawal. For this purpose they commandeered all the mission bicycles. On the 13th it was learned that the Belgians had suffered a reverse at Itaga, but gunfire sounded all night on the 14th. More German troops withdrew, but the peace negotiations were postponed.

Meanwhile, the two remaining White Fathers at Itaga Mission witnessed the moonlight battle of September 13th and 14th.[70] The Alsatian superior, Charles Grün (1873-1928) believed he was under cover, when a bullet grazed his face and flattened itself against a wall beside him. Although one hundred and fifty shells fell all around the mission, it was not hit. As the battle swept over Itaga hill towards the town, Grün and his Italian confrere, Alessandro Isola (1887-1958), took refuge with a party of Christians in the church. During the twenty-four hours they spent there they prayed for deliverance and made a vow to Saint Anthony, their patron, promising a procession in his honour. As there was nothing to eat or drink in the church, they imitated David, who ate the loaves of proposition in the Holy of Holies, by drinking holy water.[71] When the firing died down, Isola made his way to Tabora and Grün remained behind with the wounded.

Revictualling the retreating troops took place in Tabora on September 17th and the missionaries finally saw the last of the Germans on the following day. On the 19th Léonard and six White Fathers left the town in three groups, taking different directions to bring the surrender to the Belgians. On the same day, the victorious troops made their solemn entry, with band playing and colours flying. They halted outside the mission where the new administration was installed. Because of the evil reputation of the *Force Publique* and its predilection for looting and pillaging, the welcome was not as warm as it might otherwise have been. However, it was a day of liberation for the missionary internees. A sad postscript to the conquest of Tabora was the death of the doctor-catechist Augustine Mechire. He had been serving in a German medical unit and was shot in Ugunda south of the town by a Belgian patrol.[72]

The Vicariate Apostolic of Tanganyika did not have the restricted area and concentrated population of Kivu, but in many ways its war experience was similar: the alternating visits of German and Allied troops, deportation of missionaries and pillaging of mission stations. The Calvary of Tanganyika, however, was more long drawn out, lasting from the middle of 1916 almost to the last weeks of the war. General Northey began his invasion of the German colony on May 24th 1916, attacking the German border forts. These were strong and well positioned but could offer no serious resistance to the British forces from Northern Rhodesia (Zambia). As we have seen, Northey's columns were accompanied by four Missionaries of Africa, acting as chaplains and transport officers. Two of these, Joseph Mazé and Ernest Paradis were present at the three-day siege of Mwembe and the capture of Langenburg. From Rungwe, Mazé was able to visit the most south-easterly mission station of Tanganyika vicariate, Galula where the Fathers had begged for cloth and medicines. These were sent to them from Langenburg. Mazé learned at Galula that the Germans were everywhere on the run, abandoned by their porters and irregulars, the *ruga-ruga*. Ernest Paradis and Wilfrid Sarrazin took part in the battle of Lupembe in November, baptizing scores of soldier-catechumens in the trenches and bringing Holy Communion to Christians before the battle. Paradis described his work as "speaking of God, reinforcing morale and explaining the orders of the officers". During an armistice arranged by the Red Cross at Lupembe, Paradis was taken blindfolded to the German positions to bring the last sacraments to dying *Schütztruppen*. Posted to Njombe, Paradis and Sarrazin celebrated Mass for whites and blacks in the British column, hearing seven hundred confessions and distributing a thousand communions. Northey's ADC turned out to be a Catholic and invited them to celebrate Mass in his apartments. Paradis's comment was: "The *entente cordiale* really means something!"[73]

In Tanganyika vicariate the Germans made long range preparations before the invasion. Already in October 1914, French or neutral personnel in the lakeside missions of Karema, Kirando and Utinta were ordered to Kigoma and Tabora. Those in the other stations were to be regrouped inland by the commandant at Bismarckburg (Kasanga). Bishop Adolphe Lechaptois, the Vicar Apostolic happened to be at the inland station of Urirwa when the order was given and thus escaped deportation. Since the southern frontier was defended by only one German company, it was clear that they would have to retreat before the British when they came. The missionaries were ordered to precede them, evacuating the mission stations and destroying herds and crops as they went. Faced with the "complete ruin of all our stations", Lechaptois obtained a counter-order from General Wahle with the help of Monsignor Léonard in Tabora. As things turned out, there was a partial occupation by both British and German forces over a period of three months, with the missionaries' neutrality suspected now by one side, now by the other. Boats were destroyed and herds taken in four mission stations. Karema, the seat of the Bishop, lost four hundred animals and the mission's best boat.[74]

The ups and downs of Mwazye Mission, one of those nearest the southern border, illustrate what the missionaries had to go through. In early April 1915 German soldiers issued a proclamation threatening death to anyone who would help the British when they came. On April 13th the mission was designated a field hospital. On April 24th a German patrol appeared in the village pursued by a British patrol. Later, the Germans returned, saying they had repulsed the enemy and the dead body of a British soldier was found. On the following day, a wounded German soldier was brought for treatment and more wounded Germans came two days later. On April 28th and 29th successive German columns camped at the mission, and there were more German military comings and goings throughout May. On June 6th the British were rumoured to be advancing and a wounded German *ruga-ruga* was brought for treatment. On September 5th the Germans ordered the missionaries to evacuate Mwazye. On September 7th Jean Trenchard (1878-1954), who was touring the outstations, received a warning that he was behind the German lines and must not communicate with the enemies of Germany. On September 9th, the French and Belgian missionaries were ordered to Rukwa Mission, their place being taken by a German and two Dutchmen.[75] On November 3rd, Hamberger, the German superior found himself at an outstation on the British side.

In May 1916, when the British advance actually came, the Germans ordered the complete evacuation of Mwazye. Five days later, the order was rescinded. On May 27th the missionaries departed, as some eight hundred British troops descended on the mission and searched the buildings for weapons. On June 16th Trenchard and the Dutch Brother, Lambert Swyste (1873-1940), returned. Two days later, the British company commander McCarthy and his officers came to Sunday lunch. July saw further clashes between British and German patrols and an entire herd of mission cows stolen by German *ruga-ruga*. On September 12th a British officer and fourteen soldiers were billeted at the mission. On April 1st 1917 the mission was again threatened by the Germans (the Wintgens column) and the missionaries were ordered by the British to evacuate Mwazye. Two days later, the order was countermanded.[76]

From this illustration, it is easy to see that Lechaptois was somewhat unrealistic in desiring his missionaries to remain neutral in such a situation. It was obvious that missionaries would fall foul of one or other of the opposing armies. This happened to François Haugomat (1876-1956) and Marcel Maurice (1884-1934*). Haugomat and Maurice were stationed at Kala Mission, another station near the southern border, on Lake Tanganyika north of Kasanga Fort. In July 1916 some fleeing German soldiers had visited Kala, threatening Haugomat if he refused them assistance. Haugomat went to the German commander to ask what he should do. In the meantime Maurice gave them supplies. People at the mission spread the rumour that the two White Fathers had been sentenced to death, presumably for helping deserters. Fearing that the Germans would come looking for them, Haugomat fled to Kate and Maurice to Zimba. Fellow missionaries urged the two to go to Namanyere Fort and clear themselves with the German authorities, but the British took over on the following day and were immediately suspicious of their dealings with the Germans. Partly as a punishment for abandoning their mission and presumably also to remove them from danger, Lechaptois asked Etienne Larue, in the neighbouring Vicariate of Bangweolo, to take them in at Chilubula Mission, Northern Rhodesia. After this, it was not surprising that they were unwilling ever to return to Tanganyika vicariate.[77]

On June 23rd 1916 a missionary at Kate wrote: "We emerge from the most unpleasant of nightmares". Then he added, "But the unexpected return of the Germans brought the bitterest month of the war".[78] He was referring to the sudden arrival of Max Wintgens and his column in March 1917. The depredations and destruction wrought by Wintgens far surpassed anything that the Tanganyika vicariate had experienced in the previous year.[79] The German detachment which arrived at Galula Mission in the south-east of the vicariate on March 7th numbered two thousand four hundred men. The missionaries were taken at once by a German patrol to Mamba Mission where they were joined shortly afterwards by the missionaries from Mkulwe, the other station on the Rukwa Plain, and from Mwazye. All they had been allowed to take with them was a tent, two blankets, a sheet, a personal suit-case and thirty rupees.

Mwazye remained without staff for a month, but otherwise went unscathed. Galula and Mkulwe were mercilessly pillaged. When the missionaries returned to Galula on April 25th they found only the walls of the mission standing, occupied by a British supply column pursuing Wintgens. Five hundred head of cattle had been taken and all the personal belongings of the missionaries. Even cows suffering from Rinderpest were among the animals taken, thus threatening to spread the disease throughout the country. The books, mission diaries and parish registers had all been destroyed. In the wake of the attack, both Zimba and Mamba Missions were evacuated for a time. Luckily, the swollen rivers prevented the Germans reaching them, and the column passed through Ukimbu to the east of Lake Rukwa and not west of the lake where these missions were to be found. In Tabora, people were agog at the news that the famous Wintgens was marching in their direction. Then they heard on April 24th that he had been taken prisoner in Ugunda, south of the town. Two weeks later the news came that he was in Tabora hospital and his column was besieging Mkalama Fort north of Singida. There was even the fear that it might attack Ndala Mission, but fortunately this did not happen.[80] In fact, Naumann had camped a mere half-hour's journey from Turu Mission. The missionaries there were relieved when he struck camp after his attack on Singida and moved south. "The Blessed Virgin heard our prayers" was their grateful comment.[81]

Amazingly, this was not the end of the ordeal for Galula Mission. On September 19th 1918 the missionaries at Galula heard that the Germans were once more in the neighbourhood. This was von Lettow-Vorbeck on his way to Northern Rhodesia and his "end-game" at Kasama. This time the missionaries did not wait to be ejected, but fled to Mkulwe the following day, before the Germans arrived. In their absence, the German column pillaged the mission once more and took all that was left. This was not much. The missionaries valued the stolen goods at a mere two hundred rupees.

Once across the Northern Rhodesia border, Von Lettow occupied Kayambi Mission in the Vicariate Apostolic of Bangweolo from November 4th to 7th. The White Fathers and White Sisters (MSOLA) escaped in the night, living like nomads in the hills for eight days in rough and ready huts built of branches. A number of local people joined them with their herds. On their return, the mission was a sad sight. It had been thoroughly pillaged. All cloth was taken, the wheat harvest slashed, fruit and vegetables taken from the garden. Losses were estimated at twenty thousand Francs. The local people had also been robbed. In his reminiscences, von Lettow described the "wonderful, spacious and massive buildings" of Kayambi Mission, but he was irritated that the missionaries had found it necessary to flee. "The missionaries had fled quite unnecessarily", he wrote. "In the nuns' house there was a letter for me from a Catholic nun. She was a native of Westphalia and as a fellow country woman appealed to my humanity. She would certainly have spared herself many discomforts if both she herself and the other people attached to the mission had remained quietly at their posts."[82]

On November 10th von Lettow descended on Chilubula Mission where the missionaries had taken precautions before they escaped. The sacred vessels had been sent to a neighbouring station, the Mass wine buried and the salt, cloth and vestments hidden. Unfortunately, they were obliged to leave a hundred and twenty bags of salt behind. After consuming the hosts in the tabernacle, the missionaries camped at Lukulu and watched the Germans through a pair of binoculars. The invaders raised the German flag and entered the missionaries' rooms. After moving further away, the White Fathers and Sisters eventually returned to find the mission ransacked. Cassocks from the sacristy had been torn up and thrown about the courtyard. The Sisters' chapel had been rubbished. The losses were considerable – valued at forty thousand Francs, and it took three days to clear up the mess.[83]

At Kapatu Mission, the fathers fled the Germans on November 14th, having hidden salt and flour. After supper, they left with their boxes and beds to spend the night in the bush. They returned next day and vowed to place a beautiful statue of their patron, Saint Leo, over the church entrance in thanksgiving for preserving the mission. Two days later, on November 17th a German detachment under a warrant officer named Guenin appeared shortly after the missionaries had sung a *Te Deum* in the church to celebrate the end of the war. He and his forty men were on their way to capture the British forts on the Congo border and were unaware of the Armistice in Europe. The missionaries invited Guenin into their dining-room to read letters and telegrams announcing the Armistice. "A pity I did not know this news sooner", exclaimed the German. After spending the night at the mission and paying for the flour and cloth they were given, a messenger from von Lettow arrived telling them to surrender at Abercorn. The missionaries wrote a testimonial of their correct behaviour and Guenin left a gift of fifty rupees for the church.[84]

Thus ended the direct involvement of the White Father vicariates in the East African campaign. The nature of that campaign, particularly the tactics of the *Schütztruppe* in its final stages, coupled with the relative economic importance of the Catholic missions, rendered the latter obvious targets as sources of supply.

End of an Era

On July 20th 1917 Adolphe Lechaptois had written that the greatest ordeals of the Tanganyika vicariate were moral ones. Two months later his vicariate was to face its greatest moral ordeal, the unexpected death of Lechaptois himself. At the age of sixty-five, he was already feeling the accumulated fatigue of a quarter century as Tanganyika's third Vicar Apostolic. When the Allied victories on Lake Tanganyika allowed the priestly ordination of Upper Congo's first diocesan priest, Stefano Kaoze, to go ahead on July 21st 1917, it was Théophile Avon (1870-1953), his Vicar General, who represented him at Baudouinville on the other side of the lake. Lechaptois had been personally instructing a Belgian engineer called Mercenier in the Catholic faith and had been acquainted with him since the beginning of the war. On November 25th 1917 the engineer went fishing on the lake, using explosives. In the course of the expedition he blew himself up and gravely injured the captain of the vessel he was using. Mercenier's remains were wrapped in a canvas cloth and brought to Karema where they were placed in a coffin and buried on November 26th.

The Vicar Apostolic received the news of his friend's death with great emotion and shortly afterwards collapsed during a weekly council, having apparently suffered a stroke. In delirium, he continually babbled about the poor Mercenier. He was anointed in the evening, having lost consciousness and the power of speech. On the 27th he suffered a second stroke, and after leeches were applied behind his right ear there seemed to be an improvement in his condition on the 28th. The following day, however, he relapsed into a coma with a high fever and breathed his last in the evening of November 30th. His body lay in state in Karema Cathedral and he was buried on December 1st in the choir where he used to pray and recite the breviary. The vicariate being under Belgian administration, the Belgian garrison gave him military honours and the Deputy Governor-General, Justin Malfeyt (1862-1924) sent a telegram.

The death of Lechaptois was keenly felt in the vicariate and in the Society of Missionaries of Africa, of which he was one of the oldest and most accomplished members. His confreres and diocesans regarded him not merely as a father, but as a saint. Possessed of great piety, sweetness and sensitivity, he was always approachable and was widely renowned for his wise counsel. In spite of age and weakness he remained an active missionary to the last.[85] After his death, Théophile Avon took over as Pro-Vicar and Administrator of Tanganyika, with the difficult task of presiding over its post-war recovery. The appointment was confirmed by *Propaganda Fide*.

Avon, who was in his prime at forty-seven, had served the vicariate for almost as long as his lamented bishop, mostly as a teacher of trainee catechists and junior seminarians. Livinhac wrote on January 21st 1919 complimenting him on the "wisdom, piety and zeal" with which he was carrying out his functions as administrator.[86] It was obvious that Avon should be favourably considered as the successor of Lechaptois and on September 29th 1919, the General Council forwarded a *terna* to *Propaganda Fide*, with Avon as first choice. The other two being Joseph Birraux (1883-1947), and Albert Wyckaert (1881-1961).[87] Before long, it transpired that discipline in the vicariate was becoming lax. Several missionaries had taken to wearing "English shorts" instead of the White Fathers' habit, and worse still, a missionary had contracted a customary marriage with an African woman at Chala.[88] Avon, who had been insufficiently informed about the affair, allowed the supposedly repentant offender to return to Chala as superior and "repair the scandal". Priests arriving at Algiers for the Long Retreat had informed Livinhac about the case and given evidence on oath. Apparently the culprit was still supporting the lady and had given out that he had a dispensation from the Pope to get married. Naturally, he could not remain in the Society, let alone at his post, and a telegram was sent by

Livinhac to this effect. Avon himself sensed that he was no longer *persona grata* in the vicariate and that only a third of the missionaries wanted him to be their bishop. The General Council thereupon decided that Avon was not a suitable episcopal candidate and Livinhac sent a confidential letter on the subject to *Propaganda Fide*.[89]

Events moved swiftly from tragedy to farce. In April 1920 Joseph Birraux was nominated as the new vicar apostolic and Livinhac sent Avon another telegram. The message that was sent read: *Avon Kigoma Karema Birraux Vicar Apostolic Livinhac*. Unfortunately, as a result of a tiresome error in the telegraph office, the message which Avon received omitted the name of Birraux, and read: *Avon Kigoma Karema Vicar Apostolic Livinhac*. In spite of his misgivings, Avon believed he had been appointed bishop and immediately set about making arrangements, informing the Belgian authorities and his family, redecorating the bishop's chapel and announcing his episcopal consecration for October.[90] He received congratulations from the Belgian authorities, from White Father confreres and even from neighbouring bishops, before the truth became known. He also wrote to Livinhac expressing the hope that he would be a better Vicar Apostolic than Pro-Vicar, writing his signature in Episcopal fashion with a cross before his name.[91] When the mistake became apparent, Avon announced the true state of affairs with admirable simplicity and humility, but the "incident of the telegram" passed forever into White Father folklore.

The General Council helped Avon to live down his embarrassment by making him regional superior for the whole country, but he was replaced a year later and went into "exile" in Unyanyembe (Tabora) vicariate, where he died more than thirty years later, after a fall on the altar steps at Ndala in 1953, at the age of eighty-three.[92] Birraux arrived at Karema in November 1920 after a vacancy that had lasted three years, and the Belgians ceded their occupied territory to the British in the following year, retaining Rwanda-Burundi. Birraux rejoiced that the White Fathers no longer had to cope with a double jurisdiction, but he and his confreres missed the sympathetic administration of the pro-Catholic Belgians.[93]

The remainder of this book will deal mostly with the after-effects of the First World War on the White Fathers and on Africa. The first outstanding question on the Society's post-war agenda was the place of the Germans in the Missionaries of Africa. The next chapter examines this.

CHAPTER SEVEN

WHAT TO DO WITH THE GERMANS ?

The Humiliation of Germany

> *Behold, my child,*
> *the Nordic Man*
> *And be as like*
> *him as you can.* [1]

The Anglo-French author and poet, Hilaire Belloc, thus satirized the Aryan theory and other racial hypotheses, which underpinned European national stereotypes at the beginning of the twentieth century. In previous centuries dynastic and early colonial wars were distant conflicts carried out by small armies of professionals and mercenaries, which did not involve whole nations. Even the Napoleonic Wars at the beginning of the nineteenth century resulted in the demonization of Bonaparte himself, rather than the French nation as a whole. All of this changed with the Franco-Prussian War in 1871, a "foretaste of (the) total war" that was to come in 1914-1918. [2] The German annexation of Alsace-Lorraine was not justified in merely economic, strategic, or even historical terms. Its justification was ultimately ideological, a result of the drive to build big nations and to crush or paralyse lesser ones. It was in effect a battle for existence, a war between irreconcilable concepts of government, society and progress. [3] The German Empire came into existence as a consequence of the 1871 war, an authoritarian and centrist fusion of smaller states. Confronting it were the emerging democratic nationalisms of the remainder of Europe.

Their identities were further shaped by the hostile attitudes that preceded and accompanied the First World War. Prejudicial stereotypes of enemy nations were encouraged by universal conscription and by the volunteer divisions of the "New Armies". Mobilization and recruiting took place against a background of national hysteria, and of violent discrimination against enemy nationals lurking in the home country. Although the war did not directly involve civilian populations, the vast numbers of war casualties and the cult of the war dead contributed to nation-wide emotionalism. People subscribed to a "social Darwinism", the theory that force was the only law between nations and that the fittest countries would survive. [4] The aim was not merely to defeat the enemy, but to destroy its existence as a nation. German apologists believed that the future of European culture depended on a German victory. The Allies claimed that they were defending civilization.[5] It was a case of militarism versus liberalism, community versus individualism, order versus anarchy, state socialism versus capitalism.[6]

The outcome that all the belligerents envisaged was a total and punitive victory over the other, a knock-out blow.[7] The enemy was to be completely crushed and all thought of compromise or reconciliation was banished from people's minds. Because of this, Pope Benedict XV's efforts to remain neutral and to end the useless carnage were misunderstood. The belligerent nations rejected his Peace Note, because they had their own moral agendas, dominated by nationalist and militaristic passions. Benedict was regarded by all parties to the conflict as siding with the enemy, and his courageous fight for peace was only recognized when the war was over.[8]

By mid-September 1918, the tide was turning against Germany. Although its army was not defeated, broken or enveloped, the realization dawned that victory could not be achieved. German forces fell back to defensive lines within Germany itself, abandoning conquests in France and Belgium. Meanwhile, the collapse of Turkey, Bulgaria and Austria-Hungary meant that the coalition of Central Powers had fallen apart. The Allies of the *Entente* occupied German territory on the left bank of the Rhine, and bridgeheads up to fifty miles beyond the river. The formal request for an armistice was made on October 4th, and this triggered a social revolution in Germany itself. By early November the German government was ready to accept any terms in order to stem the revolutionary tide. Although the army and state remained intact, the Kaiser was obliged to abdicate. Democracy was imposed from above and Germany ceased to be an empire.

In the event, the Armistice turned into the very defeat its rulers sought to avoid. A German peace without victory became an Allied victory without peace. The Germans hoped for peace terms along the lines of President Woodrow Wilson's "Fourteen Points" which purported to conserve legitimate and "well defined" national aspirations. The Allies, however, wanted revenge as well as security from future German encroachments. During the peace negotiations in Paris visitors were taken to see the destruction wrought by the invader on the Western Front, much as people were taken to see the Berlin wall in the 1960s and 1970s in order to witness at first hand the evils of Communism. Germany was made to bear the sole guilt of the war and the harshest possible terms were imposed under the pressure of a continuing blockade and the threat of renewed hostilities.

The Armistice took the place of victory in battle. The invaded territories had to be evacuated. Alsace-Lorraine was to be restored to France. All the German colonies were lost. The iron, steel and coal industries of the Saar were surrendered and the Rhineland was to be occupied for fifteen years. On top of this, the country was to disarm, military *materiel* was to be handed over and the German navy given to Britain. In fact, the navy was scuttled before the hand-over could take place. Above all, reparation was to be paid to the Allies amounting to sixty billion marks. The peace terms caused shock and dismay in Germany. They meant the loss of thirteen percent of its territory and ten percent of its population. The reparation sum was unrealistic. General Smuts called the treaty "an impossible peace".[9]

The Germans did not admit they were beaten. They regarded the ultimatum that had been imposed on them as wicked and unfair and they had every intention of repudiating the treaty at a later date. The Treaty of Versailles was thus a direct cause of the Second World War, because the German people felt they had been wronged in 1919.   No reconciliation had taken place and Germany continued to be an enemy in Allied eyes.

The German Vice-Province of the White Fathers
Four of the eight sub-Saharan vicariates entrusted to the Missionaries of Africa lay in German East Africa, including the densely populated Kivu vicariate. Because of this, the Society had created a German Vice-Province in 1905, separate from the single European Province. Recruitment was undertaken in Germany, and German-speaking missionaries, many from Alsace-Lorraine or the Netherlands, were appointed to the region. The German language and German colonial policy were taught to those in formation. Although Germans were a small percentage of the Society, the German Vice-Province possessed four houses, all of them for formation purposes. Marienthal in Luxemburg was acquired in 1890 and served as a Brothers' formation centre as well as a house of German studies. After the war it housed a novitiate for clerics and brothers.[10] At Trier a building had been rented from the Diocese since 1903, serving as a major seminary of philosophy and theology. During the war its student numbers declined to four, but already by 1919 it boasted thirty-two seminarians, eight of them in theology.[11]   Also in 1903 a purpose-built apostolic school had been opened at Haigerloch in Hohenzollern. In 1921 it had a hundred and twelve pupils.[12] Yet another school at Altkirch in Alsace had been acquired from the De La Salle Brothers before the war, but was badly damaged during the conflict.

In German East Africa, relations between French White Fathers and their German confreres as well as with the German colonial administration had been nothing if not amicable for close on thirty years. In fact, when war was declared in August 1914 Henri Léonard, the White Father Vicar Apostolic of Unyanyembe, a Frenchman from Lorraine, and Thomas Spreiter, the German Benedictine Vicar Apostolic of Dar es Salaam from Regensburg exchanged letters, lamenting that the war in Europe threatened to place them on opposing sides of the conflict.[13] Nevertheless, in the light of the pillaging of missions and all the upheavals of the East African campaign, it would have been surprising if some French White Fathers did not adopt the language of anti-German prejudice. "The *Boches* are in Usangu", wrote the French diarist of Galula Mission, as Von Lettow and his column approached in 1918 to pillage the mission for a second time.[14]

In Algiers the General Council of the Society was beginning to have reservations about the compatibility of French and German missionaries in the Society. In August 1916 it was not thought opportune to admit an aspirant of mixed German and French parentage, but Theodore Frey (1875-1954), the Alsatian in charge of the Vice-Province, was maintained in his functions in the following month.[15] In April 1918 a French missionary, Joseph Le Clainche (1876-1920*), was not allowed to leave the mission and the Society on the grounds that some White Fathers helped the German belligerents in East Africa. Apart from the accusation being unproven, it was not a canonical reason for a dispensation.[16] Then, in April 1919 it was announced that the "Vice-Province of Trier" would not be maintained and that Frey should withdraw to Alsace, leaving Georg Steinhage (1876-1962) to look after the Society's interests in Germany. The Alsatian children at Haigerloch were to be brought by Eugene Daull (1876-1940) to Altkirch, now in France, but the German pupils were to be sent home after explaining that formation in view of the missions cannot continue.[17] A further consequence of the suppression of the Vice-Province was that Frey could not be an *ex officio* member of the 1920 General Chapter.[18]

After the war German East Africa had ceased to exist. Three of its White Father vicariates now lay in what was to be called Tanganyika Territory, administered by Britain under a League of Nations mandate. The Kivu Vicariate belonged to the mandated territory of Rwanda-Burundi, administered by Belgium. The General Council of the Society jumped to the conclusion that there was no longer a need for a German Vice-Province. After interning and eventually repatriating the German missionaries from the former German colony, the British Colonial Office issued regulations controlling the admission of foreign missionaries to British Africa. For the time being, the (first) appointment of German nationals – "those born in the German Empire" – was not approved. Livinhac's characteristic pessimism prompted his fear that the exclusion would be of indefinite duration. Hence the decision to suppress the German Vice-Province.

In the meantime, confreres who belonged to the Vice-Province campaigned for its retention. One of these was the Luxemburger, Paul Betz (1880-1955), who was made novice-master of the brothers at Marienthal shortly after the armistice in 1918.[19] According to oral tradition in the Society, it was mainly due to his efforts that the German Vice-Province was rescued from extinction.[20] He is said to have interviewed German White Fathers to ascertain their views, but no mention is made of these efforts in his official obituary notice.[21]

Eugene Daull (1876-1940), superior at Haigerloch, reacted forcefully to the General Council's decision in April 1919. He was, he said, "painfully surprised" by it, in view of the continuing German interest in missionary work, proved by the growing number of vocations and the financial support that was forthcoming. His faith in the future of the German Vice-Province was unshaken and he demanded to know the motives behind the decision. "Are German confreres superfluous and to be withdrawn?" he asked. "What are we to say to the parents of our students? Are we to break relations unilaterally with our benefactors? I see no reason for the measures. If the superiors have acted out of a well-founded fear, may I be permitted to intercede for the confreres and projects in Germany? Is it seriously proposed to repatriate German religious? Are Germans to be excluded forever from the evangelization of the world? May

God preserve humanity from such folly! Let us first see what the other congregations do. If the major superiors decide to keep the German houses and continue recruitment, then Father Frey must remain at the head of affairs." Daull ended with a plea for a gradual, not an immediate, withdrawal of the Alsatian missionaries from the German formation houses and their replacement by Germans for the sake of continuity and stability.[22]

On June 30th 1919 Frey reported in person to the General Council in Algiers and made several telling points.[23] No missionary congregation in Germany was thinking of abandoning their apostolate, even though Germany had lost her colonies and the British were not disposed to admit German missionaries to their territories. Frey believed that the exclusion would be temporary. Other congregations, including international orders and societies, were continuing their recruitment, formation and promotion programmes in Germany. Frey believed it was morally impossible to suppress White Father recruitment and formation in the country. This would make a deplorable impression on German bishops, clergy and the Catholic population. Moreover, he said, German confreres were profoundly attached to the Society and to their vocation. He asked the Council to maintain the Vice-Province provisionally.

Livinhac, however, poured cold water on Frey's positive report, basing his arguments surprisingly on French antipathy. The foundations in Germany, he argued, were only made in order to ensure that the mission could continue in the German colonies, having been pressured by the German government to send German nationals there. In the present circumstances it was "absolutely necessary to restrict our recruitment in Germany, if not suppress it completely. Moreover, the profound feelings caused in France by German aggression and the horrors of war are reasons why it is no longer possible to receive and form both French and Germans in a common novitiate, and make them live together in community in the same missions. To attempt to do this so soon after the war would make recruitment difficult, if not impossible in France." The General Council decided to open a separate novitiate for German candidates who had already completed their theological studies at Trier during the war.[24]

Three days later the Council issued the following orders: the German "region" was to be maintained provisionally, with Theodore Frey as regional and Georg Steinhage as assistant regional and delegate for relations with the German civil and religious authorities. Frey was to reside at Marienthal and open a novitiate for German clerics there. For the time being, the German communities were to vote with the Province of Europe for delegates to the 1920 General Chapter.[25]

Georg Steinhage added his voice to that of Daull in the following year. In conscience he felt bound to ask whether it was really certain that Germans would not be admitted to missionary countries and that it was useless to recruit German Missionaries of Africa? The hope was well-founded, he believed, that German White Fathers would be allowed to continue. More than thirty million practising Catholics in Germany could not be forbidden to work for the conversion of the pagans. To end recruitment and formation at the very moment when vocations were increasing and when other missionary societies were re-opening their novitiates and formation centres in Germany would be a bitter deception. Steinhage believed that the decision was premature and the real situation still unclear. He ended his memorandum with the ringing assertion that the mission of the Church was a Catholic work which should not be restricted by national frontiers. It was, he said, the duty of the superiors to find a field in which German White Fathers could work.[26]

Encouraged perhaps by this final appeal, Livinhac wrote an extraordinary letter to Willem Marinus Cardinal Van Rossum, the Dutch Prefect of the Vatican Congregation of *Propaganda Fide*. It was dated March 14th 1920.[27]

Most Eminent Lord Cardinal,
        Our Institute being destined exclusively for missionary work among the infidels of Africa, our confreres of German nationality are finding it impossible to follow their vocation. It seems, in fact, probable, if not certain, that the rulers of the countries we are evangelizing will forbid them entry.
        I therefore beg Your Eminence to be so kind as to employ them in the conversion of blacks in the United States, a work which, outside Africa, best corresponds to their aspirations.
        I have the honour, Most Eminent Lord Cardinal, in reverencing your sacred purple, to subscribe myself,
    The very humble and very obedient son and servant of Your Most Reverend
                Eminence,
                Léon Livinhac
      Bishop of Pacando and Superior General.

The letter was tabled one month later, on April 14th at the Fifteenth General Chapter of the Society together with Van Rossum's reply. Evidently, the Cardinal Prefect did not take Livinhac's counsel of despair very seriously. The request, he said, had made him smile.[28] In view of the fact that German missionaries of other congregations had been allowed to stay in British Africa, the Cardinal preferred that German White Fathers remain where their vocation had placed them.[29] The Chapter voted by thirty-six votes to one to continue the Society's work in Germany.[30] The capitulants appreciated the solid position of the Missionaries of Africa in Germany, the sacrifices made by confreres and students and the spirit of charity, loyalty and regularity which they displayed. As long as any were not allowed to return to their missions, another field of activity had to be found for them, preferably in Africa. The gaps left by the return of Alsace-Lorraine to France had to be filled, but the internationality of the Society, intended by the Founder, was not to be subjected to the vagaries of political change.

Instead of the single European Province, the Chapter decided to erect French, and Belgian Provinces. In this context, it was decided by a unanimous show of hands to create a German Province also, leaving it to the General Council to make it a reality according to circumstances.[31] In September the Council decided that it was still too early to ask *Propaganda Fide* to approve the erection of the German Province. This would depend on acquiring a field of missionary activity of its own. In July of the following year the canonical status of the German Province was still under discussion, but it was decided to seek Rome's approval.[32] Eventually in 1936 the German Province was officially erected – the first canonical province to be set up in the Society - with responsibility for the *sui juris* missions of Tukuyu, in Tanganyika Territory (Tanzania), and of Lwangwa in Northern Rhodesia (Zambia).[33]

In April 1921, while imploring "the Heavenly Father for a field of action *in tempore opportuno*", Theodore Frey reported on the progress of recruitment and formation in Germany.[34] A new apostolic school had been acquired to replace Altkirch in Alsace. This was an austere building at Rietberg in North Rhine-Westphalia. Frey reported that Haigerloch had one hundred and twelve students, and that there were already twenty-five at Rietberg. At Trier there were thirty-one seminarians, eight of whom had made their novitiate. At Marienthal, there were fourteen brother novices and eight postulants. Clearly there was no lack of vocations in post-war Germany. However, it was noted that, contrary to the pre-war experience, the recruitment of brothers was becoming more difficult. There were several reasons for this. A loss of manpower due to the war had placed a premium on the services of able-bodied men, and the abrogation of anti-clerical legislation favoured strong competition between various religious institutes. Added to this was the attraction of life in the world at a time of increasing post-war prosperity.[35]

Where Livinhac and the General Council had faltered, the 1920 Chapter stolidly supported the Society's international character and the right of German confreres to have their own province. They did not, however, alter the arrangements already in place for a separate missionary formation for Germans candidates. This was an accomplished fact, resulting from the war experience, and – as we have seen – had become an object of policy. It must be said that depriving German Missionaries of Africa of an international formation placed them at a disadvantage in a multi-national society for some years to come.

Departures from the Society in 1915-1922
There had been departures from the Society since its beginning in 1868. In fact, during the forty-six years of its existence up to 1914 – when the Society was relatively small - one hundred and forty White Fathers had left, an average of slightly more than three per year. During the First World War and in its immediate aftermath there was a marked increase in departures from the Society.[36] Of those who had taken the perpetual oath up to and including the year 1914, forty-two left in the following eight years, the period covered by this book.[37] This is a rate of more than five a year. A further twenty-four in the same category left during the twenty-seven years from 1922 to 1950, a rate of less than one per year.[38] The loyalty of German confreres to a society that had a large French majority and which was under mainly French leadership was remarkable. No less remarkable was the fact that the French, contrary to the General Council's apprehensions after the war, were not averse to sharing community life with Germans. There are only three cases known to the author

in which incompatibility between French and German played a part in the departure of a confrere.[39]

Among the forty-two who left the Society during or immediately after the war, three belonged to non-belligerent nations. They were a Dutch priest, a Dutch brother and a Swiss priest. Of the remainder, there were twenty-five French priests and four French brothers; two German priests and four German brothers; three Belgian priests and one Luxemburger priest. Twenty-four of these were under the age of forty and had seen active service. Several in their forties had also been called up as reservists. Some of those who departed had been excluded from the Society by the Superiors on account of a misdemeanour, but most were dispensed from the missionary oath at their own request, after application to the Vatican Congregation of *Propaganda Fide*. The vast majority of priests were incardinated in a diocese, following their departure.

Each departure tells a different story and we have already seen some of them in these pages. It is extremely seldom that the proximate reason for departure had anything directly to do with the missionary's war experience, even though many of those who left had a distinguished military career. In some cases, the missionary was already known to be unstable, had left and rejoined the Society or had re-applied and had been refused. Célestin Paulhe (1888-1919*) was one of those with a distinguished war record. He had been seriously wounded in the head at Verdun and had been awarded the Legion of Honour, *Croix de Guerre* and Palm. Besides the effect of his wounds, it seems that his life as an army officer had alienated him from the Society and had given him a distaste for the missionary life. He joined the Diocese of Nîmes.[40]

Gaston Duiquet (1888-1930*) and Charles Joyeux (1885-1936*) were also war heroes, but their departure from the Society took place in the 1930s and had nothing to do with their military service. Duiquet had been wounded at Verdun and received the Croix de Guerre with three stars. After the war he was allowed to work in Morocco, in the Vicariate Apostolic of Rabat. Having been refused incardination there, he re-applied to the Society, but it was felt that he had been too long out of community.[41] Joyeux was probably the most decorated White Father of World War I. He had received the Legion of Honour, *Croix de Guerre* and Palm, with five stars. He left the Society for the Archdiocese of Paris where he was formally incardinated in 1938 and died as a hospital chaplain in 1953.[42]

Looking at the age factor, many of the departures may have been connected with a mid-life crisis. Nevertheless, it must be said, in view of the numbers involved, that whatever the proximate reason for leaving the Society may have been, the departures took place against the backdrop of a traumatic war experience. This experience was certainly unsettling and may have brought other issues to the fore. However, it is not possible to generalize from the little we know about the effect of the war on the missionary vocations of White Father servicemen.

A White Father Spy?
One of the Missionaries of Africa who left the Society during the First World War was Joseph Marsigny, released from his oath on June 30th 1915.[43]

Marsigny belonged to a well to do Belgian family from Namur and was born at Ciney in 1880. Attracted by the missionary vocation, he studied with the White Fathers and entered the novitiate in 1902. He was found to be a brilliant student, but lacking in judgement. Ordained priest in June 1906, he was appointed to the Vicariate Apostolic of Upper Congo. In 1910, he was excluded from this vicariate because of inappropriate behaviour and was appointed to the White Fathers' *procure* at Antwerp, from where he applied for permission to leave the Society. This he effectively did in 1914, before his official release.

His movements at the outbreak of the war are shadowy in the extreme, but it is possible to piece together something of his life from a lengthy correspondence about him in 1988, involving the archivist of the Missionaries of Africa of the time (René Lamey). Marsigny first of all became an officer in the Belgian army, in which he seems to have performed priestly duties, without however becoming an official chaplain. With the German occupation of Belgium, he moved to the Netherlands, which had remained neutral in the conflict, and became the director of a school there for the remainder of the war. According to a tradition in his own family he worked for Allied intelligence during this time, using his position at the school as a cover. According to the family, his method of espionage was the colourful, but highly improbable one of seducing the wife of the German Ambassador at the Hague.[44] The family tradition is uncorroborated and may have been invented out of a desire to excuse Marsigny's departure from the Belgian military at the time of the German invasion.

After the war, he entered the Cistercian Monastery of Our Lady of the Lake at Oka in Quebec, Canada. He did this as a "penitent", without however taking vows as a Trappist. On leaving the White Fathers he had been authorized to find another ordinary or institute, and the Trappists seem to have recommended him to the Vicariate Apsotolic of Canton, China in 1925. Marsigny was impressed by the heroic witness of the Belgian Leper missionary, Blessed Damien De Veuster (1840-1889) at Molokai, Hawaii and he offered to take charge of the leper colony at Shek Lung in Canton. This leprosarium had been founded by Louis Lambert Conrardy who died at Hong Kong in 1914. Marsigny lived and worked among these lepers as a secular priest until his death at Canton in 1940. In spite of the dubious and reprehensible activities that marked his early life, he died a missionary hero in the mould of Father Damien.

Rescuing the German Benedictine Missions

The original Catholic evangelizers of the territory that became German East Africa were the Spiritans in the north-east (1863), followed later by the Missionaries of Africa who went to the Lakes region in the west (1878). Both these institutes were international, but with a majority of French and/or Alsatian members. Under German rule both had introduced a few German missionaries into the colony. After the German annexation in 1885, a third congregation began work there. This was the missionary Benedictine Congregation of the recently founded Abbey of Saint Ottilien near Munich in Bavaria, membership of which was almost entirely German. These Benedictines evangelized the south-east of the country, known as the Vicariate Apostolic of Dar es Salaam. It was a huge territory of more than eighty thousand square miles, stretching some four hundred miles from the Indian Ocean to the Ruaha Valley and Lake Nyasa (Malawi). In 1913 under its Vicar Apostolic, Thomas Spreiter OSB, the vicariate had been divided and the Prefecture Apostolic of Lindi created. Dar es Salaam counted eleven mission stations and Lindi six. Besides the towns of Dar es Salaam and Lindi, there were other important centres in this Benedictine territory, such as Iringa, Mahenge, Mtwara and Songea.

After the East African campaign, German missionaries were threatened by the Allies with internment and repatriation. The policy was far from consistent and the Missionaries of Africa came off lightly. As we have seen in Chapter Three, six German brothers were interned in either Egypt or India and a handful of priests were relocated to White Fathers' missions in neighbouring African countries. The Spiritans were only slightly less lucky. Three of their missionaries were obliged to withdraw from the country, along with their two bishops, Emile-Auguste Allgeyer C.S.Sp., Vicar Apostolic of Bagamoyo and Aloys-Marie-Joseph Münsch C.S.Sp., Vicar Apostolic of Kilimanjaro.[45] Bishop Thomas Spreiter OSB, however, and all the Benedictines from Bavaria were interned at Ahmednagar camp in India from where they were repatriated to Germany, leaving their vast mission field without any personnel.[46] Henri Streicher the White Father Vicar Apostolic of Uganda, agreed to release Joseph Laane (1861-1941) to organize a rescue operation.[47] Laane was an able and distinguished missionary from the Netherlands. In the Uganda vicariate he had founded several mission stations, including Mahagi, across the Congo border in the West Nile region. He spoke English and his native Dutch was useful in conversation with the South African commander-in-chief, General van Deventer who preferred to speak Afrikaans as a rule.[48]

Faced with the ruin of his mission and in desperate need of personnel, Spreiter turned to Bishop John Biermans of the Mill Hill Missionaries, Vicar Apostolic of Upper Nile (eastern Uganda). Biermans was invited to Dar es Salaam in the hope that he would accept responsibility for all the spiritual and material interests of the Benedictine mission. This he was not in a position to do. Consulted by Biermans, Streicher authorized Laane to ask for priests from the surrounding vicariates.

Laane arrived in Dar es Salaam in June 1917, living at first with the Benedictines and their Bishop, who were gathered there awaiting their journey into exile. In July Spreiter conferred the power of provisional apostolic administrator on him for a period of five years, pending approval by *Propaganda Fide*. The military authorities appointed him chaplain with the rank of honorary captain and Laane found himself in a gathering of thirteen other military chaplains from various missionary and religious congregations. These and a handful of others still up-country were the only Catholic priests serving the vast region that lay between the Indian Ocean and the lake regions and which was still a battle field.[49]. Laane hoped to secure the services of some of these chaplains as well as other recruits from the White Father vicariates.

Eventually, he was joined at different times by a total of twelve Missionaries of Africa, by a Mill Hill Missionary, some Consolata Missionaries and a German Swiss Benedictine who had escaped internment.[50]

There was always a danger, however, that bishops might withdraw their missionaries without warning, especially after the armistice and demobilization. Laane lost no time in writing at once to Livinhac for support. With the authority of *Propaganda Fide* behind him, Livinhac circularized all his vicars apostolic in Equatorial Africa, requesting not only that they should not withdraw their personnel, but that they should make further priests available to serve the seventeen thousand Christians abandoned by the Benedictines.[51]

In Dar es Salaam itself Laane visited military camps and hospitals and served the small Catholic community of Goans, Europeans and "up-country boys" who worshipped in the monumental cathedral that had been built by the Benedictines. Bishop Mathurin Guillemé, Vicar Apostolic of Nyasa, accepted responsibility for the Prefecture of Lindi and Camille de Chatouville (1871-1927) was posted to the former Benedictine mission of Kigonsera towards the end of 1917, where he was able to use the Swahili language. He was mystified by the letters "KMB" which he found inscribed on all the buildings erected by the Benedictines and learned later that they stood for "Kasper, Melchior, Balthasar" the traditional names of the three wise men venerated at Cologne.[52] In 1918 Ambroise Fauconnier (1874-1940) was put in charge of Peramiho, the most important of the four surviving stations in the prefecture.[53]

Léon Huntziger (1884-1977) and Corneille Smoor (1872-1953) were sent to Ndanda in 1919. At the outset of the war, there had been between six and seven thousand Christians, one hundred and sixty-two catechists and a hundred and forty-two schools, but the mission had suffered heavily during the campaign. Outstations had been pillaged and the church at Lukuledi destroyed by German bombardment.[54] Some twenty thousand troops were now billeted or hospitalized in buildings belonging to the mission. The two White Fathers began a clean-up, managing to revive six centres. Seven hundred Christians were traced, but the catechists declined to go back to work.[55]

In the Dar es Salaam vicariate René Claerhout was sent to Kwiro, Mahenge in November 1918, where he lived alone in the former convent of the Benedictine Sisters. There had been seven thousand Christians at Kwiro before the departure of the Benedictines, as well as three hundred catechists. Mahenge had suffered in the campaign of Von Lettow-Vorbeck, and its people, the Pogoro, had been badly treated. Barely seven hundred now attended Mass and an even smaller number received the sacraments regularly. Claerhout looked after six other centres, including Ifakara and a leprosarium with three hundred and thirty-two inmates.[56] He managed to get seven schools functioning again, but lamented the lack of a serious catechumenate at this mission. Early in the following year he was briefly joined by Henri Pineau (1897-1981) and Louis Prouvoyeur (1886-1961). They were recalled to Dar es Salaam for demobilization after a mere four weeks.[57] Pineau, however, returned in 1920 with Alphonse Boudewyn (1885-1955) to look after Kwiro and Ifakara. They described their activity there as "a crushing work".[58]

François Haugomat (1876-1956) and Bernard Schmitt (1864-1925) were sent to Tosamaganga, Iringa, in early 1919. The former Benedictine mission there resembled a medieval castle. The six or seven hundred Christians were scattered. Most did not practise their faith or had irregular marriage unions. Many, if not most, were ransomed children who had been raised in orphanages and settled after marriage by the missionaries in households that were heavily subsidized by the mission. The White Fathers were not able to re-start the hospital, flour-mill and shoe-craft industry, but left them to whichever congregation would eventually take over.[59]   Apart from regularly visiting the outstations, they could do little more than receive those who came to them and seek out a few "ship-wrecked souls". There was no money to hire catechists or open schools.[60]

In May 1920 Cardinal Van Rossum, the Prefect of *Propaganda Fide*, was urging the Missionaries of Africa to take permanent responsibility for all the former Benedictine missions. The suggestion was discussed by the General Council who offered to meet the Cardinal half way. The White Fathers would be ready to take on Dar es Salaam, but not Lindi.[61]   Then news came in March 1921 that *Propaganda Fide* had plans to hand them over to other congregations. Swiss Capuchins were to take over the Vicariate Apostolic of Dar es Salaam, while the Abbey of Uznach, a Swiss foundation of the St. Ottilien Benedictines, was to be made responsible for the Lindi prefecture. In 1922, the Prefecture Apostolic of Iringa was created and entrusted to the Consolata Missionaries of Turin, who were also at work in British East Africa. The first Swiss Capuchin Fathers and Sisters embarked at Naples for East Africa in 1921 and Laane helped the Uznach Benedictines on their way to Lindi in the following year.[62]

Meanwhile, the ever resourceful Laane founded a *procure* at Dar es Salaam and became its procurator. The building he acquired from Karimjee Jivanjee had been put up by Sultan Said Majid of Zanzibar in 1877, and was one of the oldest in the city. It was situated conveniently near the customs house, post-office and railway station and the British authorities allowed Laane to add a balcony and verandah which overhung the street. The building is still the property of the Society and has become the nucleus of the present Atiman House. The Dar es Salaam procure served six vicariates. Laane departed for Europe in June 1922, leaving the *procure* in the hands of Felix Dufays (1877-1954). After first serving for some years as Streicher's Vicar-General, a further pioneering task awaited the "saviour of the German missions in East Africa", notably the first foundation of the Missionaries of Africa in London in 1928. This was Westbrook House at Heston, opened by Laane as a *procure*, for promotion work and as a study house for missionaries following courses in Britain on educational subjects.[63]

The German "problem" was the biggest post-war challenge to the Society of Missionaries of Africa and its international character. In the case of the Benedictines, it threatened the very survival of the Catholic mission in parts of former German East Africa. The White Fathers managed to tackle the problem in their own ranks fairly well, in spite of a temporary loss of nerve by the superiors. They also helped solve the Benedictine dilemma, rendering the withdrawal of the German missionaries less detrimental, if not more beneficial, than it might otherwise have been. The following chapter tries to assess the other immediate consequences of the First World War for Africa and the Society of Missionaries of Africa.

CHAPTER EIGHT

THE AFTERMATH OF WAR

Social and Economic Consequences

In September 1921, three years after the Armistice and nearly five years after the Allied occupation of Tabora and the central region of German East Africa, a Missionary of Africa, Frédéric Salelles (1874-1956) travelled up the central railway to Kigoma, on his way to take the lake steamer to Northern Rhodesia (Zambia). He described the former German colony as "wretched and uninhabited". A few plantations were visible from the train, but they had been invaded by bush, and there was no evidence of business or trade.[1] Throughout Africa, and especially eastern Africa, the early post-war years witnessed widespread hardship. There were labour shortages and a loss of land under cultivation. This decline in agricultural production was partly due to pillage and destruction by soldiers and carriers, but much more to general depopulation.[2] Not only were there war casualties, there was extensive loss of life due to famine and disease. Of the two, famine was reckoned by the Missionaries of Africa to be worse.

Famine made its appearance in Africa early on in the war on both sides of the continent, in the Gold Coast (Ghana) and Northern Rhodesia (Zambia).[3] In Bangweolo vicariate (Northern Rhodesia) the villages were deserted. Those who were still alive spent their time in the forest searching for anything safe to eat. People were "walking skeletons". In Burundi (Kivu vicariate) starving people struggled to the mission, only to die on the doorstep, and there were corpses on all the roads and pathways. There was also famine in the southern missions of Tanganyika vicariate that had suffered most at the hands of the military. It was impossible to know how many hundreds of thousands died.[4] Famine persisted during and after the war. In 1919, every mission station in the sprawling vicariate of Tabora reported famine; and in 1921-1922 famine returned to Burundi.[5] The missionaries distributed what relief they could and deaths were certainly fewer in the vicinity of the mission stations.

As a cause of depopulation, disease came a close second to famine. Apart from dysentery, meningitis, typhoid and smallpox, all of which were widely reported in the East African region, there was a serious outbreak of bubonic plague in Uganda beginning in 1916 and lasting five years.[6] It may have been carried by returning Ugandan soldiers, since there was an outbreak early in the war among Allied troops at Karonga, Nyasaland (Malawi).[7] Much more serious, however, was the world pandemic of Spanish influenza. Unusually for influenza, which is normally a killer of the elderly and young children, the "Spanish" variety was most deadly for people in the prime of life. It carried with it a lethal pneumonia that caused a haemorrhaging that filled the lungs and suffocated the victims. The virus struck with amazing speed, killing the sufferers within hours of the first signs of infection. The pandemic circled the globe and estimates of the number of deaths it caused range from twenty to forty million worldwide. In Africa, scarcely a single village was immune.

Spanish Influenza was reported by the White Fathers in every one of their sub-Saharan vicariates. Three missionaries died of the infection in 1919 within ten days of each other in Unyanyembe and Upper Congo, Félix Maymard (1885-1919) at Mbulu, Alphonse Simon (1883-1919) at Ndala and Léandre Germain (1882-1919) at Kirungu.[8] At Segu (French Sudan) three White Fathers went down with it, but survived.[9] Seven hundred people died of the disease at Chilubula (Bangweolo) in 1919.[10] Bishop Auguste Huys reported in 1920 that an estimated ten thousand died of it in the Upper Congo vicariate and Philippe Déchaume (1879-1947) wrote in the previous year that half the population of Kate mission in Tanganyika vicariate were ill with it.[11] In Northern Rhodesia (Zambia), people were immobilized on government orders. They were told to stay on their farms to avoid contagion and not return to the village. According to Bishop Etienne Larue of Bangweolo, silence enveloped the mission stations of his vicariate for three months as a result.[12]

In February 1920 most of German East Africa, now under a British mandate, was renamed Tanganyika Territory and drawn into the political and economic sphere of Britain. The old German *rupia* was worthless, but inflation rapidly overtook the British rupee that replaced it. Prices quadrupled in 1919.[13] In Uganda the currency was devalued by fifty percent in the following year.[14] In British East Africa (Kenya) the exchange rate between the pound sterling and the rupee was ruinous.[15] In Tanganyika vicariate Bishop Birraux complained that sixteen pre-war *rupia* were now worth fifty-five post-war rupees, and he wondered if the missionary enterprise could continue under these conditions.[16] People had no money to pay tax or buy clothes, but reverted to traditional garments of animal skins, tree cotton or bark. For the time being, it was impossible to make a profit on any cash crop. Lack of manpower meant that porters were unobtainable, and as rail and road transport gradually improved, porterage and the income derived from it disappeared. By the end of the war, it was possible for missionaries to reach Entebbe (Uganda) from London, via Port Said, Cairo and Khartoum in thirty-five days, by a combination of rail, steamer and road journeys.[17]

Before the end of German rule, their East African colony had begun to be profitable. In Tanganyika Territory, however, the plantations which were taken over by British companies or Indian businessmen were never as lucrative. The outstanding achievement of the British was to develop cash crop areas farmed by Africans. In Tanganyika Territory these were principally the coffee-growing areas of regions such as Kilimanjaro, Bukoba and the Southern Highlands. Similar cash crop areas were developed in the other British colonies. Returning army veterans had the cash, the self-confidence and social standing to become entrepreneurs. Little by little peasant societies emerged and the balance of African society was altered.[18]

In 1920 British East Africa was also renamed the Colony and Protectorate of Kenya. After the war, the British Government initiated a soldier settlement scheme in the colony, offering cheap land in the highlands to British war veterans. This increased the European population from three thousand in 1912 to around ten thousand. Together, the white settlers owned the bulk of the fertile highland areas, a situation that compromised eventual African rural development.

African Attitudes to the War

Joseph Mazé (1883-1959), a British Army transport officer in the East African campaign, knew the African point of view well. After the campaign he composed a short essay, summarizing African attitudes towards the war.[19] At first, Africans did not believe the war was a reality. They suspected it was a ploy on the part of the colonial rulers to take a firmer grip on their African conquests. Soon the realization dawned that the whites were really fighting one another. Such a thing was incomprehensible. "Why", Africans asked one another "should rich white people fight each other?" They had no need to pillage the property of other whites or to make them slaves. At first it was believed that the fighting would soon be over. Then people believed it would never be over. Why was the war so fierce, when African tribal wars were quickly finished? The Africans accepted the explanations they received from missionaries and others, but did not try to understand them. Mazé's observations tally with those of other White Fathers.

At first Africans tried to hold aloof from the war. It was an affair of the whites and had nothing to do with them.[20] Then, as they were drawn into the conflict, they began to make comparisons with their own tribal wars. Even if slavery was not the ultimate purpose, this war was still a manhunt. A missionary at Galula (Tanganyika vicariate) commented that the prestige of Europeans and the moral authority of the missionaries had been diminished by the war. The Africans' "simplicity and docility is not what it was formerly."[21] An old Nyamwezi chief told Bishop Léonard in the last year of the war: "Up till now we thought all the whites were brothers, members of the same race. We Banyamwezi used to fight each other, but never for so long. When the rains started, everyone went home to take up the hoe and cultivate."[22]

Fighting with, and against, Europeans was a new experience for Africans. Having actually killed white men, it was impossible to maintain the kind of unthinking respect for them that was common before the war. In African eyes, the war was cruel, inhuman and futile, and the veterans' new self-assurance was inevitably a seed of nationalism. Indeed, in both East and West Africa the war was in many cases a first national experience. Ideas of self-determination and colonial accountability were already present in embryonic form.

In Kenya the Kikuyu Association was formed in 1919 to oppose the alienation of land and other colonial abuses. Two years later Harry Thuku (1895-1970) a young government telegraph operator aged twenty-seven, announced the foundation of a more militant organization which rejected white rule altogether. This was the Young Kikuyu Association, later called the East African Association to give it wider appeal. Thuku was arrested on March 14th 1922 and thousands of people took part in a demonstration in Nairobi, demanding his release. Armed police fired on the crowd, killing at least twenty-seven people.[23] In Mombasa, the White Fathers put the number of Nairobi demonstrators at four thousand and were at pains to emphasize that Catholics did not take part.[24] Thuku was detained for nine years as a danger to peace and good order.

Before he died in 1917, Bishop Lechaptois lamented the moral disorientation caused by the war. He felt that it had encouraged violence and dishonesty among the people and that Europeans had lost respect in the eyes of Africans.[25] He was writing at the height of his vicariate's misfortunes and without witnessing the war's long-term effects. However, he believed that Christians had managed to preserve a good reputation in the midst of the disorder and mayhem.

In African eyes the military brass band was a symbol of European power. Before the war *Beni* (Band) dance societies came into existence chiefly in German East Africa, as a kind of pantomime or satire on European authority and social structure, mimicking military drill and band formations.[26] *Beni* officials often bore German titles like *Kaiser* or *Bismarck*. In the last years of the war the dance was brought to Nairobi and continued to spread throughout eastern and central Africa, promoted especially by war veterans. The *Beni* dance societies were welfare associations, practising mutual aid. Although they were supremely irreverent, they were not politically subversive or linked to movements of protest. They combined nostalgia for the past with accommodation to a new situation and were a creative African response to post-war social disorientation. Although they were not really a form of embryonic nationalism, they gave their members the experience of a complex and widespread organization.

Both the British and the Belgians were hostile to the *Beni* dance, but there was little they could do to stop it. The Missionaries of Africa also feared it on account of alleged immoral practices. Théophile Avon (1870-1953),   as Apostolic Administrator of the Tanganyika vicariate, reported in 1919 that the *Beni* dance was like "a gunpowder trail" stretching from the sea coast to Lake Tanganyika. It was, he said, "an evil association" that preached wife-sharing and practised lascivious dances. According to Avon, the refrain of the principal *Beni* song was: "The lion is only wounded", a symbolic reference to the widespread expectation that the Germans would return. "We have to preach against the *Beni*", he added.

More directly threatening to the work of the missionaries was the appearance of African prophetical figures with a millenarian message arising from the war situation. The most important of these was Malaki Musajjakawa (c.1875-1929) in Uganda. Malaki, who claimed to be the "Apostle of God", was an Anglican school teacher and petty government chief. Having been refused baptism twice by the Anglicans, he founded his own Church, known as the Malakites, or "The

Society of the One Almighty God". The movement appeared at the beginning of the war and was particularly opposed to western medicine. Malaki also preached a return to the polygamous marriage practices of the Biblical patriarchs and invited people to come to him for baptism, without the need of any preparation. He also revived the cult of the traditional divinities and promised a golden age in which whites would become servants of the blacks. The Anglicans opposed him at first, but became more supportive in the light of his numerical success. At one moment he was joined by a hundred and twenty thousand new recruits. Seven thousand eight hundred Catholic catechumens also joined him and were baptized, lured by the ease with which they could get a Christian name.[27] The Malakites claimed a membership of ninety thousand by the early 1920s.

Malaki himself is said to have given up personal involvement in the baptisms in 1916. At the same time, his neophytes were being re-baptized by the Anglicans.[28] By 1922, the movement was in rapid decline and former Malakites accounted for half the postulants joining the Catholic catechumenates in Uganda. Only the elderly, who were happy with their new Christian name, remained loyal to him.[29] The Malakites were basically a religious group but their teaching contained seeds of anti-colonial dissent, especially where the provision of medical services were concerned. The Church was suppressed by the British when Malaki opposed a government vaccination programme and had disappeared altogether by 1930. Malaki himself died as a result of a hunger strike.[30]

Liberation and Demobilization

As the German army fell back in the last months of the war, the White Fathers in Belgium and northern France were liberated amid general scenes of euphoria. The community of the apostolic school at Gits, near Bruges in Western Flanders probably suffered the most from the military occupation.[31] Their first experience was of a German officer at the door demanding five hundred cigars at the point of a revolver. After ransacking the house, the missionaries managed to find some cigars that had been given as a present to Joseph Kindt (1872-1947). The next request was from the Captain-Commander of an aviation unit who came to billet a hundred and twenty soldiers at the school. The missionaries were each allowed to keep a room and to have the use of the chapel and a class-room. On Sunday December 13th, the Fathers celebrated Mass for the Catholic soldiers and were invited to dinner at the officers' mess. Against their wishes a photograph was taken of the occasion. As it turned out, this photograph with the enemy brought them unexpected good luck.

In January the Germans became more demanding. Requests for wine, beer, foodstuffs and other supplies were made with threats, but most of the things demanded were not in the house. Then, at the end of the month, the White Fathers were forced to leave Gits and go to Roeslare (Roulers) where they were thrown into prison. During the interrogations that followed, money was demanded as the price of their release. The missionaries explained that the money they possessed was for the evangelization of Africa, and that some of it came from a donation by the Kaiser himself, made to the Catholic missions at the time of his silver jubilee. The soldiers then changed their tune and demanded wine and liqueurs in lieu of money. All the White Fathers had was fifty litres of Mass wine and forty litres of red table wine. These did not interest their jailers. There followed a variety of accusations, mostly about rumour-mongering, slandering Germany and spreading false information. The Superior then produced the famous photo of the dinner party and the officers were surprised to see the Belgian missionaries occupying a place of honour at the German table. Next day they were freed and allowed to return to Gits.

In August the aviation company departed, but other soldiers came to demolish the school's perimeter wall and use the bricks for road making. In December 1917 the house itself was requisitioned and the missionaries were again ordered to leave. Before departing they had to hand over their herd of cows and all brass objects from the chapel. They made their way to the White Fathers' seminary at Bouchout near Brussels. The students had all been sent home and food was scarce, but the exiles from Gits were able to live there until January 1919. On their return, they found the house and property in a lamentable condition. All the doors and windows had been torn out and the orchard of three hundred fruit trees had been cut down. The house could not be occupied until it had dried out.

At the sanatorium of Autreppe, near the French border in Hainaut Province, the White Fathers' experience of military occupation was only slightly better than at Gits.[32] In 1914 the missionaries were alarmed by the fall of one Belgian town after another and they were unwilling spectators of German military parades and victory songs. After the first battle of the Marne, the frontline stabilized but there was a complete news blackout. Slowly, the occupying forces' regime was organized. Although they never starved, the missionaries waged a constant battle to fend off requisitions. The Germans wanted everything imaginable: bread, wheat, wine, beer, milk, butter, eggs, brass, mattresses, pillows, feathers, poultry, trees, horses. Food was obtained on the black market and meat was smuggled to the confreres across the French border in Lille, hidden in a hay wagon, even evading inspection at a German road block. A Dutch White Father, Henri Raeskin (1873-1956), had the house registered in the name of a civil society in the Netherlands and obtained a letter of attestation to this effect from the Dutch Consul in Brussels. The house had originally been bought by the Dutch Society of St. Charles of Boxtel, in 1905. The declaration: "We are neutral. Our property is Dutch" prevented or postponed the requisitions in most cases. The chapel bell was saved and also the wire fencing, but brass objects were prudently hidden from sight. The missionaries' worst suffering was to be deprived of any communication with the Society's superiors and with their own families.

The Fathers carried out supply work in local parishes, since many of the diocesan clergy had been arrested. Then, when the German frontline receded to Brussels in early October 1918, the White Fathers at Autreppe were caught up in the military retreat and the exodus of civilians from northern France. For the first time officers, men and horses were billeted on them. In the village, the church was pillaged and the Blessed Sacrament rescued by a fifteen year old boy, who brought the ciborium to the house. Two refugee diocesan priests and a seminarian were given White Father habits as a disguise. The firing line drew ever nearer and two bombs fell in the park. Then on the day before the Armistice British cavalry were spotted less than a mile away. The German lieutenant, who had been an unwelcome guest, bade the White Fathers farewell with the words, "You are now with the British. Goodbye".

The welcome afforded the British was euphoric. "Oh that encounter! What emotion! We laugh, we cry, we jump up and down. We would have embraced these brave sons of Albion, had they not been on horseback. We indicate the direction taken by the departing Germans. 'Alright' (was the reply)…May God bless this new era which is beginning and make this world peace last…!"

In Antwerp the occupation had been less threatening. The military had not even insisted on requisitioning brass objects, since it was a religious house. On the eve of the Armistice, German troops mutinied, forming their own councils before their departure. Four days after the Armistice, the White Fathers took part in the *Te Deum* in Antwerp Cathedral.[33] The occupation of Lille, where the Missionaries of Africa ran an apostolic school, was a different story altogether.[34] After their defeat in the first battle of the Marne, the Germans in vengeful mood descended on the town in early October 1914. As the siege began to bite, and the bombardment got under way, Eugène Kaise, "Brother Romuald" (1879-1949), who had been taken prisoner, managed to escape his captors and join the community. The first enemy troops entered the town, taking one thousand, five hundred prisoners in the process, while many French soldiers got away in civilian clothes. On October 13th the missionaries watched sixty thousand German troops parade through the town singing *Deutschland über alles*.

With fires raging in the town and the water supply cut, the enemy began taking hostages from among the clergy, the municipality and propertied classes. French prisoners were shuttled on to Germany, among them Joseph Bouniol (1884-1950). Attempts to make contact with him were to no avail. However, the missionaries were dispensed from providing billets, when the officers saw how Spartan the house was. French prisoners were paraded before the townspeople, who shouted *Vive la France* in defiance. Allied aeroplanes dropped bombs on telegraph installations and scattered propaganda leaflets and newspapers over the town. In 1916 there were mysterious explosions and fires, destroying a German arsenal, houses, factories and the city hall. Churches were requisitioned for meetings and concerts. Electric motors, church bells and organ pipes were removed, while teams of soldiers scoured the town for objects of brass. Typewriters, strong boxes, spare mattresses and pillows were all requisitioned.

The White Fathers had received from their neighbours many objects of brass or copper - candelabra and the like - for safe keeping. On November 14th 1917, the Superior was summoned by officers and soldiers to the street door at six in the morning and ordered to make a declaration of such objects. The answer was "nothing to declare". An inspection followed in which the box of chalices was closely scrutinized but the cupboard containing the candelabra was luckily overlooked. In January 1918, however, all the electric fittings had to be surrendered, since they contained copper. Only one electric lamp was allowed to remain in the house. In February, mattresses were taken and the only bell. The missionaries watched when the statue of Joan of Arc was taken down from its plinth in the square to be melted down for munitions. Soon afterwards, there was another visitation. This time not only were the copper items that had escaped notice on the previous occasion taken, but the brass door plate, door bell and door handles were all removed.

By July it was already clear that things were not going well for the Germans. In mid-September lorries were lined up in the streets and filled with furniture and other requisitioned goods ready for departure on the 29th. Males between the ages of fifteen and sixty-five were ordered to accompany the retreating soldiers. Alexandre Guérin (1864-1947) was on the point of being forced to obey this order, but was reprieved at the last minute. Before their departure, the Germans dynamited the railway, foot bridges, sluice-gates and telegraph installations. They also set fire to railway goods depots. Then on the night of the 16th/17th October they disappeared. Next day no Germans! Instead, a magnificent parade of victorious British and French troops took place and Georges Clemenceau joined the celebrations. Throughout the occupation the White Fathers' chapel had been well frequented and the Fathers had managed to keep in touch with some thirty of their pupils.

Livinhac and the General Council lost no time after the Armistice in issuing instructions to the Missionaries of Africa who were about to be demobilized. All conscripts who had taken their final missionary oath were asked to report to Maison Carrée in Algiers for a period of physical and spiritual rehabilitation. The latter was to take the form of an eight-day or thirty-day retreat. Aspirants who qualified for the novitiate were also required to come to Maison Carrée. Theology students were to report to the scholasticate at Carthage in Tunisia. But those who had been ordained priest before completing their theology studies were to follow a finishing course at Maison Carrée. Henri Gaudibert (1863-1929), one of the two White Fathers of British nationality, was also to make himself available for those who needed to brush up their English.[35]

More and more demobilized missionaries and ex-prisoners of war gathered around Livinhac in Algiers. Forty-seven made the thirty-day retreat. Many arrived in time to offer their New Year good wishes to the Superior General and to celebrate with him the Golden Jubilee of the Society. In his New Year speech, Paul Voillard hailed Livinhac as the "inspiration, regulator and co-ordinator of all (their) energies...to preside for a long time still over the new cycle of African regeneration which his sons, comforted by the retreat and spiritual exercises, will install when they return to their dear missions." Livinhac himself declared: "We must regard Africa henceforward as our true fatherland and devote ourselves generously to its salvation until death."[36] This notable post-war gathering was, in effect, a re-dedication of the Society of Missionaries of Africa.

The demobilized missionaries were given a euphoric welcome in their African vicariates. Those from Uganda, depleted by casualties and by some new appointments elsewhere, were still the largest number. Twenty-one White Fathers originally from Uganda, together with one from Nyanza, arrived in

Mombasa at the end of November 1919.[37]   The White Fathers' procure was hung with British and French flags and there were decorations in the chapel and dining-room. A jubilant letter awaited them from Henri Streicher, Vicar Apostolic of Uganda, who quoted the Book of Revelation. "Beloved and valiant confreres, I salute each and every one of you with respect, pride and love; for 'these are they who have come out of the great tribulation and have washed their garments in the blood of the lamb!'"[38] The Mombasa Times carried the headlines: "White Fathers Return from Active Service" and "Brave Chaplains Earn *Croix de Guerre*".[39]

The heroes travelled by train and steamer to Uganda. On the quayside to meet them at Entebbe were Bishop Streicher and his new auxiliary John Forbes (1864-1926), Daudi Chwa, *Kabaka* of Buganda and Stanislas Mugwanya, his Catholic minister, together with twenty confreres. On arrival, the *Marseillaise* and *God Save the King* were played. At Rubaga, the *Te Deum* and *Magnificat* were sung in church and a gala dinner followed at the mission. The menu included: *Rosbif de la Somme*, *Pommes de Terre Apostoliques*, *Legumes Alliés en Macedoine* and *Crème Maréchal Foch*. A cake bearing the battle honours had been baked by the Sisters of Mary Reparatrix and there were toasts, speeches, poems and songs. The dinner was followed by a visit to Government House, where Sir Robert Coryndon the Governor, admired a *croix de guerre* and examined a white flag signed by German parliamentarians on the occasion of the Armistice. On the Sunday following, Bishop Streicher pontificated, wearing the *cappa magna*, an archiepiscopal privilege recently bestowed on him by Benedict XV, and there was a reception hosted by John Biermans, the Mill Hill Bishop and Mugwanya.[40] It was a happy and exhilarating moment for the White Fathers and the Catholic Church in Uganda.

Changed Relationships with the Colonial Powers

The so-called "sacred union" of Church and State was an outcome of the declaration of war in 1914. Thenceforward patriotism overrode anti-clericalism in France and in the French possessions, and the former animosity disappeared when the war was over.   Relations between France and the Holy See were finalized a week after the canonization of the national heroine Joan of Arc in 1920, and her feast was declared a day of national homage. In Algeria many parishes had been closed for the duration of the war due to the clergy being mobilized. The Missionaries of Africa, however, continued in Kabylia with ten or eleven stations and some forty missionaries. Eleven priests and two brothers returned to the region after demobilization. The White Fathers' stock was high in the country, as so many had seen active service in the Zouaves and colonial infantry. Missionaries were allowed to staff schools and hospitals again, provided they had the requisite qualifications. On June 8th 1914 the government had decreed the closure of all mission schools and this was carried into effect in July. When hostilities broke out in August all the schools were allowed to reopen unconditionally, at least for the duration of the war.[41] The boarding schools and workshops run by the White Sisters (MSOLA) were especially esteemed.[42]

The missionaries hoped that anti-Christian prejudices would be diminished among Muslims as a result of their experience of the war, but legal problems still remained in spite of the disappearance of ill feeling. The civil status of Kabyle Christians in particular, under French or Muslim law, was a bone of contention.[43] Meanwhile, Henri Marchal's ideas concerning the catechumenate in the Islamic context began to be put into practice.[44] Henri Marchal (1875-1957) had been regional superior of Kabylia and Ghardaia until he was elected to the General Council of the Society in 1912. After active service, he returned in 1918 to the General Council where he remained until 1947.[45] In this long held position of authority he was able to revolutionize the White Fathers' attitude towards Muslims and promote a deeper understanding of Islam. The first fruit of these efforts consisted in the setting-up of the *Institut des Belles Lettres Arabes* (IBLA) at Tunis in 1927.

In 1919 Gustave Nouet (1878-1959) succeeded Henri Bardou (1877-1916*) who had left the society two years earlier, as Prefect Apostolic of Ghardaia (Sahara). The prefecture was not in the best of conditions. Most of the priests had been called up and only two stations remained open, Ghardaia and Wargla. Marchal's correspondent and mentor, Blessed Charles de Foucauld, had been tragically murdered by pro-Turkish dissident tribesmen on December 1st 1916 at his hermitage in Tamanrasset.[46] De Foucauld's spiritual heir, however, was Marchal whose new pastoral strategy towards Muslims was soon adopted by the Sahara communities. Ghardaia's school was allowed to continue in 1918, because it was run by a French Canadian with teaching qualifications.[47] Nouet reopened El Golea and reburied the body of Charles de Foucauld there in 1929.[48]

In the vast vicariate of French Sudan, progress had been hampered by both anti-clerical legislation and by the tyranny of distance. With the return of the conscripts and of the Vicar Apostolic, Alexis Lemaître himself, the Church found itself in a more favourable position. There was even a noticeable reaction against anti-clericalism.[49] In the west the vicariate drew its following from the Bambara and neighbouring peoples at the headwaters of the Niger and Senegal Rivers. In the east, missionary activity centred on the Kingdom of the Mossi, where Lemaître was able to found the new station of Manga. Meanwhile, a very promising centre had been founded at Pabre by the superior of Wagadugu, Joanny Thévenoud (1878-1949). Nearly five hundred acres had been acquired there and a development scheme started. Large numbers of people attended catechism and seven hundred joined the catechumenate in 1921. A parish was founded and a catechist training centre and junior seminary opened there in 1925. Pabre quickly became a model village and parish – a microcosm of evangelization among the Mossi.[50]

To concentrate the missionary effort effectively, the vicariate had to be divided. However, in Rome *Propaganda Fide* was opposed to the division as long as the Christian population was scarcely more than two thousand. The post-war years began to witness an increase. From two and a half thousand in 1914, the numbers reached three thousand in 1918 and eventually four and a half thousand in 1922. By this time, the request received added weight from the decision of the French Government in August 1919 to divide the region into the two colonies of Upper Volta (now Burkina Faso) and Upper Senegal and Niger (now Mali), with capitals at Wagadugu and Bamako respectively.[51]   A propitious moment for ecclesiastical division presented itself in 1920, with the translation of Alexis Lemaître to Carthage, as coadjutor and titular Archbishop of Cabasa.

In November 1920 the General Council of the White Fathers asked *Propaganda Fide* for a division of the vicariate into three.[52] A vicariate of "East Sudan" would correspond to the French colony of Upper Volta and a vicariate of "West Sudan" would correspond to the French colony of Upper Senegal and Niger. For Navrongo mission, which lay in the British Gold Coast colony, the "Prefecture Apostolic of Black Volta" was proposed. The names of Joanny Thévenoud, Emile Sauvant (1869-1939) and Joseph Dubernet (1875-1966) were put forward as vicars and/or prefect apostolic. In January 1921, Rome requested more information about the project and the General Council had second thoughts about the Black Volta prefecture.[53] Finally in July, Livinhac was able to announce that Sauvant and Thévenoud had been nominated heads of two new vicariates, to be called "Bamako" and "Wagadugu" respectively.[54] At the time of the division, Bamako possessed slightly more than two thousand Christians and Wagadugu just over three thousand. Compared with the statistics of Equatorial Africa, the numbers were tiny, but no one doubted the potential for growth. Needless to say, the British authorities were not happy that Navrongo was to remain in the vicariate of Wagadugu, a French colony. Thévenoud suggested that the Missionaries of Africa withdraw from the Gold Coast altogether and invite another missionary congregation to take over the mission.[55] Although the General Council agreed with this proposal, it was not followed up and the Prefecture Apostolic of "Navrongo" eventually came into existence in 1926 under the Canadian, Oscar Morin (1878-1952). At the end of 1921, the newly consecrated vicars apostolic, Sauvant and Thévenoud met at Kati, near Bamako to organize the two new vicariates and finalize their boundaries.[56]

A French government decree of 1922 made the White Fathers fear a revival of the anti-clerical Law of Associations of 1906, the application of which had been suspended. The decree stated that a permit was required from the administration in order to open a school or a church, and that the baptism of minors required a permit from the head of the family. Basically, the problem was caused by the juridical ambiguity of the Catholic Church in the French colonies. Without juridical recognition, the Church was obliged to operate under one or other cover provided by different companies or unions. After lengthy negotiations, the White Fathers' Missions became a moral person under the government and could administer the 1922 Decree themselves. Similar debates took place with regard to a Christian statutory law, especially concerning marriage. In all of these discussions the White Fathers appealed to the protocol of the Treaties of Versailles and St. Germain which guaranteed freedom of religion and the liberty of religious missions to continue their work in territories belonging to the Allies or ceded to them.[57]

In Equatorial Africa, the disappearance of the German colony and the creation of the Belgian and British mandates had far-reaching consequences for the Missionaries of Africa. The changes meant, on the one hand, that dealings with the Belgian Government became more extensive and on the other, that the bulk of the White Fathers' missions now lay in a belt of contiguous, English-speaking territories administered by Britain. On the eastern side of the continent 1922 was once again the year of ecclesiastical reorganization. The Kingdoms of Rwanda and Burundi had been ceded to Belgium as the mandated territory of "Ruanda-Urundi" and the whole region lay in the Vicariate Apostolic of Kivu. The retirement to Kabgayi of the pioneer Bishop John-Joseph Hirth (1854-1931) in 1921 was the signal for a division of the vicariate and each kingdom was given a separate circumscription. Léon Classe (1874-1945) became Vicar Apostolic of "Ruanda" and Julien Gorju (1868-1942), Vicar Apostolic of "Urundi". Classe had spent all his missionary life in Rwanda, and had been Hirth's vicar delegate there when it was still part of the Southern Nyanza vicariate. Gorju was a missionary in Uganda and was consecrated at Villa Maria by Bishop Streicher, during the latter's episcopal silver jubilee celebrations. The Christian population of Rwanda at the time of the division stood at nearly twenty-one thousand. In Burundi Christians numbered fourteen and a half thousand.

The replacement of the German administration by a Belgian government spelt the end of the German Protestant missions in Rwanda and Burundi. Moreover, the German prohibition against founding Catholic missions in the Tutsi chiefdoms was reversed. The removal of these obstacles certainly favoured the growth of the Catholic population. It must also be said that the survival of the Catholic Church after the departure of the Germans helped draw a clear distinction between missionary and colonialist.[58]

Henri Streicher's Uganda Vicariate had a hundred and four missionaries and fourteen diocesan priests in 1922. In its thirty-three mission stations there were nearly two hundred thousand baptized Christians. Four of his mission stations lay in the West Nile region of the Belgian Congo, and Streicher had asked for these to become a separate administration. While awaiting the decision of *Propaganda Fide*, and in spite of his heavy responsibilities in Uganda, he agreed in January 1921 to be administrator apostolic of the vicariate of Stanley Falls (Kisangani) in Congo.[59] In 1922 he was released from this additional burden, and the Congolese part of the Uganda vicariate became the Prefecture Apostolic of Lake Albert, with the Belgian, Alphonse Matthysen (1890-1963) as Prefect.[60] In this post-war period, therefore, the White Fathers found themselves with four vicariates or prefectures in the Belgian colonies, instead of only one.

Three of the White Father vicariates in the former German colony now found themselves in the British mandated Tanganyika Territory. The Nyanza vicariate of Bishop Joseph Sweens had twenty-one thousand Christians. After the war Joseph Mazé noted "a real and general movement of the people, and even of the chiefs themselves, towards the Catholic mission". Missionary personnel could not at first keep pace with the growth in numbers. He was also happy to see the British, unlike the Germans, giving employment to Christians as well as

Muslims.[61] Henri Léonard in Unyanyembe had around seven thousand and Joseph Birraux, appointed - as we have seen – in 1920 to the Tanganyika vicariate, had around twenty thousand. To the south, across the border with Central Africa, lay the vicariate of Bangweolo under Etienne Larue, with around thirty thousand neophytes, and the vicariate of Nyasa under Mathurin Guillemé, with around eleven thousand.

For the time being, the organization of Tanganyika Territory under its first British Governor, Sir Horace Byatt, was still rather rudimentary. Byatt had merely adapted the German system of administration. When Sir Donald Cameron became Governor in 1925, a sweeping reorganization took place, according to the ideals of "indirect rule", in which native authorities were everywhere identified and empowered. The fact, however, that Britain had replaced Germany on the East African mainland, meant that communication and co-operation were now easier across the borders of the various colonies. The first institutions to benefit were the major seminaries run by the White Fathers. The idea of a Regional Major Seminary for the vicariates of Unyanyembe, Tanganyika, Bangweolo and Nyasa, had long been a cherished project of Bishop Birraux, a former seminary professor and rector at Utinta. In 1919, it received added support and encouragement from the publication of *Maximum Illud*, the mission encyclical of Benedict XV. In this letter the Pope explicitly called for regional seminaries serving several dioceses.[62] It was decided in 1921 that the regional seminary would open that autumn at Utinta, on the lake shore of Bishop Birraux's vicariate.[63] The seminary duly opened in November with four students from Tanganyika vicariate and four from Unyanyembe.[64] In October 1922, when the bishops of the four vicariates met at Utinta, there were fifteen students. The bishops decided that the seminary should be transferred to Kipalapala, near Tabora. Rome approved the plan in 1923, and most of the new building was finished in the following year. St. Paul's Senior Seminary, Kipalapala, opened its doors in February 1925.[65] 1921 also saw the creation of an international White Fathers' region, comprising the Tanganyika, Bangweolo and Nyasa vicariates.[66]

Fired by the example of Utinta, the General Council of the Missionaries of Africa had the idea of joining Rubya Seminary, in Bishop Sweens's Nyanza vicariate, to Katigondo Seminary in neighbouring Uganda.[67] This did not happen immediately. In fact in 1929, the students from Rubya were sent to Kipalapala instead. Soon afterwards, they were switched to Katigondo and eventually returned to Kipalapala many years later in January 1967.[68]

Bishop Sweens, however, made frequent contact with the Uganda vicariate after the war. Among other things, he went to Villa Maria for the episcopal consecration of Julien Gorju in 1921. With his well known reputation for being accident-prone, the good bishop had one of his most spectacular mishaps on the journey. He was riding a donkey which wandered off the road as he was reading his breviary. As a result the venerable rider collided with the wire support of a telegraph post and nearly lost his left eye. The comment of the British resident in Bukoba was memorable: "My Lord, travelling by donkey is very dangerous".[69]

The colonial powers, it has been said, were "schizoid about Christianity".[70] On the one hand, they basked in the moral superiority which it provided. On the other hand, their aim was to build a modern progressive society which behaved as if God did not exist. After the 1914-1918 war, the Catholic missions continued providing social services in the fields of medicine and education, but they did so, very often, as paid agents of the state. They were no longer independent, as they had been in the early days of colonization, when they were ignored or opposed by governments. It was only in the seminaries that the Church was fully in control. Now, the missions began to be outpaced by secular institutions, and found themselves contributing in practice, if not in theory, to the ideal of an over-arching secularism

The Catholic Breakthrough

In the opinion of one historian of the African Church, the 1920s were the years of a "Catholic breakthrough".[71] After the First World War, the "Protestant ascendancy" was reversed and African society everywhere opened up to Catholic missionary influence more widely and more easily. It is true that missionary communication and recruitment were interrupted by the war, that Catholic vicariates were crippled by the mobilization or permanent repatriation of missionaries and that the first years after the Armistice were years of widespread hardship. However, it is also true that in the eight years covered by this book – 1914-1922 – the foundation was laid for a massive upsurge in Catholic numbers and influence.

These years also saw the consolidation of the colonial regimes, now that the "scramble for Africa" was finally over. From this point on, the European powers were masters in their own colonies, without the fear of external political rivalry, indigenous revolts or internal competition from the Church. It is often assumed that the Church's growth went hand in hand with the growth of the colonial administration, and there is no doubt that the fortunes of both were linked. However, it has also been asked whether it was not a disadvantage in the long run for Christianity to become part of the colonial project.[72] Colonialism was basically a secularizing force, which – in both French and British territories – directly or indirectly helped the advance of Islam, while remaining ambivalent towards the Church. "The end of colonial rule inhibited the expansion of Islam in Africa, whereas the opposite seems to have happened with Christianity."[73] The subversion of colonialism by Christian ideas became more and more evident as political independence drew nearer, and thereafter an even greater upsurge of Christianity took place in the continent without the Church needing to be propelled by colonial political structures. While colonialism held sway therefore, the place of Catholic Christianity in the colonial project was far from being always comfortable.

That being said, these years witnessed a growing alignment of the Catholic Church with the education policies of colonial governments. This was a process that started during and after the First World War, well before the extended tour of British Africa by Archbishop Arthur Hinsley, the Apostolic Visitor, in 1928-

1929.[74] Hinsley's message that that any conflict between evangelization and education should be resolved in favour of the latter was however an undoubted stimulus. The Missionaries of Africa had realized from the beginning that running schools was an important means of attracting converts and ensuring their steadfastness as well as training future priests. Indeed, this was originally the missionaries' major, if not their only, interest in education. After the war, both French and British administrations wanted them to enter still further into this field. Colonial regimes needed educated civil servants and professionals to implement their policies and operate their institutions and structures. They also felt the need to acquaint Africans with the intellectual and technological ethos of the west, if they were to take their place in the modern world. In 1922 a commission from the missionary inspired and privately financed Phelps-Stokes Foundation in America made recommendations to the British Colonial Office concerning education in West and South Africa. Two years later a second Phelps-Stokes commission visited East Africa, closely followed by the British government's own East Africa Commission under William George Arthur Ormsby-Gore.[75] One result of this flurry of educational investigation was the call for partnership between colonial governments and the missions. In government eyes, education was an ideal in itself that had, if possible, to be detached from the aims of religious proselytism.[76]

Catholic missionaries had already entered the field of secondary education, but they were not without interested motives. They saw the ownership of such schools as a guarantee for the future and a way to capture "the cream of the younger generation".[77] There was also a strong element of interdenominational rivalry. This was especially evident in Uganda where Catholic secondary education first made its appearance.

The Missionaries of Africa had for a long time attempted to influence the children of the traditional ruling classes through "schools for the sons of chiefs". This was the case with the court school at Nyanza in Rwanda, where the King and fifty children learned to read and write in Swahili.[78] At Mwanza, on the southern shore of Lake Victoria, the White Fathers accepted responsibility for a government "school for princes" started by the Germans. This was a boarding primary school, in which the government paid the expenses and the mission provided clothing and housing. The school became known as St. Leo's School, and Aloys Meyer (1873-1965) was appointed headmaster. There was a big turnover in school attendance. In 1920-1921 the academic year started with a hundred and eighteen pupils, but thirty-four left during the year.[79] The school survived the British occupation of Mwanza in 1916, the turmoil of the East African campaign and the change of regime.

The junior seminary that was opened in 1925 by Thévenoud at Pabre (Wagadugu Vicariate) was a secondary school, as were the long-standing junior seminaries on the other side of the continent. The first secular school at this level, opened by the White Fathers, was St. Mary's School, Rubaga. The 1906 General Chapter had already discussed the training of young Africans for administrative posts and the General Council invited Bishop Streicher to create a secondary school at Rubaga for this purpose.[80] Célestin Dupupet (1876-1949), the first French White Father in Uganda to be fluent in English, was appointed director.[81] As a fee paying school, the problem was how to attract the gifted poor. Although Streicher did not want to place himself under an obligation to the government, a subsidy was requested and granted. Already in 1910 Streicher could boast of St. Mary's impressive teaching staff and one hundred and thirty-eight pupils. The Protestant school at Budo, he wrote, "no longer has the monopoly".[82]

Vicars Apostolic became more and more convinced of the need to concentrate on education, in order to safeguard the future of the Church and confront the threat posed by successful Protestant Schools already in existence.[83] By 1913, it was clear that there was not enough room at Rubaga for the expanding school, and the General Council approved a plan to move it to a site near Entebbe, next to the Junior Seminary at Kisubi.[84] The outbreak of war, however, meant that the move had to be postponed.

During the war St. Mary's came into its own. In 1915 graduates of St. Mary's became interpreters in the KAR.[85] In 1917 three graduates were appointed interpreters for British troops and there were volunteers in other capacities for the war effort. All in all, a hundred and five served as medical orderlies, NCOs and warrant officers. Five were killed; two were decorated and two were mentioned in dispatches. "An excellent response to the Protestant super-high-school of Budo", was the comment of Balthazar Drost (1874-1959) who wrote the report.[86] St. Mary's became basically a secretarial school, and "even typewriters" were seen there by Frans Van Volsem (1893-1968) who visited in 1917.[87] Telegraphy and medicine were added to the syllabus during and after the war.

In January 1920 there were one hundred and fifty pupils and a staff of four, under the direction of the Canadian, Edouard Michaud (1884-1945). By 1922, out of two hundred and seventy alumni, a hundred and seventy were employed by the government. Of these, thirty-five were local chiefs and twenty were provincial or district Chiefs. Twenty were working in the government's telegraphy department. Altogether, St. Mary's was a focus of admiration from the Government and from the European community.[88] Eventually Canadian Brothers of Christian Instruction reopened St. Mary's at Kisubi in 1926. It has since become one of the most prestigious schools in Uganda, a model for secondary education in all the White Father vicariates.

The First World War saw the ordination of the first African diocesan priests. The first two had been ordained in Uganda in 1913. In 1917 four were ordained at Rubya for the vicariate of Nyanza and three were ordained at Kabgayi for the Kivu vicariate. In the same year, Stefano Kaoze was ordained at Baudouinville, the first African priest of Upper Congo. By 1922, the end of the period covered by this book, there were thirty-one African diocesan priests in equatorial Africa.[89] Everywhere, there appeared a real desire for the priesthood and seminaries were filled with candidates. Both the junior seminaries of Uganda and Rwanda, at Bukalasa and Kabgayi respectively, had a hundred students in 1921 and Katigondo Major Seminary in Uganda had a regular annual total of more than forty.[90] "If I died a thousand times and were reincarnated a thousand times, I would desire the priesthood a thousand times", exclaimed a Rwandan seminarian.[91]

The First World War enabled many Africans to seize the initiative in the Church. As Richard Gray pointed out, this was caused by the "beneficial removal of missionaries" through conscription or repatriation.[92] Catechists found themselves left to their own devices, running outstations on their own and teaching in places no missionary had visited. The emphasis on education helped to nourish their ambition to become teachers.[93] The White Fathers had been reluctant to give their newly ordained African priests pastoral assignments, and had kept them, in most cases, on the staff of junior seminaries. Shortages of personnel as a result of the war made it necessary to place them in parishes. In the last year of the war Victor Womeraka and John Muswabuzi, the first and third African priests of Uganda, were sent to the parish of Narozari. The appointment was a complete success and the report they made after their first year was ecstatic. In fact, it was reminiscent of the mission of the seventy-two disciples who came back rejoicing that "even the devils submit to us".[94] They had carried out a visitation of the whole parish, village by village, during twelve major tours. There had been an increase in baptisms and a notable growth of the catechumenate.[95]

The ordination of the first African priests in the Nyanza vicariate prompted a big movement of conversions which Bishop Sweens described as a "resurrection" for the diocese.[96] When one of them was appointed curate at Kagondo parish, a missionary confessed: "He understands and is understood better than us".[97] Even Stefano Kaoze, ordained in 1917 in Upper Congo, who was kept as a teacher at Lusaka junior seminary until 1928, was able to do pastoral work in the local parish and was appointed its parish priest in 1924.[98]

Perhaps the most eloquent visual symbol of the "Catholic breakthrough" was the building of Rubaga Cathedral in Kampala, Uganda. Preparations had begun as early as 1910, with the making and firing of bricks. These were carried by Christians from local brick-kilns to the building site at the top of Rubaga hill. By 1913 over six hundred thousand bricks had been brought on site.[99] Building was interrupted by the war, but the collection of money continued. In April 1917 a group of Catholic chiefs made a pledge to give a third of their income towards the project. This amounted to a total of £900.[100] In August it was the turn of the Catholic faithful to pledge a similar proportion of income. In January 1918 Bishop Henri Streicher laid the foundation stone and the building began to make rapid strides.[101] There were even premature rumours that Livinhac would come in person for the cathedral's consecration.

John Forbes (1864-1926) was closely involved with Rubaga, its prestigious St. Mary's School and with the cathedral building project. On May 19th 1918 he was consecrated coadjutor bishop of Uganda by its Vicar Apostolic, Henri Streicher. The ceremony took place in the old church, attended by the *Kabaka* of Buganda and other members of the royal family, the British Governor and members of the administration, eight Catholic chiefs and choirs from the seminaries and schools. The co-consecrators were John Neville, the Spiritan Archbishop of Zanzibar, Bishop John Biermans, the Mill Hill Vicar Apostolic of

Upper Nile and Bishop Joseph Sweens of Nyanza. The ceremony ended with the British National Anthem and a lunch provided by the Imperial Hotel.[102]

During the following year, the cathedral continued to rise slowly, but it was reckoned that the roof could not be finished until 1922. Meanwhile, Forbes went on a begging trip to Europe and Canada. In Rome he had an audience with Benedict XV who donated twenty-five thousand *lire* to the cathedral building fund and promised more if it were needed.[103] In Canada, Forbes collected a hundred and thirteen thousand dollars.[104] Meanwhile in 1921-1922, carpenters, metal workers and sculptors worked on the cathedral's furnishings, fittings and statues at St. Joseph's Technical School Kisubi. Although the arches of the crossing were incomplete and money was still needed, the unfinished cathedral was already being hailed as an unparalleled work of art.[105] Designed by Joseph van Griesven, "Brother Cyprien" (1872-1938), it has been described as a "red brick, clerestoried building in the Norman style, with twin towers (and) capable of accommodating five thousand people".[106] The Cathedral of the Sacred Hearts of Jesus and Mary, Rubaga, was consecrated at last by Bishop Streicher on October 31st 1925, in the presence of *Kabaka* Daudi Chwa and thousands of Christians from all over Uganda.[107] Alas, Bishop Forbes was not there to see it. He had been invalided back to France with heart disease in June, and died the following year at Billère in the Pyrenees on March 13th 1926.[108]

The final chapter of this book continues the story of the Society of Missionaries of Africa, as it unfolded during the last years of its first Superior General, Léon Livinhac.

CHAPTER NINE

BISHOP OF THE WHOLE SOCIETY

Livinhac and the Society 1919-1922

Paul Voillard, Livinhac's First Assistant, was seldom at a loss for words. On the occasion of the superior-general's episcopal silver jubilee in 1909, Voillard had hailed him as the "Bishop of the whole Society, the Superior of all our Bishops, Priests and Brothers. The Bishop of all our Missions."[1] When Livinhac died in 1922, he was one of sixteen White Father bishops. Eleven of them were active vicars apostolic in sub-Saharan Africa and two were active auxiliary bishops.[2] There were also two retired vicars apostolic.[3] What is more, Alexis Lemaître had just become Archbishop of Carthage. In addition, there were two prefects apostolic, who were not technically bishops.[4] Livinhac was the first Missionary of Africa to be ordained bishop and the first bishop in the interior of equatorial Africa. When he was appointed superior-general of the Society in 1890 and left Uganda for North Africa, he firmly declined the invitation to become Lavigerie's archbishop coadjutor in Carthage. He did not see his new role as compatible with that of a diocesan bishop.

Unlike Lavigerie, who combined the direction of his infant missionary society with his double role as Archbishop of Algiers and Carthage, Livinhac wanted to concentrate on his leadership of the society, then on the threshold of spectacular growth. Livinhac was completely practical. With his Uganda experience behind him, he foresaw that the management of the Society needed his undivided attention, however much he yearned to return to equatorial Africa. His diocese was to be the Society itself. Voillard was correct. Livinhac *was* "Bishop of the whole Society".

Léon Livinhac was born in 1846, in the *Massif central* region of France.[5] An orphan with delicate health, he nevertheless proved to be a good student and a hard worker. Completing his theological studies in the diocesan seminary of Rodez, he applied as a deacon to join the Missionaries of Africa in 1873. After a six month novitiate in Algiers, he was ordained priest by Lavigerie and started teaching theology at the scholasticate. Livinhac learned his missiology from Lavigerie and later was able to appreciate its relevance and practicality in Uganda. However, he learned his spirituality, that of Saint Ignatius Loyola, from his novice master, François Terrasse S.J. Lavigerie and Terrasse were the two great influences of his missionary life. Lavigerie, as he used to say, was his "father", Terrasse his "mother".

After a short period of fund-raising in France and pastoral work in Kabylia (Algeria), he returned to the scholasticate. Then, in 1878, barely five years after joining the society, he was named a member of the first caravan to Equatorial Africa and superior of the Nyanza mission, becoming its Vicar Apostolic seven years later. As bishop, he continued to share in the vicissitudes of the mission in Uganda - persecution, expulsion and restoration. Nominated Superior-General of the Society, he returned to North Africa and, after Lavigerie's death in 1892, became its unequivocal leader.

His first task was to rescue the Ugandan mission, after the country's heavy-handed annexation by Lugard on behalf of Britain. Facing the real possibility of the White Fathers being expelled as agents of French colonialism, he travelled to Britain in 1894 for an interview with the British Colonial Secretary, Lord Rosebery, and accepted the advice of his principal supporter in Britain, John Ross-of-Bladensburg, to invite the Mill Hill Missionaries to take responsibility for the sensitive region of the Nile head waters. He sent this proposal to *Propaganda Fide* which put it into effect at once.

A more insidious and far-reaching crisis was caused by the French government's anti-clerical legislation, which threatened the very existence of the Society itself. Livinhac had the delicate task of dealing with the politicians in France and Algiers, of coping with the practical consequences of the new laws, of making contingency plans and preparing his missionaries for a "worst case scenario". In the event, the Society was let off lightly and anti-clericalism was all but forgotten when war broke out in 1914.

Livinhac's next great task was to send an expedition up the Senegal River to the French West African interior, after successive attempts to cross the Sahara had failed in Lavigerie's time. Augustin Hacquard's caravan of 1894 opened up the vast territory of French Sudan to evangelization. A further achievement of Livinhac as superior-general was the promotion of vocations in Canada. Livinhac saw the value of having Canadian members of the Society to safeguard its international character and to find favour with the British authorities. He personally crossed the Atlantic in 1910 in order to visit the White Fathers' house in Quebec and to consolidate this policy.

Finally, Livinhac worked to achieve juridical status for the Society. The Constitutions were approved in 1908 and the Directory in 1914. Although Rome imposed a quasi-religious observance on the Missionaries of Africa, they remained a society of secular priests and lay auxiliaries, without religious vows, according to Lavigerie's original conception.

Livinhac was "Bishop of the Society" and a bishop is an administrator, teacher, spiritual father and focus of unity for his diocese. Livinhac was all these things for the Society of Missionaries of Africa. Administration, in his case, principally took the form of correspondence and the taking of decisions in the General Council of the Society. Not only was there official correspondence with *Propaganda Fide*, the Rome procurator, the vicars apostolic and the regional superiors, there was also the correspondence required of every

Missionary of Africa by the Constitutions.[6] Even with the minimum of one letter a year from each confrere, correspondence with a society of more than eight hundred members was a heavy burden. Until 1916, Livinhac himself answered virtually all the letters addressed to him, with the secretarial assistance of Louis Burlaton (1865-1932) and Lucien Duchêne (1857-1934). As we have seen, ill health intervened. Moreover, Burlaton and Duchêne were temporarily assigned elsewhere because of the war.[7] Thereafter, Livinhac was obliged to share the writing of these letters with his assistants Paul Voillard and Joseph Malet (1872-1950).

The General Council of the Society operated roughly on a weekly basis. Livinhac personally chaired all the meetings until five months before his death. His last attendance was on June 14th 1922. Thereafter, it was noted that he was "unavoidably absent".[8] Livinhac put his stamp on all the meetings he attended and sometimes his personal opinion was minuted in full. The General Council dealt with questions of varying importance from matters of great moment to the most trivial. It was concerned with the opening and closing of formation houses and procures in Europe and elsewhere. It dealt with reports, financial requests and disciplinary matters from bishops and regionals, with proposals for the division of vicariates and the nomination of vicars apostolic. It had a special interest in Kabylia and in the communities of North Africa dependent on the mother house at Algiers. Its regular business also included nominations and calls to the missionary oath and major orders, as well as the disciplinary cases of individual missionaries. Whereas Lavigerie only had first hand knowledge of North Africa, Livinhac had personal experience of both North Africa and equatorial Africa. This was immensely valuable for the General Council's work of directing the Society from day to day. However, Livinhac was unable to revisit his sub-Saharan missions. His plan to do this, after succeeding Lavigerie, was thwarted by *Propaganda Fide*. In 1902 another proposed journey received Roman approval, but had to be abandoned because of French anti-clerical legislation.

The General Council scrutinized all new inventions and trends towards modernity. The bicycle was being introduced into the missionary regions during these years. The Council did not question the enthusiasm of Bishop Henri Léonard who hailed the bicycle as the "instrument especially given by Providence for the salvation of the Nyamwezi" because it "suppresses distances and allows the missionaries to perform the miracle of bilocation".[9] Léonard believed that the introduction of the bicycle and motorcycle had made the sacraments of the sick more generally available.[10] The Council had no difficulty in permitting the use of the bicycle and even allowed the Priory, Bishop's Waltham, to buy twelve of them in 1914.[11] However, it was notably less keen on the motorcycle and refused the same community permission to buy one the following year, on the grounds that others might also want to have one.[12] In 1916, however, Jean-Marie Stéphant (1876-1938), was allowed to buy a second-hand motorcycle.[13] In 1915 the agricultural community at Thibar was allowed to use a motor car "only in cases of the most urgent necessity", but permission for a motor lorry was refused in the following year because of expense, the danger of accidents and its limited usefulness.[14]

Livinhac was a remarkable focus of unity for the Society. Not only was he personally known to all who had received their formation in North Africa, but he was in communication with them, as we have seen, through personal correspondence. Most of his teaching and spiritual guidance however was exerted through the circular letters he addressed to the whole society and which were highly appreciated. In the four years of life remaining to him after the war he produced a further fourteen circular letters. The first of these was the lengthy letter he wrote in celebration of the Society's Golden Jubilee in 1919.[15] It took him five months to compose. In it he retold the entire history of the White Fathers, beginning with the arrival of Lavigerie in Algiers in 1867 and concentrating especially on the story of the Uganda mission and the part he himself played in it. He was not afraid to mention the astonishment of the Spiritans at the unexpected arrival of the White Fathers in the African interior. The Spiritan plan to link hands across the continent from coast to coast was taking too long and was being overtaken by the Protestants. The peoples of the interior, he said, proved more receptive to the Gospel than those at the coast. Then there was the story of Upper Congo and the struggle against the slave traders led by Joubert.

These were the reminiscences of a great missionary pioneer and they ended with an affecting account of Lavigerie's death and his legacy to the Society he had founded. The success of the latter was due, Livinhac claimed, to the impulse and intercession of Lavigerie. Then, as the privileged exponent of the founder's teaching, Livinhac summed it up under five points: personal sanctification, prayer, charity, catechetical strategy and knowledge of languages. The continued success of the Missionaries of Africa depended on retaining the founder's spirit and on being penetrated more and more by Lavigerie's teachings. The circular was a remarkable summary of Livinhac's life and the expression of his deepest convictions as a missionary.

Livinhac returned to the historical theme the following year in a speech on his patronal feast day. The first caravan to equatorial Africa, which he had led in 1878, was no doubt "bold", but it had been vindicated, he said, by the fact that there were now a thousand Catholic missionaries at work between the Indian and Atlantic Oceans.[16] Pope Benedict XV, who received a copy of the Jubilee Circular, was so impressed by it, that he wrote Livinhac a hand written appreciation in reply to this "edifying letter".[17] Cardinal Van Rossum, Prefect of *Propaganda Fide*, also wrote and both letters were presented by Livinhac in subsequent circulars.[18] In November 1919 Benedict XV published the first papal missionary encyclical *Maximum Illud*. The main thrust of the letter concerned the formation of indigenous clergy and the renunciation of nationalism. Livinhac presented the encyclical in his first circular of 1920.[19] He placed the emphasis on two points: the fact that missionaries are not working for their countries of origin and the need for co-operation between vicariates and between different missionary congregations. There were other circulars on the Uganda Martyrs, the decisions of the 1920 General Chapter (both of which are discussed below), on devotion to St. Joseph, on the prevailing economic crisis and its relevance for apostolic poverty and on the modification of the Constitutions in the light of the 1920 Chapter and the new Code of Canon Law.[20]

Typically, his final circulars reflected his concern for the spirituality of his missionaries. Whenever Livinhac spoke in public, he included an exhortation to personal holiness through fidelity to the rule and "duties of state"[21]. He and the General Council insisted that the methods of St. Ignatius Loyola be used in the novitiate and scholasticate.[22]   Livinhac was assiduous about the eight-day annual retreat and the thirty-day retreat after some years of missionary experience. When Bishop Streicher in Uganda made difficulties over sending older missionaries to Algiers for the thirty-day retreat, the General Council laid down a procedure for such invitations, involving agreement between the vicar apostolic, the regional superior and Maison Carrée.[23]

Benedict XV's nomination of St. Ignatius Loyola as patron of all spiritual exercises in the Church was music to the ears of Livinhac, and he devoted his ante-penultimate circular to the subject, even though he could only dictate his message to others.[24] "The end of my pilgrimage is not far off", he declared, before reminding his readers that the founder had appointed Jesuits as the Society's first spiritual guides and stressing that "St. Ignatius should be the inspiration in all our retreats". Once again he turned to the rule as the principal means of sanctification and the spiritual exercises that it laid down. In February 1922 Livinhac returned to the subject of Lavigerie's recommendations, on humility, mortification, poverty and chastity.[25]   His final circular was a brief message of greeting, due – as he said – to tiredness.[26]

At the end of the war there were eight hundred and sixty-three members of the Society. When Livinhac died four years later, there were well over nine hundred. Membership reached four figures in 1925. After the inevitable slowing-down during the war years, the Society began to pick up again. Recruitment slowly increased. Visitors began again to besiege Maison Carrée, and the printing presses again took up the production of books in African vernaculars. Only four such books were produced in the war years. Between 1918 and 1922 twenty-five were printed, a prelude to the impressive lists of the mid-1920s onwards.[27]

Livinhac was always happy to correspond with African seminarians and newly ordained African priests. Victor Womeraka had written to him from Uganda at the time of his ordination in 1913, and in September 1917 he received a letter from one of the Rwandan ordinands, Baltasar Gafuku.[28] The new priests looked upon him as their spiritual grandfather. Livinhac was also overjoyed to welcome African visitors to Algiers. Barely two months before the outbreak of war, he received some Baganda celebrities, the Catholic minister Stanislas Mugwanya, his son, a senior chief and a royal prince.[29] In 1919, immediately the war was over, there were more African visitors: two Catholic Senegalese Riflemen and the first African priest of the Congo, Stefano Kaoze.[30]   These were followed in 1920, by two young sons of the Mogho Naba, King of the Mossi.[31]

The General Chapter of 1920

The war had prevented convening a general chapter of the Society. The last to be held had been in 1912 and the chapter that was due in 1918 had to be postponed. In 1919 Livinhac lost no time in announcing the delayed assembly. It was to open on April 15th 1920.[32] The state of the Society on the eve of the chapter was hopeful. Numbers had dropped for two years after 1917, through death and departures, but membership was now showing an increase for the first time since the war.[33] In Europe, Canada and North Africa there were twenty-five houses. France had seven. Belgium and Germany each had four. Student numbers were looking hopeful in 1920.[34] In Philosophy, there were forty-three at the newly acquired French seminary of Kerlois, twenty at Trier, sixteen at Bouchout and fifteen at Boxtel. In spite of the loss of ten to fifteen aspirants who gave their lives in the war, the novitiate at Maison Carrée had seventy-seven novice clerics and nineteen novice brothers. The following year the novitiate included eight Canadians, one of them already a priest and there were already more than forty Canadian members of the Society. In Marienthal there were thirteen novice clerics and nine novice brothers by 1921. In Theology there were twenty-eight students at Carthage, all but four of them demobilized war veterans, and eight at Trier. There were a dozen apostolic schools with rising numbers of pupils, one of them being the Priory Bishop's Waltham which was now permitted to recruit boys from Britain.[35]

Only two of the thirty-eight elected or official capitulants were unable to attend the chapter.[36] Six vicars apostolic and one prefect apostolic were present. Together with Livinhac, his four assistants and nine regional superiors they formed a body of twenty-one officials. There were fifteen elected delegates. Livinhac had once again tendered his resignation to *Propaganda Fide* before the chapter opened. Once again it was refused. The assistants elected by the chapter were Paul Voillard (1860-1946), Pierre Michel (1855-1926), Antoine Constantin (1874-1950) and Henri Marchal (1875-1957). It was foreseen, that in the event of Livinhac's death before the next General Chapter which was due in 1926, Voillard should govern the Society as Vicar-General.

Apart from the future of the German Vice-Province, already discussed in Chapter Seven, the meeting's deliberations focussed on the related question of erecting other new provinces, on the adaptation of the society's constitutions to the new Code of Canon Law and on relations between White Fathers and African diocesan priests. France and Belgium were to become provinces in their own right, with Switzerland joined to France. As we have seen, a German Province was to be created as soon as it was feasible to do so. Work on the eventual creation of a Dutch Province was also to begin, but in the meantime the Netherlands and Britain were to be dependents of the mother house, along with Canada, the North African houses and the procures in Rome and Africa.

In the discussions about African diocesan priests, the vicars apostolic who had already ordained them carried considerable weight. Predictably, in view of his negative outlook on African psychology, Bishop Victor Roelens of Upper Congo argued for separate living arrangements. Henri Streicher of Uganda was anxious that there should be no gulf between European and African clergy, while Joseph Sweens of Nyanza stressed the importance for bishops of knowing well their seminarians. Livinhac and Voillard both made a strong plea for White Fathers to have the formation of the local clergy very much at heart. Missionaries had to make sacrifices in this regard, even to the extent of giving up their mother tongue. African priests should not be placed with missionaries who were not welcoming. There was a wide ranging discussion on the merits of integrated communities, of placing African priests in an outstation, or of allowing them to staff a mission station of their own. Much of this debate was academic, seeing that African priests were already either living in an integrated community, as was Stefano Kaoze at Lusaka (Upper Congo), or running missions of their own, as were Womeraka and Muswabuzi in Uganda. The chapter also endorsed Benedict XV's advocacy of regional or inter-vicarial seminaries, especially in the British colonies. For female religious, it was noted that – apart from Uganda – there were many disappointments and few hopes. Rome wanted pious associations first of all, rather than religious congregations.

With regard to the Constitutions, the chapter was anxious that, whatever modifications were required by the new Code, the traditional practices of the apostolate and of community life should be maintained, as far as possible without change. Superiors however were exhorted to be more vigorous in imposing their authority. On a lighter note, a costume had to be found for bicycle riders. The chapter proposed a short khaki cassock (*gandourah*)! Having voted the amendments to the Constitutions, the General Chapter closed, after two weeks, on April 27th. A fortnight after its closure, Livinhac communicated its decisions to the Society in a circular letter. Its emphasis was on African priests and on the Constitutions. No mention was made of the sensitive German problem.[37] In the following year a further circular communicated the reactions of *Propaganda Fide*.[38]

The Fifteenth General Chapter was Livinhac's last. He had attended all of them except for four held during his absences in East Africa between 1878 and 1889.[39] The importance of the 1920 Chapter lay in its positive approach to post-war problems, its introduction of multiple provinces and its endorsement of the teachings of Benedict XV in his encyclical *Maximum Illud*. This was the only general chapter of the Society to take place in his pontificate, but Benedict's influence was important and lasting.

Benedict XV and the Uganda Martyrs

Benedict XV was virtually unknown to Catholics until Joseph Ratzinger, on becoming pope in 2005, evoked his memory by taking the same name. Benedict XV was the "unknown pope", "the forgotten pope", "the most invisible pope" of the twentieth century. Only now is his stature as peace-maker appreciated, and only today is it clear that he helped to lay the foundations for the Church's massive presence in Africa.[40] Giacomo Della Chiesa was born prematurely on November 21st 1854. He was small, frail and walked with a limp. As a child he was unable to play games. His appearance was unattractive, with a sallow complexion and prominent teeth. In fact everything about him was crooked: his nose, his mouth, his eyes and shoulders.[41] And he was notoriously tone-deaf. In short, he had what is nowadays called "an image problem". Mentally, however, he was sharp and precise. He had a neat, ordered mind, and a taste for unobtrusive and unrelenting hard work. In the *Curia*, where he was nicknamed *piccoletto*, he gained the reputation of being a discreet powerbroker.

At the age of twenty-seven he met Mariano Rampolla del Tindaro, the Nuncio in Spain, who immediately appreciated his talents. Rampolla took him as his secretary to Madrid, and returned with him to Rome when he was made Secretary of State by Leo XIII in 1887. As Rampolla's *minutante*, Della Chiesa got to know the Church. He also came to know the missions and especially the Society of Missionaries of Africa, the founder of which was Rampolla's friend Lavigerie, and of which Rampolla himself became the Cardinal Protector at Lavigerie's death. In 1901 Della Chiesa became Under-Secretary of State, but two years later St. Pius X became pope and Rampolla was effectively disgraced, being appointed Archpriest of St. Peter's by his successor as Secretary of State, Rafael Merry del Val. Barely four years later, Della Chiesa was also sidelined and made Archbishop of Bologna.

The Archbishopric of Bologna normally carried with it a cardinal's hat, but Della Chiesa, as Rampolla's associate, was suspected of being a Modernist sympathiser, and it was not until Rampolla died in 1913, that Merry del Val considered it safe to accede to demands from Bologna and allow Pius X to make its archbishop a cardinal. Della Chiesa was devastated by Rampolla's death, but had little time to grieve. In just four months time, at the end of August 1914, the newly appointed cardinal was elected the successor of St. Pius X. The Cardinals' choice of Della Chiesa probably had more to do with the anti-modernist controversy than with concerns about the war. They wanted a moderate with both curial and pastoral experience, someone with a reputation of being soft on Modernism. Peace however was the motto of St. Benedict, and the choice of name both distanced the new pope from the policies of the previous pontificate, and suggested that peace making would be his major preoccupation.

There was no grandeur about Benedict's wartime election. Even the smallest of the three white cassocks prepared for the new pope was too big for him. His coronation took place quietly in the Sistine Chapel and his first papal blessing was delivered from an internal *loggia* to a congregation inside St. Peter's. It is said that Benedict discovered a denunciation of himself as a Modernist among his predecessor's papers.[42] Be that as it may, he quietly dismantled the anti-modernist apparatus and restored freedom of theological debate. His first encyclical called for concord and an end to the witch hunt. Nevertheless, two days after his inauguration he also issued an exhortation to the belligerent nations to put an end to armed conflict, sincerely believing that peace was the foremost doctrine of Jesus Christ. "Like truth", it has been said, Benedict himself "was one of the first casualties of war."[43]

Something has already been said about his attempts to end the war and to mitigate its horrors – attempts which were almost universally misunderstood. In his Christmas messages of 1915 and 1916 he declared that the world had become "a hospital and a charnel house" and that the war was the "suicide of civilized Europe".[44]   His appeals fell on deaf ears and his peace initiatives provoked scorn and abuse. Part of the problem was that the Vatican's sovereignty was not yet recognized and that, while Germany and Austria had access to the Holy See, France, Britain and most other European nations had no regular diplomatic representation. After the war, Benedict was critical of the Versailles Treaty and the humiliation of Germany. Above all, he strove to persuade the warring nations to forget their former hostilities.

The Missionaries of Africa were among those who knew Benedict and welcomed his election. Louis Burtin (1853-1942), their long-serving procurator in Rome, had known Della Chiesa for more than a quarter of a century and was a personal friend.[45]   There is even a tradition in his family that he was approached by the anti-clerical French government of the day to provide a window of information in the Vatican and that he had the temerity to mention this to the Pope.[46] On numerous occasions Benedict expressed his admiration for the Society, singled out White Fathers at audiences for a special word or blessing, and made generous donations to the Society's projects and to famine relief in Africa. After the war, the uncertain fate of the missions in the former German colonies convinced Benedict of the dangers of European nationalism and imperialism for Catholic missionary work. Missions had too often become the religious "colonies" of nationalistic missionary institutes or provinces. There was a risk of "territorial feudalism", to use the phrase coined by Celso Constantini at *Propaganda Fide*.[47]   Hence Benedict's anxiety to prepare the post-colonial future of the missions by the formation of an indigenous clergy and by stressing the need for co-operation between vicariates and missionary congregations in this work. These were major themes of *Maximum Illud*, a text that has been called the "most important and most significant" papal document until Paul VI's *Evangelii Nuntiandi* of 1976.[48] Hence also his reason for founding the Ethiopian College in 1919 in the Vatican City itself, and in addition his predilection for international missionary societies, such as that of the White Fathers.

It is in this context that Benedict's beatification of the Uganda Martyrs in 1920 must be seen. The cause of twenty-two Catholic young men, most of them servants or officials of the royal court of Buganda, who died for their faith in 1885-1886, had already begun in the pontificate of Leo XIII.[49] Steps towards their eventual beatification had been taken as early as 1887 with the gathering of oral testimonies from witnesses and written testimonial references. The cause had been officially introduced in Rome in 1912. Thereafter, the validation process continued at sessions held in Villa Maria during the war until 1916.[50] In that year, Michele Franco (1874-1955), the Italian Rector of Katigondo Seminary, carried the precious documents to Rome. The Acts of the Apostolic Process had been placed in a container closed with the seal of Bishop Henri Streicher. It was important that the seal should be unbroken when the container was handed over to the Congregation of Rites, as evidence that the contents had not been tampered with. Franco took the precaution of obtaining a legal declaration concerning the container's contents from the Italian Consul at Mombasa before boarding the boat for Naples. In spite of this, on his arrival the

Italian Customs wanted to open the container, and Franco needed all his powers of persuasion to prevent this happening.[51]

Simultaneously with that of the Uganda Martyrs, the cause of an Algerian martyr, the Venerable Geronimo, was also introduced in Rome, and there was a single procurator and *ponent* for the two causes. In principle, the two proceedings were separate, but there was a considerable overlap in practice. There is also the unavoidable suspicion that the cause of Geronimo suffered in the long run from unfavourable comparison with that of the Ugandans. It is necessary, therefore, to say something first of all about the Geronimo story.[52]

Our information about Geronimo derives principally from Diego de Haëda's *Topography and History of Algiers*.[53] De Haëda was a Spanish monk, Abbot of Fromesta, whose book appeared some seventy years after Geronimo's death. De Haëda had collected accounts of the sufferings of Christian captives in Algiers, among them the story of a small boy of four, taken by Spaniards in a foray on a local tribe around the year 1536. The boy was brought to Oran, where the Vicar-General Juan Caro, raised him as a Christian and gave him the name Geronimo. During the plague of 1542 the boy escaped and returned home. However, as a young man in his early twenties, he came back to Oran in 1559, was received again by Caro and returned to the practice of his Christian faith. Having married an Arab Christian girl, he joined an armed gang that raided a village by the sea and was again captured and sold as a slave, this time in Algiers. There he was forced to choose between renouncing his Christian faith and being buried alive. Geronimo chose death. On September 18th 1569 he was thrown alive into one of the great cases of adobe concrete, from which blocks were being made for the Fort of the Twenty-Four Hours. The block was subsequently built into a wall of the fort, but its position was remembered by the Christian Master-Mason, Michael of Navarre.

Although de Haëda's authorship was later disputed, and details of his story impugned by Muslim apologists, it received dramatic confirmation from a discovery made in 1853, when the French demolished the fort. During the demolition, a block was split open, revealing human bones. Moreover, a plaster cast of the cavity left by the decomposed body provided evidence of the death throes of a man who had been bound and suffocated. The remains were assumed to be those of Geronimo.[54] Antoine Pavy, Lavigerie's predecessor as Bishop of Algiers, obtained a rescript from Pius IX declaring Geronimo "Venerable", and the bones were enshrined in Algiers Cathedral in 1854. When Lavigerie became Archbishop of Algiers after Pavy's death, he took the matter up with enthusiasm. The Missionaries of Africa, founded by him, were even briefly called "The Society of Missionaries of the Venerable Geronimo" in 1869, a discreet reference to their Muslim apostolate.[55] At the same time, the process for beatification was begun in Rome. However, the dossier seems to have been mislaid in the upheavals accompanying the capture of Rome in 1870 and the process was interrupted for some forty years.

On June 12th 1912 the cause of Geronimo was reintroduced in Rome at the same time as that of the Uganda Martyrs. In 1913 the plaster cast of his body (afterwards placed in the Museum of Algiers) was exhibited in the parlour of the

White Fathers' novitiate at Maison Carrée and a young Kabyle girl in Ouadias was allegedly cured through his intercession in the following year.[56]   A preparatory meeting of the Congregation of Rites in 1915 requested an exhaustive refutation of Muslim objections and at another meeting in March 1917 some of the consultors still had last minute difficulties with the Muslim apologetic.[57]   At the end of 1918 a "neo-preparatory" congregation was held to discuss doubts about Geronimo's cause. Louis Burlaton (1865-1932), a keen supporter of the cause, had provided more evidence and Burtin sent an optimistic telegram to the Archbishop of Algiers: *Congregation favourable.*[58] The Congregation requested an extraordinary grace or miracle wrought at the Venerable Geronimo's intercession and it was decided to present the cure of the Maltese Bishop of Sfax, Tunisia, Monsignor Polomeni. Burlaton was to compile a final substantiation of the martyrdom and authentication of the relics.[59]

Burtin's optimism, alas, was not borne out. A General Congregation on the martyrdom, signs and miracles of the Venerable Geronimo was held on December 2nd 1919 in the presence of Benedict XV himself. The consultors were not satisfied with the heavenly favours cited, and the Pope personally requested that the beatification of Geronimo should be deferred until an undoubted miracle had been worked by the venerable martyr. "May our confreres unite with us to obtain one from heaven", was Burtin's pious – but by now desperate – wish.[60]   Swallowed up in the avalanche of enthusiasm for the Uganda Martyrs that swept the Society and the African Church during and after 1920, the wish was not heeded and no further mention of Geronimo appeared in the records of the Missionaries of Africa.

By contrast, the progress of the Uganda Martyrs was triumphant. On July 3rd 1917, the validity of the process was attested by the Congregation of Rites meeting at the Vatican and on July 8th 1919 a Preparatory Congregation for the beatification took place.[61] The "miraculous signs" cited in the documents were principally the mass conversions to Christianity in Uganda which followed the martyrdoms. On February 10th 1920 a General Congregation was held in the presence of Benedict XV. The beatification was approved unanimously and the postulator was invited by the Pope to make the official request at a solemn session on February 29th. This was done and the decree issued. The beatification was to take place on June 6th and Benedict requested that preparations begin immediately. In normal circumstances two more decrees were required, but the Pope waived all further bureaucracy, famously declaring: "The cause of the Uganda Martyrs is my cause". Nothing was to delay its progress. When Bishop Mathurin Guillemé of the Nyasa vicariate visited Rome in December, Benedict told him: "I wanted to beatify them this year myself so as to show the Catholic world that the black race, like the white race, can be raised by divine grace to the altars".[62]

Burtin had three months in which to make the arrangements.[63] The artist Luigi Bartolini was engaged to paint the picture of the martyrs that would be placed in Bernini's "glory", and Professor Ballerini painted the banners for the Bronze Doors and the *Loggia*. A book on the lives of the martyrs was written and seven thousand copies printed. Twenty thousand holy pictures were produced in three sizes for distribution in St. Peter's and at the Vatican congregations. Apart from Archbishop Leynaud of Algiers and Bishop Roelens of Upper Congo, who were given rooms at a neighbouring convent, all the guests of the White Fathers, including bishops, were to be lodged at the *procure* in Via degli Artisti , two or three to a room.

Livinhac had dearly wanted to be present, but his state of health did not permit a journey to Rome. Instead, he was represented by Ludovic Girault (1853-1941), the only other survivor of the First Caravan to Uganda. He had himself baptized three of the martyrs.[64] Arthur Prentice (1872-1964) accompanied two Ugandan confessors of the faith, now in their forties: Joseph Nsingirisa or Mbubi, who had been imprisoned with the martyrs, and Denis Kamyuka who, at the last minute, had been spared the fire of Namugongo itself. Three MSOLA (White Sisters) and a Congolese party that included Stefano Kaoze arrived with them. On Thursday June 3rd Benedict received Streicher and the two Ugandans in audience. The latter were made Knights Commander of the Order of St. Gregory. The Pope also revealed that he himself had been cured of rheumatism in his right arm at the intercession of the martyrs.

The beatification was preceded by a *triduum* organized by Propaganda Fide at the Church of Sant' Andrea delle Frate. At this, a panegyric of the martyrs was preached each day, followed by Benediction of the Blessed Sacrament. On Sunday, June 6th, the beatification itself took place. In the morning the decree was read in St. Peter's in the presence of five White Father vicars apostolic; the Archbishop of Algiers; the Greek Melchite Patriarch; Henry Hanlon, first Mill Hill bishop in Uganda, and the superior-general of the Society of African Missions (SMA). A Solemn *Te Deum* was sung and Mass was celebrated by Cardinal Merry del Val (now – with poetic justice – a successor of Rampolla as Archpriest of St. Peter's).[65]

The papal ceremony was scheduled for five-thirty in the afternoon and the basilica was already full by four. Among the guests were the ambassadors of France and Britain. Benedict XV entered wearing a red *mozetta*. He was accompanied by nineteen cardinals and thirty bishops. A bouquet from the Rome Carmel was offered by Louis Burtin, the postulator of the cause, and the two Ugandan confessors presented the biography of the martyrs and a reliquary of Blessed Charles Lwanga, which the Pope kissed. Henri Streicher delivered an address of thanksgiving to the Pope and this concluded the simple ceremony. Leaving the basilica, the two Ugandans were besieged on all sides by bishops, prelates and members of the faithful, eager to embrace them, touch them or to kiss their hands. Throughout the following week there was a procession of cardinals, prelates and religious who came to the Via degli Artisti to meet the two confessors. The two also received an enthusiastic welcome at the Gregorian University and the Roman Seminary.

At a subsequent papal audience, Bishop Roelens presented Stefano Kaoze to the Pope who said he had already spotted him near the altar at the beatification; and Burtin presented the Pope with pictures of the martyrs. Benedict's comment was: "These at least are real black faces. I noticed that in the banner in St.

Peter's on the day of the beatification the painter had made them nearly white!"[66]

Pierre Roche (1861-1943) conducted the two Ugandans to Naples where they visited the major seminary and prepared their return journey to Mombasa. Honoured by the Pope and fêted by Catholic clergy and laity alike, the two confessors were refused berths by the British steamship company, whose racist policy did not admit black passengers. At length an Italian company gave them places in the lowest class.[67] The contrast between an inclusive Church and a discriminatory colonial system could not have been starker.

In Uganda a pilgrimage to Namugongo, the major site of the martyrdoms, took place on the day of the beatification, and there was a *triduum*, like the one in Rome, as well as a *Te Deum* at Rubaga. This example was copied in many dioceses and vicariates. Even Algiers Cathedral, last resting place of Geronimo who had been eclipsed by his brothers from the equator, was the scene of a joyous *Te Deum*. In May 1921, the Feast of the Martyrs on June 3rd was proclaimed.[68] The impact of the beatification on the Christians of Uganda and Africa generally was striking. It signalled a growth of spiritual awareness and an enhanced appreciation of the virtues for which the martyrs stood: faith, purity and forgiving love. Livinhac, in his circular on the martyrs saw it as a renewal for the whole Society.[69] Certainly, it placed before the Missionaries of Africa the ultimate goal of their evangelistic endeavour in no uncertain terms. Taking a wider perspective, the beatification coincided with the imminent upsurge of the Catholic Church in Africa, just as the canonization of these same martyrs by Paul VI in 1964 coincided with an even more rapid rise of Catholicism after political independence.

Benedict XV died on January 22nd 1922, at the comparatively early age of sixty-seven, after a reign of only seven years and five months. His last words were: "I offer my poor life to God for the peace of the world". The editor of the White Fathers' bulletin *Petit Echo* summed up the feelings of his confreres. "Our little Society in particular will never forget the marks of esteem and paternal affection with which it was honoured by Benedict XV."[70] Achille Ratti, the newly elected pope, who took the name of Pius XI, had been virtually groomed by Benedict to be his successor. All Benedict's policies, especially where missionary work was concerned, were followed by him. He had met Louis Burtin in 1888, when the latter accompanied Lavigerie to Milan during the Anti-Slavery Campaign. After his election, he told Burtin how moved he had been by the painting of the Uganda Martyrs that hung in the *procure* at Via degli Artisti.[71] But Pius XI was not Benedict XV and the Missionaries of Africa never again enjoyed the papal esteem they had during the pontificate of Della Chiesa.

Archbishop of Oxyrhynchus

Those who encountered Léon Livinhac came away with two basic impressions: his universal kindness and his outstanding holiness.[72] After World War I his leadership of the Missionaries of Africa was at an all-time high. He was not just the distant hero of the first caravan to Equatorial Africa, but a warm-hearted person, deeply concerned for the spiritual and material welfare of the missionaries in his charge. He was someone whom everybody thought they knew. Mathurin Guillemé expressed the thoughts of many, when he wrote to Voillard after receiving the news of Livinhac's death. White Fathers, he said, had become so accustomed to him, after his thirty year superiorate, that they thought he would be there forever. It was difficult to imagine the Society without him.[73]

Livinhac's proverbial kindness was not just part of his nature. It was cultivated through personal self-conquest. His instincts tended towards impatience, even irascibility, but he quickly suppressed all such feelings, especially when interrupted by an unexpected visitor. Visitors were received in the kindest possible way, and went away ravished by the consideration he had shown them. Livinhac was able to adapt himself to everyone. His experience of North Africa, of Equatorial Africa and of formation work gave him something in common with every member of the Society. He showed an interest in everyone's conversation during recreation and was completely at ease with the novices and scholastics. He made a point of remembering the feast days of the confreres in the community and paid special attention to the sick at the sanatorium, visiting them once or even twice a day. He had absolutely no interest in politics or world events. His was a simple, uncomplicated goodness.

Linked to this goodness was a characteristic spirit of humility. Livinhac spoke so disparagingly about himself on so many occasions, that one is left with the impression that he had a low self-esteem. But this was not really the case. Although he was quite sure of his opinions and of the decisions he had to make, he really did believe that he was not the best person for the task he was doing. This made him all the more certain of God's guidance in the affairs of the Society. He declined honours and sought release from responsibilities for which he felt unqualified, but he also believed that God's grace was given to those who were obedient to their superiors and faithful to their "duties of state".

In a tribute paid to him after his death, a preacher declared "one day he will be called 'Saint'", but there were many who called him thus in his own lifetime.[74] For Alexandre Le Roy, Superior General of the Spiritans, Livinhac was the most saintly person he had ever encountered, and the Prioress of the Rome Carmel described his calling at her convent as "the visit of a saint".[75] A Dutch brother, Antoon Stootman - "Brother Boniface" – (1869-1968), who lived to be nearly a hundred and who had been with Livinhac in his early days at Maison Carrée and at the end of his life, always believed he had been in the presence of a saint.[76] In the tradition of the Society, Lavigerie was known as the "venerable founder", but his successor was always "the holy Monsignor Livinhac".[77] Miraculous cures, which he refused to acknowledge, were even attributed to him in his lifetime.[78]

The Anglican missionary, Philip O'Flaherty, met him in Uganda and wrote of him: "Livinhac I love. He and I have many long walks, talking of the deep things of God – those delightful things that refresh the spirit. And O the spirit needs to be refreshed in this dry parched land. We take a mutual pleasure in each other's company".[79]

In what did the holiness of Livinhac consist? There is no doubt that – apart from his characteristic kindness - Livinhac saw a scrupulous fidelity to the rule as the indispensable means of sanctification. This was linked to the interior life, the spiritual exercises and accepted practices of piety. These were mentioned again and again, in his spoken and written exhortations to confreres, and it was by these principles that he himself lived. A striking example of his fidelity to the rule was given by Victor Lardeux, "Brother Félicien" (1890-1960), one of the infirmarians who nursed him at Maison Carrée during his last illness. The brother was talking quietly with Joseph Petibou (1881-1942), his fellow infirmarian, outside the room, when Livinhac rose from his sick bed, opened the door and said, "We do not talk like this in the corridors. Go to your room to say what you have to say".[80]

Livinhac's asceticism was not extreme, but was part and parcel of his obedience to the rule. He slept on a modest camp bed, a reminder possibly of his Spartan missionary existence in Uganda, and rose without fail at four in the morning. The community found him already in silent prayer before the Blessed Sacrament when they came to chapel. He abhorred unnecessary luxuries and this was the basic reason for his intolerance of tobacco. He exploded with wrath on hearing that a missionary had ordered thousands of francs' worth of cigars from a factory in Europe. It was, he said, "a grave fault of scandalous expense that could cause scandal to the benefactors."[81] Towards the end of his life he became more and more sensitive to infringements of the rule and this explains other pronouncements of his which appear quirky to us today. During the war, missionaries serving at the front became used to wearing longer hair and being clean shaven. Livinhac demanded immediate conformity to the rule which laid down that missionaries should have closely cropped hair and wear long beards. The razor, he declared, "is an instrument that should not even appear among a missionary's possessions."[82] In the very last year of his life he became embroiled in a controversy concerning Eucharistic practice. The rule laid down that retreatants should abstain from receiving Communion during the first three days of the annual retreat, but to some missionaries this seemed to be at odds with the practice of frequent Communion introduced by Pope St. Pius X. Livinhac insisted on the abstention and was only convinced of the contrary when *Propaganda Fide* intervened on the side of the innovators.[83]

Livinhac had great respect for the rubrics of the Mass and the divine office. He prayed the breviary, the *angelus* and the rosary every day almost until his death. In his final illness he received a faculty from Rome to replace the breviary by the rosary, but insisted that those who nursed him should continue to recite the divine office for him. Health permitting, he visited the cemetery every Sunday in order to pray for deceased confreres. He said grace over everything he ate or drank and even in his final delirium did not fail to bless the medicines he was taking. Above all, Livinhac was faithful to meditation and the Ignatian spiritual exercises. On his deathbed, the *Suscipe* of St. Ignatius Loyola was among the favourite prayers he recited.[84]

In 1921 the four General Assistants of the Society decided that the time had come to ask the Pope to grant Livinhac the title of archbishop. Alexis Lemaître had already been made Archbishop-Coadjutor of Carthage with right of succession in July 1920. Was it thought fitting that, if Livinhac were to remain "Bishop of the whole Society" and Superior of all its bishops, he too should have archiepiscopal status? Or was it simply a desire to honour the man now entering upon his thirtieth year as superior-general? Voillard, who followed Livinhac, was to rule the Society for fourteen years without becoming a bishop, let alone an archbishop.[85] Whatever the motivation, the plot was hatched behind Livinhac's back in order to present him with a *fait accompli*. Had he known about it, he would have refused the honour in no uncertain terms. Louis Burtin made the request in the name of the General Council. This he did in spite of a violent agitation by Mussolini's Fascists on the streets of Rome. On his way to the Vatican the Fascists made him alight from the tram and continue his journey on foot. Under a hail of bullets, Burtin was forced to take cover until the police arrived. He was miraculously unscathed, but others with him were wounded. After this dramatic adventure, the request was handed in, and received a favourable response.[86]

On July 27th 1921 a telegram arrived at Algiers from Burtin with the news. Livinhac received it without enthusiasm, fixing an accusing look on Voillard and his fellow conspirators.[87] The title was officially granted at a Secret Consistory of November 21st. Up to this point, Livinhac's episcopal title had been Bishop of Pacando.[88] Now he was titular Archbishop of *Oxyrhynchus*, a designation relinquished by John MacIntyre on becoming Archbishop of Birmingham in England.[89] The curious and inelegant name *Oxyrhynchus* referred to an Egyptian town on the Nile, at the end of the western desert. In Pharaonic times it had been a focus for the cult of a "sharp-nosed" fish, the *Oxyrhynchus*, or Bronze Nile Perch, which featured in a disagreeable myth concerning the god Osiris.[90] Oxyrhynchus, the town, (now Al-Bahnasa or Behnesa) had become an important Christian centre and metropolitan see. It was said to have had more monasteries than private houses and there was a legend that the Holy Family had visited it during the flight into Egypt. Archaeological excavations had taken place at the site in 1896 and 1907, and fragments of New Testament papyri of the third century had been found there.

A dinner was held at the novitiate to celebrate Livinhac's new honour and Voillard was forced to do some explaining. He pulled out all the stops in a witty speech to which not even Livinhac could object.[91] The General Council, he said, was not to blame. It was a plot laid in heaven itself by the Uganda Martyrs who wanted their grandfather *Vinyaki* to share their honour by having another row of tassels added to his episcopal hat.[92] The Martyrs had asked the *Namasole* (Queen Mother) Mary to support them and as her ambassadors they appeared in a vision to Benedict XV. As a result, the Pope had decided to change Livinhac's title from distant Pacando (in Turkey) to a place on the river that flows from Lake Nyanza, in which the Martyrs were baptized. Voillard succeeded in bringing Lavigerie into the story and all the first missionaries and deceased vicars-apostolic. The tale ended with the approval of Jesus himself! Voillard added somewhat lamely that if his story was an exaggeration, it was certainly true that this recompense for Livinhac's labours was not made without the intercession of the Martyrs and the desire of the Blessed Virgin.

In his reply, Livinhac put the best face on it that he could. The honour was not for him. "What am I? An old man, an unknown. It is to our Society that this honour is addressed. The Society is archbishop, not me!" "Pacando was enough", he told the novices later, on the Feast of the Immaculate Conception.[93] The whole episode was a final test of Livinhac's meekness and obedience. Voillard congratulated himself on the success of his ploy. "I found the means", he wrote, "of showing everyone how this favour of the Holy See was legitimate. I did it with the dessert, in such a way that *Monseigneur* appeared to accept it willingly. In the evening he seemed happy with the day and everyone shared his happiness. May God be praised!"[94]   However, *Monseigneur* remained suspicious and mildly resentful, writing to Burtin in January "the culprit is perhaps you".[95] In the event, the incident was overshadowed by the death of Benedict XV and the election of his successor.

The Last Days

Livinhac was a tall man and continued to carry himself well, but he was becoming more and more frail, and his bouts of fatigue became longer and more frequent. He spoke often of his old age and approaching death. "I have an illness called seventy-five years", he joked in 1921.[96] At the New Year celebration of 1922 he also spoke of his great age, which gave him the right to quote the words of St. Paul: *cupio dissolvi*, "I long to be dissolved and to be with Christ".[97] In April he entered his fiftieth year in Africa and in June the seventy-seventh year of his life. His confreres looked forward to his Golden Jubilee of priesthood in 1923, but all that interested Livinhac himself was the grace of a good death. He cut short his working hours and spent more time in front of the Blessed Sacrament. In May he had another bout of tiredness, but by mid-July he was back again in chapel and at dinner with the community.[98] In August he became too weak to celebrate Mass even in his private oratory and he kept more or less continually to his room. An altar was set up in his office for Girault to say Mass and give him Communion. When asked about his condition, he replied, "I do not suffer, but I feel I am on the way to eternity…I feel a kind of collapse of the spirit as well as of the body".[99]

At the end of October Livinhac took to his bed and did not rise again.[100] His chronic fatigue was now aggravated by intestinal and other disorders. A doctor visited him regularly and prescribed injections, but they afforded no relief and the patient asked for them to be stopped. Every day an infirmarian read passages to him from the Old and New Testaments in Latin and French, and at the prescribed time for spiritual reading, a passage from a spiritual author. Joseph Mercui (1854-1947) was performing this service on November 4th but Livinhac asked him to stop. "My poor head cannot bear any more. I cannot follow." From Sunday November 5th he found it impossible to take solid food and relied only on a few mouthfuls of milk and vegetable soup. In the afternoon, Voillard anointed him in the presence of confreres representing the various communities of Maison Carée. Livinhac was conscious and made the responses aloud.

Afterwards, he blessed those present and the whole Society with visible affection. Archbishop Leynaud of Algiers visited him in the evening and Livinhac told him: "I am going! In accordance with God's will; as he wills and when he wills."

In due course, he began to lose the sense of time and thought it was always evening. He would recite the *angelus* and his favourite prayers with the infirmarians. "I have done nothing!" he exclaimed on one occasion "and yet I assumed great responsibility. But I abandon myself to the infinite mercy of God." Then on Wednesday, he received the Viaticum after Morning Prayer and asked the infirmarian to help him make his thanksgiving, only ending his recollection when he was assured that the allotted time was up. He was full of praise and gratitude. "How good God is! He comes to visit me in my poor room." Afterwards, he received a telegram from Burtin with the Papal Blessing. "How good of the Holy Father to think of me!" was his response. Repeatedly he thanked the infirmarians who nursed him: "Thank you, dear Father, thank you! God will bless you in this world and the next…May the good God…reward you for all you do for such a difficult and disagreeable old man."

As the delirium increased, he kept on talking: "I can do no more. O My God, have mercy on me," and "How cold it is". An ejaculatory prayer that he was fond of repeating was his own episcopal motto in honour of Our Lady for whom he always had a tender devotion: *Totus tuus sum ego, Maria*, "I am all yours Mary". On the evening of Friday, November 10th he lapsed into semi-consciousness and the agony lasted a full day. Although he did not respond to what was said, he kept repeating: "Jesus, Mary, Joseph". The community assembled in his room after evening prayer on Saturday November 11th and Mass was celebrated once more. The dying man's breathing was free and regular, but death was visibly approaching. At eight forty-five, he breathed his last. Voillard gave the absolution and closed the eyes. Then he and all present kissed Livinhac's hand.

Throughout Sunday, November 12th the body lay in state in the chapel of the Brothers' Novitiate, where the novices kept vigil and kissed the "feet that trod the murderous path of the caravans".[101] The Funeral Mass was sung by Bishop Durand of Oran in the chapel of the Mother House on Monday November 13th. Archbishop Leynaud delivered the allocution in which he recalled, among other things, the episcopal consecration of Livinhac by Cardinal Lavigerie at which he had himself been present. The novices then had the honour of bearing the coffin to the cemetery where it was laid in a brick-lined grave. A striking panegyric was preached by Prosper Repeticci, Parish Priest of Maison Carrée, at the commemorative Requiem one month later.[102] Its major theme was that the work of Cardinal Lavigerie, however energetic and inspired, required the prudence and holiness of Archbishop Livinhac to bring it to completion. Genius was not enough. Only kindness could ultimately make it fruitful.[103]

Livinhac had made his will in December 1914.[104] Half of the two thousand francs that he left was given to the Missionaries of Africa for their general account and for Masses to be offered. The rest went in small bequests to relatives and to the parish of his birth. All his possessions, except his chalice and his episcopal insignia, went to three great-nephews, his watches, alarm clock and a few books. Finally eight books by spiritual authors were left to Voillard. The will was proved in January 1923. It was the will of a poor African missionary.

The cemetery of Maison Carrée was not destined to be Livinhac's final resting place. In April 1970 the urban planning office of Algiers municipality ordered the removal of the cemetery to make way for a motorway. Livinhac's remains were exhumed and enclosed in an urn. This was transported by funeral hearse to the Basilica of Our Lady of Africa, where it was placed in a vault beneath the Chapel of St. Augustine.[105] In 1975 Archbishop (later Cardinal) Emmanuel Nsubuga of Kampala came to Algiers to take possession of the remains, with a view to interring them in the newly constructed Martyrs' Shrine at Namugongo in Uganda, together with the other "ancestors in the faith" who were members of the first caravan to Uganda in 1878-1879.[106] The vault was opened on April 14th in the presence of Archbishop Nsubuga and Bishop Jaquier, Auxiliary of Algiers, and the casket was flown to Kampala the same evening.[107] On June 3rd 1975 the Namugongo Shrine was dedicated by a specially appointed Papal Legate, Sergio Cardinal Pignedoli. Léon Livinhac's casket was carried in procession to the shrine in African fashion, being held aloft on the head of the bearer, amidst the joyful acclamations of a huge crowd. In the procession of bishops and clergy walked Monsignor Victor Womeraka Mukasa, the first priest of equatorial Africa. It was a historic homecoming for "Grandfather *Vinyaki*".[108]

EPILOGUE

At the beginning of this book it was asked what impact the Great War had on the Society of Missionaries of Africa and on the Catholic Church in Africa, in so far as it was committed to the care of the Society. There is no doubt that in the short term the impact of the war and its aftermath was devastating. The carnage and destruction, as well as the loss of life through famine and disease, was overwhelming. The war and its aftermath caused social and economic disorientation. Lives were lost. Missionary vocations were abandoned. Material was destroyed. Christian numbers diminished or remained temporarily static. Africans were right to point to the cruelty and futility of the war. It was truly a "great storm" that wrecked lives and ruined relationships. In particular, it poisoned international affairs in Europe for the greater part of the twentieth century, resulting in a second world war and subsequent cold war. One can rightfully ask whether all the nobility and valour of the battlefield – the heroic sacrifice of young lives, white and black – was worth it. Unjustified it may have been, but were disorder and turmoil the only eventual outcomes of the conflict? It would seem not. During the eight years (1914-1922) covered in this history the outcome may have been in doubt, but by the end of the period the situation was beginning to stabilize and, in the long term, the future looked hopeful.

To begin with, the war had brought changed relationships and new outlooks. Probably its most positive and far-reaching outcome, as far as the White Fathers were concerned, was the fact that missionaries and African Christians were drawn closer together, and were less of a mystery to each another. The experience of war had brought better mutual understanding. Friendship forged in conditions of hardship is the strongest tie, and the two parties now had a better understanding of each other's aspirations. For White Fathers, as Livinhac had said, Africa was now a "fatherland" in a much more real sense, transcending and relativizing their nationalities of origin. There was a missionary awareness of embryonic African nationalism, and the seed of eventual political co-operation in the mid-twentieth century had been sown. Africans, for their part, were surer of the missionaries' intentions than they had been before the war. They had shared war experiences with them and had ample proof of their kindness. They now knew better where they themselves stood with them and what they had come to Africa for.

Colonialism was a by-product of the competing European nationalisms that had caused the war. Yet the conflict had brought about a new relationship between the Missionaries of Africa and the colonial powers. The Allied nations,

Belgium, Britain and France, were the principal colonial beneficiaries of the war. Their colonies had been strengthened and enlarged, and in most cases they were grateful for the missionaries' loyalty and co-operation in the struggle with Germany. For the French anti-clericalism was effectively a thing of the past. The European powers now offered the prospect of partnership in the colonial project, especially in the field of education. This was an opportunity that the White Fathers, for one, were glad to seize. However, the war had damaged the reputation of colonialism; and for those who thought deeply about it, its long-term future was far from secure. While co-operating with colonialism, many Missionaries of Africa also sought to distance themselves from the inequality, subjection and exploitation that it promoted. They feared its secularism and its pragmatic support of Islam. They opposed its espousal of unjust cultural traditions, especially those which concerned marriage and the status of women. They resisted racial discrimination, both implicit and explicit, as well as the imposition of forced labour. They could also afford to ignore colonial frontiers in their own regional re-organization and the introduction of an inter-vicarial seminary system.

The First World War had jeopardized the Society's internationality. This was always a compromise between the nationalistic requirements of the colonial powers and the Society's own geography of recruitment, quite apart from the demands of a practical Catholicity that favoured local communities of mixed nationality. The post-war antagonism between French and Germans was a grave threat, but fortunately good sense prevailed. Helped especially by the presence of French-speaking Canadians, the Society's international character was strengthened in the long run.

Crucial to the recovery of the Missionaries of Africa after the war, was the influence of two outstanding personalities, Léon Livinhac and Giacomo Della Chiesa, Benedict XV. Unlike Charles Lavigerie, the founder of the Society, Livinhac was not himself a missionary strategist in the strict sense. However, he held doggedly to the missionary principles he had learned from Lavigerie, and his thirty-year superiorate (1892-1922) represented an unbroken link with the Founder and the Society's origins. Livinhac lived in Lavigerie's shadow, as it were, and his lengthy reign conferred continuity and stability on the Society's leadership. What is more, Paul Voillard, who can be said, in his turn, to have lived in Livinhac's shadow, continued the tradition after his death for another fourteen years. Livinhac put Lavigerie's ideas into practice and completed the organization of the Missionaries of Africa which the founder had left unfinished.[1]   He was also in himself the model missionary, who had lived the life of every ordinary member of the Sociery.[2]   The quality of Livinhac's personal leadership reached new heights during and after the war. In the minds of most White Fathers, he was identified with the Society itself and its early history, both in North Africa and at the Equator. His leadership was a practical day to day affair, exercised through decision-making and correspondence. It was also a truly spiritual leadership that resonated with the suffering of the confreres in the trenches, and encouraged its sublimation in their interior life. Livinhac's personal sanctity reinforced all he said or wrote about missionary holiness.

Benedict XV took the longer view of missionary evangelization. He was undoubtedly a missionary strategist, operating at the highest possible level. His conclusions were drawn from a long association with the Society of Missionaries of Africa and all that they stood for. Benedict drew out the implications of White Father policies. Already foreseeing the end of colonialism, he strongly advocated the formation of an indigenous clergy. The Missionaries of Africa were already committed to this, and Benedict threw all the weight of his authority behind it. He also appreciated the White Fathers' internationalism and played down the nationalistic divisions that led to World War I. Mission territories, in which so many nationalities jostled one another were the ideal setting for a Catholicism that transcended every nationality.

Benedict's priorities were confirmed by the ongoing ordinations of African priests that took place during and after the war in White Father vicariates in Uganda, Tanganyika Territory, Rwanda and Congo, and the initiation of these priests to parish work. His respect for the African reached a climax in the beatification of the Uganda Martyrs. Their cause had been promoted by the Missionaries of Africa almost from the moment of their deaths, especially by Livinhac who had carried the early testimonials from Uganda in 1890, and who had personally edited the documents of the process in Algiers. Benedict, however, had made their cause his own. The beatification of June 6th 1920 was the most sublime tribute the Church could pay to the people of Africa and to the quality of their faith. It was also a magnificent compliment to Livinhac and the Society of which he was the head.

The 1914-1918 war led to a spiritual rebirth of the Missionaries of Africa, and also served as the launch base for soaring Catholic growth in the 1920s and 1930s. Ultimately, the First World War, in spite of all its horrors, the terrible memories it evoked and the trail of disasters that followed in its wake, was a stimulus for the quantitative and qualitative growth of African Christianity in the mission territories of the White Fathers.

APPENDIX I

World War I – Those Who Died

Introduction

This is a list of Missionaries of Africa who, having taken the missionary oath or being still in formation, died as a result of the war. It includes those who were killed on the field of battle, those who died of wounds inflicted on the battlefield and those who died as a result of infections or conditions sustained while on active service, as internees or under enemy occupation. The deadly Spanish Influenza was rife among servicemen in the last year of the war and its spread was associated with troop movements and with the soldiers' low resistance to the pandemic. It is said that nearly half a million German soldiers succumbed to the disease at its first outbreak. In Macedonia, malaria, caused ten casualties among the allies for every one casualty inflicted by the enemy, and the allied base at Salonika has been called one "vast hospital". Medical orderlies, like many of the White Fathers, were exposed to such infections from their hospital work.

The condition of a young stroke victim (46) may have been a brain disorder attributable to "shell-shock" or post-traumatic stress. Some other missionaries on active service, who nevertheless survived, seem to have suffered from post-traumatic stress disorder.

This list includes forty-six Frenchmen, nine Germans and five Belgians. Among them are fourteen fathers, eleven brothers, eleven scholastics (including one deacon), fourteen novices (including one priest) and ten aspirants. Since there were no regular necrological notices for aspirants, their list may not be complete. It has been estimated that between ten to fifteen aspirants died in the war.[1] The total of 60 individuals given in this list is therefore a conservative one. The list includes the name of Fr. Eloi Falguières (22) who, although he did not die on active service, eventually succumbed to the long-term effects of asphyxiating phosgene gas on September 28th 1924. In four cases, Joseph Buatois (9), Georges Maeyaert (35), Léon Pignide (46), and Antoine Toulemonde (55) it is not clear how far war conditions affected the cause of death. Their names have been included in default of evidence to the contrary.

Of the thirty-seven Frenchmen who died in action thirty-five have been found on the official data-base of the French Ministry of Defence.[2] This gives a facsimile of the official record in each case. There are discrepancies of name, age and dates of birth/death in many records. There are also frequent erasures and corrections. On the whole, the list given here reproduces the names and dates found in the archives, publications, necrological notices and calendars of the Missionaries of Africa. Some variants in the official records are noted.

Those who Died

1. **Apitz**, Gustave (Ludger), German Brother aged 20. Born in Cologne 1895. Called up in 1914. Died in hospital at Châtel (Rhône), August 28th 1915.

2. **Béraud**, Jean-Baptiste, (Baptiste-François-Joseph), French Scholastic aged 24. Born in St. Privat d'Allier (Haute Loire) in the Diocese of Le Puy, on September 26th 1891. Corporal in the First African Regiment of Foot.[3] "Valiant and devoted". Killed in the Dardanelles on June 21st 1915, in an act of courage, leading an assault on recently occupied trenches. Received a bullet through the right eye and died instantly. Buried in the night. When called up, he was due for ordination.

3. **Berthoumieux**, Gabriel, (Jean-Gabriel-François-Joseph), French Scholastic aged 22. Born in Antoire (Lot), Diocese of Cahors, on October 6th 1893. Corporal in the First African Regiment of Foot.[4] Died of wounds on 17th November 1915 at Strumitza Station in Serbia. "A saint". He received a bullet in the stomach during a reconnaissance patrol at Planus on November 16th. He asked his confreres not to risk their lives in carrying him back. Fr. Jean-Baptiste Blin (1887-1977) gave him the last sacraments and he died in the first aid post at the railway station in the early hours of November 17th. He was buried in the cemetery of Strumitza. Fr.Arsène Sabau (1887-1974) visited his grave later in the month.

4. **Boissay**, Alphonse, Pascal (Martial), French Novice Brother aged 23. Born in Orléans on March 19th 1891. Private First Class in the First Regiment of Zouaves, Mounted Troop. Killed by enemy fire at the Pas de Calais stables (Arras) on October 24th 1914.[5] He refused to be carried to the first aid post, saying: "I am fatally wounded. I feel I am going to die. I want to be left alone to prepare to appear before God." He had declined the Military Medal.

5. **Boyer**, Adrien, (Adrien-François-Germain), French Novice Cleric, aged 20. Born in St. Christophe-Vallon (Aveyron), Diocese of Rodez on September 5th 1895. Private Second Class in the Fourth Regiment of Zouaves. Died in the

Military Hospital at Nice on June 16th 1915 from wounds sustained at the Dardanelles front.[6]

6. **Brauchle**, Gustave (Albert), German Brother aged 25. Born in Furamoos (Rottenburg) 1889. He served as an ostler in a German mounted unit. Killed at Ypres, Belgium, on December 5th 1914.

7. **Bros**, Jean, Paulin, Marius, French Aspirant in Philosophy at Binson aged 25. Born in St. Bauzile (Lozère) on November 23rd 1893. Sergeant in the 142nd Infantry Regiment. Went missing at the Somme (Moreuil) on April 4th 1918.[7]

8. **Brossier**, Léon, (Marie), French Father aged 36. Born at Cholet (Maine et Loire), Diocese of Angers, on June 21st 1882. Missionary in Uganda. Sergeant Stretcher-Bearer in the 116th Alpine Regiment. Fought at Verdun, in the retaking of Douaumont. Killed on 18th September 1918, at the Vosges, by a splinter from an exploding shell.[8] He received the *Croix de Guerre* and was four times mentioned in dispatches. He had written on November 13th 1916: "I return safe and sound from Verdun for the second time, thanks be to God. How many times did my heart not cast an appeal to the Blessed Mother of Heaven and our dear saints of Buganda?"

9. **Buatois**, Joseph, French Father aged 31. Born in Ratte (Saône et Loire), Diocese of Autun on March 5th 1884. He took his oath in 1909 and was ordained priest the following year, working first in Jerusalem and then as bursar at Thibar, Tunisia. After call-up as a medical orderly in 1914, he was assigned to the care of sick soldiers in Teboursouk military prison, Tunisia. He was working with a road gang near Thibar when he collapsed on May 30th 1915, and died six days later of "brain fever" or cerebral malaria on June 5th 1915 at Teboursouk Hospital. He was the first priest of the Society to die at Thibar.[9]

10. **Cadet**, Léon, French Father aged 37.[10] Born in Steenbecque (Nord), Diocese of Cambrai, on July 14th 1878. Missionary in Uganda. Stretcher-bearer in the 290th Infantry Regiment. Killed at Verdun by the direct hit of a shell on the cellar (Hill 304) where he was taking cover on April 27th 1916. The explosion took off one foot, broke the other leg in two places and wounded him in the chest. He lived for three hours. He was buried in the church cemetery of Jubecourt (Meuse). He was described as possessing "untiring goodness". In his last letter of April 24th 1916, he wrote: "Our ordeals accepted by us are the path that leads to future glory and an eternal reward...If God wishes to keep me for Uganda, he will. Those he keeps are well kept. If he wishes to call me more quickly to his side, I will not be any less happy." His name is engraved on the front of the high altar, in the chapel of the Douaumont Ossuary.

11. **Capelle**, Clovis-Hubert-Joseph, French Scholastic aged 29. Born in Cléty (Pas-de-Calais), Diocese of Arras, on November 1st 1888. Second Lieutenant in the First African Infantry Regiment.[11] Wounded in the arm at the Dardanelles,

but continued to care for his men. Died on April 17th 1917 at Dihovo, Serbia, while begging his unit to leave him and withdraw. He was killed by a bullet in the head, while lobbing grenades at the (Bulgarian) enemy to give cover for his troops. He was awarded the *Croix de Guerre*, the Silver Medal for Bravery and the Legion of Honour. On May 28th 1916 he had taken part in the funeral of Régis Delabre in Macedonia.

12. **Carmoi**, Léon-Auguste-Marie, French Novice Cleric aged 29. Born in Breteil (Ille et Vilaine), Diocese of Rennes, on September 5th 1890. Sergeant in the 3rd Regiment of Zouaves. He was killed at Crouy on the Aisne, in the Battle of the Somme, near Soissons, on September 30th 1914.

13. **Chiron**, Henri-Léon-Benjamin, French Novice Cleric aged 26. Born in Landes Genusson (Vendée), Diocese of Luçon, on December 15th 1889. Warrant Officer in the 7th Regiment of Zouaves. Died on February 10th 1915 in hospital at Poitiers from typhoid contracted in the trenches.

14. **Clavel**, Joseph, French Father aged 31. Born in Duingt (Haute Savoie), Diocese of Annecy, on May 9th 1888. He took his oath in 1914 and was a deacon, finishing his scholasticate, when called up at the beginning of the war. He served in a Zouave Regiment, and was afterwards transferred to a medical unit, working in the military hospital of Teboursouk, Tunisia. In 1915 he was ordained priest in Algiers together with four other soldier-deacons. He took part in the Battle of the Somme, but was invalided from the front and died in hospital at Versailles of Spanish Influenza on August 1st 1919. He was the 23rd scholastic of Carthage to die as a result of the war. His brother, Auguste Clavel (1895-1979), was a veteran of the Macedonian campaign and a hero of the Russian Civil War, taken prisoner by the Bolsheviks in 1919.

15. **Courant**, Alfred, Ambroise, French Father aged 38. Born in Quimper (Finistere) on January 20th 1880. He worked as a missionary in Zambia, and was called up on returning to France in 1914 for a rest. Private Second Class in the 15th Medical Section. He contracted broncho-pneumonia on the Serbian front and died in a field hospital at Veles (Serbia) on November 2nd 1918. He was buried in the French cemetery at Veles.

16. **Courmont**, Jean-Pierre, French Father, aged 33. Born in Beaumetz-les-Cambrai (Pas-de-Calais), Diocese of Arras, on May 2nd 1883. He had worked as a missionary in Uganda. Private Second Class Stretcher-Bearer in the First Military Medical Section. Killed at Harvillers in the Battle of the Somme on July 29th 1916, when the dug-out in which he was sheltering under heavy bombardment, collapsed on top of him and forty of his comrades, burying them alive. Fr. Joseph Ménard (1880-1967) found his grave in the cemetery of a nearby village and erected a cross.

17. **De Boninge**, Lode (Louis), Belgian Novice Cleric aged 22. Born in Wekelgem, Antwerp, Diocese of Malines-Brussels 1896. Stretcher-bearer in the Belgian Army. He was killed by a shell in Flanders, while on his way to care for the wounded, on May 7th 1918. He died instantly. His statue adorns the Flemish Ijser memorial at Diksmuide. He was buried in the military cemetery of Duinhoek (De Panne). In 1921 his remains were removed to the civil cemetery of Wekelgem. In 1936 permission was given for them to be transferred to the crypt of the Ijser memorial at Diksmuide.

18. **De Langhe**, Auguste, Henri (Liévin), Belgian Brother (temporarily professed), aged 26. Born in Wortegem, Diocese of Ghent 1890. Stretcher-bearer in the 65th Belgian Division. He was killed by a shell burst near Ramscapelle in Flanders on August 24th 1917. He had been only a few hours in the trenches, when a piece of the exploding shell pierced his heart.

19. **Declerck**, Jean-Jules-Joseph, French Aspirant in philosophy at Binson aged 21. Born in Roubaix (Nord), Diocese of Cambrai, on October 21st 1894. Private Second Class in the Second African Infantry Regiment (Zouaves). He served in the Dardanelles, where he was wounded in an assault. He died on the boat taking him from Mudros to Bizerta in July 1915.[12]

20. **Delabre**, Régis, Hippolyte, French Scholastic aged 27. Born in St. Thout (Haute Loire), Diocese of Le Puy, on February 12th 1889. He was due to be ordained at Carthage when he was called up. He served as a Sergeant with the First Regiment of African Infantry (Zouaves) in Macedonia. On the evening of Saturday May 27th 1916, he took shelter with a warrant officer in a trench at Doiray on the Serbian front under a hail of enemy shells. The fox-hole in which he lay received a direct hit. The shell virtually beheaded him and took off his right arm. Fr. Joseph Delmer identified the body at midnight and conducted the burial early on Sunday morning, assisted by Frs. Sabau, Blin and Farrussenq and the students Capelle, Verdouck, Huguet and Clavel (Auguste). A cross was erected with the inscription: "Died for France". Delmer had spent the afternoon of the previous day with him and had brought him Communion on the morning of the day he died. He was "always joyful and faithful to his duty". In his last letter, written on April 17th 1916, he lamented the two years of studies he had lost, but abandoned himself to Providence. "God loves me and is a better judge than me of what is good or bad for me." "From now on my barometer is always set fair", he wrote. "…all is accepted in advance."

21. **Delarse**, Ernest, French Scholastic aged 35. Born in Lurcy-Levis (l'Allier), Diocese of Moulins, on April 21st 1881. A Senior Warrant Officer in a Regiment of Riflemen, he was wounded at Arras in June 1915, and then took part in the Battle of Verdun in the following year. Three weeks before he died, he wrote: "It is our turn to enter the furnace. Generously, I make the sacrifice of my life, if it is God's holy will…if I fall there, it is the holy names of Jesus and Mary and of the Society that will be found on my lips at my last breath, with the

only regret that I am not (yet) a priest or a White Father". On the day before he died, he wrote to Fr.Voillard: "As for me I am entirely submitted to God's will. I know that the least little shell burst or single bullet will not touch me without God's permission...This very evening we are going back to the same place, at the moment one of the most dangerous on the front. If I remain there, Father, rest assured that my last thought will be for our dear Society, which I have wanted to join, and for its venerable superiors. Please present my respectful good wishes to Mgr. the Superior General and ask him to bless me." He disappeared at Esnes (Meuse) on May 19th 1916. No trace of him was ever found.

22.   **Falguières**, Jean-Marie-Joseph-Eloi, French Father aged 37. Born in Bozouls (Aveyron), Diocese of Rodez, 1887. After ordination he taught at Bishop's Waltham. He was called up in 1914 and served as a Corporal Stretcher-Bearer in the 22nd Medical Division. He was involved in conflicts at Malmaison in 1917 and on the Somme in 1918. He was captured at the Chemin des Dames and suffered a harsh imprisonment. He was released in November 1918 and demobilized the following year. Although he was appointed again to Bishop's Waltham and afterwards to St. Laurent d'Olt, he was still suffering from the effects of asphyxiating phosgene gas. After seven years of suffering he died of suffocation at Pau on September 28th 1924.

23. **Gaillard**, Pierre, French Aspirant at St. Maurice aged 20. Born at Iffendie (Ille et Vilaine), Diocese of Rennes, on November 10th 1897 He served as a Private 2nd Class in the Second Regiment of Colonial infantry and fought at Verdun, where his left leg was shattered by a shell on October 8th 1917. He died in hospital at Roanne (Rhône-Alps) on October 20th 1917.

24. **Gomé**, Lucien (Barnabé), French Novice Brother,aged 29. Born in the Diocese of Chalons 1889. After serving with the Third Zouaves, he joined the Eighteenth Regiment of Artillery at the end of 1915, and worked in a munitions factory. He died of Spanish Influenza on October 7th 1918 at Castelsarrasin Hospital (Carcassone). Medical care had been left too late.

25. **Grison**, Joseph, Jean-Baptiste, French Deacon aged 26. Born in Baisieux (Nord), Diocese of Lille, on April 11th 1889. He served as a Sergeant in the Fourth Regiment of Zouaves. His thigh was shattered by a shell on the River Ijser at Ypres on April 30th 1915. He received absolution from Fr. Charles Joyeux (1885-1936*) in the expectation of a total amputation, but died of his wounds in hospital at Dunkirk on the same day. He expected to be promoted a warrant officer.

26. **Guibert**, Henri-Louis-Marie, French Novice Cleric aged 30. Born in La Planche (Loire Inférieure), Diocese of Nantes, on May 25th 1888. He was a Sergeant Stretcher-bearer in the Ninth Regiment of Zouaves. He took part in early engagements at Verdun and was killed at Landifay in the Aisne offensive

on October 30th 1918 by a shell splinter through the heart. He was in the act of reconnoitring a forward site for a First Aid Post. Buried at Landifay. He had received the *Croix de Guerre*.

27. **Guillou**, Adrien, French Novice Cleric aged 28. Born in Ste-Lumine-de-Coutais (Loire Inférieure), Diocese of Nantes, on November 27th 1889. He served as a Second-Lieutenant in the 1st Mixed Regiment of Zouaves/Riflemen, and was killed at Beaulne et Chivy on the Aisne, (Chemin des Dames) on May 11th 1917. One version states he was killed by a machine-gun bullet in the head, as he went "over the top". A more reliable account from the chaplain-stretcher-bearer (Albert Claverie) who carried him from the front, is that he was killed by a grenade. He was buried at Vendresse. He had asked for Livinhac's blessing before departing for the front and declared that he had no other ambition than to devote himself entirely to the African missions.

28. **Huguet**, Pierre-Marie, French Scholastic aged 27. Born in Herbignac (Loire Inférieure), Diocese of Nantes, on September 1st 1889. He served as a Corporal in the First African Infantry Regiment. Wounded at the Dardanelles, he went on to Macedonia after his recovery. He was wounded again in an engagement with the Bulgarians at Elvrina railway-station on September 20th 1916 and died of his wounds the following day, after being anointed by Fr. Farrussenq (1889-1953). In his last letter he wrote: "I submit myself entirely to God's will. Whatever happens, I have already said my *Fiat*." Paul Verdouck (1889-1932) wrote of him: "He died a saint. He is now with God and the Blessed Virgin Mary. He died for France, the Church, the Society and the dear scholastics. He was my companion at Binson, in the Novitiate, at Carthage and my brother in arms".

29. **Jory**, Alban-Félix, French Aspirant, aged 20. Born in Lanuéjols (Gard), Diocese of Nîmes, on June 21st 1898. Private 2nd Class in the 156th Infantry Regiment. serving in the infantry was killed by enemy fire on May 28th 1918 at Braine in the Battle of the Aisne (Chemin des Dames). He wrote on May 27th 1918 that he was going up to the front and nothing more was heard of him.

30. **Jouve**, Louis (Daniel), French Novice Brother aged 23. Born in St. Julien du Tournel (Lozère) Diocese of Mende 1892. He served with the Second Regiment of Zouaves and was wounded at Quennevières in 1915. After a month in hospital, he rejoined his regiment for the Champagne offensive in August. He wrote his final letter to his novice master under bombardment on September 23rd. Two days later the assault began in which he was killed on September 27th 1915.[13]

31. **Le Cléac'h**, Pierre, French Scholastic aged 25. Born in Quimper (Finisterre) 1889. He was due for ordination when called up in 1914. He served as a Warrant Officer in the Zouaves and went missing in Champagne on October 5th 1914. Presumed dead.[14]

32. **Le Devédec**, Louis, French Father aged 34. Born in Kerfourn (Morbihan), Diocese of Vannes 1882. He served as a missionary in Uganda. In the army he was a medical orderly, and after spending several months nursing at Neufchâteau, he was posted to Greece, where he died of typhoid fever in a hospital in Salonika, on October 7th 1916. After his ordination in 1907 he briefly contemplated becoming a Benedictine, but this was not realized.

33. **Lhomme**, Pierre-Marie, French Father aged 30. Born in Médréac (Ille et Vilaine), Diocese of Rennes, on October 21st 1886. After ordination in 1912, he was on the staff of the apostolic school of St.Laurent d'Olt. He served as a Private stretcher-bearer in the 206th Infantry Regiment. He was killed by machine-gunfire in the Anglo-French offensive at Ypres, in the Cerny sector of the Bourg et Comin road, on July 31st 1917. For his outstanding courage he was awarded the *Croix de Guerre*. Two of his sayings: "The will of God is more important than such honours." "In the face of death it is difficult to be bad."

34. **Loiseau**, Joseph (Pierre), French Brother aged 37. Born in Frossay (Loire Atlantique), Diocese of Nantes, 1881. He served as a Corporal in the Fourth Regiment of Zouaves, and at the Dardanelles was mentioned in dispatches for having held a conquered enemy trench. He died in the Military Hospital at Tunis on November 26th 1918 of a double abscess on the neck..

35. **Maeyaert**, Georges, Belgian Father aged 32. He was born at Wijngene St. Amand (Diocese of Bruges) on April 16th 1884. He was ordained in 1911 and, after doctoral studies in Rome, became a seminary professor at Bouchout on October 1st 1913. When war broke out, he was transferred to Antwerp. He fell ill and died in German occupied Antwerp on February 13th 1917. A note signed by G. de Vulders (presumably a doctor) found in his personal dossier speaks of an (unspecified) illness "with frightful wounds that are only the beginning" and in which "complications can occur at any moment". Up to two or three months before his death "he has not lacked what is necessary". There is no indication of how the military occupation of Antwerp affected his condition.[15]

36. **Malavieille**, Albert, French Novice Cleric, aged 24. Born in Arzenc de Randon (Lozère), Diocese of Mende, on September 4th 1892. He served as Private Second Class with the Ninth Regiment of Zouaves in Flanders. After being wounded (shrapnel in the buttocks) in July 1915, he was sent to Verdun in the following year and was killed in the fighting around Douaumont on March 5th 1916, hit by a grenade in the head. The official record lists him as "missing".[16] His name is inscribed on the front of the high altar in the chapel of the Douaumont Ossuary at Verdun. "He had the soul of a saint."

37. **Margot-Duclos** (sometimes Duclot), Marie-Joseph, French Novice Priest aged 35.[17] Born in Villarobert near Gap (Hautes Alpes), Diocese of Gap, on August 22nd 1881. He was ordained a diocesan priest in 1904. After further studies and pastoral work at the cathedral parish of his diocese, he entered the

novitiate of the Missionaries of Africa in 1914, and was immediately called up, serving as a Nurse/Chaplain and then as a Private stretcher-bearer in the 200th Regiment of Infantry. After the dissolution of his regiment, he was appointed Chaplain to the fortification of Froide-Terre at Verdun. On June 23rd 1916 he went to the help of a wounded officer, but was machine-gunned through the head, heart and kidneys. The bullet that pierced his heart passed through a pyx containing the Blessed Sacrament that he was carrying. He was buried in the courtyard of the fortification and his grave was honoured by General Charles Mangin. A plaque commemorates all who died there.[18]

38. **Mechau**, Arthur (Fulgence), German Brother aged 41. Born in Meissen. On April 21st 1916 German troops made a short stop at Mibirisi Mission in Rwanda. They were surprised by soldiers of the invading Belgian army from Congo. A fire fight developed around the mission from which the German force retreated. During the exchange of fire Brother Fulgence was mortally wounded, became unconscious and died the same evening. The mission diary and other sources for his death are extremely discreet and the implication seems to be that Brother Fulgence died from "friendly" Belgian fire.

39. **Meyronin**, Louis-Félix, French Aspirant in philosophy at Binson, aged 20. He was born in Malzieu-Ville (Lozère), Diocese of Mende, on November 24th 1895. He served as a Private Second Class in the Second Regiment of Colonial Infantry and saw action with a machine-gun company in Champagne, where he was mentioned in dispatches. He was wounded there by a bullet in the stomach and died in the field hospital at Souain on 27th 1915. He was buried in the cemetery at Suipes.

40. **Moussié**, Joseph-Benjamin-Marie-Barthélémy, French Scholastic aged 26. Born in Toulouse, on March 29th 1889, he studied philosophy in Toulouse Major Seminary and applied to the novitiate in 1912 after two years military service. He was called up from Carthage in 1914 and served as Private Second Class in the Ninth Zouaves. He was "literally blown to pieces" by a bomb in the Pas de Calais on the Arras front on January 25th 1915.[19] Virtually nothing recognizable remained. His commanding officer described it as "a horrible death", adding "we only found a little piece of him.[20]

41. **Müller**, Nicolaus (Ubald), German Brother, aged 30. Born in Trier 1885. He took his temporary oath in 1911. Although he hoped to avoid call-up, he was mobilized in 1914. He died at Lens (Pas de Calais) in northern France on May 9th 1915. A man of "great piety and spirit of faith".

42. **Nalbach**, Jakob, (Othon), German Brother,aged 24. Born in Trier 1891. He took his temporary oath in 1910. He was called up in 1914 and was killed at Loos on March 31st 1915.

43. **Nilges**, Jacob, German Novice Cleric, aged 28. Born in Trier 1887. He was interned as an enemy alien at Fort l'Empereur, Algiers. During his internment he contracted tuberculosis and died in hospital at Mustapha, Algiers on April 29th 1916. "One of our best seminarians."

44. **Pecheberty** (sometimes Pechberty), Georges-Louis-Joseph-Charles, French Aspirant, aged 21. Born in Algiers, on August 24th 1894. Served as Private Second Class with the Second Regiment of Zouaves. He was wounded on the eve of a French assault at Choisy-au-Bac (Aisne) and died the same day, June 7th 1915.

45. **Pignide**, Joseph, Laurent, French Aspirant, aged 23. Born in St. Chely d'Apcher (Lozère), Diocese of Mende, December 18th 1895. Served as Corporal in the Ninth Regiment of Zouaves, in the Dardanelles, then in Champagne-Ardennes, where he was killed on September 30th 1918 at Romain (Marne), in the attack on Courlandon, near Fismes.

46. **Pignide**, Léon, French Aspirant, younger brother of Joseph. He saw active service in France. On home leave from the army, he suffered a stroke and drowned when swimming in the river La Truyère, near St.Laurent d'Olt on July 20th 1917. The occurrence of a stroke in a twenty-year old may have been due to a brain disorder caused by post-traumatic stress.[21]

47. **Potier**, Jean-Jacques-Ernest, French Scholastic aged 30. Born at La Charité (Nièvre), Diocese of Nevers, on June 3rd 1888. He served as a Sergeant in the Fourth Regiment of Zouaves. In 1917 he took part in the Battle of Verdun, where he was wounded within ten minutes of a "frightful, unimaginable bombardment", carrying a wounded soldier under fire and living "moments which belong neither to life nor death". The following year he was killed by a bullet in the forehead while "brilliantly" leading an attack at Orvillers (Oise) on the Champagne front, on Maundy Thursday March 28th 1918. "One of our best scholastics."

48. **Renaudier**, François-Marie, French Father aged 27. Born in Rennes 1890. He was ordained on June 27th 1914 and was called up the following November. He served as Nurse-Chaplain in several parishes of France and Switzerland before being sent to Salonika in March 1916. He suffered recurrent fevers and was invalided back to France, where he died in a hospital at Rennes on October 18th 1917, offering his life for his confreres and for the non-Christians of Africa. He was buried in the parish cemetery of All Saints, Rennes.

49. **Robert**, Jean-Baptiste, French Father, aged 29. Born in Montbel (Lozère), Diocese of Mende, May 15th 1887. He was one of the newly ordained priests of 1914, called up as a medical orderly, and served as a Private Second Class in the Fourth Mixed Regiment of Zouaves and Riflemen. He took part in the Battle of Verdun and was continuously at the front from the end of 1914 until his death in

1916. He received the *Croix de Guerre* and was renowned for his courage. He was fatally wounded at Douaumont on October 26th 1916 and died the following day in Field Hospital 6/4. He was a frequent correspondent with the Motherhouse and left several striking descriptions of battle scenes.

50. **Saclier**, Pierre, French Father, aged 41. Born at Poisson (Saône-et-Loire), Diocese of Autun 1876. He served as a missionary in Uganda and was called up in November 1914 as a Medical Orderly. He was posted to the military hospital in Dijon. During the six months he was there, the hospital treated 4,350 wounded soldiers and he administered the last rites to 220 who were dying. Exhausted, he went to recuperate at his family home in Paray-le-Monial in May 1915. After more than a year's rest, he was back at Dijon in December 1916, but he collapsed and died in the hospital six months later, on May 31st 1917.

51. **Schmid**, Anton (Théotime), German Brother, aged 26. Born in Regensburg 1888. He took his temporary oath in 1910 and afterwards did a year of military service. He was called up again in 1914 and was killed almost immediately at Mulhouse on August 7th 1914. "This young man is for us a perfection !"

52. **Schröder**, Werner, (Thierry), German Brother aged 21. Born in Trier 1894. He took his temporary oath in 1913 and was called up at the outbreak of war the following year. He was killed at Faye-en-Haye, Lorraine, on April 7th 1915. "Joyful, but a little timid."

53. **Souton**, Marius-Joseph-Louis, French Aspirant. Born in Malzieu-Ville (Lozère), Diocese of Mende, on January 11th 1893. He had just completed his philosophy studies at Binson when he was called up in 1914. He served as a Private in the 416th Infantry Regiment. He was wounded by an exploding shell at Mount Kemmel in Flanders on April 29th 1918, and died after a long agony in a field hospital at Abeele. His name is inscribed on the French monument at Mount Kemmel.[22]

54. **Sylvestre**, Adrien-Julien-Jean-Marie (Alexis), French Brother, aged 30. Born in Guenrouët (Loire Inférieure), Diocese of Nantes, on May 9th 1887. After taking his missionary oath in 1906 he was posted to St.Anne's Jerusalem. He served as a Private Second Class in the Fourth Regiment of Zouaves. He was wounded in the left arm and left thigh at the Somme in 1916 and remained immobilized in a trench. He attributed his survival to the intercession of (the as yet uncanonized) Thérèse of Lisieux, whose shrine he visited while convalescing after a painful operation. "I am happy", he wrote, "that God has asked of me a little of my blood for France, the Church and our Society". "...if he wants my life, it will be my happiness to give it." He went missing in the German lines at Boulogne-la-Grasse, west of Lassigny, on Maundy Thursday, April 15th 1918.[23] He was seen praying the rosary after being fatally wounded, but the first-aid post where he was being looked after was overrun by the enemy.

55. **Toulemonde**, Antoine, French Novice Cleric, aged 21. Born at Tourcoing (Nord) on January 23rd 1893, he studied philosophy at Cambrai Major Seminary and applied for the novitiate in August 1913. He was one of the fifteen French novices called up in August 1914 and served in the First Regiment of Zouaves. He died in uniform barely a month later in Orléansville Hospital (Elaçnam) Algeria, on October 4th 1914 after a short but fatal illness. The cause of his death was "a pernicious fever" brought about by extreme fatigue. His parents, two of whose other sons were killed in the war, only learned of Antoine's death in September 1918.[24]

56. **Valléau**, Pierre-Jean-Marie French Novice Cleric aged 23. Born in Péaule (Morbihan), Diocese of Vannes, on August 8th 1892. Corporal in the Fourth Regiment of Zouaves. Having been mentioned in dispatches, he went missing at Lizerne (Flanders) on the banks of the Ijser on April 30th 1915.[25] His body was discovered in the following year during the digging of a trench, together with letters and his identity disc. He was buried under a small cross amidst the many shell-holes. Brother Victor Vuylsteke (1892-1962), then a soldier in the Belgian army, saw the grave and added the words *Père Blanc* to the inscription.

57. **Valette**, François-Léon, French Novice Cleric aged 27. Born in Ségur (Aveyron). Diocese of Rodez, on December 31st 1888. He served as a Corporal in the First Infantry Regiment of Riflemen. He went missing at Langemark, on the river Ijser in Flanders on April 30th 1915.[26]

58. **Van Der Wegen**, Frans, Belgian Aspirant. He studied philosophy at Bouchout and Antwerp and was called up to serve in the Belgian Army as a Stretcher-Bearer. He wrote to Livinhac in July 1918, from the Belgian camp at Auvours where he was convalescing, asking permission to spend some leave with the Vincentians at Preston in England. Livinhac consented, sending him a comforting message in August. Less than a month after his return, he was killed in France on September 29th 1918 by a bullet through the skull. His last words were: "My God I love you with all my heart!"[27]

59. **Vanlaere**, Emile, Belgian Scholastic, aged 26. Born at Dottignies, Western Flanders, on January 22nd 1892. He completed philosophy at Bouchout and applied to join the novitiate in July 1913. He served as a Stretcher-Bearer in the Belgian army and was killed by a shell, while returning between the lines from a patrol near Nieuport on the Yser front on April 9th 1918. Found among the wounded and dying, with left leg and arm broken, he was taken to the central aid post at Nieuport and given a blood transfusion. He died after suffering for five to six hours in the presence of several confreres who administered the last rites. "It is for Jesus and the poor souls", he told those around him. He died repeating the names Jesus and Mary.[28]

60. **Weissgerber**, Joseph (Oscar), German Brother aged 27. Born in Trier 1890. He made his temporary oath on November 1st 1911. He died in France on March 31st 1918. The news reached the Motherhouse via Switzerland.

APPENDIX II

World War I - Wounded Survivors

Introduction

The following is a select list of twenty-nine Missionaries of Africa who were wounded and/or disabled as a result of active service in the First World War. There were many more than these. In fact, already in 1914 at the very beginning of the war, the Mother House received news of a total of twelve wounded confreres. This list, however, gives the reader an idea of the nature and variety of the wounds and the suffering they caused. Many of these men were wounded twice, even three times.

Wounded Survivors

1. **Châles**, Louis (1891-1969). His hip was fractured by pieces of shrapnel, the last piece being removed several years later. He suffered inflammation and abscesses. Throughout his life he had a stiff leg which made walking and sitting difficult.

2. **Chevalier**, Armand (1882–1953). Seriously wounded during an action in Champagne in 1915. He had three subsequent, painful operations.

3. **Cormerais** Camille (1894-1979). In April 1917 he was hit by machine gun bullets in his right arm and shoulder. He remained with part of the *humerus* missing. No natural joint was possible. He wore an appliance for the rest of his life and had difficulty in moving his arm. He suffered severe headaches throughout his life.

4. **Cormerais**, Jean-Baptiste (1890-1941). He was wounded in the thigh on the Serbian front, and suffered thirty years of discomfort thereafter.

5. **Darot**, Léon (1890-1958). On the Serbian front he had the top of his right ear taken off by either a bullet or piece of shrapnel. (He did not know which.) Later, he received a sabre blow on his helmet. This affected his spine and crushed nerves in the back. He was in pain all his life. At the end of his life a paralysis developed.

6. **Delmer**, Joseph (1891-1969). Wounded three times in the thigh at the Dardanelles in 1915, and wounded again in Macedonia in 1916.

7. **De Maeght**, Joseph, (1894-1963). Wounded in the left shoulder and right leg.

8. **Duiquet**, Gaston (1888–1930*). At Verdun in 1916, he received two shell splinters in his right side, and had a double operation in a field hospital. The wound took longer to heal than expected. Eventually, he was reassigned by the army to Dahomey (Benin) and placed in charge of recruits from Congo Brazzaville.

9. **Falguières**, Jean-Marie-Joseph-Eloi (1887-1924). He suffered the long-term effects of phosgene gas poisoning which destroyed his respiratory tract. He died as a result of the condition six years after the war.

10. **Farussenq**, Etienne (1889-1953). He was wounded in 1915 at the Dardanelles.

11. **Gallerand**, Pierre (1887-1976). He was wounded in the arm at Verdun in 1916, then seriously wounded again in the last German offensive of 1918, receiving shell splinters in the chest, right elbow and hip. He had painful operations in various French hospitals.

12. **Henry**, André, a French Aspirant at Bishop's Waltham (between 1912-1915*). He was wounded in France by shrapnel that passed through the hip, lodged in the stomach and perforated his intestines. He had a serious operation and eventually retired to his family home in Algiers. He did not continue his formation.

13. **Jaureguy**, Martin (1886-1965). He was wounded at the Chemin-des-Dames in 1917 by shell splinter that entered his right side. He was operated on at a hospital in Dunkirk. In 1918 on the Somme, he was wounded again near Beauvais. A bullet passed through his upper and lower jaw. He was treated in several hospitals and had a painful operation without anaesthetic to reset his lower jaw. The wound caused a speech impediment throughout the rest of his life.

14. **Joyeux**, Charles (1885-1936*). He was wounded at the Aisne by a shell splinter that passed through his belt and clothes into the kidney region.

15. **Laroche**, Emile (1890-1979). A machine gun bullet fractured his right femur and severed some nerves. The operation at Rouen shortened his leg by six centimetres and the wound caused a generalized atrophy of the leg. His apostolate was deeply marked by the wound and subsequent illness.

16. **Lautour**, Joseph (1875-1943). At Verdun in 1916, a shell explosion collapsed a communication trench and buried him alive. He managed to get out, but his eyesight and hearing were impaired. Because of this, he was run down

by a German military car in occupied France in 1943, and died of a fractured skull.

17. **Lebouc**, Léon, Brother Euthyme, (1879-1919*). He was called up in 1915. In the same year he was wounded at the Dardanelles in the neck, head and eye. The eye was luckily saved. He left the Society in 1919.

18. **Le Doaré**, Xavier (1887-1941). He was wounded in Serbia by a bullet in his left shoulder. Moving his arm was difficult afterwards and there was a tendency towards paralysis.

19. **Marcant**, René (1882-1961). His shoulder was shattered by a shell at Arras. After hospital in Paris, he was invalided out of the army in 1916.

21. **Pagès**, Jules (1887-1984). He was wounded in the final German offensive of 1918.

22. **Paulhe**, Céléstin (1888-1919*) In 1916 at Verdun he received two shell splinters in the face and jaw, luckily missing his left eye. One crushed his lower left jaw. The other lodged behind his eye cavity. They were extracted without further complication.

23. **Quéinnic**, Hervé (1896-1946). He was injured by a bomb from an enemy war-plane at Fleury in June 1916, being wounded in the arm and head. Afterwards, he had a trepanning operation. At the time, he was an aspirant from Bishop's Waltham.

24. **Rollin**, Joseph, Brother Maxime (1881-1961). In Morocco in 1916, he received a sniper's bullet in the back. Presumably because of his back-pack, the bullet did not penetrate his body and the wound was luckily no more than a burn.

25. **Sabau** (Sabeau), Arsène (1887-1974). In September 1916, he was seriously injured in Macedonia, when going to assist a wounded soldier under machine-gun fire. A shell burst a yard from him and he received splinters in the arm, leg and back. Because of delayed treatment, the arm became gangrenous and had to be amputated in a hospital at Salonika. The other wounds took a long time to heal. During the rest of his life he was well-known for using a tricycle as a means of getting about.

26. **Valex**, Pierre (1888-1972). He was wounded at the Dardanelles in 1915 and had to be evacuated to Bizerta. In Salonika, he suffered from persistent malaria, jaundice and bronchitis. This caused a history of palpitations, dizziness, breathlessness and cramps throughout his life.

27. **Van Reeth**, Ludovic (1913-1960). Serving in France, he was buried by a shell explosion together with two companions who died as a result. He sustained a flesh wound in the right forearm and was taken to hospital in Coburg.

28. **Verdouck**, Paul (1889-1932). He was wounded by shrapnel in the thigh at the Dardanelles in 1915 and evacuated by hospital ship. He was wounded again in Serbia in an engagement with the Bulgarians in 1917, this time in the arm. After a lengthy delay he was evacuated back to France for convalescence.

29. **Viel**, François, Brother Camille (1884-1955). In 1917 at Verdun, he was wounded by a large shell splinter in the left thigh.

APPENDIX III

Departures from the Society During, or Immediately After World War I – 1915-1922

Introduction
This is a list of the 42 Missionaries of Africa who took the perpetual oath in or before 1914 and who departed from the Society during or immediately after World War I between 1915-1922. Of the combatant nations, there are 25 French Fathers and 4 French Brothers, 2 German Fathers and 4 German Brothers, 3 Belgian Fathers and 1 Luxemburger Father. Of the non-combatants, there are 1 Dutch Father, 1 Dutch Brother and 1 Swiss Father. The Society was, of course, predominantly French at the time. In 1914, the French, Belgians and Germans were liable to call up, and some in the list are known to have played a prominent role on active service. A few others who were prominent as servicemen in the war left the Society considerably later.

Possible reasons for this unprecedented number of departures is discussed in Chapter Seven. It is noteworthy that 42 pre-1914 missionaries should have departed in the eight years 1915-1922. (23 others, who joined the Society before World War I, left in the twenty-seven years 1923-1950.) Individuals left for various reasons, only a few of them apparently directly or indirectly connected with the experience of war. World War I however was the background against which all these departures took place.

Departures from the Society 1915-1922 – Name, Date of Departure, Age
1. **Bardou**, Henri, French Father (former PA Ghardaia), June 30th 1916, aged 39.
2. **Bertin**, Joseph, French Father, March 12th 1921, aged 41.
3. **Blass**, Jean-Pierre, German Brother, March 2nd 1916, aged 31.
4. **Bodin**, Louis, French Father, May 1st 1919, aged 52.
5. **Brutel**, Emile, French Father, April 1st 1919, aged 45.
6. **Chayriguès**, Casimir, French Father, March 1st 1919, aged 47.
7. **Chevrat**, Claude, French Father, January 5th 1921, aged 35.
8. **Chuzeville**, Jean-Pierre, French Father, June 30th 1919, aged 40.
9. **Delévaux**, Léon, French Father, July 15th 1919, aged 39.
10. **Dumahut,** Victor, French Father, March 1st 1919, aged 43.
11. **Folliot**, Albert, French Father, August 1st 1920, aged 37.
12. **Galand**, Désiré, Belgian Father, October 17th 1922, aged 49.
13. **Gaudillière,** Désiré, French Father, June 3oth 1918, aged 36.
14. **Glass, Louis**, French Father, June 1st 1919, aged 33.
15. **Hamberger**, Aloys, German Father, August 1st 1921, aged 47.
16. **Hugonnet**, Alexandre, French Father, June 30th 1921, aged 42.

17. **Itsweire**, Paul, French Brother, December 1st 1919, aged 35.
18. **Kutscher**, Valentin, German Brother, October 13th 1919, aged 31.
19. **Le Clainche**, Joseph, French Father, June 30th 1920, aged 44.
20. **Lebouc**, Léon, French Brother, November 10th 1919, aged 40.
21. **Lepelletier,** Ludovic, French Father, September 1st 1923, aged 61.
22. **Marc**, Louis, French Father, June 30th 1919, aged 37.
23. **Marsigny**, Joseph, Belgian Father, June 30th 1915, aged 35.
24. **Meyer**, Joseph, French Brother, January 19th 1920, aged 36.
25. **Moh**r, Philippe, German Brother, June 30th 1919, aged 35.
26. **Molitor**, Henri, Luxemburger Father, December 16th 1916.
27. **Op den Kamp**, Jan, Dutch Brother, December 1st 1915, aged 26.
28. **Palz**, Jacques, German Father, October 31st 1919, aged 32.
29. **Paulhe**, Célestin, French Father, September 1st 1919, aged 31.
30. **Perrot**, Alphonse, French Father, June 30th 1918, aged 44.
31. **Portet**, Martin, French Father, May 1st 1919, aged 42.
32. **Rebours**, Pierre, French Father, June 30th 1920, aged 41.
33. **Thézé**, Auguste, French Father, January 1st 1920, aged 30.
34. **Toulet**, Jean-Baptiste, French Father, June 1st 1920, aged 40.
35. **Tritsche**r, Eugène, French Father, June 30th 1919, aged 33.
36. **Van der Stay**, Lambert, Dutch Father, June 30th 1919, aged 31.
37. **Van Geen**, Hubert, Belgian Father, June 30th 1922, aged 33.
38. **Vanhoove**, Maurice, French Father, July 1st 1919, aged 31.
39. **Verger**, Louis, French Father, June 30th 1919, aged 35.
40. **Wahl**, Anton, French Brother, October 1st 1919, aged 34.
41. **Wahle**, Wilhelm, German Brother, January 1st 1920, aged 48.
42. **Zarn**, Antoine, Swiss Father, September 11th 1916, aged 38.

APPENDIX IV
GLOSSARY

Askari, Swahili: "Soldier".

Aspirant: candidate for formation as a missionary priest.

Angelus, Latin: "angel" (prayer in honour of the incarnation recited three times daily).

Beni, Swahili: "band" (type of dance).

Bismarck, (German nineteenth century statesman), official of the *Beni* dance.

Boches, French: term of opprobrium for Germans, cf. "Huns".

Burnous, North African cloak, part of the White Fathers' habit.

Cappa Magna, Latin: "great cloak", silk cloak with train worn by archbishops etc.

Carrier: military porter; carrier corps: unit of military porters.

Catechumen: candidate for baptism,

Catechumenate: candidacy for baptism; residence of catechumens.

Chasseurs Alpins: French mountain regiment.

Chechia: North African red felt fez, (part of the White Fathers' habit).

Chemin des Dames, French: "Ladies' Way" (Battlefield in the Nivelle Offensive).

Chevalier, French: Knight.

Chicote, French: Hippopotamus hide whip used in the Congo.

Chiwaya, Chichewa: "machine-gun".

Ciborium, Latin: sacred vessel for consecrated hosts.

Communards, French: inhabitants of a *commune*.

Corps Expéditionnaire d'Orient, French: "Eastern Expeditionary Force".

Credo, Latin: "I believe", i.e. creed.

Croix de Guerre, French: "War Cross".

Cupio dissolvi, Latin: "I wish to be dissolved" (Phil.1:23).

Deutschland über alles, German: "Germany over all", German National Anthem.

Echos Binsonnais, French: Echos of Binson (Bulletin of Binson Priory Seminary).

Entente, entente cordiale, French: "Cordial Understanding", Anglo-French/Allied pact.

Études, French: "Studies" (theological periodical).

Ex voto, Latin: votive gift, tablet etc.

Force Publique, French: "Public Force", Congolese Army.

Gandourah, North African tunic or gown, part of the White Fathers' habit.

Gloria, Latin: "Glory (to God in the highest)".

Humerus, Latin: bone of the upper arm.

In tempore opportuno, Latin: "at the opportune time".

Jihad, Arabic: "Holy War".

Kabaka, Luganda: "King" of Buganda.

Kaiser, (German Emperor), official of the *Beni* dance.

Kyrie, Greek: "Lord have mercy".

Landstürm, German: Territorial Assault Reserve.

Landswehr, German: Territorial Defence Reserve.

Livre d'Or, French: "Golden Book".

Loggia, Italian: "balcony".

Luganda, language of the Baganda, or Ganda people.

Magisterium, Latin: Church's teaching authority.

Marabout, Muslim holy man, healer.

Matériel, French: military stores, weapons, ammunition.

Maximum Illud, Latin:"The Great (and most holy mission)" Papal Mission Encyclical.

Melkite: Arabic-speaking Catholic of Greek rite.

Minutante, Italian: "secretary".

Missions d'Afrique, French: "African Missions".

Monument aux Morts, French: "Monument to the Dead", War memorial in Dakar.

Mozetta, Italian: red silk shoulder cape.

Namasole, Luganda: Queen Mother.

Nataka Mungu, Swahili: "I want God (Baptism)".

Neophyte, newly converted/baptized Christian.

Ngoma, Swahili: "drum", "dance".

Notices nécrologiques, French: "obituary notices".

Notre Dame du Retour, French: "Our Lady of the Return".

Novice: candidate in the spiritual year.

Novitiate: house/community of novices.

Nyau, Chichewa: secret dance society.

Ouvrage, French: fortification or redoubt.

Pères Blancs, French: "White Fathers".

Petit Communiqué, French: "Little Communication", Livinhac's war time bulletin.

Petit Echo, French: "Little Echo" (internal bulletin of the Missionaries of Africa).

Piccoletto, Italian: "tiny one".

Poilu, French: "hairy one", French soldier.

Ponent, Latin: first proposer.

Postulancy: community of postulants.

Postulant: candidate for formation as a missionary brother.

Prie-dieu, French: wooden kneeler.

Procure: centre for fund-raising, forwarding and handling the Society's business.

Profession: missionary oath, final missionary commitment.

Propaganda Fide, or *Pro Propaganda Fide*, Latin: Vatican Mission Secretariat.

Rapports Annuels, French: "Annual Reports".

Razzia, armed raid, usually slave-raid.

Reconnaissance Française, French: "French gratitude/recognition", a French medal.

Regional: (religious) superior of a missionary region.

Ruga-ruga, Swahili: irregular soldier(s).

Rupia, Swahili: "rupee".

Sakalani, nickname of Tom von Prince.

Scholastic: student of theology.

Scholasticate: theology seminary.

Schütztruppe, German: "Defence Force", German colonial army.

Schütztruppen, German: Soldiers of the German colonial army.

Sepoy, Hindustani: Indian soldier.

Sui Juris, Latin: "in its own right".

Suscipe, Latin: "Take", "Receive". Prayer of St.Ignatius Loyola.

Te Deum, Latin: "(We praise) Thee, O God", Hymn of Thanksgiving.

Tenga-tenga, Chichewa: Carrier, porter.

Terna, Latin: "three"; the three names submitted as candidates to be bishop.

Theologate: theology seminary.

Tirailleurs: French: Riflemen.

Totus tuus sum ego Maria, Latin: "I am all yours, Mary" (Livinhac's motto).

Triduum, Latin: "three days" (celebration).

Union sacrée, French: "Sacred Union", national solidarity during the 1914-1918 War.

Vicar Apostolic: bishop of a missionary diocese.

Vicariate: missionary diocese.

Vive la France, French: "Long live France".

Zouave: North African (Algerian) regiment.

APPENDIX V

ABBREVIATIONS

ADC	*aide de camp*
AGMAfr.	*Archivio Generale dei Missionari d'Africa*, Rome.
ANZAC	Australian and New Zealand Army Corps.
CSSp.	Congregation of the Holy Spirit, Spiritans.
DACB	*Dictionary of African Christian Biography*
IBMR	*International Bulletin of Missionary Research*
IMC	Consolata Missionaries.
KAR	King's African Rifles.
KMB/CMB	Kasper, Melchior, Balthasar, *Custodiat Mansionem Benedictam*.
M.Afr.	Society of Missionaries of Africa.
Mgr.	Monsignor, *Monseigneur*.
MHM	Mill Hill Missionaries.
MSOLA	Missionary Sisters of Our Lady of Africa – "White Sisters".
NCO	Non-Commissioned Officer
OFM Cap.	Capuchin Franciscans.
OSB	Order of Saint Benedict, Benedictines.
SGA	*Société Generale pour l'Administration*.
SMA	Society of African Missions.
WF	"White Fathers".

APPENDIX VI

SELECT BIBLIOGRAPHY

Abbott, Peter and Raffaele Ruggeri, *Armies in East Africa 1914-1918*, Oxford, Osprey 2002.

Anderson, Ross, C., *The Battle of Tanga*, Stroud, Tempus, 2002

Anderson, Ross, C., *The Forgotten Front: The East African Campaign*, Stroud, Tempus, 2004.

Andries Debeir: *Omdat zijn hart zo ruim was..., Lode De Boninge (1896-1918), Een Levensverhaal*, Maarkedal, Ceres, 1979, (*Because his Heart was so Big...Lode De Boninge (1896-1918), The Sacrifice of a Life*).

Benoist, Joseph Roger de, *Eglise et Pouvoir Colonial au Soudan Français*, Paris, Karthala, 1987.

Bouniol, Joseph, *The White Fathers and their Missions*, London, Sands, 1929.

Burgman, Hans, *The Way the Catholic Church Started in Western Kenya*, London, Mission Book Service, 1990.

Burlaton, Louis. *Le Vénérable Géronimo, le Martyr du Fort des XXIV Heures à Alger*, Pères Blancs, Algiers, Maison Carrée, 1931.

Ceillier, Jean-Claude, *A Pilgrimage from Chapter to Chapter, The First General Chapters of the Society of Missionaries of Africa*, 1874-1900, Missionaries of Africa – History Series, no.1, Rome, 2002.

Clifford, Hugh, *The Gold Coast Regiment In The East Africa Campaign*, London, John Murray, 1920.

Croegaert, Luc, *Les Pères Blancs au Rwanda – Jalons et Balises*, unpublished MS, n.d.

Daye, Pierre, *Avec les Vainqueurs de Tabora, Notes d'un Colonial Belge en Afrique Orientale Allemande*, Paris, Perrin 1918.

Duff, Hector, *African Small Chop*, London, Hodder and Stoughton, 1932.

215

Ewans, Martin, *European Atrocity, African Catastrophe – Leopold II, the Congo Free State and its Aftermath*, London, Routledge Curzon, 2002.

Faupel, J.F., *African Holocaust, The Story of the Uganda Martyrs*, Nairobi, St.Paul's Publications Africa, 4th edition, 1984.

Finn, Peter, *History of the Priory Bishop's Waltham*, Winchester, Hedera Books, 2002.

Foden, Giles, *Mimi and Toutou Go Forth: The Bizarre Battle of Lake Tanganyika*, London, Penguin Books, 2005.

Fox, Douglas, "The 1918 Spanish Influenza Pandemic", *Science*, vol.293, September 2001, p. 1,842.

Gardner, Brian, *German East – The Story of the First World War in East Africa*, London, Cassell, 1963.

Gray, Richard, "Christianity", in A.D.Roberts (ed.) *The Cambridge History of Africa 1907-1940*, Vol.7, 1986, Chap.3, p.175.

Hastings, Adrian, *The Church in Africa*, Oxford, Clarendon Press, 1994.

Heremans, Roger, *L'Education dans les Missions des Pères Blancs en Afrique Centrale 1879-1914*, Brussels, Editions Nauwelaerts, 1983.

Hetherwick, Alexander, *Robert Hellier Napier in Nyasaland – Being His Letters to his Home Circle*, Edinburgh and London, William Blackwood and Sons, 1925.

Hinfelaar, Hugo, *History of the Catholic Church in Zambia*, Lusaka, Zambia, Bookworld Publishers.

Hochschild, Adam, *King Leopold's Ghost*, London, Pan Macmillan, 2002.

Hodges, GWT, *The Carrier Corps*, Greenwood Press Inc, Connecticut, 1986.

Hodges, Geoffrey, "Military Labour in East Africa and its Impact on Kenya", in Page, Melvin.E. (ed.), *Africa and the First World War*, London, Macmillan, 1987.

Holmes, J. Derek, "Benedict XV and the First World War", *The Papacy in the Modern World*, London, Burns and Oates, 1981.

Holt, Tonie and Valmai, *The Western Front – North, Battlefield Guide*, Pen and Sword Military, Barnsley, 2004.

Hordern, Charles, *Military Operations, East Africa,* Vol. I, London, Battery Press, 1941.

Ignatius, Loyola, *The Spiritual Exercises*, London, Burns Oates and Washbourne, 1952.

Ilboudo, Jean, *"La Christianisation du Moogo (1899-1949), la Contribution des 'Auxiliaire Indigenes'"*, in Ilboudo, Jean S.J. (ed.), Burkina 20000 – *Une Eglise en Marche vers son Centenaire*, Ouagadougou, Presses Africaines, 1993.

Iliffe, John, *Tanganyika under German Rule*, Cambridge University Press, 1969.

Iliffe, John, *A Modern History of Tanganyika*, Cambridge University Press, 1979.

Iliffe, John, *Honour in African History*, Cambridge University Press, 2005.

Kabeya, John B., *Adriano Atiman, Katekista na Mganga*, Tabora, Tanganyika Mission Press and Arusha, Eastern Africa Publications, 1977.

Keegan, John, *The Face of Battle*, London, Jonathan Cape 1976 (Pimlico 1991).

Keegan, John, *The First World War*, London, Hutchinson (Pimlico), 1998 (1999).

Kimpinde, Amando Dominique *et al.*, *Stefano Kaoze, prêtre d'hier at d'aujourd'hui*,
Kinshasa, Editions St. Paul Afrique, 1982.

Ki-Zerbo, Joseph, *Alfred Diban, Premier Chrétien de Haute Volta*, Paris, Cerf, 1983.

Lawrence, T.E., *Seven Pillars of Wisdom*, "Oxford Text" of 1922, Fordingbridge, Hants, J. and N. Wilson, 2004.

Lettow Vorbeck, Paul, Von, *My Reminiscences of East Africa*, London, Hart and Blackett, 1920.

Linden, Ian with Linden, Jane, "John Chilembwe and the New Jerusalem", *Journal of African History*, vol.xii, no. 4, 1971.

Linden, Ian with Linden, Jane, *Catholic Peasants and Chewa Resistance in Nyasaland 1889-1939*, Berkeley and Los Angeles, University of California Press, 1974.

Livinhac, Mgr. Léon, *Lettres Circulaires*, Algiers, Maison Carée, 1912-1922.

Lunn, Joe Harris, "Kande Kamara Speaks: an Oral History of the West African Experience in France 1914-1918", in Page, Melvin.E. (ed.), *Africa and the First World War*, London, Macmillan, 1987.

Lunn, Joe Harris, *Memoirs of the Maelstrom: A Senegalese Oral History of the First World War*, Oxford, James Currey, 1999, p.146.

Macmillan, Margaret, *The Peacemakers*, London, John Murray, 2001.

Malishi, Lukas, *Kipalapala Seminary 1925-1975*, Tabora, TMP, 1975.

Marben, Rolf, (tr. Claud W. Sykes), *Zeppelin Adventures*, London, John Hamilton, 1932.

Matthews, James K., "Reluctant Allies: Nigerian Responses to Military Recruitment 1914-1915", in Page, Melvin E. (ed.), *Africa and the First World War*, London Macmillan 1987.

Max, Arthur, *Forgotten Voices of the Great War*, London, Ebury Press, 2002.

Meinertzhagen, Richard, *Army Diary 1899-1926*, Edinburgh and London, Oliver & Boyd, 1960.

Miller, Charles, *Battle for the Bundu - The First World War in East Africa*, London Macdonald, 1974.

Mohlamme, J.S., "Soldiers Without Reward", The South African Military History Society, *Military History Journal*, vol.10, no.1, *scribe@samilitaryhistory.org*.

Moorman, Theodore, *Histoire des Origines de la Société*, Typescript volume, Monteviot House, Jedburgh, Scotland, n.d.

Morrow Jr., John H., *The Great War – An Imperial History*, London, Routledge, 2004.

Moyse-Bartlett, H, *The King's African Rifles, A Study in the Military History of East and Central Africa 1890-1945*, Aldershot, Gale and Polden, 1956.

Nolan, Francis, Patrick, *Christianity in Unyamwezi 1878-1928*, Cambridge Ph. D. Dissertation, 1977.

Oliver, Roland, *The Missionary Factor in East Africa*, London, Longmans 1952.

Ousby, Ian, *The Road to Verdun*, London, Jonathan Cape (Pimlico), 2002 (2003).

Page, Ivan "Alexis Lemaître, Général de Brigade, Missionnaire d'Afrique, Archevêque de Carthage", typescript, n.d. (contribution to a dictionary of the French Generals of World War I, as yet unpublished).

Page Malcolm, *A History of the King's African Rifles and the East African Forces*, London, Leo Cooper, 1998.

Page, Melvin E., *The Chiwaya War – Malawians and the First World War*, Boulder Colorado, Westview Press, 2000

Paice, Edward, *Lost Lion of Empire. The Life of Cape-to-Cairo Grogan*. London, Harper-Collins, 2001.

Paice, Edward, *Tip and Run. The Untold Tragedy of the Great War in Africa*, London Weidenfeld and Nicholson, 2007.

Parsons, Timothy, *The African Rank and File, Social Implications of Colonial Military Service in the King's African Rifles*, 1902-1964, London, Heinemann, 1999.

Pelletier, Raynald, *Bishop John Forbes (1864-1926), Coadjutor Vicar Apostolic of Uganda, The First Canadian White Father*, Missionaries of Africa – History Series, no.2, Rome, 2003.

Pichard, Gabriel, *Dii Alfred-Simon Diban Ki-Zerbo: Témoin de Dieu...Fondateur de l'Église*, Bobo Dioulasso, Imprimérie Savane, 1997.

Pineau, Arthur, *Le Vicariat du Tanganyika Durant la Guerre 1914-1918*, MS, n.d. AGMAfr. P 169/20.

Pinguilly, Yves, *Verdun 1916, Un Tirailleur en Enfer* ("A Rifleman in Hell"), Paris, Nathan, 2003.

Pollard, John F., *The Unknown Pope, Benedict XV (1914-1922) and the Pursuit of Peace*, London, Geoffrey Chapman, 1999.

Prost, André, *Les Missions des Pères Blancs en Afrique Occidentale avant 1939*, (mimeographed) 1939.

Rabeyrin, Claudius, *Les Missionnaires du Burundi Durant la Guerre des Gentilshommes en Afrique Orientale 1914-1918*, M.Afr. Private Printing Langéac, 1978.

Ranger, Terence Osborn, *Dance and Society in Eastern Africa 1890-1970: The Beni Ngoma*, London, Heinemann Educational, 1975.

Repeticci, Prosper, *Oraison Funèbre de Sa Grandeur Monseigneur Livinhac, 16 Décembre 1922*, Algiers 1923.

Sanneh, Lamin, *Whose Religion is Christianity ? The Gospel beyond the West*, Grand Rapids, Michigan, Eerdmans, 2003.

Saul, Mahir and Royer, Patrick, *West African Challenge to Empire. Culture and History in the Volta-Bani Anticolonial War*. Athens (U.S.A.), Ohio University Press, 2001.

Shepperson, George and Price, Thomas, *Independent African, John Chilembwe and the Origins, Setting and Significance of the Nyasaland Native Uprising of 1915*, Edinburgh, University Press, 1958.

Shorter, Aylward, "Christian presence in a Muslim Milieu: The Missionaries of Africa in the Maghreb and the Sahara", *IBMR*, vol. 28, no.4, October 2004.

Shorter, Aylward, *Chiefship in Western Tanzania. A Political History of the Kimbu*. Oxford, Clarendon, 1972.

Simkins Peter, Jukes Geoffrey and Hickey Michael, *The First World War*, Oxford, Osprey, 2003

Société des Missionnaires d'Afrique *(Pères Blancs), Directoire des Constitutions*, Algiers, Maison Carrée, 1914.

Société des Pères Blancs, *Publications en Langues Africaines*, Algiers, Maison Carrée, 1928.

Strachan, Hew, *The First World War*, vol.1, *To Arms*, Oxford, OUP, 2001.

Strachan, Hew, *The First World War*, London, Simon and Schuster, 2003.

Strachan, Hew, *The First World War in Africa*, Oxford, OUP, 2004.

Taylor, A.J.P., *The First World War*, London, Hamish Hamilton, 1963.

Taylor, John Vernon, *The Growth of the Church in Buganda. An Attempt at Understanding,* London, SCM Press, 1958.

T.E. Lawrence Society, *Journal of the T.E. Lawrence Society*, vol.ix, no.1, Autumn 1999, "French Soldiers in the Arab Revolt".

Tourigny, Yves, *So Abundant a Harvest, The Catholic Church in Uganda 1879-1979*, London, Darton, Longman and Todd, 1979.

Zwemer, Samuel, *The Law of Apostasy in Islam,* London, Marshall Brothers, 1924.

References - Introduction

[1] Strachan, Hew, *The First World War in Africa*, Oxford, O.U.P., 2004, p.3.

[2] The two names are used interchangeably throughout this book. The Society was founded by (Cardinal) Charles Lavigerie, Archbishop of Algiers in 1868.

[3] Shorter, Aylward, *Cross and Flag in Africa. Catholic Missionaries and the Colonial Scramble. The White Fathers 1892-1914*, New York, Orbis Books, 2006.

[4] These may now be consulted online.

[5] The author spent a semester in 2003 as a Yale Research Associate and Senior Mission Scholar at the Overseas Ministry Study Center, New Haven, CT.

References - Chapter One

[1] Keegan, John, *The First World War*, London, Hutchinson (Pimlico), 1998 (1999), p.3.

[2] *Rapports Annuels*, no.16, 1920-1921, p.102.

[3] Cf. Keegan *op.cit.*, pp.452-453.

[4] Lunn, Joe, *Memoirs of the Maelstrom: A Senegalese Oral History of the First World War*, Oxford, James Currey, 1999, p.146.

[5] Parsons, Timothy, *The African Rank and File*, Oxford, James Currey, 1999, p.19.

[6] Fox, Douglas, "The 1918 Spanish Influenza Pandemic", *Science*, vol.293, September 2001, p. 1,842.

[7] The number 60 represents the recorded names of priests, brothers, scholastics, novices and aspirants of the White Fathers who lost their lives because of the war. There is a further unknown number of aspirants and postulants (students) who died in battle, and whose names are unrecorded. It is thought to be between 10 and 15. Also, there were missionaries who died later of the long-term after effects of war.

[8] AGMAfr. 119029-054.

[9] Casier, Jacques, *Développement de la Société*, AGMAfr.MS, 1961, estimates that in 1914 there was a total membership of 899, composed of 658 priests and 241 brothers. This is a considerable but unexplained advance on Voillard's figures.

[10] Cf. AGMAfr. 122011 for the distinction between "genuine" Germans and Alsatians.

[11] AGMAfr. 119042, Voillard to Commandant August 19th 1914.

[12] Cf. Ousby, Ian, *The Road to Verdun*, London, Jonathan Cape (Pimlico), 2002 (2003), pp.148-149, 183-184. One White Father from Lorraine, with German nationality and French sympathies, was Bishop Henri Léonard, Vicar Apostolic of Unyanyembe, German East Africa.

[13] Casier, *loc.cit.*

[14] AGMAfr. 119003, Mobilization Statistics; The *Livre d'Or*, AGMAfr. 121, gives the slightly lower figure of 363 French conscripts.

[15] Finn, Peter, *History of the Priory Bishop's Waltham*, Winchester, Hedera Books, 2002, pp.49-52.

[16] *Rapport Annuels*, no.14, 1918-1919, p.59.

[17] There is no official record of aspirants who died before joining the novitiate. Ten are known for certain to have died in the war.

[18] This account of events is based on letters from Moullec to Livinhac AGMAfr. 087603, October 23rd 1914 and 087604, November 8th 1914; Grange to Livinhac AGMAfr. 84265-184271, September 14th to December 14th 1914; Uganda Provincial Archives, Grange's circulars of September 13th and 28th 1914; Streicher to Livinhac AGMAfr. 082393-082395, August 5th to November 30th/December 1st 1914.

[19] AGMAfr. 84268, Grange to Livinhac November 9th 1914.

[20] Uganda Provincial Archives, Grange to confreres September 13th and 28th.

[21] AGMAfr. 84266 Grange to Livinhac October 5th 1914; *Rapports Annuels*, no.10, 1914, p.199-200, Report of Amédée Goulet (1879-1957), Entebbe.

[22] AGMAfr. 084267, Grange to Livinhac, November 5th 1914; 087604, Moullec to Livinhac November 8th 1914.

[23] AGMAfr. 84266, Grange to Livinhac October 5th 1914.

[24] AGMAfr. 087603, Moullec to Livinhac, October 23rd 1914; 087604, November 8th; 84267 Grange to Livinhac, November 5th 1914; 84268, November 9th and enclosure.

[25] AGMAfr. Streicher/Livinhac 082393, August 5th 1914; 082394, September 8th.

[26] AGMAfr. 082395, Streicher to Livinhac, November 30th/December 1st 1914; 084271, Grange to Livinhac, December 14th 1914.

[27] AGMAfr. 84267 Grange to Livinhac, November 5th 1914; 084268, Grange to Livinhac, November 9th. *Rapports Annuels*, no.10, 1914, pp.182-3 (Report by Mgr.Streicher), pp.199-200 (Report by Amédée Goulet); *Lettres Circulaires*, Mgr. Livinhac, Maison Carée, Algiers, 1912-1922, no. 109, 1915, p.14 states that the British Government paid 6,000 Francs for the travel and food of mobilized French missionaries in Uganda. Louis Hamon described the excitements and hardships of the journey by rail and steamer in *Missions d'Afrique*, no.229, 1915, pp.2-7.

[28] *Rapports Annuels*, vol.33, 1938-1939, pp.55*-61*.

[29] National Archives, Kew, Colonial Office/Uganda, CO 536 70, 71, 73, 74.

[30] AGMAfr. Grange to Livinhac, 084266, October 5th 1914.

[31] The only references to the White Fathers in 1914 concern the request on behalf of Streicher for an advance of £400, because drafts on Brussels were blocked by the war. In the end, Colonial Secretary, Viscount Lewis Harcourt, suggested a draft on London, rather than through Entebbe, CO 536/71/42923/176; 536/74/42532/325-328. The records show that the Colonial Office held the White Fathers in high esteem.

[32] *Munno*, December 1914, p.200. I am grateful to Ivan Page for drawing my attention to this reference.

[33] *Petit Echo*, 1917, no.43, p.91.

[34] *Rapports Annuels*, no.13, (1917-1918), p.56.

[35] *Rapports Annuels*, no.10, 1914, p.6; *Petit Echo*, no.25, 1915, pp.122-123; no.37, 1916, p.297.

[36] Information from Hugo Hinfelaar, M.Afr.

[37] *Rapports Annuels*, no.13, 1917-1918, p.480.

[38] *Rapports Annuels*, no.11, 1915, p.25-27.

[39] *Petit Echo*, no.29, 1916, pp. 33, 40.

[40] *Petit Echo*, no. 547, April 1964, pp.270-272.

[41] *Petit Echo*, no.37, 1916, pp.293-294.

[42] Keegan, *op.cit.*, pp.20-21.

[43] Blass, Jean-Pierre, AGMAfr. Personal Dossier, no.489; Minutes of the General Council, p.1179, February 12th 1917.

[44] AGMAfr.Mwazye Mission Diary 1910-1928, May 25th 1915.

[45] *Ibid.*, November 20th 1915.

[46] *Rapports Annuels*, 1949-1951, *Notices Nécrologiques* 1951, p.86.

[47] *Rapports Annuels*, 1958-1959, *Notices Nécrologiques* 1958-1959, pp.43-44.)

[48] *Petit Echo*, no.41, February 1917, p.51; no.46, July 1917, p.200.

[49] AGMAfr. Charles Umbricht, Personal Dossier.

[50] Cf. Ousby , *op.cit.*, p.203.

[51] They were: Boudewyn, Alphonse (1885-1955); Claerhout, René (1888-1964); Debbaudt, Antoine (1886-1963); Dumortier, Augustin (1878-1951); Feys, Egide (1886-1960); Hérenthals, Jules (1884-1961); Roy, Raphaël (1879-1943); Tielmans, Alphonse (1884-1938); Van den Tillaert, Joseph (1880-1948); Verbeke, Cyrille (1883-1928); Weghsteen, Joseph (1873-1962).

[52] Page, Melvin E., *The Chiwaya War – Malawians and the First World War*, Boulder Colorado, Westview Press, 2000, p.112.

[53] *Rapports Annuels*, no.12, 1916-1917, p.307.

[54] Swiss Capuchins eventually took over Dar es Salaam and Mahenge, and the Italian Consolata missionaries, Iringa. The Benedictines were finally allowed back to Lindi and Peramiho in 1922, when the British recognized their St.Ottilien Swiss province as a separate congregation.

[55] Gray, Richard, "Christianity", in A.D.Roberts (ed.) *The Cambridge History of Africa 1907-1940*, Vol.7, 1986, Chap.3, p.175.

[56] This interpretation is based on the figures given in the annual reports.

[57] Communication from M. Rooijackers, January 6th 2006.

[58] Gray, *op.cit.* , p.174-175.

[59] *Rapports Annuels* no.17 1921-1922, p.28.

[60] The figures quoted in this section are taken from relevant numbers of *Rapports Annuels*, and *Petit Echo*.

[61] *Petit Echo,* no.69, July 1919, p.136.

[62] *Petit Echo*, no.93, July 1921, p.114.

[63] *Petit Echo*, no.85, November 1920, p.260.

[64] *Petit Echo*, no.46, July 1917, p.185; *Rapports Annuels*, no.13, 1917-1918, p.47; no.17, 1921-1922, p.90.

[65] AGMAfr. General Council Minutes, September 18th 1914, p.1076.

[66] *Petit Echo*, no.52, January 1918, p.3.

[67] Casier, *op.cit.* p.1.

[68] *Rapports Annuels*, no.16, 1920-1921, p.42; *Petit Echo*, no.85, November 1920, p.261.

[69] AGMAfr. 41027, "Post-War Problems" , Steinhage, Memo; 15th General Chapter of 1920, *Chapitres Généraux*, Casier 358, p.330.

[70] *Petit Echo*, no.32, 1916, p.160.

[71] Casier, *op.cit.* In 1925: 1,010. In 1934: 1,540. In 1939: 2,045.

References – Chapter Two

[1] *Petit Echo*, no.42, March 1917, p.78.

[2] *Petit Echo*, no.35, 1916, p.248.

[3] Auguste Clavel (1895-1979) served in the war against the Bolsheviks in Ukraine in 1919 and Sebastian Zehetmaier (1894-1969) served with the Turkish army against the Russians in the Caucasus. Apart from these, there is no apparent evidence that any White Father served on the Eastern or Russian Front.

[4] The permanent exhibitions of the Imperial War Museum, London, (especially the "Trench Experience") give an excellent idea of trenches and trench warfare. The *Musée des Abris*, at Albert on the Somme, displays the most extensive collection of artefacts and memorabilia. The "In Flanders Fields" Museum at the Cloth Hall in Ypres offers an impressive multi-media experience. There are many examples of surviving trenches on the Western Front. A good example is the "Trench of Death" on the Ijser Dyke near Diksmuide, Belgium.

[5] Cf. Keegan, *op.cit.*, pp.217-219

[6] *Petit Echo*, no.32, 1916, p.131.

[7] Cf. Keegan *op.cit.*,pp.300-308; Ousby *op.cit.*, *passim*; Taylor, A.J.P., *The First World War*, London, Hamish Hamilton, 1963, pp.119-126.

[8] Cf. Keegan, op.cit., pp.308-321, also Keegan, John, *The Face of Battle*, London, Jonathan Cape 1976 (Pimlico 1991), pp.204-284.

[9] Keegan, *op.cit.* (1998), p.321.

[10] *Petit Echo*, no.56, 1918, p.113.

[11] *Petit Echo*, no.29, 1916, p.51.

[12] *Petit Echo*, no.31, 1916, pp.112-113.

[13] *Petit Echo*, no.34, 1916, p.203; no.64, 1919, p.38.

[14] See pp.55-56, and fn.100, for the Zouaves.

[15] *Petit Echo*, no.34, 1916, pp.205-206.

[16] *Petit Echo*, no.34, 1916, p.207.

[17] *Petit Echo*, no.34, 1916, p.215.

[18] *Petit Echo*, no.37, 1916, p.305.

[19] *Petit Echo*. no.41, February 1917, pp.41-44.

[20] *Ibid.*, pp.46-47.

[21] Keegan, op.cit.(1998), pp.393-395.

[22] Pierre Lhomme (1886-1917) and Auguste De Langhe (1890-1917).

[23] Keegan, *op.cit.*, pp.253-269; Taylor, *op.cit.*, pp.79-84; Strachan, Hew, *The First World War*, London, Simon and Schuster, 2003, pp.113-121; Simkins, Peter; Jukes, Geoffrey and Hickey, Michael, *The First World War*, Oxford, Osprey, 2003, pp.291-301.

[24] *Petit Echo*, no.22, 1915/3, p.37.

[25] *Petit Echo*, no.609, 1970/6, pp.257-260.

[26] *Petit Echo*, no.21, 1915, pp.12-20.

[27] *Petit Echo*, no.23, 1915, pp.60-69.

[28] *Petit Echo*, no.23, 1915, p.69; no.27, 1915, p.196.

[29] This necessarily brief account relies on Keegan *op.cit.*, (1998), pp.164-168, 269-276

[30] *Petit Echo*, no.27, 1915, pp.192-196.

[31] *Petit Echo*, no.26, p.169.

[32] *Petit Echo*, no.28, 1916, p.23.

[33] *Petit Echo*, no.30, 1916, p.88.

[34] *Petit Echo*, no.34, 1916, pp.222-223.

[35] Keegan *op.cit.*, (1998), pp.454-455; Taylor, *op.cit.*, p.100; Strachan *op.cit.* 2003, p.296; Macmillan, Margaret, *The Peacemakers*, London, John Murray, 2001, pp.442-445.

[36] Lawrence, T.E., *Seven Pillars of Wisdom*, "Oxford Text" of 1922, Fordingbridge, Hants, J. and N. Wilson, 2004; cf. Keegan *op.cit.* (1998), pp.444-445.

[37] *Rapports Annuels*, vol.23, 1927-1928, pp.52*-56*.

[38] Lawrence, *op.cit.*, p.508.

[39] *Rapports Annuels*, no.15, 1919-1920, p.83; *Petit Echo*, no.53, February 1918, pp.100-101.

[40] *Petit Echo*, no.21, June 1915, p.4.

[41] *Petit Echo*, no. 34, June 1916, p.209. The horror had been compounded for him by being wounded.

[42] *Petit Echo*, no.38, 1916, p.330.

[43] *Petit Echo*, no.36, 1916, pp.271-272.

[44] *Petit Echo*, no.38, 1916, pp.325-327.

[45] *Petit Echo*, no.38, 1916, p.330.

[46] *Petit Echo*, no.31, 1916, p.120.

[47] *Petit Echo*, no.31, 1916.

[48] *Petit Echo*, no.32, 1916, p.152.

[49] *Petit Echo*, no.32, 1916, p.149.

[50] *Petit Echo*, no.631, 1972/7, pp.337-341.

[51] *Petit Echo*, no.706, 1980/1, pp.32-37.

[52] *Petit Echo*, no.48, 1917, p.250.

[53] *Petit Echo*, no.36, 1916, p.275.

[54] *Petit Echo*, no.22, 1915, p.46.

[55] *Petit Echo*, no. 21, 1915, p.15.

[56] *Petit Echo*, no. 25, 1915, p.136.

[57] *Rapports Annuels*, 1939-1945, Supplement, *Notices Nécrologiques*, pp.110-113.

[58] *Petit Echo*, no.21, June 1915, p.4; no. 38, 1916, p.322.

[59] *Petit Echo*, no. 21, June 1915, pp.7-8.

[60] *Petit Echo*, no.21, June 1915, p.14.

[61] *Petit Echo*, no. 23, August 1915, p.70-71.

[62] *Petit Echo*, no.25, October 1915, pp.138-139.

[63] *Petit Echo*, no. 31, 1916, pp.114-115.

[64] Cf. Arthur, Max, *Forgotten Voices of the Great War*, London, Ebury Press, 2002, p.243.

[65] *Petit Echo*, no. 28, 1916, p.18.

[66] *Petit Echo*, no.41, February 1917, pp.49-50.

[67] *Petit Echo*, no. 40, January 1917, p.20.

[68] *Petit Echo*, no. 29, 1916, p.52.

[69] *Petit Echo*, no.36, 1916, p.272.

[70] Arthur, *op.cit.*, p.85.

[71] *Petit Echo*, no.28, 1916, p.12.

[72] Cf. Arthur, *op.cit.* p.97.

[73] This account of poison gas warfare relies on Keegan, *op.cit.* 1998, pp.213-215; and internet articles from *The National Archives Learning Curve*.

[74] *Petit Echo*, no.25, October 1915, p.130.

[75] *Petit Echo*, no.28, 1916, p.3.

[76] *Petit Echo*, no.29, 1916, pp.44-45.

[77] *Petit Echo*, no.29, 1916, p.52.

[78] *Petit Echo*, no.29, 1916, p.53.

[79] *Petit Echo*, no.29, 1916, pp.53-54.

[80] *Petit Echo*, no.31, 1916, p.118.

[81] *Petit Echo*, no.38, 1916, p.329.

[82] *Petit Echo*, no.56, May 1918, p.113.

[83] *Petit Echo*, no.58, July 1918, p.159.

[84] *Petit Echo*, no.704, 1979/9, pp.562-566; *Rapports Annuels*, no. 19, pp.25*-26*.

[85] This account of aerial warfare uses Keegan, *op.cit.*, (1998) pp.157, 240, 386, 240 and 435; Strachan, *op.cit.* 2003, p.57 and internet articles from the Zeppelin Library, *WWIAviation.com* and *Air Power/WWI_Bombing*.

[86] *Rapports Annuels*, no.11, 1915, p.51; Finn, *op.cit.*, pp.54-55.

[87] *Petit Echo*, no.30, 1916, p.87; no.31, 1916, p.122.

[88] *Petit Echo*, no.31, 1916, p.119.

[89] This description is included here because of its intrinsic interest.

[90] *Petit Echo*, no.43, 1917, p.105, Letter from Henri Le Veux March 21st 1917.

[91] As a child, the author watched the Graf Zeppelin fly over Carshalton, Surrey in 1938.

[92] *Petit Echo*, no.30, 1916, p.85; no. 31, 1916, p.109; no.32, 1916, p.144.

[93] *Petit Echo*, no.34, 1916, p.204.

[94] *Petit Echo*, no.35, 1916, p.247.

[95] *Ibid.*, p.251.

[96] *Petit Echo*, no.38, 1916, pp.328-329.

[97] *Petit Echo*, no.41, 1917, p.41.

[98] *Rapports Annuels*, no.13, 1917-1918, pp.27-31.

[99] *Petit Echo*, no.44, May 1917, p.120.

[100] *Rapports Annuels*, 1958-1959, *Notices Nécrologiques* 1957-1958, pp. 18-32.

[101] *Petit Echo*, no.23, 1915, pp.76-77.

[102] *Rapports Annuels*, no.14, 1918-1919, p.42.

[103] *Petit Echo*, no.37, 1916, p.310.

[104] *Petit Echo*, no.56, 1918, p.115. General information from *Zouave* internet sites.

[105] *Petit Echo*, no.41, February 1917, p.40.

[106] *Petit Echo*, no.52, 1984/7, pp.413-417.

[107] *Petit Echo*, 42, 1917, p.72.

[108] *Petit Echo*, no.32, 1916, p.151.

[109] *Petit Echo*, no. 23, 1915, p.43.

[110] *Rapports Annuels*, vol.33, 1938-1939, pp.55*-61*.

[111] *Petit Echo*, no.22, 1915, p.34; *Rapports Annuels*, 1958-1959, *Notices Nécrologiques* 1957-1958, pp.124-130.

[112] *Petit Echo*, no.34, 1916, pp.215-217.

[113] *Petit Echo*, no. 23, 1916, p.59.

[114] *Petit Echo*, no.34, 1916, p.219.

[115] *Petit Echo*, no.22, 1915, p.34.

[116] *Petit Echo*, no.48, 1917, p.251.

[117] *Petit Echo*, no.30, 1916, pp.76-80.

[118] *Petit Echo*, no. 22, 1915, p.38.

[119] *Petit Echo*, no.25, 1917, pp.134-135.

[120] *Petit Echo*, no.41, 1917, p.52.

[121] *Petit Echo*, no.33, 1916, pp.176-177.

[122] *Petit Echo*, no.46, 1917, p.200.

[123] *Petit Echo*, no.48, 1917, p.242.

[124] *Rapports Annuels*, no.14, 1918-1919, p.146.

[125] *Petit Echo*, no.21, June 1915, pp.7-8.

[126] *Petit Echo*, no. 27, 1915, p.202.

[127] *Petit Echo*, no. 32, 1916, p.141.

[128] *Petit Echo*, no.44, 1917, p.143.

[129] *Petit Echo*, no.29, 1916, p.41.

[130] *Petit Echo*, no.35, 1916, p.237.

[131] *Petit Echo*, no.23, 1915, p.72.

[132] *Petit Echo*, no.28, 1916, pp.20-21.

[133] *Petit Echo*, no.27, 1915, p.186; no.32, 1916, pp.153-154; no.46, 1917, p.196. Also AGMAfr Dossier of Charles Umbricht, typescript biography, pp.5 and undated newspaper cutting.

References – Chapter Three

[1]   AGMAfr 119003; 119071 121. The statistics were amended in the course of preparing the "Golden Book". Livinhac ordered that a "Golden Book" be made, cf. *Petit Echo* no.62, 1918, p.242. In spite of this, no printed copy survives in AGMAfr, unlike the Golden Book of the 1939-1945 War.

[2] The complete list is given in Appendix I.

[3] AGMAfr. records list him as a sergeant. The official record of the French Ministry of Defence lists him as corporal.

[4] *Rapports Annuels*, Vol.19, 1923-1924, pp.25*-26*.

[5] AGMAfr, Nilges Jakob, Personal Dossier.

[6]   AGMAfr Mibirizi Mission Diary 1912-1913, p.13; *Petit Echo*, no.35, 1916, p.229; *Rapports Annuels*, no.11, 1915, p.87.

[7] This is not the same number 43 found in the Golden Book. It includes 10 Germans and 3 Belgians.

[8] Details given here are from reports in *Petit Echo*, and from AGMAfr 119 007.

[9] Strictly speaking it was not one of the Verdun forts, but a fortification or redoubt (*ouvrage*).

[10] AGMAfr. Personal Dossier, notebook, June 22nd 1916.

[11] *Petit Echo*, no.37, 1916, p.304; no.39, 1916, p.377.

[12] *Petit Echo*, no.55, 1918, p.88; no.56, 1918, p.114; no.61, 1918, p.231.

[13] *Petit Echo*, no.39, 1916, p.371; no.40, 1917, p.14; no.61, 1918, p.228; *Rapports Annuels*, no.13 1917-1918, p.482.

[14] *Petit Echo*, no.33, 1916, pp. 166-167; no.39, 1916, p. 378.

[15] *Petit Echo*, no.57, 1918, p.134.

[16] The author visited the monument at Diksmuide on June 9th 2005. De Boninge's story is told by Andries Debeir: *Omdat zijn hart zo ruim was..., Lode De Boninge (1896-1918), Een Levensverhaal,* Maarkedal, Ceres, 1979, (*Because his Heart was so Big...Lode De Boninge (1896-1918), The Sacrifice of a Life*); also by Jaques Casier in "Souvenirs Historiques 22", Annexe to *Nuntiuncula,* no. 447, April 1988.

[17] *Petit Echo*, no.48, 1917, p.247.

[18] *Petit Echo*, no.34, 1916, pp.220, 222-223.

[19] Petit Echo, no.62, 1918, pp. 254, 257.

[20] *Petit Echo*, no.57, 1918, p.121.

[21] The author visited the monument on June 9th 2005.

[22] *Petit Echo*, no.45, 1917, p.157.

[23] *Petit Echo*, no.23, 1915, p.52; no.31, 1916, pp.107, 113; no.32, 1916, p.148.

[24] *Rapports Annuels*, no.10, 1916, p.17.

[25] *Rapports Annuels*, no.11, 1915, p.8; AGMAfr. 119 007.

[26] *Petit Echo*, no.37, 1916, p.296.

[27] AGMAfr. 119 007.

[28] AGMAfr.119 007; *Petit Echo*, no.32, 1916, pp.139-140.

[29] *Petit Echo*, no.37, 1916, p.302; no.38, 1916, p.338; no.39, 1916, pp.379-380, 382. It was typical of the time for French M.Afr. conscripts to place "France" before the Church and the Society in the intentions of those who offered their lives.

[30] AGMAfr. 119 007; Rapports Annuels, no. 10 Supplement, 1914-1915, pp. 9-13.

[31] *Petit Echo*, no.56, p.108.

[32] Cf. Elam, Kathy, "News from the Western Front", *Genealogists' Magazine*, vol.28, no.5, March 2005, p.224.

[33] Cf. Holt, Tonie and Valmai, *The Western Front – North, Battlefield Guide*, Pen and Sword Military, Barnsley, 2004, p.208.

[34] *Petit Echo*, no.59, 1918, p.173.

[35] *Petit Echo*, no. 34, 1916, pp.202-203.

[36] *Petit Echo*, no.59, 1918, p.172.

[37] *Petit Echo*, no.64, 1919, p.38.

[38] *Petit Echo*, no. 36, 1916, p.276; no. 37, 1916, p.307; no.56, 1918, p.109

[39] Petit Echo, no.64, 1919, p.38.

[40] *Petit Echo*, no.38, 1916, p.322; no.42, 1917, p.73.

[41] See Appendix II

[42] *Rapports Annuels*, vol. 21, 1925-1926, pp.45*-48*.

[43] *Petit Echo*, no.606, 1970/3, pp.119-122.

[44] *Petit Echo*, no.706, 1980/1, pp.32-37.

[45] *Rapports Annuels*, 1939-1945 Supplement, *Notices Nécrologiques*, pp.69-73.

[46] He was not sure if it was a bullet or a piece of shrapnel.

[47] *Rapports Annuels*, 1958-1959, *Notices Nécrologiques*, pp.56-58; *Petit Echo*, no.22, 1915, p.42; no.28, 1916, pp.28-29; no.38, 1916, p.336.

[48] *Rapports Annuels*, vol.16, 1920-1921, pp.8*-12*.

[49] *Petit Echo*, no.672, 1976/7, pp.385-391.

[50] *Petit Echo*, no.562, November 1965, pp.510-514; also no. 25, 1915, p.126; no.36, 1916, p.272; no.56, 1918, p.118; no.57, 1918, p.140 and *Rapports Annuels* no.12, 1916-1917, p.21.

[51] Petit Echo, no.705, 1979/10, pp. 614-617.

[52] *Rapports Annuels*, 1939-1945, Supplement, *Notices Nécrologiques*, pp.64-67.

[53] *Petit Echo*, no.28, 1916, pp.10-11; no.522, January 1962, pp.56-57.

[54] *Petit Echo*, no.56, 1918, p.114; no. 52, 1984/7, pp.413-417.

[55] *Petit Echo*, no.635, 1972/11, pp.532-535.

[56] *Petit Echo*, no.22, 1915, p.44; no.44, 1917, p.129; Rapports *Annuels*, vol.27, 1931-1932, pp.154-157.

[57] *Petit Echo*, no.35, 1916, pp.231, 240, 246-247.

[58] Bouniol, Joseph, *The White Fathers and their Missions*, London, Sands, 1929.

[59] *Rapports Annuels*, 1949-1951, *Notices Nécrologiques*, 1951, pp.82-85; *Petit Echo*, 22, 1915, p.41; no.27, 1915, pp.204-205, no.29, 1916, p.63; no.63, 1919, pp.6-7.

[60] *Petit Echo*, no.28, 1916, pp.30-31; no.36, 1916, p.282; no. 43, 1917, p.108; no. 45, 1917, p.161; no.59, 1918, p.175; no. 72, 1919, p.203; AGMAfr, Auguste Thézé, Personal Dossier cf. letter from Ivan Page, Archivist, February 8th 2005.

[61] Bellaue was provincial treasurer. The reason for his imprisonment is not recorded. It may have had something to do with a German demand for money, as happened at Gits.

[62] *Petit Echo*, no. 64, 1919, p.30; *Rapports Annuels*, no.8, 1915, p.52; no.14, 1918-1919, p.87; AGMAfr. 43464 postcard from Rheinbach Prison, Bellaue to Superior of St. Maurice, Switzerland, June 2nd 1918; 43465 and 43466 heavily censored letters from Limburg Prison: Bellaue to Livinhac July 10th and July 28th 1918.

[63] Petit Echo, no. 562, 1965, pp.503-509. I am indebted to Peter Crocker of the Royal Welch Fusiliers Regimental Museum, Caernarfon Castle, for details of Howell's service record. Letter of March 13th 2006.

[64] *Petit Echo*, no. 56. 1918, p.110; no.59, 1918, pp.175, 190; no.60, 1918, p.205; no.63, 1919, pp.6-7; no.64, 1919, p.30.

[65] *Petit Echo*, no.38, 1916, p.336; 46, 1917, p.205.

[66] *Petit Echo*, no. 42, 1917, p.70; no.43, 1917, p.97.

[67] *Petit Echo*, no. 28, 1916, p.6; no.35, 1916, p.229; no.36, 1916, p.260; *Rapports Annuels*, no. 11, 1915, pp. 71, 80, 87, 96; no.12, 1916-1917, p.189; no. 13, 1917-1918, p.316.

[68] *Petit Echo*, no. 42, 1917, p.69; *Rapports Annuels*, no.11, 1915, p.76; no.12, 1916-1917, p.252.

[69] He was allowed to return to the Iraqw, where he died almost immediately in 1919.

[70] *Petit Echo*, no.10, 1914 (1916), pp.182, 199; no.36, 1916, p.265; *Rapports Annuels*, 12, 1916-1917, pp.240, 241, 243. AGMAfr. Alois Hamberger Personal Dossier and Letter from Ivan Page, Archivist, January 25th 2005.

[71] *Petit Echo*, no.47, 1917, p.221; *Rapports Annuels*, no.12, 1916-1917, pp.241-243; 1949-1951, *Notices Nécrologiques*, 1951, p.86.

[72] *Rapports Annuels*, 1958-1959, *Notices Nécrologiques*, pp.43-44; vol. 19, 1923-1924, pp.29*-31*.

[73] Rapports Annuels, no.10 1914 (1916), pp.9-10; no.11, 1915, pp.8-9.

[74] The fullest account of Clavel's ordeal in the Ukraine is in *Petit Echo*, no.75, 1920, pp.16-18. His obituary is in *Petit Echo*, no.704, 1979/9, pp.562-566. Other references are: *Rapports Annuels*, no.13, 1917, p.25; no. 16, p. 9; *Petit Echo*, no. 67, 1919, p.109; no.77, 1920, p.37; no.89, 1921, p.41.

[75] *Petit Echo*, no.70, 1919, p.157.

[76] Cf. Saint Ignatius, *The Spiritual Exercises*, no.23, London, Burns Oates and Washbourne, 1952, p.13.

[77] *Petit Echo*, no. 38, 1916, p.332; no.40, 1917, p.22; Ps. 115:1 (V.113b), *"Non nobis Domine, sed nomine tuo da gloriam."*

[78] *Petit Echo*, no.36, 1916, p.268.

[79] *Petit Echo*, no. 36, 1916, p.269.

[80] *Petit Echo*, no. 39, 1916, p.367.

[81] *Petit Echo*, no. 23, 1915, p.57.

[82] *Petit Echo*, no. 25, 1915, p.139; no. 49, 1917, p.272.

[83] *Petit Echo*, no. 42, 1917, p.71.

[84] *Petit Echo*, no. 25, 1915, p.126; AGMAfr. 119071 121.

[85] AGMAfr. 119071 121.

[86] AGMAfr. 119071 121 gives an original figure of 4, correcting it to 8.

[87] *Petit Echo*, no. 21, 1915, p.4; no. 28, 1916, p.21; no. 36, 1916, p.268.

[88] *Petit Echo*, no. 87, 1921, p.5.

[89] AGMAfr. 119071 121 gives 11 as the original figure, correcting it to 16.

[90] *Petit Echo*, no. 38, 1916, p.334; AGMAfr. 119071 121.

[91] AGMAfr. 119071 121.

[92] *Petit Echo*, no. 43, 1917, p.108.

[93] Petit Echo, no. 117, 1923, p.74; AGMAfr. personal dossier. De Paepe finally left the Society in 1941.

[94] *Petit Echo*, no. 38, 1916, p.323.

[95] *Petit Echo*, no. 37, 1916, p.304.

[96] *Petit Echo*, no.74, 1919, p.261.

[97] *Petit Echo*, no. 66, 1919, p.92.

[98] *Petit Echo*, no. 91, 1921, p.76.

[99] *Petit Echo*, no. 525, April, 1962, pp.236-240.

[100] This account is based on *Rapports Annuels*, no.10, 1914 (1916), pp.48-62.

[101] They had asked for Champagne and were surprised that there was none in the house.

[102] *Petit Echo*, no. 32, 1916, pp.132-133, 149; no. 33, 1916, pp.163, 173-174; no. 35, 1916, p.245; no. 39, 1916, 379.

[103] *Rapports Annuels*, no.12, 1916, p.41; AGMAfr. 119014-119019 contains a complete set of all the issues.

[104] *Petit Echo*, no. 37, 1916, p.287.

[105] *Petit Echo*, no.43, 1917, p.88.

[106] *Petit Echo*, no. 28, 1916, p.3.

[107] *Petit Echo*, no. 41, 1917, p.34; no. 42, 1917, p.63; no. 44, 1917, p.119; *Rapports Annuels*, no. 13, 1917-1918, p.41.

[108] *Rapports Annuels*, no. 13, 1917, pp.40-44; *Petit Echo*, no. 58, 1918, p. 149; no. 59, 1918, p.175; no. 60, 1918, pp.196-197; *Echos Binsonnais*, January 13th 1919, AGMAfr. 119 019.

[109] *Rapports Annuels*, no. 12, 1916, p.31.

[110] *Petit Echo*, no.61, 1918, p.220.

[111] *Petit Echo*, no. 24, 1915, p.85.

[112] *Petit Echo*, no. 53, 1918, p.43. The original letter is in AGMAfr. Fontugue's personal dossier. Fontugue who received the *Croix de Guerre* and bronze medal for Epidemics, dropped out of missionary formation in 1919.

[113] *Petit Echo*, no. 53, 1918, pp.43-44.

[114] *Petit Echo*, no. 47, 1917, pp235-236; *Rapports Annuels*, 1949-1951, Notices Nécrologiques 1951 (2nd Series) pp.36-39.

[115] Lawrence, *op.cit.,* p.418.

[116] "French Soldiers in the Arab Revolt", *Journal of the T.E.Lawrence Society*, vol. .ix, no.1, Autumn 1999, ISSN 0963 1747.

[117] *Petit Echo*, no. 57, 1918, pp.142-144; no. 686, 1978/1, pp.40-47.

[118] *Petit Echo*, no. 59, August 1918, p.171.

References – Chapter Four

[1] *Petit Echo*, no.30, 1916, p.81.

[2] *Petit Echo*, no. 32, 1916, p.145.

[3] *Société des Missionnaires d'Afrique (Pères Blancs), Directoire des Constitutions*, Maison Carrée, Algiers, 1914, no.105.

[4] *Petit Echo*, no.20, 1914, p.130; no. 21, 1915, p.1.

[5] The originals of many of these letters are to be found in AGMAfr. personal dossiers.

[6] *Petit Echo*, no. 28, 1916, p.1.

[7] *Petit Echo*, no. 30, 1916, p.65; no. 32, 1916, p.129.

[8] *Petit Echo*, no. 32, 1916, p.152.

[9] *Ibid.*, p.145.

[10] *Petit Echo*, no.34, 1916, p.211.

[11] *Petit Echo*, no. 26, 1915, pp.173-174.

[12] *Ibid.*, p. 212. *Priest in the Army* was a periodical published specially for priests and seminarians in the frontline.

[13] *Petit Echo*, no. 36, 1916, p.276.

[14] *Petit Echo*, no. 40, 1917, p.28.

[15] E.g. *Petit Echo*, no. 34, 1916, p.211.

[16] *Petit Echo*, no. 30, 1916, p. 84.

[17] *Petit Echo*, no.27, 1915, p. 186.

[18] *Petit Echo*, no.29, 1916, p.43.

[19] *Petit Echo*, no. 34, 1916, p.214.

[20] *Petit Echo*, no. 36, 1916, p.283.

[21] *Petit Echo*, no. 21, 1915, p.6.

[22] *Petit Echo*, no. 28, 1916, p.8.

[23] *Petit Echo*, no 40, 1917, p.215.

[24] *Petit Echo*, no. 21, 1915, p.6.

[25] *Petit Echo*, no. 21, 1915, p.19; no. 32, 1916, p.151; no. 36, 1916, p.276.

[26] *Petit Echo*, no. 33, 1916, p.174.

[27] *Petit Echo*, no. 26, 1915, p.166.

[28] *Petit Echo*, no. 34, 1916, p.215.

[29] *Petit Echo*, no. 40, 1917, pp.15-16. "Africans", original: *infidèles*, not a pejorative term.

[30] *Petit Echo*, no. 40, 1917, p.29.

[31] Songs, 6:4 and 10; *Petit Echo*, no. 41, 1917, pp.47-48.

[32] *Petit Echo*, no. 26, 1915, p.155; no. 28, 1916, p.28.

[33] *Petit Echo*, no.34, 1916, p.209.

[34] *Petit Echo*, no. 34, 1916, p.222

[35] *Rapports Annuels*, no. 15, 1919-1920, p.477.

[36] The three older missionaries were: Brother Artémon Galendrin (1840-1922), Father Jean-Joseph Richard (1841-1917) and Father Pierre Viven (1844-1933).

[37] In 1872 Saint Daniel Comboni became Vicar Apostolic of "Central Africa", a vicariate that was limited in practice to Northern Sudan. In 1883 Raoul de Courmont CSSp became Vicar Apostolic of Zanzibar, presiding over a group of missions at the East African coast and its hinterland. Livinhac's elevation in 1885 to the Vicariate of Nyanza, in the East African interior, can therefore be said to have made him the first Bishop of Equatorial Africa.

[38] Livinhac, L., *Lettres Circulaires* 1912-1922, Maison Carrée, Algiers, no. 108, August 5th 1914.

[39] *Ibid.*, no. 109, February 2nd 1915, p.22.

[40] Livinhac, *op.cit.*, no. 109 of February 2nd 1915; no. 111 of May 24th 1915; and no.117 of February 2nd 1918.

[41] Livinhac, *op.cit.*, no. 111 of May 24th 1915, pp.22-25.

[42] Livinhac, *op.cit.*, no.112 of February 2nd 1916, pp.24-25.

[43] Livinhac, *op.cit.*, no.113, of May 12th 1916, pp.1-8.

[44] Livinhac, *op.cit.*, no.115, of February 2nd 1917, p.4.

[45] Livinhac. *op.cit.*, no. 116, of May 17th 1917, p.3.

[46] Livinhac, *op.cit.*, no.117, of February 2nd 1918.

[47] Lechaptois died at 65. He was appointed Vicar Apostolic of Tanganyika in 1891 and had held this post for 28 years.

[48] AGMAfr. 119 068, Circulars to mobilized missionaries.

[49] They are to be found in *AGMAfr.*, Livinhac I, iv, Letters to Confreres.

[50] Pierre Viel (1879-1964).

[51] Cf. *Petit Echo*, no. 32, 1916, p.129; no. 52, 1918, p. 2; no. 55, 1918, p.75.

[52] *Petit Echo*, no. 40, 1917, p.1.

[53] *Petit Echo*, no. 24, 1915, p.98; no. 26, 1915, p.169.

[54] *Petit Echo*, no. 34, 1916, p.213.

[55] *Petit Echo*, no. 34, 1916, p.213.

[56] *Petit Echo*, no.39, 1916, p.377.

[57] *Petit Echo*, no. 39, 1916, p.377; no.64, 1919, p.33.

[58] *Petit Echo*, no. 35, 1916, p.238; no. 36, 1916, p.273.

[59] *Petit Echo*, no. 40, 1917, pp.15-16.

[60] *Petit Echo*, no. 34, 1916, p.213; no. 35, 1916, p.239.

[61] *Petit Echo*, no. 36, 1916, p.279.

[62] *Petit Echo*, no. 35, 1916, p.242.

[63] *Petit Echo*, no. 40, 1917, p.12.

[64] *Petit Echo*, no. 32, 1916, p.147.

[65] *Petit Echo*, no.561, September-October 1956, pp.442-446.

[66] *Petit Echo*, no, 28, 1916, p.12.

[67] *Petit Echo*, no. 30, 1916, p.92; no. 33, 1916, p.206.

[68] *Petit Echo*, no. 34, 1916, p.206.

[69] *Petit Echo*, no. 38, 1916, p.331; no. 39, 1916, p.379.

[70] *Petit Echo*, no. 29, 1916, p.40; no. 44, 1917, p.123.

[71] *Petit Echo*, no. 35, 1916, p. 250.

[72] *Petit Echo*, no. 38, 1916, p.343.

[73] *Petit Echo*, no. 25, 1915, pp.134-135.

[74] *Petit Echo*, no. 22, 1915, p.25; AGMAfr. General Council Minutes, 1171, 27th November, December 4th 1916.

[75] *Petit Echo*, no. 69, 1919, p.136.

References – Chapter Five

[1] This introduction is based on Strachan, *op.cit.* 2003, pp.80-94; Morrow Jr., John H., *The Great War – An Imperial History*, London, Routledge, 2004, *passim*; Lunn, Joe, *Memoirs of the Maelstrom: A Senegalese Oral History of the First World War*, Heinemann 1999, *passim*; Mohlamme, J.S., "Soldiers Without Reward", The South African Military History Society, *Military History Journal*, vol.10, no.1, *scribe@samilitaryhistory.org*.

[2] There were also a small number of units from the West Indies, which included black soldiers. Names of the missing from these units are inscribed on the Menin Gate at Ypres.

[3] The estimate for the number of African soldiers on the Western Front varies from 140,000, to 170,000 or 180,000.

[4] *Petit Echo*, no. 31, 1916, p.108.

[5] Mangin, Charles, *La Force Noire*, Paris, Librairie Hachette, 1910.

[6] Lunn, *op.cit.*, pp.2-3, 24-48.

[7] Lunn, *op.cit.*, p.33.

[8] Morrow, *op.cit.*, p.96.

[9] This account of Diagne is based chiefly on Lunn, *op.cit.* and Morrow, *op.cit.*

[10] This account of the East African *Schütztruppe* is based on Strachan, *op.cit.* 2003, pp.80-94; Morrow, *op.cit.*, pp.58-60, 99, 145-147; Gardner, Brian, *German East – The Story of the First World War in East Africa*, London, Cassell, 1963, pp.9-13, 59, 76-77; Page Malcolm, *A History of the King's African Rifles and the East African Forces*, London, Leo Cooper, 1998, pp.25, 27, 33; Parsons, Timothy, *The African Rank and File, Social Implications of Colonial Military Service in the King's African Rifles*, 1902-1964, London, Heinemann, 1999, p.19.

[11] Cf. Shorter, Aylward, Chiefship in Western Tanzania. A Political History of the Kimbu, Oxford, Clarendon, 1972, pp.276-279. The term *ruga-ruga* was already current among the Nyamwezi and Kimbu of Tanzania in the mid-19th century. It referred to young, unmarried, professional soldiers. The name probably derives etymologically from the Nyamwezi *iluga*, "penis". It would seem that they wore the genitals and other parts of their enemy's bodies as trophies.

[12] Lettow Vorbeck, Paul, Von, *My Reminiscences of East Africa*, London, Hart and Blackett, 1920, pp.320-321.

[13] The author himself served as an officer in the 3rd Kenya Battalion of the KAR in Kenya and Malaysia from 1951-1952.

[14] This account of KAR logistics is based on Gardner, *op.cit.*, pp.8, 13-15, 20, 43-46; Strachan, *op.cit.* 2003, pp.86-88, 91; Morrow, *op.cit.*, pp.59-60, 99, 145-146; Page, *op.cit.*, pp.25-49; Parsons, *op.cit.*, pp.14-19; Lettow, Von, *op.cit.*, pp.319-321.

[15] Lettow, Von, *op.cit.*, p.318.

[16] Parsons, *op.cit.*, pp.53-61; Page, Malcolm, *op.cit.*, *passim*.

[17] This section on the KAR in Central Africa is based on: Page, Melvin E., *The Chiwaya War: Malawians and the First World War*, Boulder, Westview Press, 2000, pp.28-37 and Hinfelaar, Hugo, *History of the Catholic Church in Zambia*, Lusaka, Zambia, Bookworld Publishers, 2004, pp.82-84.

[18] Ewans, Martin, *European Atrocity, African Catastrophe – Leopold II, the Congo Free State and its Aftermath*, London, Routledge Curzon, 2002, pp.116-117.

[19] Hochschild, Adam, *King Leopold's Ghost*, London, Pan Macmillan, 2002, pp.127, 129, 190, 278.

[20] Paice, Edward, *Lost Lion of Empire. The Life of Cape-to-Cairo Grogan*. London, Harper-Collins, 2001, pp.264-268, 273-274.

[21] Page, Malcolm, *op.cit.*, pp.41-42; Page, Melvin, *op.cit.*, pp. 35-111; Parsons, *op.cit.*, pp.63-64.

[22] *Petit Echo*, no. 37, 1916, p.297.

[23] *Petit Echo*, no. 34, 1916, p.199; *Rapports Annuels*, no. 11, 1915, p.102; no. 12, 1916, p.92; no. 13, 1917, p.295.

[24] Lettow, Von, *op.cit.*, p.321.

[25] *Petit Echo*, no. 41, 1917, p.39.

[26] Strachan, *op.cit.* 2003, p.82.

[27] *Petit Echo*, no. 31, 1916, p.103; *Rapports Annuels* no. 12, 1916, pp. 127, 192-193.

[28] Anderson, Ross, *The Forgotten Front: The East African Campaign*, Stroud, Tempus, 2004, p.187.

[29] Strachan, *op.cit.* 2003, p.83.

[30] Page, Malcolm, *op.cit.*, p.41; *Rapports Annuels*, no. 12, 1916, p.78.

[31] Strachan, Hew, *The First World War in Africa*, Oxford, O.U.P., 2004, pp.6-9, 167.

[32] Anderson, *op.cit.*, p.172.

[33] *Petit Echo*, no. 66, 1919, p.88.

[34] *Petit Echo*, no. 40, 1917, p.8.

[35] *Rapports Annuels*, no.13, 1917, p.295.

[36] *Petit Echo*, no. 58, 1918, p.157.

[37] The British officially admitted the deaths of 44,000 carriers, clearly a gross underestimate.

[38] Hodges, Geoffrey, "Military Labour in East Africa and its Impact on Kenya", in Page, Melvin.E. (ed.), *Africa and the First World War*, London, Macmillan, 1987, p.148.

[39] In 1914 there was also the Egba revolt in Nigeria which did not affect the Missionaries if Africa. Cf. Matthews, James K., "Reluctant Allies: Nigerian Responses to Military Recruitment 1914-1915", in Page, Melvin E. (ed.), *Africa and the First World War*, London Macmillan 1987, pp.95-114.

[40] Saul, Mahir and Royer, Patrick, *West African Challenge to Empire. Culture and History in the Volta-Bani Anticolonial War*. Athens (U.S.A.), Ohio University Press, 2001, pp.127-128, 141-172; Morrow, *op. cit.*, pp.97-98, 144-145.

[41] Interview with Fr.Gilles De Rasilly at Wagadugu on February 24th 2004. He was familiar with the judicial transcripts of the subsequent trials. Alien chiefs had also been imported into the region, according to Fr. Joseph Roger de Benoist. Interview at Dakar on February 3rd 2004.

[42] Benoist, Joseph Roger de, *Eglise et Pouvoir Colonial au Soudan Français*, Paris, Karthala, 1987, p.243.

[43] Petit Echo, 31, 1916, p.100.

[44] Ki-Zerbo, Joseph, *Alfred Diban. Premier Chrétien de Haute Volta*, Paris, Cerf, 1983, p.53.

[45] *Petit Echo*, no. 31, 1916, p.100. The report states that the offender's legs were "smashed". It does not say how.

[46] Ki-Zerbo *op.cit.*, pp.53-55; Pichard, Gabriel, *Dii Alfred-Simon Diban Ki-Zerbo: Témoin de Dieu...Fondateur de l'Église*, Bobo Dioulasso, Imprimérie Savane, 1997, p.22.

[47] *Rapports Annuels*, no.12, 1916-1917, pp.398-424; Benoist, de, *op.cit.*, p.246.

[48] *Rapports Annuels*, no. 12, 1916-1917, p.398; Petit Echo, no. 86, 1920, p.280.

[49] The literature on John Chilembwe and his rising is extensive, beginning with the classic biography: Shepperson, George and Price, Thomas, *Independent African, John Chilembwe and the Origins, Setting and Significance of the Nyasaland Native Uprising of 1915*, Edinburgh, University Press, 1958. A Catholic viewpoint is provided by Linden, Ian with Linden, Jane, "John Chilembwe and the New Jerusalem", *Journal of African History*, vol.xii, no. 4, 1971, pp.629-651; and *Catholic Peasants and Chewa Resistance in Nyasaland 1889-1939*, Berkeley and Los Angeles, University of California Press, 1974, pp.75-102.

[50] Linden, *op.cit.*, 1974, p.100.

[51] The accounts of the Blantyre meeting published by the Missionaries of Africa are: *Petit Echo*, no. 26, 1915, p.152; no. 27, 1915, p.182; *Rapports Annuels*, no. 10, 1914 (1916), p.359.

[52] *Petit Echo*, no. 27, 1915, p. 152.

[53] This account of the Riflemen's war is largely based on Lunn, *op.cit.*, pp.120-192 and Morrow, *op.cit.*, pp.83, 127-128, 131, 159-60, 183-184, 186, 268-269, 310-311.

[54] Lunn, *op.cit.*, p.138.

[55] A picture of the sufferings endured by the Riflemen is given by Pinguilly, Yves, *Verdun 1916, Un Tirailleur en Enfer* ("A Rifleman in Hell"), Paris, Nathan, 2003; and by Joe Harris Lunn, Kande Kamara Speaks: an Oral History of the West African Experience in France 1914-1918", in Page, Melvin.E. (ed.), *Africa and the First World War*, London, Macmillan, 1987, pp.28-53.

[56] One of these was *Banania*, a family breakfast food made with cereal, bananas and cocoa. *Banania* tins are available in French World War I souvenir shops.

[57] *Petit Echo*, no. 21, 1915, p.12; no. 23, 1915, pp.72, 79.

[58] *Petit Echo*, no. 35, 1916, p.234; no.43, 1917, p.102.

[59] *Petit Echo*, no. 35, 1916, p.243.

[60] *Petit Echo*, no.45, 1917, p.166.

[61] *Petit Echo*, no. 46, 1917, p.199.

[62] *Petit Echo*, no.37, 1916, p.289.

[63] *Petit Echo*, no.45, 1917, p.149.

[64] *Petit Echo*, no. 43, 1917, p.102; no. 24, 1915, p.98; no. 27, 1915, pp.199-200; no. 29, 1916, p.59.

[65] *Petit Echo*, no. 34, 1916, pp.216-217; no. 46, 1917, p.203.

[66] *Rapports Annuels*, no. 13, 1917, pp.22-24.

[67] *Rapports Annuels*, no. 14, 1918, p.32.

[68] This account is based mainly on the essay by Ivan Page, "Alexis Lemaître, Général de Brigade, Missionnaire d'Afrique, Archevêque de Carthage", typescript, pp.1-5. The essay was commissioned for a dictionary of the French Generals of the First World War, as yet unpublished. The essay uses material in AGMAfr, particularly correspondence between Lemaître, Livinhac and Voillard.

[69] *Rapports Annuels*, no. 12, 1916-1917, p.35.

[70] Page, *op.cit.*, p.3; *Petit Echo*, no.56, 1918, p.102.

[71] *Petit Echo*, no. 60, 1918, p.195; no. 62, 1918, p.246.

[72] AGMAfr. General Council Minutes, 1266, May 13th 1919; Livinhac, 123009-043; Page, *op.cit.*, pp.3-4.

[73] *Petit Echo*, no. 66, 1919, p.89.

[74] *Petit Echo*, no.69, 1919, p.138.

[75] AGMAfr. 009457, Antoine Delpuch (Vice-Procurator) to Livinhac, May 24th 1920.

[76] *Ibid.*

[77] Page op.cit., p.4; *Petit Echo*, no.84, 1920, p.245, which states that the nomination was dated July 2nd.

[78] *Petit Echo*, no.103, 1922, p.75.

[79] AGMAfr. 006158, Livinhac to Burtin, April 5th, 1922; 006156, Voillard to Burtin, February 22nd 1922.

[80] Cf. also AGMAfr., 00212 Voillard to Burtin, January 22nd 1922, and March 22nd 1922.

[81] AGMAfr. Livinhac 122215.

[82] AGMAfr. General Council Minutes, 1274, June 16th 1919; 1289, October 6th 1919; 1296, December 5th 1919; 1331, may 31st 1920; 1348, July 25th 1920; 1444, August 26th 1921.

[83] AGMAfr. General Council Minutes, 1125, November 8th 1915; Livinhac 113 362.

[84] *Rapports Annuels*, no.13, 1917-1918, pp.378-379.

[85] *Rapports Annuels*, no. 11, 1915, p.102.

[86] *Petit Echo*, no.22, 1915, p.29; no.32, 1916, p.136.

[87] *Petit Echo*, no.34. p.200.

[88] *Petit Echo*, no. 43, 1917, p.93.

[89] *Rapports Annuels*, no. 12, 1916, pp.222-223.

[90] *Petit Echo*, no. 65, 1919, pp.57-58.

[91] *Rapports Annuels*, no. 13, 1917-1918, pp.378-379.

[92] *Petit Echo*, no. 63, 1919, pp.57-58.

[93] *Petit Echo*, no. 43, 1917, p.92.

[94] *Petit Echo*, no. 31, 1916, p.105.

[95] Page, Melvin, *op.cit*, p.112.

[96] Page. Melvin, *ibid*.

[97] Duff, Hector, *African Small Chop*, London, Hodder and Stoughton, 1932, pp.58-59. Duff preserves the French: *Ah c'est égal, mon capitaine, ne vous inquiétez pas; je tire si mal, je n'attrape jamais personne."*

[98] He also refers to oral evidence of his own, without any specific charges.

[99] Hetherwick, Alexander, *Robert Hellier Napier in Nyasaland – Being His Letters to his Home Circle*, Edinburgh and London, William Blackwood and Sons, 1925, p.86.

[100] *Petit Echo*, no. 57, 1918, p.126.

[101] Hastings, Adrian, *The Church in Africa*, Oxford, Clarendon Press, 1994, p.559.

References – Chapter Six

[1] Iliffe, John, *A Modern History of Tanganyika*, Cambridge University Press, 1979, p.241. The phrase refers particularly to von Lettow-Vorbeck's brilliant campaign in East Africa.

[2] Strachan, Hew, *The First World War in Africa*, Oxford, O.U.P., 2004, p.1.

[3] The best complete accounts are: Strachan, Hew, *The First World War in Africa*, Oxford, O.U.P., 2004 and the the original version of this in Strachan, *The First World War, Volume I: To Arms*, pp.495-643, *The Dark Continent: Colonial Conflict in Sub-Saharan Africa*, Oxford O.U.P., 2001. Summary accounts of the various campaigns in Germany's African colonies are given by Keegan *op.cit.*, pp.224-230; Morrow, *op.cit.*, pp.58-60; Strachan, *op.cit.* 2003, pp.80-94 and Taylor, *op.cit.*, pp.45-46.

[4] Nigeria and French Equatorial Africa: Chad, Central Africa, French Congo and Gabon.

[5] Strachan, *op.cit.* 2004, pp. 34-35; Iliffe, John, *Honour in African History*, Cambridge Univerity Press, 2005, pp.235-236.

[6] In fact, Uganda in 1916 had more than six times that number of neophytes. Cf. *Rapports Annuels*, no. 12, 1915-1916, Uganda Statistical Table.

[7] *Petit Echo*, no. 25, 1915, pp.140-141; no. 31, 1916, pp.125-126; no. 33, 1916, pp.190-191; no.38, 1916, p.345; no.41, 1917, pp.55-57.

[8] French Sudan in 1916 had less than 3,000 neophytes, *Rapports Annuels*, no.12, 1916-1917, French Sudan Statistical Table.

[9] AGMAfr. General Council Minutes, p.1326, May 10th 1920.

[10] Strachan, *op.cit.*,2003, p.85.

[11] Strachan *op.cit.*, 2004, pp.132-133.

[12] Strachan *op.cit.*, 2004, p.64.

[13] Macmillan, Margaret, *Peacemakers, Six Months that Changed the World*, London, John Murray, 2001, p.110.

[14] Statistics from *Rapports Annuels*. no. 9, 1913-1914, p.365.

[15] Statistics from *Rapports Annuels*, no. 8 , 1912-1913, p.354.

[16] Statistics from *Rapports Annuels*, no. 11, 1914-1915, p.256.

[17] Statistics from *Rapports Annuels*, no. 11, 1914-1915, Supplement, p.22.

[18] The Missionaries of Africa had a *procure* in Mombasa, but no missions in Kenya. Nor did they have any mission in Mozambique.

[19] Statistics from *Rapports Annuels*, no. 12, 1916-1917, (1915), p.307.

[20] Statistics from *Rapports Annuels*, no.10, 1914 (1916), p.181.

[21] Statistics from *Rapports Annuels*, no. 11, 1915, pp.240-241.

[22] Cf. *Rapports Annuels*, no. 10, 1914 (1916), p.270; no. 11, 1915, p.101; no.17, 1921-1922, p.104.

[23] Statistics from *Rapports Annuels*, no. 10, 1914 (1916), p.310; no. 11, 1915, p.132.

[24] No attempt is made to give a full account of the campaign here. This can be found in e.g. Strachan, Hew, *The First World War in Africa*, Oxford, O.U.P., 2004, pp.93-184; Anderson, Ross, *The Forgotten Front. The East African Campaign*, 1914-1918, Stroud, Tempus, 2004; Gardner, Brian, *German East – The Story of the First World War in East Africa*, London, Cassell, 1963; the popular

history by Charles Miller, *Battle for the Bundu - The First World War in East Africa*, London Macdonald, 1974; and Paice, Edward, *Tip and Run – The Untold Tragedy of the Great War in Africa*, London, Weidenfeld and Nicholson, 2006.

[25] Cf. Burgman, Hans, *The Way the Catholic Church Started in Western Kenya*, London, Mission Book Service, 1990, pp.82-84.

[26] *Sakalani* or *Sakarani* is said to mean a "warrior in a state of reckless exaltation".

[27] On September 9th/10th 1965, the author shared a railway compartment, between Mwanza and Tabora, with an elderly German from Berlin, who had served at Tanga under *Sakalani* at the age of twenty-four. Aylward Shorter, East African Journal (MS), Vol.2, p.42.

[28] After the Allies gained control of Lake Tanganyika, the steamer was repaired and refloated under the new name *Vengeur*.

[29] Foden, Giles, *Mimi and Toutou Go Forth: The Bizarre Battle of Lake Tanganyika*, London, Penguin Books, 2005 (2004). A light hearted account of the Lake Battle and the subsequent history of the ships involved.

[30] In 1952 it underwent a major overhaul. In 1978 it was fitted with diesel engines and still continues to serve as a motor vessel ferry on Lake Tanganyika. Cf. Foden *op.cit.*, p.311.

[31] Strachan, *op.cit.*, 2004, p.135.

[32] Communication from Hugo Hinfelaar M.Afr. October 12th 2005.

[33] Iliffe, op.cit., p.246, quoting Hordern, Charles, *Military Operations, East Africa*, London 1941.

[34] Iliffe, *op.cit.*, pp.251-252.

[35] The Belgians were concerned to use the conquered territory as a bargaining counter with Germany in Europe, should the war end in stalemate; or, if the allies won, to compensate the British for a deal with Portugal that would transfer the southern bank of the lower Congo from Angola in exchange for southern German East Africa. Cf. Iliffe, *op.cit.*, p.246.

[36] Daye, Pierre, *Avec les Vainqueurs de Tabora. Notes d'un Colonial Belge en Afrique Orientale Allemande*, Paris, Perrin 1918, pp.198-220.

[37] *Petit Echo*, no. 94, 1921, p.122.

[38] Kabeya, John B., *Adriano Atiman .Katekista na Mganga*, Tabora, Tanganyika Mission Press and Arusha, Eastern Africa Publications, 1977, pp.61, 95.

[39] The well-known big game hunter and naturalist, Capt. F.C. Selous, was killed at Behobeho on January 4th 1917. The Selous Game Park is named after him.

[40] Abbott, Peter and Raffaele Ruggeri, *Armies in East Africa 1914-1918*, Oxford, Osprey 2002, p.3.

[41] Strachan, *op.cit.*, 2004, pp.118-119, 102-103, 123-125, 178-179.

[42] Miller, *op.cit.*, p.283.

[43] Strachan *op.cit.*, 2004, p.177.

[44] von Lettow-Vorbeck, *op.cit.*, pp.315-321.

[45] Anderson, *op.cit.*, p.294.

[46] Cf. Gardner, *op.cit.*, p.194; Iliffe, *op.cit.*, p.246.

[47] *Petit Echo*, no.41, 1917, p.36.

[48] *Petit Echo*, no. 37, 1916, p.301.

[49] Rabeyrin, Claudius, *Les Missionnaires du Burundi durant la Guerre des Gentilshommes en Afrique Orientale 1914-1918*, M.Afr. private printing Langéac, 1978, p.33.

[50] *Petit Echo*, no. 26, 1915, p.150.

[51] *Petit Echo*, no. 34, 1916, pp.197

[52] *Rapports Annuels*, no. 10, 1914 (1916), pp. 282-283.

[53] *Ibid.*, pp.298-300.

[54] *Rapports Annuels*, no. 11, 1915, p.125.

[55] *Petit Echo*, no. 34, 1916, p.199.

[56] *Rapports Annuels*, no. 11, 1915, p.79.

[57] *Rapports Annuels*, no. 12, 1916-1917, pp.239-242.

[58] *Rapports Annuels*, no.12, 1916-1917, p.243.

[59] This necessarily brief account is based on the diaries of the affected mission stations, the *Rapports Annuels* and *Petit Echo* for 1916-1917.

[60] In Rwanda: Save, Murunda and Mibirisi were requisitioned. In Burundi: Buhonga and Kanyinya.

[61] He later returned to Kabgayi.

[62] *Petit Echo*, no. 37, 1916, pp.293-294.

[63] Rabeyrin, *op.cit.*, pp. 15-17, 36.

[64] *Rapports Annuels*, no. 13, 1917-1918, pp.298-299.

[65] Rabeyrin, *op.cit.*, pp. 19-21.

[66] *Petit Echo*, no. 36, 1916-1917, pp.260-265.

[67] *Rapport Annuels*, no. 12, 1916-1917, p.289.

[68] *Rapports Annuels*, no. 11, 1915, p.73; no.12, p.221.

[69] AGMAfr. Tabora Mission Diary, entries for July 3rd to September 20th 1916.

[70] *Rapports Annuels*, no. 12, 1916-1917, pp.247-248.

[71] 1 Sm. 21: 2-7.

[72] *Rapports Annuels*, no. 11, 1915, p.102; *Petit Echo*, no. 48, 1917, p.292.

[73] *Petit Echo*, no. 42, 1917, pp.69-71; no. 43, 1917, pp.94-98.

[74] *Petit Echo*, no. 37, 1916, p.296; *Rapports Annuels*, no. 12, 1916-1917, pp.189-191.

[75] Alois Hamberger, Adrien Teurlings and Lambert Swyste.

[76] This sequence of events is taken from AGMAfr. Mwazye Mission Diary 1910-1928.

[77] AGMAfr. 122185-122186, Larue to Livinhac 7th October 1916, Haugomat to Livinhac 6th October 1916; Minutes of the General Council, 1175, 8th January 1917; Zimba Mission Diary 1909-1924, p.63, July 15th and August 3rd 1916.

[78] *Petit Echo*, no. 37, 1916, pp.295-296.

[79] The story is told in AGMAfr. Galula Mission Diary, vol.2, May 1917 to December 3rd 1919, and by Lechaptois in *Rapports Annuels* no.12, 1916-1917, p.192.

[80] AGMAfr.Tabora Mission Diary, entries for April 24th 1917, June 6th 1917.

[81] *Rapports Annuels*, no. 13, 1917-1918, p.191.

[82] *Petit Echo*, no. 64, 1919, p.34; von Lettow-Vorbeck, *op.cit.*, pp.312-313.

[83] *Petit Echo*, no.64, 1919, pp.34-35; no. 65, pp.69-71.

[84] *Petit Echo*, no. 65, 1919, pp.66-68.

[85] *Rapports Annuels*, no. 13, 1917-1918, pp.201-205; *Notices Nécrologiques*, vol. 3, pp.268-282.

[86] *Notices Nécrologiques*, 1953, p.27.

[87] AGMAfr. General Council Minutes, 1288, September 29th.

[88] AGMAfr. General Council Minutes, 1297, December 9th 1919; 1309-1313, February 17th, 18th 1920.

[89] *Ibid.*; AGMAfr. 8404, Burtin to Livinhac, March 14th 1920.

[90] *Petit Echo*, no. 80, 1920, p.181; *Notices Nécrologiques*, 1953, p.27.

[91] AGMAfr. 104048, Avon to Livinhac May 27th 1920 and 104097 "the fateful telegram".

[92] The author gathered oral information about him at Tabora in 1977-1980.

[93] *Rapports Annuels*, no. 16, 1920-1921, p.106.

References – Chapter Seven

[1] Belloc, Hilaire, "Ladies and Gentlemen", p. 15 in *Cautionary Verses*, London, Duckworth, 1940.

[2] Cf. Ousby, *op.cit.*, pp.174-175.

[3] Strachan, *op.cit.*, 2001, p.1115.

[4] Ousby, *op.cit.*, p. 191.

[5] Strachan, *op.cit.*, 2001, p. 1122.

[6] *Ibid.*, p.1139.

[7] Taylor, *op.cit.*, p.238.

[8] Pollard, John F., *The Unknown Pope, Benedict XV (1914-1922) and the Pursuit of Peace*, London, Geoffrey Chapman, 1999, pp.87-93, 215; Holmes, J.Derek, "Benedict XV and the First World War", *The Papacy in the Modern World*, London, Burns and Oates, 1981, pp.1-31.

[9] Macmillan, *op.cit.*, pp.474-475.

[10] *Rapports Annuels*, no.16, 1920-1921, p.144.

[11] *Rapports Annuels*, no.16 1920-1921, p.145.

[12] *Petit Echo*, no.90, 1921, p.58.

[13] Correspondence seen in Tabora Archdiocesan Archives. Communication from Jean-Claude Ceillier July 26th 2005.

[14] AGMAfr. Galula Mission Diary, Vol.2, September 19th 1918.

[15] AGMAfr. General Council Minutes, 1157, August 14th 1916; 1162, September 25th 1916.

[16] AGMAfr. General Council Minutes, 1226, April 29th 1918.

[17] AGMAfr. General Council Minutes, 1261, April 22nd 1919.

[18] AGMAfr. General Council Minutes, 1265, May 9th 1919.

[19] He afterwards became novice-master at Maison Carée and superior of Carthage.

[20] AGMAfr. 41024, John McNulty (1919-2004) to François Richard (1940-). McNulty had it from Johannes Fuchs (1900-1994) who was a student and eye-witness at the time.

[21] *Rapports Annuels, Notices Nécrologiques*, 1954-1956, pp.65-70.

[22] AGMAfr., 41026, April 17th 1919.

[23] AGMAfr., General Council Minutes, 1276, June 30th 1919.

[24] AGMAfr., General Council Minutes, 1277, June 30th, 1919.

[25] AGMAfr., General Council Minutes, 1277, July 3rd 1919.

[26] AGMAfr., 41027, Memorandum of Georg Steinhage, 1920.

[27] AGMAfr., 41027, Livinhac to Van Rossum, March 14th 1920.

[28] AGMAfr., 8408, Burtin to Livinhac, April 13th 1920.

[29] AGMAfr., Casier 358, *Chapitres Généraux*, 15th General Chapter of 1920, p.330.

[30] Since the ballot was secret, we do not know who cast the single negative vote. It may have been Livinhac himself.

[31] AGMAfr., Casier 358, *Chapitres Généraux*, 15th General Chapter of 1920, p.330-333.

[32] AGMAfr., General Council Minutes, 1359, September 20th 1920; 1430, July 5th 1921. The Netherlands and Great Britain were attached to the mother house in Algiers, while Switzerland was joined to the French Province.

[33] Tukuyu became a prefecture and eventually the Diocese of Mbeya. Lwangwa also became a prefecture and eventually the Diocese of Abercorn, now Mbala.

[34] *Petit Echo*, no. 90, April 1921, p.58.

[35] *Rapports Annuels*, no. 17, 1921-1922, p.92.

[36] See Appendix III.

[37] Brothers who had taken a temporary oath were of course free to leave when the period expired.

[38] This figure does not include the departures of those who took the perpetual oath after 1914.

[39] They were: Jean-Pierre Blass (1885-1916*), German brother; Aloys Hamberger (1874-1921*), German priest and Joseph Le Clainche (1876-1920*), French priest. The first was excluded from the Society. The other two left at their own request.

[40] Malet to Livinhac August 20th 1919, cited by Ivan Page in a communication of January 25th 2005.

[41] Birraux to *Propaganda Fide* (undated draft) cited by Ivan Page in a communication of January 25th 2005.

[42] Communication from Ivan Page, January 25th 2005.

[43] Biographical information and correspondence concerning Marsigny is to be found in his AGMAfr. dossier, Casier 314.

[44] René Lamey doubted this detail and the entire spy story. AGMAfr. Casier 314, Lamey to Promper April 21st 1988 and April 25th 1988.

[45] *Petit Echo*, no.78, April 1920, p.159.

[46] *Petit Echo*, no. 43, April 1917, p.116.

[47] *Petit Echo*, no. 46, July 1917, p.185.

[48] *Petit Echo*, no. 50, 1917, p.289.

[49] *Petit Echo*, no. 43, April 1917, p.116.

[50] *Ibid.*; *Petit Echo* no. 46, July 1917, p.185.

[51] Livinhac to Vicars Apostolic, November 28th 1919, AGMAfr., Printed Circulars 4, II b.

[52] *Petit Echo*, no. 52, January 1918, p.10. Even today the three letters are found above the entrances of many houses in Germany. Usually, however, Kasper is spelt "Caspar" and CMB is the usual form of the letters. Originally, CMB stood for *Custodiat Mansionem Benedictam* - "May he (God) keep the house blessed". Communication from Hans Schrenk M.Afr.

[53] *Petit Echo*, no. 57, June 1918, p.128.

[54] Not to be confused with Lukuledi in Malawi.

[55] *Petit Echo*, no. 69, July 1919, p.140.

[56] *Petit Echo*, no. 67, May 1919, p.107.

[57] *Petit Echo*, no. 65, March 1919, p.56.

[58] *Petit Echo*, no. 82, August 1920, p.218.

[59] *Petit Echo*, no. 68, June 1919, p.116, Haugomat to Livinhac.

[60] *Petit Echo*, no. 75, January 1920, p.6.

[61] *AGMAfr.*, General Council Minutes, 1331, May 31st 1920.

[62] *Petit Echo*, no. 89, March 1921, p.43; no. 93, July 1921, p.116; no. 105, July 1922, p.108.

[63] Bouniol, Joseph, *The White Fathers and their Missions*, London, Sands, 1929, p.311.

References – Chapter Eight

[1] *Petit Echo*, no. 95, September 1921, p.140.

[2] *Rapports Annuels* no. 13, 1917-1918, p.300; *Petit Echo*, no. 28, 1916, p.7; cf. also Iliffe *op.cit.*, 1979, pp.273-317; Morrow, *op.cit.*, pp.309-312.

[3] *Petit Echo.*, no. 22, March 1915, p.28; no. 32, 1916, p.137.

[4] *Rapports Annuels*, no. 12, 1916-1917, p.87; no. 13, 1917-1918, p.227; *Petit Echo*, no. 55, April 1918, p.84; no. 58, July 1918, p.156.

[5] *Rapports Annuels*, no. 14, 1918-1919, p.229; no.17, 1921-1911, p.563.

[6] *Petit Echo*, no. 39, December 1916, p.367; no. 40, January 1917, p.127; no. 90, April 1921, p.63.

[7] *Petit Echo*, no.44, May 1917, p.127

[8] *Petit Echo*, no.65, March 1919, p.49 gives Ndala as the place of Germain's death, whereas the Society's Necrological Calendar gives it as Ushirombo.

[9] *Rapports Annuels*, no. 14, 1918-1919, p.500.

[10] *Petit Echo*, no. 70, August 1919, p.175.

[11] *Rapports Annuels*, no. 15, 1919-1920, p.146; *Petit Echo*, no. 67, May 1919, p.80.

[12] *Rapports Annuels*, no. 14, 1918-1919, p.458.

[13] *Petit Echo*, no. 65, March 1919, p.49.

[14] *Petit Echo*, no. 99, January 1922, p.14.

[15] *Rapports Annuels*, no. 14, 1918-1919, p.107.

[16] *Rapports Annuels*, no. 17, 1921-1922, p.145.

[17] *Petit Echo*, no. 59, August 1918, p.180.

[18] Iliffe, *op.cit.*,1979, pp.274-301.

[19] Mazé, Joseph, *La Guerre de Azungu*, mimeographed MS, AGMAfr. 122215.

[20] *Rapports Annuels*, no. 10, 1914 (1916), p.329.

[21] *Rapports Annuels*, no. 13, 1917-1918, p.228.

[22] *Rapports Annuels*, no. 14, 1918-1919, p.231.

[23] This was the official estimate. Unofficial estimates put the figure at 150.

[24] *Rapports Annuels*, no.17, 1921-1922, p.64. Thuku is spelt "Suku".

[25] Pineau, Arthur, *Le Vicariat du Tanganyika Durant la Guerre 1914-1918*, MS, n.d., AGMAfr. P 169/20, Supplement p. 9.

[26] Ranger, Terence Osborn, *Dance and Society in Eastern Africa 1890-1970: The Beni Ngoma*, London, Heinemann Educational, 1975.

[27] *Rapports Annuels*, no. 10, 1914 (1916), p.185; no. 13, 1917-1918, p.95; *Petit Echo*, no. 25, September 1915, pp.89-90; no. 27, 1915, p.182

[28] *Petit Echo*, no. 29, 1916, p.36.

[29] *Petit Echo*, no.104, 1922, p.96.

[30] See entry for Malaki Musajjakawa by Norbert C. Brockman in the *Dictionary of African Christian Biography* (<dacb.com>).

[31] *Rapports Annuels*, no.14, 1918-1919, pp.65-82.

[32] *Ibid.*, pp.83-92.

[33] *Ibid.*, pp.93-94.

[34] *Ibid.*, pp.38-57.

[35] *Petit Echo*, no. 62, December 1918, p.241; no. 63, January 1919, p.1; *Rapports Annuels* no 15, 1919-1920, p.7; no. 16, 1920-1921, p.6.

[36] *Petit Echo*, no. 66, April 1919, pp. 76-78.

[37] *Petit Echo*, no. 70, August 1919, p.161; no. 73, November 1919, pp.234-235.

[38] Revelation 7:14.

[39] *Mombasa Times*, Thursday September 4th 1919, p.3.

[40] *Rapports Annuels*, no. 14, 1918-1919, pp.17*-21*.

[41] *Rapports Annuels*, no. 10 , 1914 (1916), p.97.

[42] *Rapports Annuels*, no. 15, 1919-1920, p.96.

[43] *Rapports Annuels*, no. 13, 1917-1918, p.58.

[44] *Rapports Annuels*, no. 12, 1916-1917, p.48.

[45] *Rapports Annuels*, no. 14, 1918-1919, p.6; Shorter, Aylward, "Christian presence in a Muslim Milieu: The Missionaries of Africa in the Maghreb and the Sahara", *IBMR*, vol.28, no.4, October 2004, pp.159-164.

[46] Charles de Foucauld was beatified by Pope Benedict XVI on November 13th 2005.

[47] *Rapports Annuels*, no. 13, 1917-1918, p.80.

[48] *Rapports Annuels*, 1958-1959, *Notices Nécrologiques*, pp.12-18.

[49] *Rapports Annuels*, no. 16, 1920-1921, pp.228-229.

[50] *Rapports Annuels*, no. 16, 1920-1921, p.233; *Petit Echo*, no.40, January 1917, p.8; no. 43, April 1917, p.90; no. 87, January 1921, p.14; no. 88, February 1921, p.31; no. 90, April 1921, p.70; Ilboudo, Jean, "*La Christianisation du Moogo (1899-1949), la Contribution des 'Auxiliaire Indigenes*'", in Ilboudo, Jean S.J. (ed.), *Burkina 20000 – Une Eglise en Marche vers son Centenaire*, Ouagadougou, Presses Africaines, 1993, p.107. The author visited the village, parish and seminary of Pabre on February 17th 2004.

[51] *Petit Echo*, no.70, August 1919, p.175.

[52] AGMAfr. General Council minutes, 1368, November 29th 1920.

[53] AGMAfr., General Council minutes, 1374, January 11th 1921.

[54] *Petit Echo*, no. 93, July 1921, p.109.

[55] AGMAfr., General Council minutes, 1485, February 27th 1922.

[56] *Petit Echo*, no. 98, December 1921, p.178.

[57] Benoist, *op.cit.*, pp. 261-264; 276-281; Prost, André, *Les Missions des Pères Blancs en Afrique Occidentale avant 1939*, (mimeographed) 1939, pp.120-123; personal communication from Gilles de Rasilly at Wagadugu on February 24th 2004.

[58] Rabeyrin, *op.cit.*, pp.34-35.

[59] AGMAfr., General Council minutes, 1374, January 11th 1921.

[60] *Rapports Annuels*, no. 17, 1921-1922, p.353.

[61] Mazé, Joseph, "Vicariats de Mwanza et de Bukoba", AGMAfr. P 169/6, (1930?), p.70.

[62] *Maximum Illud*, 39.

[63] *Rapports Annuels*, no. 16, 1920-1921, p.105, AGMAfr., General Council minutes, 1381, January 25th 1921

[64] *Rapports Annuels*, no. 17, 1921-1922, pp.152-155.

[65] Malishi, Lukas, *Kipalapala Seminary 1925-1975*, Tabora, TMP, 1975, pp.21-23.

[66] AGMAfr., General Council minutes, 1471, December 26th 1921.

[67] AGMAfr., General Council minutes, 1460, November 7th/8th 1921.

[68] Malishi, *op.cit.*, p.25. The author witnessed their arrival in 1967, and was later on the staff of Kipalapala Seminary from 1977 to 1980.

[69] *Petit Echo*, no.109, November 1922, p.160.

[70] Sanneh, Lamin, *Whose Religion is Christianity ? The Gospel beyond the West*, Grand Rapids, Michigan, Eerdmans, 2003, p.19.

[71] Hastings, Adrian, *The Church in Africa*, Oxford, O.U.P., 1994, p.559.

[72] Sanneh, *op.cit.*, pp.18-19.

[73] *Ibid.*

[74] Oliver, Roland, *The Missionary in East Africa*, London, Longmans 1952, pp.274-275.

[75] Oliver, *op.cit.*, pp.264-266, 270-271; Tourigny, *op.cit.*, pp.92, 120, 126-127.

[76] Benoist, *op.cit.*, p.257; Heremans, Roger, *L'Education dans les Missions des Pères Blancs en Afrique Centrale 1879-1914*, Brussels, Editions Nauwelaerts, 1983, pp.3, 396-420.

[77] Oliver, *op.cit.*, p.276.

[78] Croegaert, Luc, *Les Pères Blancs au Rwanda – Jalons et Balises*, unpublished MS, n.d., AGMAfr Casier 341, p.131.

[79] *Rapports Annuels*, no.12, 1916-1917, p.285; no. 16, 1920-1921, p.455.

[80] AGMAfr. General Council minutes, 729, July 9th 1906.

[81] AGMAfr. General Council minutes, 1023, June 23rd 1913.

[82] *Rapports Annuels*, no. 6, (1910-1911), p.172.

[83] *Rapports Annuels*, no. 15, 1919-1920, pp.359, 407.

[84] AGMAfr. Minutes of the General Council, 1023, June 23rd 1913; 1051-1054, January 12th 1914.

[85] *Rapports Annuels*, no. 11, 1915, p.243.

[86] *Petit Echo*, no. 54, March 1918, p.58; *Rapports Annuels*, no. 17, 1921-1922, pp.364-366.

[87] *Petit Echo*, no. 46, July 1917, pp.192-3.

[88] *Rapports Annuels*, no. 17, 1921-1922, p.356.

[89] 14 in Uganda; 8 in Nyanza; 5 in Rwanda; and 4 in Upper Congo.

[90] *Rapports Annuels*, no. 17, 1921-1922, p.528; *Petit Echo*, no. 97, November 1921, p.165.

[91] *Rapports Annuels*, no. 17, 1921-1922, p.529.

[92] Gray, Richard, "Christianity", Roberts, A.D. (ed.), *The Cambridge History of Africa 1907-1940*, vol.7, Cambridge University Press, 1970, chap.3, p.175-176.

[93] Nolan, Francis Patrick, Christianity in Unyamwezi, 1878-1928, Cambridge Ph.D. Dissertation 1977, pp.314-316.

[94] Luke 10:17

[95]*Rapports Annuels*, no. 17, 1921-1922, pp.466-467

[96] *Petit Echo*, no.52, January 1918, p.4.

[97] *Petit Echo*, no.94, August 1921, p.126.

[98]Kimpinde, Amando Dominique *et al.*, *Stefano Kaoze, prêtre d'hier at d'aujourd'hui*, Kinshasa, Editions St.Paul Afrique, 1982, pp.135-138.

[99]Tourigny, Yves, *So Abundant a Harvest, The Catholic Church in Uganda 1879-1979*, London, Darton, Longman and Todd, 1979, p.89.

[100] Tourigny, *op.cit.*, p.97; *Petit Echo*, no. 43, April 1917, p.86.

[101] *Petit Echo*, no. 52, January 1918, p.4; no. 54, March 1918, p.57.

[102] *Rapports Annuels*, no. 13, 1917-1918, p.88-93; Pelletier, Raynald, *Bishop John Forbes (1864-1926), Coadjutor Vicar Apostolic of Uganda, The First Canadian White Fathers*, Missionaries of Africa – History Series, no.2, Rome, 2003, p.52.

[103] *Petit Echo*, no. 98, December 1921, p.173.

[104] *Pelletier*, op.cit., p.63.

[105] *Rapports Annuels*, no. 16, 1920-1921, p.321; *Petit Echo*, no. 102, April 1922, p.65.

[106] Tourigny, *op.cit.*, p.114.

[107] Tourigny, *op.cit.*, p.115.

[108] Pelletier, *op.cit.*, pp.71-73.

References – Chapter Nine

[1] *Jubilé Episcopal de sa Grandeur, Mgr. Léon Livinhac*, Maison Carrée, Algiers 1909, in AGMAfr. Dossier Miscellanea, Maison Carée, 6, p.533.

[2] The Vicars Apostolic were: Sauvant (Bamako), Thévenoud (Wagadugu), Streicher (Uganda), Roelens (Upper Congo), Sweens (Nyanza), Léonard (Unyanyembe), Birraux (Tanganyika), Classe (Ruanda), Gorju (Urundi), Larue (Bangweolo), Guillemé (Nyasa). The auxiliaries were Huys (Upper Congo) and Forbes (Uganda).

[3] Joseph Dupont, formerly Vicar Apostolic of Nyasa, retired at Thibar, Tunisia and John-Joseph Hirth, formerly Vicar Apostolic of Kivu, retired at Kabgayi, Rwanda.

[4] The Prefects Apostolic were: Nouet (Ghardaia), Matthysen (Lake Albert). Oscar Morin became Prefect Apostolic of Navrongo after Livinhac's death.

[5] A fuller biography is given in Chapter 1 of Shorter, Aylward, *Cross and Flag in Africa. Catholic Missionaries and the Colonial Scramble. The White Fathers 1892-1914*. New York, Orbis Books, 2006.

[6] Société des Missionnaires d'Afrique (Pères Blancs), *Directoire des Constitutions*, Maison-Carrée, Algiers, 1914, 105.

[7] *Petit Echo*, 30, 1916, p.65.

[8] *absent empeché.*

[9] *Rapports Annuels*, no. 11, 1915, p.250.

[10] *Rapports Annuels*, no. 17, 1921, p.353.

[11] AGMAfr. General Council Minutes, 1059, March 16th 1914.

[12] AGMAfr. General Council Minutes, 1098, April 19th 1915.

[13] AGMAfr. General Council Minutes, 1146, May 15th 1916.

[14] AGMAfr. General Council Minutes, 1121, October 11th, 1915; 1171, December 11th 1916.

[15] Livinhac, Léon, *Lettres Circulaires*, 1912-1922, Maison Carrée, Algiers, no. 121, July 2nd 1919.

[16] *Petit Echo*, no. 78, April 1920, p.155.

[17] *Rapports Annuels*, no. 15, 1919-1920, p.36.

[18] Livinhac, *Lettres Circulaires*, no. 123, November 1st 1919; no. 124, December 8th 1919.

[19] Livinhac, *Lettres Circulaires*, no. 125, January 6th 1920.

[20] Livinhac, *Lettres Circulaires*, no. 126, March 6th 1920; no. 127, May 13th 1920; no. 129, February 2nd 1921; no. 130, May 26th 1921; no. 131, May 31st 1921.

[21] A phrase commonly used in writing about the religious or missionary life. It refers to the tasks that were demanded by the life.

[22] AGMAfr., General Council Minutes, 1126, November 27th 1915.

[23] AGMAfr. General Council Minutes, 1383, February 7th 1921.

[24] Livinhac, *Lettres Circulaires*, no. 132, June 3rd 1922.

[25] Livinhac, *Lettres Circulaires*, no. 133, February 2nd 1922.

[26] Livinhac, *Lettres Circulaires*, no. 134, May 8th 1922.

[27] Société des Pères Blancs, *Publications en Langues Africaines*, Maison Carrée, Algiers 1928.

[28] *Petit Echo*, no. 52, January 1918, p.7.

[29] *Petit Echo*, no. 15, March 1914, pp.30-31.

[30] *Rapports Annuels*, no. 15, 1919-1920, pp.9-10.

[31] *Petit Echo*, no. 78, April 1920, p.154.

[32] Livinhac, *Lettres Circulaires*, no. 120, May 12th 1919.

[33] Membership in 1920 was 863. In 1918 there had been a fall of 10 and in 1919 a fall of 42. Casier, Jacques, *Développement de la Société*, MS in AGMAfr. General Secretariat, Statistical Reports.

[34] The figures given here are from the various issues of *Petit Echo* in 1919-1920.

[35] *Rapports Annuels*, no. 14, 1918-1919, pp.59-61.

[36] This account is based on the acts of the chapter in *Chapitres Généraux*, AGMAfr. Casier 358, 15th General Chapter of 1920, pp. 310-371.

[37] Livinhac, *Lettres Circulaires*, 127, May 13th 1920.

[38] Livinhac, *Lettres Circulaires*, 131, May 31st 1921.

[39] Livinhac was not present at the chapters of 1878, 1880, 1883 and 1886. He attended that of 1885 as a newly ordained bishop and the second session of 1889 as newly appointed Superior-General. Cf. Ceillier, Jean-Claude, *A Pilgrimage from Chapter to Chapter, The First General Chapters of the Society of Missionaries of Africa, 1874-1900*, Missionaries of Africa – History Series, no.1, Rome, 2002.

[40] This account of the life and pontificate of Benedict XV is based on Pollard, *op.cit.*, and Holmes, *op.cit.*,

[41] Pollard, *op.cit.*, p.16.

[42] Pollard, *op.cit.*, p.44.

[43] Holmes, *op.cit.*, p.1. Holmes uses the word "victims", rather than the more usual "casualties".

[44] Holmes, *op.cit.*, p.3.

[45] *Rapports Annuels*, no. 10, 1914 (1916), pp.30-39.

[46] Letters from Burtin's distant cousin Joseph Portier M.Afr. to the author, November 17th and December 1st 2005. According to the family, the Pope took the suggestion good humouredly, saying: "If you were not Father Louis Burtin, I would expel you from my office right away without explanation". There is no reference to such a suggestion in Burtin's correspondence with Livinhac. Being very correct, he would certainly have raised the matter, if he had taken it seriously.

[47] Holmes, *op.cit.*, p.23.

[48] Pollard, *op.cit.*, p.204.

[49] Faupel, J.F., *African Holocaust, The Story of the Uganda Martyrs*, Nairobi, St.Paul's Publications Africa, 4th edition, 1984. This is the best complete account of the martyrdoms.

[50] AGMAfr. Y15, Beatification, *Acta* 1 & 2.

[51] *Rapports Annuels*, no. 11, 1915, pp.31, 61.

[52] This account is based on Moorman, Theodore, *Histoire des Origines de la Société*, Typescript volume, Monteviot House, Jedburgh, Scotland, n.d.; Zwemer, Samuel, *The Law of Apostasy in Islam*, London, Marshall Brothers, 1924; and references in *Petit Echo* and *Rapports Annuels*.

[53] Diego de Haëda, *Topographia e Historia General de Argel*, 1632.

[54] Burlaton, Louis, *Le Vénérable Géronimo – Martyr du Fort des XXIV Heures à Alger*, Pères Blancs, Maison Carrée, 1931, summarizes the arguments in favour of the identification, pp.79-92.

[55] Moorman, *op.cit.*, pp.18-19.

[56] *Petit Echo*, no. 6, April 1913, p.60; no. 13, January 1914, p.5; Zwemer, *op.cit.*, p.89.

[57] *Rapports Annuels*, no. 11, 1915, pp.22-23; *Petit Echo*, no. 44, May 1917, p.118.

[58] *Petit Echo*, no.60, September-October 1918, p.201; no. 62, December 1918, p.247.

[59] *Rapports Annuels*, no. 14, 1918-1919, p.30; *Petit Echo*, no. 60, September-October 1918, p.201; no. 74, December 1919, p.261.

[60] *Rapports Annuels*, no. 15, 1919, p.37; *Petit Echo*, no. 65, March 1919, p.51; no. 74, December 1919, p.261. Burlaton, *op.cit.*, p. 75, was still appealing for miracles in 1931.

[61] *Rapports Annuels*, no. 14, 1918-1919, p.30; *Petit Echo*, no. 47, August 1917, p.215; no. 65, March 1919, p.51.

[62] *Petit Echo*, no. 86, December 1920, p.272.

[63] Sources for the beatification ceremony and related events are: *L'Osservatore Romano*, 7th June 1920,   8th June 1920;   *La Croix*, no.11331, Tuesday March 2nd, 1920 (for the decree);   *Rapports Annuels*, no. 15, 1919-1920, pp.36-46; *Missions d'Afrique des Pères Blancs*, 1920, pp.201-211, (article by Julien Gorju); Tourigny, op.cit., pp.103-104. Numerous other references in *Petit Echo*.

[64] Matia Mulumba, Luke Banabakintu and Pontiano Ngondwe.

[65] He was also Secretary of the Holy Office.

[66] *Rapports Annuels*, no. 16, 1920-1921, p.13.

[67] *Rapports Annuels*, no. 15, 1919-1920, pp.90-91.

[68] *Petit Echo*, no. 98, May 1921, p.73.

[69] Livinhac, *Lettres Circulaires*, 126, March 6th 1920.

[70] *Petit Echo*, no. 100, February 1922, pp.21, 24-25.

[71] *Petit Echo*, no. 102, April 1922, p.58; *Rapports Annuels*, no. 17, 1921-1922, p.25.

[72] The character sketch presented here is based mainly on comments and letters of condolence at the time of his death in *Rapports Annuels*, no. 18, 1922-1923, pp.6-29 and *Petit Echo*, no. 111, December 8th 1922, pp.177-188.

[73] AGMAfr. 106-4; 106500, Guillemé to Livinhac, November 14th 1922; 106501, Guillemé to Livinhac, December 26th 1922.

[74] AGMAfr. *Dossier Miscellanea*, Maison Carrée 6, Prosper Repeticci, *Oraison Funèbre de Sa Grandeur Monseigneur Livinhac*, Algiers 1923, p.569.

[75] *Petit Echo*, no. 111, December 1922, p.179; *Rapports Annuels*, no. 18, 1922-1923, p.29.

[76] Brother Boniface was cared for in the novitiate at s'Heerenberg and the author heard about Livinhac from him there in 1957-1958. Boniface was at Maison Carrée in 1897-1902, 1905 and 1921-1922.

[77] Cf. AGMAfr. Chapitres Généraux, p.454, Opening Speech of 1947 Chapter by Mgr. Durrieu: *le saint Mgr. Livinhac, le Vénéré Père Voillard et le si regretté Mgr. Birraux.*

[78] *Foyer Chrétien*, no. 8, November 1922, p.122; AGMAfr. contains detailed accounts of two cures attributed to Livinhac after his death: Brother Désiré (1923) and Brother Hélie (1924), Livinhac, 3, 1.

[79] Taylor, John Vernon, *The Growth of the Church in Buganda. An Attempt at Understanding*, London, SCM Press, 1958, p.59, quoting Philip O'Flaherty December 25th 1881, in the *Church Missionary Intelligencer*, 1882, p.95.

[80] AGMAfr., Livinhac, 2, Testaments.

[81] *Petit Echo*, no. 90, April 1921, p.53.

[82] *Petit Echo*, no. 87, January 1921, p.1.

[83] *Petit Echo*, no. 95, September 1921, p.133; no. 99, January 1922, p.1.

[84] AGMAfr. Livinhac, 2, Testaments.

[85] Voillard was followed as superior-general by two bishops, Birraux and Durrieu.

[86] *Rapports Annuels*, no. 17, 1921-1922, pp.23-24.

[87] *Rapports Annuels*, no. 17, 1921-1922, p.6; *Petit Echo* no. 99, January 1922, p.1.

[88] Pacando or Pacanden was a town in Cilicia, modern Turkey.

[89] AGMAfr., 002 13B10, Bull of Promotion, November 21st 1921.

[90] Cf. Internet articles on the subject. The fish had reputedly eaten the phallus of Osiris after the dismemberment of his body by Seth, his son.

[91] *Petit Echo*, no.99, January, 1922, pp.3-8, where the speech and Livinhac's reply are given in full.

[92] A bishop's heraldic hat has six tassles, an archbishop's, ten tassles.

[93] *Rapports Annuels*, no. 17, 1921-1922, p.14.

[94] AGMAfr., 002 14B10, Voillard to Burtin (?), December 9th 1921.

[95] AGMAfr., 006152. Livinhac to Burtin, January 20th 1922.

[96] *Rapports Annuels*, no. 17, 1921-1922, p.6.

[97] *Ibid.*, p.14; Philippians 1:23.

[98] *Petit Echo*, no. 110, December 1922, p.166.

[99] *Ibid.*, p.168.

[100] A lengthy account of Livinhac's death and funeral was published in *Petit Echo*, no. 110, December 1st 1922 . The following issue, no. 111, December 8th 1922 was devoted to letters of condolence. Further notes and tributes were published in *Rapports Annuels*, no. 18, 1922-1923, pp.6-29, and *Missions d'Afrique*, no. 294, December 1922, pp.353-362. Notes by the Brother infirmarians, Félicien and Chanel (Jan Willebrands 1890-1952) are preserved with articles, press

cuttings and testamentary provisions in AGMAfr. Livinhac, 2, Testaments. The account given here relies on all of these.

[101] *Rapports Annuels*, no. 18, 1922-1923, p.16.

[102] Repeticci, Prosper, *Oraison Funèbre de Sa Grandeur Monseigneur Livinhac, 16 Décembre 1922*, Algiers 1923. AGMAfr. Dossier Miscellanea, Maison Carrée 6, pp.567-582.

[103] The play on the words *genie* and *gentillesse* in French cannot be reproduced in English.

[104] AGMAfr. Livinhac, 2, Testaments.

[105] *Petit Echo*, no. 614, 1970, pp.489-490.

[106] This was the original intention which has not been carried out up to the time of writing.

[107] *Petit Echo*, no. 661, 1975, pp.386-388.

[108] The author was present on that occasion and took part in the procession. At the time of writing (2005), Livinhac's casket still lies in the Chapel of the Cardinal's house at Rubaga, Kampala and is carried in the liturgical procession at Namugongo each year on the Martyrs' Feast. There are no plans at present for re-interment. Communications from Richard Nnyombi M.Afr., Provincial of Uganda, October 27th and November 2nd 2005.

References - Epilogue

[1] Burlaton, Louis, "Le role providential de Mgr. Livinhac dans notre Société", typescript, AGMAfr., 4, III.

[2] *Ibid.*

References – Appendix I

[1] *Petit Echo*, no.72, October 1919, p.203.

[2] *Ministre de la Défense, Secrétariat general pour l'administration* (SGA). *Mémoire des Hommes. Les morts pour la France de la guerre 1914-1918.* The only names missing are Daniel Jouve (30) and Pierre Le Cléach (31).

[3] *Notices Nécrologiques, Rapports Annuels*, no.10, p.14* specifies "4th Zouaves".

[4] *Notices Nécrologiques, Rapports Annuels*, no.10, p.7* specifies "4th Zouaves".

[5] SGA gives October 23rd.

[6] SGA gives June 15th.

[7] SGA gives August 6th.

[8] SGA September 19th.

[9] AGMAfr. *Notices Nécrologiques*, vol. 3, 1909-1921, pp.199-100 and personal dossier.

[10]SGA gives three other Christian names that are scarcely legible. They may be "Angel-Henri-Paul".

[11] *Notices Nécrologiques, Rapports Annuels*, no. 11, 1915-1916, p.61* specifies "4th Zouaves".

[12] This is the account in *Notices Nécrologiques, Rapports Annuels*, no. 10, 1914-1915, p.8*. SGA gives a different account and date, *viz.* "Missing", June 21st 1915.

[13] No SGA *fiche* was found.

[14] No SGA *fiche* was found.

[15] AGMAfr. personal dossier.

[16] Cf. SGA *fiche*.

[17] A variant spelling in both MAfr and SGA records is "Duclot".

[18] However, individuals are not mentioned by name and there is no indication that any graves are still there. The author visited Froide Terre on June 7th 2005.

[19] SGA gives the date of death as March 24th 1915.

[20] AGMAfr. personal dossier, undated letter from Lieut. Ferré to Malet (1915?).

[21] There is no personal dossier in AGMAfr. His exact age is unknown, but his elder brother was 23 when he was killed.

[22] He is presumably buried in the cemetery there.

[23] SGA states he died at Orvillers (Oise) on March 10th 1918.

[24] AGMAfr. personal dossier: Antoine Senior to "Superior", September 19th 1918.

[25] SGA gives April 25th as date of death.

[26] SGA gives April 22nd 1915 as the date of his disappearance.

[27] Little is known about him. The correspondence with Livinhac is all there is in his AGMAfr. personal dossier.

[28] Details and correspondence with Malet in AGMAfr. personal dossier.

INDEX